THE
IMPOSSIBILITY
OF
GOD

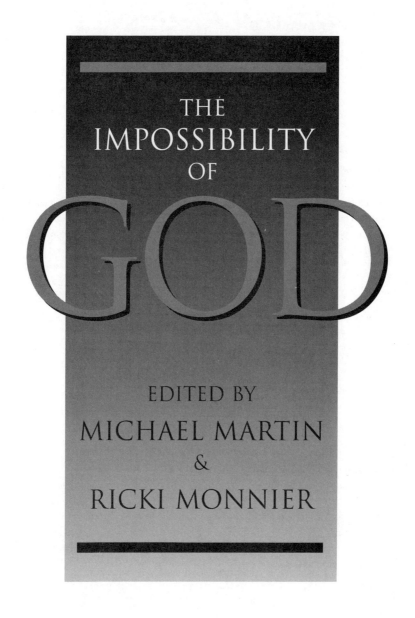

THE
IMPOSSIBILITY
OF
GOD

EDITED BY
MICHAEL MARTIN
&
RICKI MONNIER

 **Prometheus Books**

59 John Glenn Drive
Amherst, New York 14228–2197

Published 2003 by Prometheus Books

Inquiries should be addressed to
Prometheus Books
59 John Glenn Drive
Amherst, New York 14228–2197
VOICE: 716–691–0133, ext. 207
FAX: 716–564–2711
WWW.PROMETHEUSBOOKS.COM

07 06 05 04 03   5 4 3 2 1

Library of Congress Cataloging-in-Publication Data

The impossibility of God / edited by Michael Martin and Ricki Monnier.
    p. cm.
Includes bibliographical references.
ISBN 1–59102–120–0
    1. Atheism—History. 2. God—Proof—History of doctrines. 3. Theodicty—History of doctrines. 4. Religion—Philosophy—History. I. Martin, Michael, 1932 Feb. 3– II. Monnier, Ricki.

BL2747.3.I49 2003
212'.1—dc22
        2003020943

Printed in the United States of America on acid-free paper

To those who question and wonder.

CONTENTS

PART 2. DEDUCTIVE EVIL DISPROOFS
OF THE EXISTENCE OF GOD

PART 3. DOCTRINAL DISPROOFS
OF THE EXISTENCE OF GOD

PART 4. MULTIPLE ATTRIBUTES DISPROOFS
OF THE EXISTENCE OF GOD

PART 5. SINGLE ATTRIBUTE DISPROOFS
OF THE EXISTENCE OF GOD

APPENDIX

PREFACE

This anthology is the indirect result of many years of stimulating talks and lively discussions among the participants of *The Disproof Atheism Society*, an independent network of disproof atheists founded in 1994. We are indebted to the authors whose previously published papers and book selections formed the basis of those talks and discussions and are collected here. We thank the various publishers for granting us permission to republish these materials and Steven L. Mitchell, editor in chief of Prometheus Books, for assistance in publishing this anthology. We are grateful, above all, to our families for their patience, encouragement, and support.

Michael Martin
Ricki Monnier

2002

INTRODUCTION

The standard approach to the philosophy of religion is to consider arguments for the existence of God. Typically covered are the ontological, cosmological, teleological, and moral arguments; the arguments from religious experience and miracles; and perhaps a few other minor arguments. But, with the notable exception of the argument from evil, the standard approach tends to ignore arguments for the nonexistence of God.

To many people the very idea of an argument for the nonexistence of God is shocking and implausible. Such an idea is usually a source of amusement, if not derision. How can there be a serious argument for the nonexistence of God when so many people "simply know" that God exists? How can there be a successful proof that God does not exist when it is "common knowledge" that you cannot prove a negative? Indeed, almost everyone in the world today—theist, agnostic, and atheist alike—believes that God is, at the very least, possible. But almost everyone might be mistaken.

Arguments for the nonexistence of God have a long history, dating back to the earliest philosophers. Epicurus (c. 341–270 BCE), for example, is credited with formulating a version of the argument from evil. The first extensive presentation of such arguments appeared in 1770, when Paul Thiry d'Holbach (1723–1789) published *The System of Nature* (see the appendix of this anthology for an excerpt). In 1948, J. N. Findlay (1903–1987) published "Can God's Existence Be Disproved?" a paper that initiated what has become a burgeoning series of papers and books formulating, developing, and critically evaluating arguments for the nonexistence of God.

There are basically two kinds of arguments for the nonexistence of God: arguments for the improbability of God and arguments for the impossibility of God. Briefly, an argument for the improbability of God assumes that God *can* exist but argues that the weight of the evidence is against God's *actual* existence; an argument for the impossibility of God argues that the concept of God is *logically contradictory* and therefore God, like a square circle, *cannot* exist.

This anthology collects in one volume most of the important arguments for the *impossibility* of God that have been published since 1948. In the interest of clarity and to facilitate discussion, these arguments have been arranged into five main groups: Part 1 contains *definitional disproofs* based on an inconsistency in the definition of God; Part 2 contains *deductive evil disproofs* based on an inconsistency between the existence of God who has certain attributes and the existence of evil; Part 3 contains *doctrinal disproofs* based on an inconsistency between the attributes of God and a particular religious doctrine, story, or teaching about God; Part 4 contains *multiple attributes disproofs* based on an inconsistency between two or more divine attributes; and Part 5 contains *single attribute disproofs* based on an inconsistency within just one attribute. If readers are unsatisfied with this classification system or the assignment of a particular argument, they are welcome to make changes.

Each of the five parts begins with an introduction by the editors that briefly summarizes the papers and book selections that follow. Within each paper and book selection itself, the author identifies the concept of God and specific elements within that concept that are being considered; argues that those elements are contradictory in some way and therefore God, so conceived, does not and cannot exist; and then usually replies to some possible objections. In a few cases there is a follow-up paper that clarifies and develops the argument in response to published objections.

The reader might wonder why there are so many arguments for the impossibility of God. Wouldn't just one argument, if sound, be sufficient to establish that God is impossible? There are two answers to this question. First, arguments for the impossibility of God must contend with a variety of concepts of God. Since the world's major religions and leading theologians have different concepts of God, a single argument directed at one concept might not apply to other concepts. Second, arguments for the impossibility of God probe different combinations of conflicting elements within a given concept of God. Such arguments are of interest individually and make a stronger case collectively.

This anthology is an invitation to explore and ponder the possibility of God. Is the concept of God what d'Holbach called "an ocean of contradictions"? Is theism built upon the very idea that disproves it? Arguments for the impossibility of God are not about certainty but rather about rational justification. They challenge us to think deeply and critically about the coherence of an idea that has preoccupied much of humanity.

Recommended books presenting arguments for the nonexistence of God:

Drange, Theodore M. *Nonbelief and Evil: Two Arguments for the Nonexistence of God.* Amherst, N.Y.: Prometheus Books, 1998.

Kenny, Anthony. *The God of the Philosophers.* Oxford: Clarendon Press, 1979.

Mackie, J. L. *The Miracle of Theism: Arguments For and Against the Existence of God.* Oxford: Clarendon Press, 1982.

Martin, Michael. *Atheism: A Philosophical Justification.* Philadelphia: Temple University Press, 1990.

Schellenberg, J. L. *Divine Hiddenness and Human Reason.* Ithaca and London: Cornell University Press, 1993.

Weisberger, A. M. *Suffering Belief: Evil and the Anglo-American Defense of Theism.* New York: Peter Lang Publishing, 1999.

PART 1

DEFINITIONAL DISPROOFS OF THE EXISTENCE OF GOD

INTRODUCTION

This section contains previously published papers presenting and defending definitional disproofs of the existence of God. A definitional disproof of God's existence is a deductive argument based on a contradiction within the definition of God. Definitional disproofs are sometimes called ontological disproofs because they are inspired by Anselm's famous ontological argument for God's existence, although they arrive at the opposite conclusion.

Standard definitions of God include:

God is the perfect being.
God is the being most worthy of worship.
God is the adequate object of religious attitudes.
God is that than which nothing greater can be conceived.

A definitional disproof of God's existence takes the following general form:

1. If God exists,
    then the definition of God is self-consistent.
2. The definition of God is not self-consistent.
3. Therefore, God does not and cannot exist.

Here are brief summaries of the papers contained in this section.

J. N. Findlay in a classic 1948 paper "Can God's Existence Be Disproved?" argues that defining God as the adequate object of religious attitudes leads irresistibly, by the sheer logic of this definition, to the conclusion that God's existence is necessary. However, in light of the hypothetical nature of necessary predications, necessary existence is a contradiction in terms, and therefore God does not and cannot exist.

In a 1949 paper "God's Non-Existence: A Reply to Mr. Rainer and Mr. Hughes," Findlay discusses the context in which the 1948 disproof was developed and responds to several objections.

John L. Pollock in a 1966 paper "Proving the Non-Existence of God," in which God is defined as that than which nothing greater can be conceived, exposes a fallacy in ontological arguments for the existence of God that renders them invalid. Pollock goes on to demonstrate that when this fallacy is removed, an ontological argument that God exists can be transformed into an ontological argument that God does not and cannot exist.

Douglas Walton in a 1999 paper "Can an Ancient Argument of Carneades on Cardinal Virtues and Divine Attributes Be Used to Disprove the Existence of God?" presents a definitional disproof of God's existence that draws on an argument by Carneades (c. 213–128 BCE) that perfection and virtue are incompatible. Walton argues that God, defined as a being than which no greater being can be thought, must be both all-virtuous and incapable of suffering pain or destruction, but a being can only be virtuous if it is capable of suffering pain and destruction, and thus God does not and cannot exist. Walton evaluates the strength of this disproof relative to each of the four cardinal virtues.

James Rachels in a 1997 paper "God and Moral Autonomy," a chapter from *Can Ethics Provide Answers? And Other Essays in Moral Philosophy* (1997), examines the concept of worship as applied to God defined as a being worthy of worship, a being believed to be the infinitely good, wise, and powerful creator of the universe. Rachels argues that the recognition of any being as God requires, as a matter of logic, the worshiper's *total* subordination to that being, including the worshiper's total abandonment of moral autonomy. However, given the importance of moral autonomy in moral philosophy, this requirement that the worshiper totally abandon moral autonomy makes God *unworthy* of worship. Replying to objections, Rachels argues further that in order to recognize any being as God, a worshiper must both *exercise* moral autonomy to ensure that that being is God and *abandon* moral autonomy in acknowledgment that that being is God. In short, the definition of God as a being worthy of worship is contradictory, and therefore God does not and cannot exist.

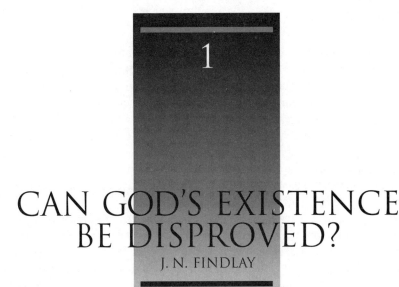

CAN GOD'S EXISTENCE
BE DISPROVED?
J. N. FINDLAY

The course of philosophical development has been full of attempted proofs of the existence of God. Some of these have sought a basis in the bare necessities of thought, while others have tried to found themselves on the facts of experience. And, of these latter, some have founded themselves on *very general facts*, as that something exists or that something is in motion, while others have tried to build on *highly special facts*, as that living beings are put together in a purposive manner, or that human beings are subject to certain improbable urges and passions, such as the zeal for righteousness, the love for useless truths and unprofitable beauties, as well as the many specifically religious needs and feelings. The general philosophical verdict is that none of these "proofs" is truly compelling. The proofs based on the necessities of thought are universally regarded as fallacious: it is not thought possible to build bridges between mere abstractions and concrete existence. The proofs based on the general facts of existence and motion are only felt to be valid by a minority of thinkers, who seem quite powerless to communicate this sense of validity to others. And while most thinkers would accord weight to arguments resting on the special facts we have mentioned, they wouldn't think such arguments successful in ruling out a vast range of counter possibilities. Religious people have, in fact, come to acquiesce in the total absence of any cogent proofs of the Being they believe in: they even find it positively satisfying that something so far surpassing

From *Mind* 57 (1948): 176–83. Copyright © 1948 by Oxford University Press. Reprinted by permission of Oxford University Press.

clear conception should also surpass the possibility of demonstration. And non-religious people willingly mitigate their rejection with a tinge of agnosticism: they don't so much deny the existence of a God, as the existence of good reasons for believing in Him. We shall, however, maintain in this essay that there isn't room, in the case we are examining, for all these attitudes of tentative surmise and doubt. For we shall try to show that the Divine Existence can only be conceived, in a religiously satisfactory manner, if we also conceive it as something inescapable and necessary, whether for thought or reality. From which it follows that our modern denial of necessity or rational evidence for such an existence amounts to a demonstration that there cannot be a God.

Before we develop this argument, we must, however, give greater precision to our use of the term 'God'. For it is possible to say that there are nearly as many 'Gods' as there are speakers and worshipers, and while existence may be confidently asserted or denied of *some* of them, we should feel more hesitant in the case of others. It is one thing, plainly, to pronounce on God's existence, if He be taken to be some ancient, shapeless stone, or if we identify Him with the bearded Father of the Sistine ceiling, and quite another matter, if we make of Him an "all-pervasive, immaterial intelligence," or characterize Him in some yet more negative and analogical manner. We shall, however, choose an indirect approach, and pin God down for our purposes as the "adequate object of religious attitudes." Plainly we find it possible to gather together, under the blanket term 'religious', a large range of cases of possible action, linked together by so many overlapping[1] affinities that we are ready to treat them as the varying 'expressions' of a single 'attitude' or 'policy'. And plainly we find it possible to indicate the character of that attitude by a number of descriptive phrases which, though they may err individually by savoring too strongly of particular cases, nevertheless permit us, in their totality, to draw a rough boundary round the attitude in question. Thus we might say, for instance, that a religious attitude was one in which we tended to abase ourselves before some object, to defer to it wholly, to devote ourselves to it with unquestioning enthusiasm, to bend the knee before it, whether literally or metaphorically. These phrases, and a large number of similar ones, would make perfectly plain the sort of attitude we were speaking of, and would suffice to mark it off from cognate attitudes which are much less unconditional and extreme in their tone. And clearly similar phrases would suffice to fix the boundaries of religious *feeling*. We might describe religious frames of mind as ones in which we felt ready to abase ourselves before some object, to bend the knee before it, and so forth. Here, as elsewhere, we find ourselves indicating the *felt* character of our attitudes, by treating their inward character as, in some sense, a concentrated and condensed substitute for appropriate lines of action, a way of speaking that accords curiously with the functional significance of the inward.[2] But not only do we incorporate, in the meanings of our various names for attitudes, a reference to this readiness for appropriate lines of action: we also incorporate in these meanings a reference to *the sorts of things or situations to which these attitudes are the normal or appropriate responses*. For, as a matter of fact, our attitudes are not indifferently evoked in *any* setting: there is a range of situations in which they normally and most readily occur. And though they may at times arise in circumstances which are not in this range, they are also readily dissipated by the consciousness that such circumstances *are* unsuitable or unusual. Thus, fear is an attitude very readily evoked in situations with a character of menace or potential injury, and it is also an attitude very readily allayed by the clear perception that a given situation isn't really dangerous. And anger, likewise, is an attitude provoked very readily by perverse resistance and obstructive difficulty in some object and is also very readily dissipated, even in animals, by the consciousness that a given object is innocent of offense. All attitudes, we may say, *presume* characters in their objects, and are, in consequence, strengthened by the discovery that their objects *have* these characters, as they are weakened by the discovery that they really haven't got them. And not only do we find this out empirically: we also incorporate it in the *meanings* of our names for attitudes. Thus attitudes are said to be 'normal', 'fully justified', and so forth, if we find them altered in a certain manner (called 'appropriate') by our knowledge of the actual state of things, whereas we speak of them as 'queer' or 'senseless' or 'neurotic', if they aren't at all modified by this knowledge of reality. We call it abnormal, from this point of view, to feel a deep-set fear of mice, to rage maniacally at strangers, to greet disasters with a hebephrenic giggle, whereas we think it altogether normal to deplore deep losses deeply or to fear grave dangers gravely. And so an implicit reference to some standard object—which makes an attitude either normal or abnormal—is part of what we ordinarily mean by all our names for attitudes, and can be rendered explicit by a simple study of usage. We can consider the circumstances in which ordinary speakers would call an attitude 'appropriate' or 'justified'. And all that philosophy achieves in this regard is merely to push further, and develop into more considered and consistent forms, the implications of such ordinary ways of speaking. It can inquire whether an attitude would still seem justified, and its object appropriate, after we had reflected long and carefully on a certain matter and looked at it from every wonted and unwonted angle. And such consideration may lead philosophers to a different and more reasoned notion of the appropriate objects of a given attitude than could be garnered from our unreflective ways of speaking. And these developments of ordinary usage will only seem unfeasible to victims of that strange modern confusion which thinks of attitudes exclusively as hidden processes "in our bosoms," with nothing but an adventitious relation to appropriate outward acts and objects.

How then may we apply these notions to the case of our religious attitudes?

Plainly we shall be following the natural trends of unreflective speech if we say that religious attitudes presume *superiority* in their objects, and such superiority, moreover, as reduces us, who feel the attitudes, to comparative nothingness. For having described a worshipful attitude as one in which we feel disposed to bend the knee before some object, to defer to it wholly, and the like, we find it natural to say that such an attitude can only be fitting where the object reverenced *exceeds* us very vastly, whether in power or wisdom or in other valued qualities. And while it is certainly possible to worship stocks and stones and articles of common use, one does so usually on the assumption that they aren't merely stocks and stones and ordinary articles, but the temporary seats of "indwelling presences" or centers of extraordinary powers and virtues. And if one realizes clearly that such things *are* merely stocks and stones or articles of common use, one can't help suffering a total vanishing or grave abatement of religious ardor. To feel religiously is therefore to presume surpassing greatness in some object: so much characterizes the attitudes in which we bow and bend the knee, and enters into the ordinary meaning of the word 'religious'. But now we advance further—in company with a large number of theologians and philosophers, who have added new touches to the portrait of deity, pleading various theoretical necessities, but really concerned to make their object worthier of our worship— and ask whether it isn't wholly anomalous to worship anything *limited* in any thinkable manner. For all limited superiorities are tainted with an obvious relativity and can be dwarfed in thought by still mightier superiorities, in which process of being dwarfed they lose their claim upon our worshipful attitudes. And hence we are led on irresistibly to demand that our religious object should have an *unsurpassable* supremacy along all avenues, that it should tower *infinitely* above all other objects. And not only are we led to demand for it such merely quantitative superiority: we also ask that it shouldn't stand surrounded by a world of *alien* objects, which owe it no allegiance or set limits to its influence. The proper object of religious reverence must in some manner be *all-comprehensive*: there mustn't be anything capable of existing, or of displaying any virtue, without owing all of these absolutely to this single source. All these, certainly, are difficult requirements, involving not only the obscurities and doubtful significance of the infinite but also all the well-worn antagonisms of the immanent and transcendent, of finite sinfulness and divine perfection and preordination, which centuries of theological brooding have failed to dissipate. But we are also led on irresistibly to a yet more stringent demand, which raises difficulties which make the difficulties we have mentioned seem wholly inconsiderable: we can't help feeling that the worthy object of our worship can never be a thing that merely *happens* to exist, nor one on which all other objects merely *happen* to depend. The true object of religious reverence must not be one, merely, to which no *actual* independent realities stand opposed: it must be one to which such opposition is totally *inconceivable*. God mustn't merely cover the territory of the actual, but also, with equal comprehensiveness, the territory of the possible. And not only must the existence of *other* things be unthinkable without Him, but His own nonexistence must be wholly unthinkable in any circumstances. There must, in short, be no conceivable alternative to an existence properly termed 'divine': God must be wholly inescapable, as we remarked previously, whether for thought or reality. And so we are led on insensibly to the barely intelligible notion of a Being in Whom Essence and Existence lose their separateness. And all that the great medieval thinkers really did was to carry such a development to its logical limit.

We may, however, approach the matter from a slightly different angle. Not only is it contrary to the demands and claims inherent in religious attitudes that their object should *exist* 'accidentally': it is also contrary to those demands that it should *possess its various excellences* in some merely adventitious or contingent manner. It would be quite unsatisfactory from the religious standpoint, if an object merely *happened* to be wise, good, powerful, and so forth, even to a superlative degree, and if other beings had, *as a mere matter of fact*, derived their excellences from this single source. An object of this sort would doubtless deserve respect and admiration, and other quasi-religious attitudes, but it would not deserve the utter self-abandonment peculiar to the religious frame of mind. It would deserve the δουλεία canonically accorded to the saints, but not the λατρεία that we properly owe to God. We might respect this object as the crowning instance of most excellent qualities, but we should incline our head before the qualities and not before the person. And wherever such qualities were manifested, though perhaps less eminently, we should always be ready to perform an essentially similar obeisance. For though such qualities might be intimately characteristic of the Supreme Being, they still wouldn't be in any sense inalienably His own. And even if other beings had, in fact, derived such qualities from this sovereign source, they still would be *their own* qualities, possessed by them in their own right. And we should have no better reason to *adore* the author of such virtues, than sons have reason to adore superior parents, or pupils to adore superior teachers. For while these latter may deserve deep deference, the fact that we are coming to *participate* in their excellences renders them unworthy of our *worship*. Plainly a being that possesses and imparts desirable qualities—which other things might nevertheless have manifested though this source were totally absent—has all the utter inadequacy as a religious object which is expressed by saying that it would be *idolatrous* to worship it. Wisdom, kindness, and other excellences deserve respect wherever they are manifested, but no being can appropriate them as its personal perquisites, even if it does possess them in a superlative degree. And so we are led on irresistibly, by the demands inherent in religious reverence, to hold that an adequate object of our worship must possess its various qualities *in some necessary manner*. These qualities must be intrinsically incapable of belonging to anything except in so far as they belong primarily to the object of our worship. Again we are led on to a queer and barely intelligible scholastic doctrine, that God isn't merely good, but is in some manner indistinguishable from His own (and anything else's) goodness.

What, however, are the consequences of these requirements upon the possibility of God's existence? Plainly they entail (for all who share a contemporary outlook) not only that there isn't a God, but that the Divine Existence is either senseless[3] or impossible. The modern mind feels not the faintest axiomatic force in principles which trace contingent things back to some necessarily existent source, nor does it find it hard to conceive that things should display various excellent qualities without deriving them from a source which manifests them supremely. Those who believe in necessary truths which aren't merely tautological think that such truths merely connect the *possible* instances of various characteristics with each other: they don't expect such truths to tell them whether there *will* be instances of any characteristics. This is the outcome of the whole medieval and Kantian criticism of the Ontological Proof. And, on a yet more modern view of the matter, necessity in propositions merely reflects our use of words, the arbitrary conventions of our language. On such a view the Divine Existence could only be a necessary matter if we had made up our minds to speak theistically *whatever the empirical circumstances might turn out to be*. This, doubtless, would suffice for some, who speak theistically, much as Spinoza spoke monistically, merely to give expression to a particular way of looking at things or of feeling about them. And it would also suffice for those who make use of the term 'God' to cover whatever tendencies toward righteousness and beauty are actually included in the makeup of our world. But it wouldn't suffice for the full-blooded worshiper, who can't help finding our actual world anything but edifying, and its half-formed tendencies toward righteousness and beauty very far from adorable. The religious frame of mind seems, in fact, to be in a quandary; it seems invincibly determined both to eat its cake and have it. It desires the Divine Existence both to have that inescapable character which can, on modern views, only be found where truth reflects an arbitrary convention, and also the character of "making a real difference" which is only possible where truth doesn't have this merely linguistic basis. We may accordingly deny that modern approaches allow us to remain agnostically poised in regard to God: they force us to come down on the atheistic side. For if God is to satisfy religious claims and needs, He must be a being in every way inescapable, One Whose existence and Whose possession of certain excellences we cannot possibly conceive away. And modern views make it self-evidently absurd (if they don't make it ungrammatical) to speak of such a Being and attribute existence to Him. It was indeed an ill day for Anselm when he hit upon his famous proof. For on that day he not only laid bare something that is of the essence of an adequate religious object, but also something that entails its necessary nonexistence.[4]

The force of our argument must not, however, be exaggerated. We haven't proved that there aren't beings of all degrees of excellence and greatness, who may deserve attitudes approximating indefinitely to religious reverence. But such beings will at best be instances of valued qualities which we too may come to exemplify, though in lesser degree. And not only would it be idolatrous for us to worship them, but it would also be monstrous for them to exact worship, or to care for it. The attitude of such beings to our reverence would necessarily be deprecating: they would prefer cooperative atheists to adoring zealots. And they would probably hide themselves like royal personages from the anthems of their worshipers, and perhaps the fact that there are so few positive signs of their presence is itself a feeble evidence of their real existence. But whether such beings exist or not, they are not divine, and can never satisfy the demands inherent in religious reverence. And the effect of our argument will further be to discredit generally such forms of religion as attach a uniquely sacred meaning to existent things, whether these things be men or acts or institutions or writings.

But there are other frames of mind to which we shouldn't deny the name 'religious', which acquiesce quite readily in the nonexistence of their objects. (This nonexistence might, in fact, be taken to be the "real meaning" of saying that religious objects and realities are "not of this world.") In such frames of mind we give ourselves over unconditionally and gladly to the task of indefinite approach toward a certain imaginary focus[5] where nothing actually is, and we find this task sufficiently inspiring and satisfying without demanding (absurdly) that there should be something actual at that limit. And the atheistic religious attitude we have mentioned has also undergone reflective elaboration by such philosophers as Fichte and Erigena and Alexander. There is, then, a religious atheism which takes full stock of our arguments, and we may be glad that this is so. For since the religious spirit is one of reverence before things greater than ourselves, we should be gravely impoverished and arrested if this spirit ceased to be operative in our personal and social life. And it would certainly be better that this spirit should survive, with all its fallacious existential trimmings, than that we should cast it forth merely in order to be rid of such irrelevances.

NOTES

1. This word is added to avoid the suggestion that there must be *one* pervasive affinity linking together all the actions commonly called 'religious'.

2. Whatever the philosophical 'ground' for it may be, this plainly is the way in which we *do* describe the 'inner quality' of our felt attitudes.

3. I have included this alternative, of which I am not fond, merely because so many modern thinkers make use of it in this sort of connection.

4. Or 'nonsignificance', if this alternative is preferred.

5. To use a *Kantian comparison*.

2

GOD'S NON-EXISTENCE
A REPLY TO MR. RAINER AND MR. HUGHES
J. N. FINDLAY

I am grateful to the able articles of Mr. Hughes and Mr. Rainer, which have forced me to restate and re-examine some of the points raised in my article on the nonexistence of God. I anticipated the general line of their criticisms, and I entirely welcome them. For there can be nothing really "clinching" in philosophy: "proofs" and "disproofs" hold only for those who adopt certain premises, who are willing to follow certain rules of argument, and who use their terms in certain definite ways. And every proof or disproof can be readily evaded, if one questions the truth of its premises, or the validity of its type of inference, or if one finds new senses in which its terms may be used. And it is quite proper, and one's logical duty, to evade an argument in this manner, if it leads to preposterous consequences. And Mr. Hughes and Mr. Rainer are within their rights in thinking my conclusions preposterous: only I don't agree with them. I may say further, that I only brought in references to a "contemporary outlook," "modern approaches," and so on, because I wanted to be frank and modest, and not because I thought such descriptions honorific. I merely wished to indicate for *what* classes of person I hoped that my argument would hold water, instead of claiming (absurdly) that it would hold for all persons, whatever they might assume, and however they might choose to use their terms.

From *Mind* 58 (1949): 352–54. Copyright © 1949 by Oxford University Press. Reprinted by permission of Oxford University Press.

I think, however, that my article will be better understood if I mention the circumstances in which I first conceived it. Its central idea occurred to me as long ago as 1932, when I was not at all strongly influenced by "verificationism" or "logical empiricism." The main point of my article can be simply stated as a development of the Kantian treatment of the Ontological Proof, which I was considering at the time: I am surprised, in fact, that it hasn't occurred to other persons. And it is strange that Kant, who found so many antinomies in our notion of the 'World', found none at all in our notion of God. For Kant said that it couldn't be necessary that there should ever *be* anything of any description whatsoever, and that *if* we included 'existence' in the definition of something—Kant, of course, didn't think we *should* so include it, as existence "wasn't a predicate"—we could only say, *hypothetically*, that *if* something of a certain sort existed, then it *would* exist necessarily, but not, categorically, that it actually existed. And he also said that if one were willing to deny the existence of God, one couldn't be compelled to assert any property of Him, no matter how intimately such a property formed part of His 'nature'. Now, Kant, of course, didn't make existence (or necessary existence) part of God's nature,[1] but I have argued that one *ought* to do so, if God is to be the adequate object of our religious attitudes. So that for all those who are willing to accept *my* account of an adequate religious object, and also Kant's doctrine of the hypothetical character of necessary predications, it must follow inevitably that there cannot be an adequate object for our religious attitudes.

Now I admit to the full that my argument *doesn't* hold for those who have no desire to say that God exists in some necessary and inescapable manner. And hence Mr. Rainer is saying nothing to the point when he remarks that Broad and Russell (mentioned as typical modern thinkers) have not thought there was anything *impossible* in the existence of God. For neither Broad nor Russell thought of God as something whose nonexistence *should* be inconceivable. And my argument also *doesn't* hold for those who regard the Ontological Proof (or some other a priori proof) as a valid argument. Nor will it hold for those who are willing to say, with Mr. Rainer, that one might *come* to perceive the necessity of God's existence in some higher mystical state, nor for those who say, with Mr. Hughes and St. Thomas, that God himself can perceive the 'necessity' of His own 'existence', though both this 'existence' and this 'necessity' are something totally different from anything that we understand by these terms. I should indeed be naive if I thought I could trap the analogical eel[2] in my dialectical net. But my argument holds for all those thinkers—who may properly be called 'modern' in no narrow or 'tendentious' sense—who accept Kant's view that there aren't any necessary facts of existence and who also can be persuaded to hold that a God who is "worth His salt" must either exist necessarily (in the same sense of 'necessary') or not at all. The force of my argument doesn't depend, moreover, on any recent analysis of necessity in terms of tautology: it holds on *any* account of the necessary that can be squared with the above conditions.

My argument is, however, exposed to much more serious difficulties than those raised by Mr. Rainer and Mr. Hughes. For the "really modern philosopher" might doubt whether there was any genuine difference between my sort of atheism and the analogical theism of my opponents. And my argument has certainly suggested that there *was* some important difference between the two positions. For my opponents would admit, as I do, that one can never hope to have the Divine "fully before one," so as to be able to say "Lo, here!" of it, in the same way that one says this of one's friend Jones or the Eiffel Tower. They would say with me that one can't ever hope to meet with more than "expressions," "approximations," or "analogies" of the Divine, that it is in the nature of the Divine to outsoar and elude one. And I, for my part, should be willing to accord to my *focus imaginarius* that same attitude of unquestioning reverence, that my critics accord to their existent God: it is, in fact, *because* I think so highly of certain ideals, that I also think it unworthy to identify them with anything existent. And there is nothing absurd in having any number of emotional or other attitudes to objects that one thinks of as imaginary. The 'god' of the atheist will indeed be slightly different from the God of the theist—Mr. Rainer has taught me this—but He will only be so by an addition of "brackets." And the atheist might also admit the existence of something that I should describe (with great trepidation) as a "godward trend" in things: certainly there are *some* facts in our experience which are (one might say) *as if* there were a God. And when theists say that their God exists in some sense quite different from created objects, there seems but a hairsbreadth between them and such atheists as place their ideal, with Plato and Plotinus, ἐπέκεινα τῆς οὐσίας.

In reply to *such* criticisms (if anyone were to raise them) I could give no better reason for preferring *my* atheistic formulations than that they suited me from a *moral* and *religious* standpoint. For I am by temperament a Protestant, and I tend toward atheism as the purest form of Protestantism. By 'Protestantism' I mean the conviction—resting, as it seems to me, on elementary truisms—that it isn't *essential* in order to be a sound or 'saved' person, that one should pay deference to institutions, persons, books, ceremonies, and so forth, or do anything more than develop those qualities in which being a sound or 'saved' person consists. (Not that I think meanly of ceremonies, books, persons, and so forth, if *not* regarded as essential.) Now I don't doubt that theism *can* be so held as not to involve any idolatrous implications, but I think it *hard* to be a theist without falling into idolatry, with all its attendant evils of intolerance and persecution. And this is particularly the case in a religion like Christianity, where the Divine is *identified* with a particular historical person, who existed in no analogical manner, but precisely as you and I do. I am not, however, a religious genius, nor do I know how to replace the existential formulations of our present religion with nonexistential formulations that would prove equally effective, whether in stimulating endeavor or in damming up the tide of cruelty and injustice. For these reasons I am not at all keen to shake faiths or overturn altars (if indeed I were able to do so).

NOTES

1. Perhaps he does, however. See Immanuel Kant, *Critique of Pure Reason*, trans. Norman Kemp Smith (New York: Macmillan, 1929), A 676/B 704.

2. This term isn't used disrespectfully: I approve of eels.

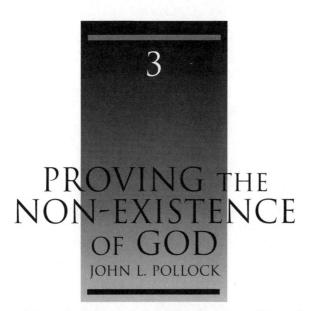

PROVING THE NON-EXISTENCE OF GOD

JOHN L. POLLOCK

In many religions, including I believe the Christian religion, the principal deity is conceived as existing necessarily. In other words, in such religions, the concept of God is such that, if there is such a being, then He exists necessarily. Symbolizing 'God' by 'g', 'x exists' by 'Ex', and the modal operator of logical necessity by '$\Box$',[1] we can say that the concept of God which we are considering is such that $(Eg \supset \Box Eg)$. I now propose to show that, simply as a matter of logic, such a being cannot exist.

In order to prove the nonexistence of God, it is convenient to begin by considering one of the most interesting of the arguments that purport to prove that God does exist—the Ontological Argument. One of the standard versions of the Ontological Argument begins by defining God to be the being more perfect than whom none can be conceived. A being that exists is more perfect than one that does not exist. Hence, if God did not exist, we could conceive of a greater being—namely, one that exists. Therefore, it follows from the definition of 'God' that He exists. We can symbolize the steps of this argument as follows:

(1) $\qquad g =_{Df}$ (the x such that Px);

(2) therefore, Pg;

(3) $\qquad \Box(x)(Px \supset Ex)$;

From *Inquiry* 9 (1966): 193–96. Copyright © 1966 by Taylor & Francis Group. Reprinted by permission of Taylor & Francis Group.

(4) therefore, $\Box(Pg \supset Eg)$;
(5) therefore, Eg.

Here we have taken 'Px' to be the predicate of absolute perfection.

The most common way of attacking this argument is due to Hume and Kant and consists in attacking (3) by denying that existence is a perfection. This is often put in a misleading way by saying that existence is not a predicate, but the arguments adduced do not support that conclusion.

In his recent article on the Ontological Argument, Norman Malcolm[2] claims to find a second version of the Ontological Argument in Anselm's writings, in which 'Ex' is replaced throughout by '$\Box Ex$'. It is then argued that although existence may not be a perfection, necessary existence is a perfection, and the conclusion of the argument is that God exists necessarily:

(1) $g =_{Df}$ (the x such that Px);
(2)   therefore, Pg;
(3') $\Box(x)(Px \supset \Box Ex)$;
(4')   therefore, $\Box(Pg \supset \Box Eg)$;
(5')   therefore, $\Box Eg$.

Unfortunately, this argument (and also the first argument) relies upon a simple logical fallacy; (2) does not follow from (1). In general, if we define 'a' by stipulating that $a =_{Df}$ (the x such that Ax), we cannot automatically conclude that Aa. To see this, suppose we let 'Ax' be 'Bx & $\sim Bx$'. Then we would have, purely by definition, 'Ba & $\sim Ba$'. In other words, we would have a contradiction following logically from a definition, in which case the contradiction would be logically true. But of course, that is absurd. What we *can* prove is that if there is a unique thing satisfying 'Ax', then 'Aa' will be true. But to say that there is a unique thing satisfying 'Ax' is just to say that a exists, that is, that Ea. If there isn't anything that can properly be called 'the x such that Ax', then clearly we can't conclude anything about a. In general, the strongest conclusion we can get from the definition '$a =_{Df}$ (the x such that Ax)' is '$\Box(Ea \supset Aa)$'.

Now let us apply these considerations to the Ontological Argument. The corrected argument now becomes:

(1) $g =_{Df}$ (the x such that Px);
(2')   therefore, $\Box(Eg \supset Pg)$;
(3') $\Box(x)(Px \supset \Box Ex)$;
(4')   therefore, $\Box(Pg \supset \Box Eg)$;
(5')   therefore, $\Box(Eg \supset \Box Eg)$.

In other words, if God exists, then He must exist necessarily. But it was just His existence that was in question in the first place, so it seems that this version does not succeed in establishing that God exists any more than the first version.[3]

Note that this argument can be repeated no matter what we put in for 'Px'. We can never get more than '$\Box(Eg \supset \Box Eg)$' for a conclusion. But next note that, as '$\Box(Eg \supset Pg)$' is the strongest conclusion we can obtain from the definition '$g =_{Df}$ (the x such that Px)', if there were any formally valid argument by which we could obtain 'Eg' from the definition of 'g', then an argument of the form of the Ontological Argument whereby we obtain it from '$\Box(Eg \supset Pg)$', together with a premise of the form '$\Box(x)(Px \supset \Box Ex)$', or more generally, of the form '$\Box(x)(Px \supset \phi x)$', which specifies what the logical nature of 'P' is, would have to be valid. Furthermore, assuming an essentially Fregean theory of logical necessity, 'Eg' is entailed by the definition '$g =_{Df}$ (the x such that Px)' if and only if, by specifying the logical nature of 'P' through the addition of premises of the form '$\Box(x)(Px \supset \phi x)$', we can obtain a formally valid argument having 'Eg' as the conclusion. As we have just seen, this cannot be done, and so it follows that the definition of 'g' does not entail 'Eg'. On the other hand, we have seen that the definition of 'g' does entail '$\Box(Eg \supset \Box Eg)$'. If we write '$P \rightarrow Q$' for 'P entails Q', then these conclusions can be symbolized as:

(6) $(g =_{Df}$ the x such that $Px) \rightarrow \Box(Eg \supset \Box Eg)$;

(7) $\sim [(g =_{Df}$ the x such that $Px) \rightarrow Eg]$.

The most common analysis of logical necessity is to say that a proposition is necessarily true if and only if it is true by virtue of the meaning of its constituent terms. This means that the proposition that God exists is necessarily true just in case the meaning of 'God' requires that He exist, that is, just in the case the definition of 'God' entails that He exists:

(8) $\Box Eg \equiv [(g =_{Df}$ the x such that $Px) \rightarrow Eg]$.

But then from (7) we can conclude that

(9) $\sim \Box Eg$.

Next recall that our concept of God is such that if He exists, then He must exist necessarily (by (6)), that is, $Eg \supset \Box Eg$. But then, simply by *modus tollens* from (9), $\sim Eg$, that is, God does not exist. Furthermore, this is a conclusion we have *proven* by logical means, so it is not just true, but necessarily true, that is, $\Box \sim Eg$. Thus, it is necessarily true that God does not exist. *The existence of God is a logical impossibility.*

One possible reply to this argument is that when people have spoken of God's necessary existence, they have not meant logical necessity. This may well be true, in which case we are talking about two different kinds of supreme being, only one kind of which I have attempted to show cannot exist. However, if by 'necessity' these people do not mean *logical* necessity, then I am afraid that I do not understand what they do mean. They clearly cannot mean *physical* necessity. It seems to me that the burden of proof is on them to explain a bit more clearly just what sort of necessity they have in mind.

NOTES

1. Thus '$\Box P$' is read 'It is necessarily true that P.'

2. Norman Malcolm, "Anselm's Ontological Argument," *Philosophical Review* 69 (1960): 41–62.

3. I think that this analysis of what is wrong with the Ontological Argument is essentially the same as the first of Kant's three objections to the Ontological Argument (*Critique of Pure Reason,* A 593–95).

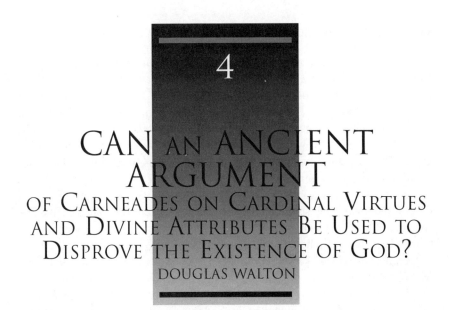

CAN AN ANCIENT ARGUMENT

OF CARNEADES ON CARDINAL VIRTUES AND DIVINE ATTRIBUTES BE USED TO DISPROVE THE EXISTENCE OF GOD?

DOUGLAS WALTON

T his essay discusses the question of whether one may coherently attribute ethical virtues—and in particular, the traditional so-called cardinal virtues of courage, wisdom, justice, and temperance—to a Divine being. First, some arguments ascribed by Sextus Empiricus and Cicero to the ancient philosopher Carneades are presented and analyzed. These arguments seem to run counter to such an attribution of ethical virtues to a Divine being. From these arguments, a deductively valid chain of reasoning is constructed that is shown to be a reductio ad absurdum of the attribution. What the Carneadean argument shows is that the assumption that a Divine being is both virtuous and perfect leads to a logical contradiction.

It is shown how the Carneadean argument is highly significant, both in philosophy of religion, where it can be shown to be importantly related to St. Anselm's ontological argument, and also in ethics, where it raises difficult questions on how the cardinal virtues should be defined.

CARNEADES THE PHILOSOPHER

Carneades (c. 213–128 BC) was the head of the third Platonic Academy, or so-called New Academy, that flourished in the second century BC. Born in Cyrene,

From *Philo* 2, no. 2 (1999): 5–13. Copyright © 1999 by Western Michigan University. Reprinted by permission of *Philo*.

Cyrenaica (now in Libya), Carneades, according to Hankinson, had an unparalleled reputation in the ancient world as a "master dialectician" and is "one of the great figures in the history of philosophy."[1] He lived to be around eighty-five years old, becoming blind in his old age.[2] Very little is known about his life, and he left no writings.[3] According to Diogenes Laertius, other than some letters he wrote, "everything else was compiled by his pupils; he himself left nothing in writing."[4] His pupil Clitomachus wrote many books—according to Diogenes Laertius, Clitomachus wrote more than four hundred treatises—but none of these survived either.[5] Carneades' successor Philo of Larissa, was the teacher of Cicero, and many interesting arguments attributed to Carneades are described by Cicero.[6] What knowledge we have about the opinions and arguments of Carneades is mostly to be found in the writings of Sextus Empiricus and Cicero.

Carneades was a skeptic who attacked the views of the Stoics and other leading "dogmatic" philosophical opinions of the ancient world. Carneades did not think we can have knowledge, but unlike prior skeptics, he was not content to advocate suspension of judgment. Instead, he proposed a criterion for rational acceptance based on what appears to be true. This criterion was his famous theory of "probability" (*to pithanon*), perhaps better translated as "plausibility." According to Long, this term, translated into Latin by Cicero as *probabile*, literally means 'persuasive' or 'trustworthy'.[7] At any rate, the term 'probability' is not used here in the modern statistical sense, but as more akin to what we might call 'plausibility' or 'appearing to be true'. Cicero describes it as "the sense impression which the wise man will use if nothing arises which is contrary to that probability."[8] In modern terms, it would be called plausible reasoning.[9] Carneades would not have seen his arguments as settling an issue conclusively, but as raising doubts that shift a burden of proof dialectically.

SKEPTICAL ARGUMENTS ABOUT
VIRTUES AND DIVINE BEINGS

Many interesting skeptical arguments about views of God (or the gods) advocated by other ancient philosophers are attributed to Carneades. There is quite a range of them covered in Sextus and in Cicero.[10] In Sextus[11] we find the following argument.

Premise 1: If the Divine exists, it is all-virtuous.
Premise 2: If the Divine is all-virtuous, it possesses the virtue of courage.
Premise 3: A being cannot be courageous unless there are things that are hard for it to endure.
Premise 4: If there are some things that are hard for a being to endure, there are some things that cause it vexation.

It is not hard to see where this argument is going. It implies that the Divine being has to be less than perfect, which appears to go against the kind of theological view that Carneades is questioning. The argument carries on as follows:

> And if there are some things which are hard for God to abstain from and hard to endure, there are some things which are able to change him for the worse and to cause him vexation. But if so, God is receptive of vexation and of change for the worse, and hence of decay also. So if God exists, he is perishable; but the second is not true; therefore the first is not true.[12]

The argument even appears to imply a kind of contradiction in the given notion of the all-virtuous God.

The general thrust of Carneades' line of argument has been summarized by Hallie in a form that articulates the contradiction inherent in the notion of an all-virtuous God:

> [God] is supposed to be virtuous and perfect, but virtue involves overcoming pains and dangers, and only for a being who can suffer or be destroyed are there pains and dangers. Neither suffering nor destructibility is consistent with perfection, so God cannot be both virtuous and perfect.[13]

This diagnosis of the fault in the set of theological assumptions that leads to the contradictory outcome pointed out by Carneades' argument is the ascription of virtue, a human quality, to a Divine being who is supposed to be perfect. Zeller articulated the crux of the problem posed by Carneades' argument: since every virtue presupposes an imperfection, ascribing a virtue like courage to God is problematic.[14]

This interesting argument raises not only theological questions about the nature of a perfect Divine being but also a number of questions of an ethical nature on how the concept of a virtue should be defined. How should courage be defined? Does courage require an overcoming of things that are hard to endure? Or should courage be defined as the overcoming of fear? Does courage imply a kind of imperfection or lack of complete power in an agent who may properly be said to be courageous? It poses some issues that are, even in light of contemporary ethical theory, difficult to deal with. The dialectical power of the argument reveals the stature of Carneades as a skeptical philosopher.

THE CONSTRUCTION OF A DISPROOF
OF THE EXISTENCE OF GOD

Carneades' skeptical argument is not only very powerful as a device for raising doubts or questions. It can be extended to generate a proof for the nonexistence of God, constructed below. This disproof does more than raise questions about the hypothesis that the Divine being is all-virtuous. It can be deployed as a positive argument supporting the conclusion that an all-virtuous Divine being does not exist. This positive argument is not actually expressed by the sources that report Carneades' arguments. But it can be constructed from them, providing an extension of them that reveals the dialectical power that these arguments have in ethics and theology.

1. God is (by definition) a being than which no greater being can be thought.
2. Greatness includes greatness of virtue.
3. Therefore, God is a being than which no being could be more virtuous.
4. But virtue involves overcoming pains and danger.
5. Indeed, a being can only be properly said to be virtuous if it can suffer pain or be destroyed.
6. A God that can suffer pain or is destructible is not one than which no greater being can be thought.
7. For you can think of a greater being, that is, one that is nonsuffering and indestructible.
8. Therefore, God does not exist.

This argument has an Anselmian spin on it, because it flows from the definition laid down in the first premise, which expresses a notion of perfection after the manner of Anselm's ontological argument. But then the argument goes on to exploit Carneades' notion of the incompatibility of virtue and perfection, using this notion to prove the nonexistence of a God who is said to be virtuous in the sense expressed in the fourth premise.

Anselm's ontological argument can be expressed as a chain of logical reasoning that is deductively valid. Once this has been done, the question of how to evaluate it centers on the individual premises, on whether they are plausible, on the definitions of the terms used in them, and on other informal matters, like whether the argument might be circular or might commit other fallacies.[15] The casting of the argument in a deductively valid form does not prove that the conclusion is true or has been proved to be true. It merely has a dialectical function of shifting the burden of proof onto anyone who does not accept the conclusion to cite which premise is not acceptable or contains dialectical problems. So too with the Carneadean argument above. The fact that it can be expressed in a deductively valid chain of reasoning has a dialectical function of leading to discussion. But before examining the premises, the question of the validity of the argument needs to be discussed.

It is not hard to prove that the argument is valid, but some of the inferences in the sequence could be criticized. Some might say that the argument sloppily moves from "a being than which no greater can be thought" at Premise 1 to simple "greatness" itself in Premise 2. Is this a problem? To investigate, the following symbolization of Premises 1 and 2 is given below, along with the conclusion 3 that follows from them in classical deductive logic. Here g is used as a name for God (the Divine being), and the expression x > y is taken to stand for the predicate "x is greater than y." The expression $x >_v y$ is taken to stand for the predicate "x is greater than y with respect to virtue."

Premise 1: $(\forall x)[(x = g) \supset \neg (\exists y)(y > g)]$
Premise 2: $(\forall x)(\forall y)[(x > g) \supset (x >_v y)]$
Conclusion: $(\forall x)[(x = g) \supset \neg (\exists y)(y >_v g)]$

This argument is easily shown to be deductively valid in classical first-order logic. Using comparable symbolizations, the remaining premises can be adjoined to the three propositions above in a sequence of reasoning that is deductively valid and has proposition 8 as its ultimate conclusion.

The validity of the Carneadean argument makes it function as a dialectical counterpart to Anselm's ontological argument, the argument that a being greater than which none can be thought must exist, since its failure to exist would mean that it would be less than perfect. That is, there would be the possibility of a greater being, one that actually exists. This reductio argument is valid, but it is open to the Carneadean objection that the idea of such a Divine being is problematic, since if its perfection is taken to include its being all-virtuous, it must be capable of suffering pain, vexation, and so on. Generally, theology wants or needs to see perfection as including all-virtuousness, because an omnipotent Divine being that was not virtuous, or whose virtue we could not be assured of, is a somewhat frightening prospect. Presumably, those who advocate the ontological argument want to view Divine perfection as including an ethical aspect—that is, seeing the Divine being as all-virtuous—and therefore the Anselmian ontological argument is open to the Carneadean argument, which attaches to it as a kind of extension or corollary that destroys it.

Two aspects of the Carneadean argument make it dialectically powerful—its deductive validity and the plausibility of its premises. As noted above, the first two premises are assumptions that fit in with or are required by the theological assumptions in the Anselmian ontological argument. And they do seem to be assumptions that are important, even vital for theology. But what about the other premises? Premises 4 and 5 are about virtue. Premise 4 claims that virtue involves overcoming pain and danger. This claim plausibly seems true of some of the main virtues, and especially the virtue of courage. Premise 5 extends this claim to say that a being can only be properly said to be virtuous if it can suffer pain or be destroyed. This claim seems plausible enough, but depends on how a virtue like courage should be defined, raising the kinds of ethical questions cited above, at the end of section 2.

DEFINING THE CARDINAL VIRTUES

How the Carneadean argument should be evaluated with respect to the acceptability of premises 4 and 5 depends on how the virtues should be specified and defined in ethical theory. The cardinal virtues are the four principal virtues—wisdom, temperance, courage, and justice—upon which the other moral virtues turn or are hinged (from *cardo*, or hinge).[16] The origin of the fourfold system is Socratic, but an influential account of two of the four cardinal virtues was given by Cicero in the *De Inventione*. Courage is "the quality by which one undertakes dangerous tasks and endures hardships."[17] Temperance is "a firm and well-considered control exercised by the reason over lust and other improper impulses of the mind."[18] The virtue of wisdom is most often associated with Aristotle's notion of *phronesis*, or practical wisdom, which involves judging how to act prudently in a variable situation where no exact form of calculation is applicable. Finally, justice has to do with judging claims and allegations in a way that is equitable or fair to all parties involved. And according to Jonsen and Toulmin, justice involves human perceptiveness and discernment in the application of moral and legal rules.[19] All four cardinal virtues are distinctively human in that all of them require balance in an uncertain and difficult situation, where hardships and dangers—either physical dangers, or the danger of making a bad decision under pressure—need to be overcome, or at least dealt with.

So how should the part of the Carneadean argument that depends on claims about the virtues be evaluated? The argument is deductively valid (or, as shown above, can be expressed in a deductively valid form), so the best point of dialectical examination is to question what appears to be the weakest premise. This weakest point for questioning would seem to be premise 4. Is it true of all the cardinal virtues that they involve overcoming pains and danger?

Clearly the virtue that most perfectly fits premise 4 is courage, which makes no sense other than as a virtue of overcoming pains and danger for a good purpose.[20] The virtue of temperance also fits premise 4 quite well—certainly as defined by Cicero it does. But what about wisdom and justice? Do they make premise 4 come out true? Perhaps all that needs to be said here is that even if they don't, on all theories of ethics, on the best accounts, they do involve elements of balance and striving for a prudent line of action in an uncertain situation.[21] And these human aspects may be enough to make questionable their compatibility with a perfect and omniscient thinker in the role of the decision-maker. Even these human aspects of wisdom and justice as cardinal virtues lend some support to the Carneadean argument.

On balance, however, support for the Carneadean argument against the existence of God is mixed. The cardinal virtue of courage gives the argument its strongest support, while the support given by the other three cardinal virtues is questionable. Even this mixed outcome, nevertheless, gives enough support to the argument to raise questions about the logical consistency of the concept of a God who is both virtuous and perfect.

One way out is to deny that courage is a cardinal virtue. But this avenue is not a line of argument that will be pursued here. Nor does it seem plausible, in line with Cicero's account of the virtues and the traditions flowing from that account. Cicero's precise definitions of the cardinal virtues given in the *De Inventione*[22] were so succinctly stated that they became classics for subsequent writers on morality, right up until modern times. These traditions are right to accord courage a place of importance as a fundamental virtue, and no account of the cardinal virtues could be compelling without according courage a place of prominence. A virtuous being must be a courageous being. And if so, the Carneadean argument is not only valid, but has premises that are all strongly representative of a theological position that not only had adherents in the time of Carneades, but has since become the official theological view.

The next point to be taken up is how the virtue of courage should be defined. There are two different ways of attempting to define 'courage'.[23] One way is to say that courage is the overcoming of fear, so that in order for someone to be acting in a truly courageous way, this person has to have fear in the given situation and has to overcome that fear. The other way is to say that courage is doing the right thing in a situation where it is markedly dangerous or difficult to do that thing. Sometimes fear is such an obstacle. However, on the second conception, but not on the first, it is possible for the courageous person not to exhibit fear.

This point of issue is significant with respect to the Carneadean argument, as can be seen when the following addition to it is noted.

> Further, in addition to the foregoing arguments, if God is all-virtuous he possesses courage; and if he possesses courage he possesses "knowledge of things fearful and not fearful and of things intermediate"; and if so, there is something which is fearful to God.[24]

This extended Carneadean argument is based on the assumption that courage is defined in the first way, as requiring fear or the awareness or knowledge of fear. But if 'courage' is defined in the other way, as not requiring fear, this extension of the argument is not applicable.

WHAT DOES THE CARNEADEAN ARGUMENT SHOW?

It is worth noting that the Anselmian ontological argument expresses its main premise in a negative format. It does not say that the Divine being is perfect, but that the Divine being is that than which nothing greater can be thought. This careful way of expressing the main premise accommodates the assumption that the Divine nature may be, in some respects, beyond our comprehension as persons. Aquinas is similarly circumspect when he writes in the *Summa Theologiae* that virtue cannot be predicated of God in the same way we would ascribe virtue to a person:

> Reply Obj. 1: Virtue and wisdom are not predicated of God and of us univocally. Hence it does not follow that there are accidents in God as there are in us.[25]

This reply indicates the awareness of Aquinas of the assumption that if we are to attribute virtue to God, it must be in a special sense. It would appear then that Western theology has been well aware of the limitations required by the kind of objection that can be posed through the Carneadean type of argument.

Still, the posing of the Carneadean argument in a chain of reasoning that has a deductively valid form, with premises that are initially plausible, is a worthwhile dialectical exercise which points the way to the necessity for the making of some distinctions by theologians. What is particularly attractive is the matching of the Carneadean argument to the ontological argument as an opposed and equally compelling counterargument. What needs to be shown is how the Anselmian ontological argument can be accepted without leading to the Carneadean argument.

What is shown is that if the Divine being is to be conceptualized as that than which nothing greater can be thought, the relation "greater than" does not necessarily imply "greater than with respect to virtue" in exactly the same sense of the term "virtue" that applies to human agents. The Carneadean argument shows that it is meaningful to attribute virtue to God only in a special sense, a sense that does not imply the difficulties revealed by the Carneadean argument. It follows that when we speak of the Divine being as courageous, prudent, loving, just, and so forth, we can do so only in a sense that is analogical to the meanings these terms normally have in ethics, when we are speaking of human agents, who typically have to act under uncertainty, depend on luck, and overcome obstacles and difficulties, even obstacles posed by their own personal failings and inadequacies.

What is shown is that there appear to be epistemological limits about what can be known by human thinkers on the basis of logical reasoning about the nature of the Divine being. These limits are staked out by the Carneadean argument. But the argument should also be seen as showing something about the dialectical development of the disputation between the believers and the doubters. It shifts a burden of proof. If theology is to defend the conception of the Divine being as that than which nothing greater can be thought, some further account needs to be given of the sense in which such a being can be virtuous.[26]

NOTES

1. R. J. Hankinson, *The Skeptics* (London: Routledge, 1995), p. 94.

2. Philip P. Hallie, "Carneades," *The Encyclopedia of Philosophy* (New York: Macmillan, 1967), p. 33. Diogenes Laertius, *Lives of Eminent Philosophers*, vol. 1, Loeb Classical Library (Cambridge, Mass.: Harvard University Press, 1931), p. 65.

3. Edouard Zeller, *Stoics, Epicureans and Skeptics* (London: Longman, Green and Co., 1982), p. 537.

4. Diogenes Laertius, *Lives of Eminent Philosophers*, vol. 1, p. 65.

5. A. A. Long, *Hellenistic Philosophy: Stoics, Epicureans, Skeptics* (London: Duckworth, 1974), p. 94. Long cites Diogenes Laertius, p. 94.

6. Hankinson, *The Skeptics*, p. 94.

7. Long, *Hellenistic Philosophy*, p. 97.

8. Marcus Tullius Cicero, *Academica*, trans. H. Rackham, Loeb Classical Library (Cambridge, Mass.: Harvard University Press, 1961), II: 99.

9. Nicholas Rescher, *Plausible Reasoning* (Assen: Van Gorcum, 1976).

10. Sextus Empiricus, *Against the Physicists*, trans. R. G. Bury, Loeb Classical Library (Cambridge, Mass.: Harvard University Press, 1937), I: 149–74. Marcus Tullius Cicero, *De Natura Deorum,* trans. H. Rackham, Loeb Classical Library (Cambridge, Mass.: Harvard University Press, 1961), III: 28–40.

11. Sextus Empiricus, *Against the Physicists*, I: 152–58.

12. Ibid., I: 157–58.

13. Hallie, "Carneades," p. 34.

14. Zeller, *Stoics, Epicureans and Skeptics*, p. 547.

15. Douglas Walton, "The Circle in Ontological Argument," *International Journal for Philosophy of Religion* 9 (1978): 193–218.

16. John Rickaby, "Cardinal Virtues," *The Catholic Encyclopedia*, vol. 3 (New York: Robert Appleton, 1908), p. 343.

17. Marcus Tullius Cicero, *De Inventione*, trans. Loeb Classical Library (London: William Heinemann, 1949), II: 163.

18. Ibid., II: 164.

19. Albert R. Jonsen and Stephen Toulmin, *The Abuse of Casuistry* (Berkeley: University of California Press, 1988), p. 9.

20. Douglas Walton, *Courage: A Philosophical Investigation* (Berkeley: University of California Press, 1986).

21. Jonsen and Toulmin, *The Abuse of Casuistry*.

22. Ibid., p. 87.

23. Walton, *Courage*.

24. Sextus Empiricus, *Against the Physicists*, I: 158–59.

25. St. Thomas Aquinas, *Summa Theologiae*, vol. 1, trans. the Dominican Fathers (Westminister: New York, Benziger Brothers, 1948), Pt. 1, Q.3, Art. 6.

26. I would like to thank the University of Winnipeg for granting me study leave in 1996–97 and the Oregon Humanities Center for inviting me to the University of Oregon as Distinguished Visiting Research Associate in 1997. Part of the work was supported by a Research Grant from the Social Sciences and Humanities Research Council of Canada and by the Department of Philosophy of the University of Western Australia.

5

GOD AND MORAL AUTONOMY

JAMES RACHELS

> Kneeling down or groveling on the ground, even to express your reverence for heavenly things, is contrary to human dignity.
>
> —Kant

God, if he exists, is worthy of worship. Any being who is not worthy of worship cannot be God, just as any being who is not omnipotent or perfectly good cannot be God.[1] This is reflected in the attitudes of religious believers who recognize that whatever else God may be, he is a being before whom we should bow down. Moreover, he is unique in this; to worship anyone or anything else is blasphemy. But can such a being exist? In what follows I will present an argument against the existence of God that is based on the conception of God as a fitting object of worship. The argument is that God cannot exist, because there could not be a being toward whom we should adopt such an attitude.

WORSHIP

The concept of worship has received surprisingly little attention from philosophers of religion. When it has been treated, the usual approach is by way of referring to God's awesomeness or mysteriousness: to worship is to "bow down in

From James Rachels, *Can Ethics Provide Answers? And Other Essays in Moral Philosophy* (New York: Rowman & Littlefield Publishers, 1997), pp. 109–23. Copyright © 1997 by Rowman & Littlefield Publishers. Reprinted by permission of Rowman & Littlefield Publishers.

silent awe" when confronted with a being that is "terrifyingly mysterious."[2] But neither of these notions is of much help in understanding worship. Awe is certainly not the same thing as worship; one can be awed by a performance of *King Lear*, by witnessing an eclipse of the sun or an earthquake, or by meeting one's favorite film star without worshiping any of these things. And a great many things are both terrifying and mysterious that we have not the slightest inclination to worship—the Black Death probably fits that description for many people. So we need an account of worship that does not rely on such notions as awesomeness and mysteriousness.

Consider McBlank, who worked against America's entry into the Second World War, refused induction into the army, and went to jail. He was active in the "ban the bomb" movements of the 1950s; he made speeches, wrote pamphlets, led demonstrations, and went back to jail. He opposed the war in Vietnam; and in old age he angrily denounced the short-lived Gulf War. In all of this McBlank acted out of principle. He thinks that all war is evil and that no war is ever justified.

We might note three features of McBlank's pacifist commitment. (1) He recognizes that certain facts are the case. History is full of wars; war causes the massive destruction of life and property; in war people suffer on a scale hardly matched in any other way; the large nations now have weapons that, if used, could virtually wipe out the human race; and so on. These are just facts that any normally informed person will admit without argument. (2) But of course they are not *merely* facts that people recognize to be the case in some indifferent manner. They are facts that have special importance to human beings. They form an ominous and threatening backdrop to people's lives—even though for most people they are a backdrop only. But not so for McBlank. He sees the accumulation of these facts as having radical implications for his conduct; he behaves in a very different way from the way he would behave were it not for these facts. His whole style of life is different; his conduct is altered, not just in its details, but in its pattern. (3) Not only is his overt behavior affected, so are his ways of thinking about the world and his place in it. His self-image is different. He sees himself as a member of a race with an insane history of self-destruction, and his self-image becomes that of an active opponent of the forces that lead to this self-destruction. He is an opponent of militarism just as he is a father or a musician. When the existentialists said that we "create ourselves" by our choices, they may have had something like this in mind.

The worshiper has a set of beliefs about God that function in the same way as McBlank's beliefs about war. First, the worshiper believes that certain sorts of things are the case: for example, that the world was created by an all-powerful, all-wise being who knows our every thought and action; that this being cares for us and regards us as his children; that we are made by him in order to return his love and live in accordance with his laws; and that if we do not live in a way pleasing to him, we may be punished. (I use these beliefs as my example. But I do not mean that these particular beliefs are accepted, in just this form, by all religious people. They are, however, the sorts of beliefs that are required for the business of worshiping God to make sense.)

Second, like the facts about warfare, these are not facts that one notes with an air of indifference. They have important implications for one's conduct. An effort must be made to discover God's will both for people generally and for oneself in particular; and to this end, the believer consults the church authorities and the theologians, reads the scripture, and prays. The degree to which this will alter his behavior will depend, of course, on exactly what he decides God would have him do and on the extent to which his behavior would have followed the prescribed pattern in any case.

Finally, the believer's recognition of these facts will influence his self-image and his way of thinking about the world and his place in it. The world will be regarded as having been made for the fulfillment of divine purposes; the hardships that befall men will be regarded either as "tests" in some sense or as punishments for sin; and most important, the believer will think of himself as a child of God and of his conduct as reflecting either honor or dishonor upon his Heavenly Father.

Wittgenstein's View

What will be most controversial in what I have said so far (to some philosophers, though perhaps not to most religious believers) is the treatment of claims such as "God regards us as his children" as in some sense factual. Wittgenstein is reported to have thought this a misunderstanding of religious belief, and others have followed him in this.[3] Religious utterances, it is said, do not report putative facts. Instead, we should understand such utterances as revealing the speaker's *form of life*. To have a form of life is to accept a language game; the religious believer accepts a language game in which there is talk of God, Creation, Heaven and Hell, a Last Judgment, and so forth, which the skeptic does not accept. Such language games can be understood only in their own terms; we must not try to assimilate them to other sorts of games. To see how this particular game works, we need only to examine the way the language of religion is used by actual believers; in its proper habitat the language game will be "in order" as it stands. We find that the religious believer uses such utterances for a number of purposes—for example, to express reasons for action, to show the significance that she attaches to various things, to express her attitudes, and so on—but not to state facts in the ordinary sense. So when the believer makes a typically religious assertion and the nonbeliever denies the same, *they are not contradicting one another;* rather, the nonbeliever is simply refusing to play the believer's (very serious) game. Wittgenstein (as recorded by his pupils) said:

> Suppose that someone believed in the Last Judgment, and I don't, does this
> mean that I believe the opposite to him, just that there won't be such a thing? I
> would say: "not at all, or not always."
>
> Suppose I say that the body will rot, and another says "No. Particles will
> rejoin in a thousand years, and there will be a Resurrection of you."
>
> If some said: "Wittgenstein, do you believe in this?" I'd say: "No." "Do
> you contradict the man?" I'd say: "No."[4]

Wittgenstein goes on to say that the difference between the believer and the
skeptic is not that one holds something to be true that the other thinks false but
that the believer takes certain things as "guidance for life" that the skeptic does
not—for example, that there will be a Last Judgment. He illustrates this by reference to a person who "thinks of retribution" when he plans his conduct or
assesses his condition:

> Suppose you had two people, and one of them, when he had to decide which
> course to take, thought of retribution, and the other did not. One person might,
> for instance, be inclined to take everything that happened to him as a reward or
> punishment, and another person doesn't think of this at all.
>
> If he is ill, he may think: "What have I done to deserve this?" This is one
> way of thinking of retribution. Another way is, he thinks in a general way when-
> ever he is ashamed of himself: "This will be punished."
>
> Take two people, one of whom talks of his behavior and of what happens
> to him in terms of retribution, the other does not. These people think entirely
> differently. Yet, so far, you can't say they believe different things.
>
> Suppose someone is ill and he says: "This is punishment," and I say: "If
> I'm ill, I don't think of punishment at all." If you say: "Do you believe the oppo-
> site?"—you can call it believing the opposite, but it is entirely different from
> what we would normally call believing the opposite.
>
> I think differently, in a different way. I say different things to myself. I have
> different pictures.[5]

But it is not at all clear that this account is true to the intentions of those who
engage in religious discourse. If a believer (at least, the great majority of those
whom I have known or read about) says that there will be a Last Judgment and
a skeptic says that there will not, the believer certainly will think that he has been
contradicted. Of course, the skeptic might not think of denying such a thing
except for the fact that the believer asserts it; and in this trivial sense, the skeptic
might "think differently"—but that is beside the point. Moreover, former believers who become skeptics frequently do so because they come to believe that
religious assertions are *false*; then they consider themselves to be denying
exactly what they previously asserted.

Moreover, a belief does not lose its ordinary factual import simply because it occupies a central place in one's way of life. McBlank takes the facts about war as guidance for life in a perfectly straightforward sense; but they remain facts. I take it that just as the man in Wittgenstein's example thinks of retribution often, McBlank thinks of war often. So, we do not need to give religious utterances any peculiar interpretation in order to explain their importance for one's way of life.

Finally, we do not need a view of religious belief that is deep and difficult. If the impact of religious belief on conduct and thinking can be explained by appeal to nothing more mysterious than putative facts and their impact on conduct and thinking, then the need for a more obscure theory is obviated. And if people believe that, as a matter of fact, their actions are subject to review by a just God who will mete out rewards and punishments on a day of final reckoning, that will explain very nicely why they think of retribution when they reflect on their conduct.

The Point of the Ritual

Worship is something that is done; but it is not clear just what is done when one worships. Other actions, such as throwing a ball or insulting one's neighbor, seem transparent enough, but not so with worship. When we celebrate Mass in the Roman Catholic Church, for example, what are we doing (apart from eating a wafer and drinking wine)? Or when we sing hymns in a Protestant church, what are we doing (other than merely singing songs)? What is it that makes these acts of *worship*? One obvious point is that these actions, and others like them, are ritualistic in character; so before we can make any progress in understanding worship, perhaps it will help to ask about the nature of ritual.

First, we need to distinguish the ceremonial form of a ritual from what is supposed to be accomplished by it. Consider, for example, the ritual of investiture for an English prince. The prince kneels; the queen (or king) places a crown on his head; and he takes an oath: "I do become your liege man of life and limb and of earthly worship, and faith and trust I will bear unto thee to live and die against all manner of folks." By this ceremony the prince is elevated to his new station, and by this oath he acknowledges the commitments that, as prince, he will owe the queen. In one sense, the ceremonial form of the ritual is unimportant; it is possible that some other procedure might have been laid down, without the point of the ritual being affected in any way. Rather than placing a crown on his head, the queen might break an egg into his palm (that could symbolize all sorts of things). Once this was established as the procedure, it would do as well as the other. It would still be the ritual of investiture, so long as it was understood that by the ceremony a prince is created. The performance of a ritual, then, is in certain respects like the use of language. In speaking, sounds are uttered, and, thanks to the conventions of the language, something is said, or affirmed, or done; and in a ritual performance, a ceremony is enacted, and, thanks to the conventions associated with the ceremony, something is done, or affirmed, or celebrated.

How are we to explain the point of the ritual of investiture? We might explain that certain parts of the ritual symbolize specific things; for example, that the prince's kneeling before the queen symbolizes his subordination to her (it is not merely to make it easier for her to place the crown on his head). But it is essential that in explaining the point of the ritual as a whole, we include that a prince is being created, that he is henceforth to have certain rights in virtue of having been made a prince, and that he is to have certain duties that he is now acknowledging, among which are complete loyalty and faithfulness to the queen, and so on. If the listener already knows about the complex relations between queens, princes, and subjects, then all we need to say is that a prince is being installed in office; but if he is unfamiliar with this social system, we must tell him a great deal if he is to understand what is going on.

So, once we understand the social system in which there are queens, princes, and subjects, and therefore understand the role assigned to each within that system, we can sum up what is happening in the ritual of investiture in this way: someone is being made a prince, and he is accepting that role with all that it involves. Similar explanations could be given for other rituals, such as the marriage ceremony: two people are being made husband and wife, and they are accepting those roles with all that they involve.

The question to be asked about the ritual of worship is what analogous explanation can be given of it. The ceremonial form of the ritual may vary according to the customs of the religious community; it may involve singing, drinking wine, counting beads, sitting with a solemn expression on one's face, dancing, making a sacrifice, or what have you. But what is the point of it?

As we have already observed, the worshiper thinks of himself as inhabiting a world created by an infinitely wise, infinitely powerful, perfectly good God; and it is a world in which he, along with other people, occupies a special place in virtue of God's intentions. This gives him a certain role to play: the role of a "child of God." In worshiping God, one is acknowledging and accepting this role, and that is the point of the ritual of worship. Just as the ritual of investiture derives its significance from its place within the social system of queens, princes, and subjects, the ritual of worship gets its significance from an assumed system of relationships between God and human beings. In the ceremony of investiture, the prince assumes a role with respect to the queen and the citizenry. In marriage, two people assume roles with respect to one another. And in worship, a person accepts and affirms his role with respect to God.

Worship presumes the superior status of the one worshiped. This is reflected in the logical point that there can be no such things as mutual or reciprocal worship, unless one or the other of the parties is mistaken as to his own status. We can very well comprehend people loving one another or respecting one another, but not (unless they are misguided) worshiping one another. This is because the worshiper necessarily assumes his own inferiority; and since inferiority is an asymmetrical relation, so is worship. (The nature of the 'superiority' and 'inferiority' involved here is of course problematic; but in the account I am presenting, it may be understood on the model of superior and inferior positions within a social system.) This is also why humility is necessary on the part of the worshiper. The role to which he commits himself is that of the humble servant, "not worthy to touch the hem of his garment." Compared to God's gloriousness, "all our righteousnesses are as filthy rags."[6] So in committing oneself to this role, one is acknowledging God's greatness and one's own relative worthlessness. This humble attitude is not a mere embellishment of the ritual: on the contrary, worship, unlike love or respect, requires humility. Pride is a sin, and pride before God is incompatible with worshiping him.

The function of worship as "glorifying" or "praising" God, which is often taken to be primary, may be regarded as derivative from the more fundamental nature of worship as commitment to the role of God's child. "Praising" God is giving him the honor and respect due to one in his position of eminence, just as one shows respect and honor in giving fealty to a king.

In short, the worshiper is in this position: He believes that there is a being, God, who is the perfectly good, perfectly powerful, perfectly wise Creator of the universe; and he views himself as the child of God, made for God's purposes and responsible to God for his conduct. And the ritual of worship, which may have any number of ceremonial forms according to the customs of the religious community, has as its point the acceptance of, and commitment to, this role as God's child, with all that this involves. If this account is accepted, then there is no mystery as to the relation between the act of worship and the worshiper's other activity. Worship will be regarded not as an isolated act taking place on Sunday morning, with no necessary connection to one's behavior the rest of the week, but as a ritualistic expression of, and commitment to, a role that dominates one's whole way of life.[7]

ACTING CONSISTENTLY WITH ONE'S ROLE AS GOD'S CHILD

An important feature of roles is that they can be violated: we can act and think consistently with a role, or we can act and think inconsistently with it. The prince can, for example, act inconsistently with his role as prince by giving greater importance to his own interests and welfare than to the queen's; in this case, he is no longer her liege man. And a father who does not attend to the welfare of his children is not acting consistently with his role as a father, and so on. What would count as violating the role to which one is pledged in virtue of worshiping God?

In Genesis two familiar stories, both concerning Abraham, are relevant. The first is the story of the near-sacrifice of Isaac. We are told that Abraham was "tempted" by God, who commanded him to offer Isaac as a human sacrifice. Abraham obeyed—he prepared an altar, bound Isaac to it, and was about to kill him until God intervened at the last moment, saying, "Lay not thine hand upon the lad, neither do thou any thing unto him: for now I know that thou fearest God, seeing thou hast not withheld thy son, thine only son from me" (Gen. 22:12). So Abraham passed the test. But how could he have failed? What was his temptation? Obviously, his temptation was to disobey God; God had ordered him to do some thing contrary both to his wishes and to his sense of what would otherwise have been right. He could have defied God, but he did not—he subordinated himself, his own desires and judgments, to God's command, even when the temptation to do otherwise was strongest.

It is interesting that Abraham's record in this respect was not perfect. We also have the story of him bargaining with God over the conditions for saving Sodom and Gomorrah from destruction. God had said that he would destroy those cities because they were so wicked; but Abraham gets God to agree that if fifty righteous men can be found there, the cities will be spared. Then he persuades God to lower the number to forty-five, then forty, then thirty, then twenty, and finally ten. Here we have a different Abraham, not servile and obedient, but willing to challenge God and bargain with him. However, even as he bargains with God, Abraham realizes that there is something radically inappropriate about it: he says, "Behold now, I have taken upon me to speak unto the Lord, which am but dust and ashes. . . . Oh let not the Lord be angry" (Gen. 18:27, 30).

The fact is that Abraham could not, consistent with his role as God's subject, set his own judgment and will against God's. The author of Genesis was certainly right about this. We cannot recognize any being *as God* and at the same time set ourselves against him. The point is not merely that it would be imprudent to defy God, since we certainly can't get away with it. Rather, there is a stronger, logical point involved—namely, that if we recognize any being as God, then we are committed, in virtue of that recognition, to obeying him.

To see why this is so, we must first notice that 'God' is not a proper name like "Richard Nixon" but a title like "president of the United States" or "king."[8] Thus, "Jehovah is God" is a nontautological statement in which the title 'God' is assigned to Jehovah, a particular being, just as "Richard Nixon is president of the United States" assigns the title "president of the United States" to a particular man. This permits us to understand how statements like "God is perfectly wise" can be logical truths, which is problematic if 'God' is regarded as a proper name. Although it is not a logical truth that any particular being is perfectly wise, it nevertheless is a logical truth that if any being is God (that is, if any being properly holds that title), then that being is perfectly wise. This is exactly analogous to saying that although it is not a logical truth that Richard Nixon has the authority to veto congressional legislation, nevertheless it is a logical truth that if Richard Nixon is president of the United States, then he has that authority.

To bear the title 'God', then, a being must have certain qualifications: he must be all-powerful and perfectly good in addition to being perfectly wise. And in the same vein, to apply the title 'God' to a being is to recognize him as one to be obeyed. The same is true, to a lesser extent, of 'king'; to recognize anyone as king is to acknowledge that he occupies a place of authority and has a claim on one's allegiance as his subject. And to recognize any being as God is to acknowledge that he has unlimited authority and an unlimited claim on one's allegiance. Thus, we might regard Abraham's reluctance to defy Jehovah as grounded not only in his fear of Jehovah's wrath but as a logical consequence of his acceptance of Jehovah as God. Albert Camus was right to think that "from the moment that man submits God to moral judgment, he kills Him in his own heart."[9] What a man can "kill" by defying or even questioning God is not the being that (supposedly) *is* God but his own conception of that being as God. That God is not to be judged, challenged, defied, or disobeyed is at bottom a truth of logic. To do any of these things is incompatible with taking him as one to be worshiped.

As a sidelight, this suggestion might also provide some help with the old problem of how we could, even in principle, verify God's existence. Skeptics have argued that even though we might be able to confirm the existence of an all-powerful cosmic superbeing, we still wouldn't know what it means to verify that this being is *divine*. And this, it is said, casts doubt on whether the notion of divinity and related notions such as 'sacred', 'holy', and 'God' are intelligible.[10] Perhaps this is because in designating a being as God, we are not only describing him as having certain properties (such as omnipotence), but we are also ascribing to him a certain place in our devotions and taking him as one to be obeyed, worshiped, and praised. If this is part of the logic of 'God', we shouldn't be surprised if God's existence, insofar as that includes the existence of divinity, is not empirically confirmable. But once the reason for this is understood, it no longer seems such a serious matter.

THE MORAL AUTONOMY ARGUMENT

So the idea that any being could be worthy of worship is much more problematic than we might have at first imagined. In saying that a being is worthy of worship, we would be recognizing him as having an unqualified claim on our obedience. The question, then, is whether there could be such an unqualified claim. It should be noted that the description of a being as all-powerful, all-wise, and so on would not automatically settle the issue; for even while admitting the existence of such an awesome being, we might still question whether we should recognize him as having an unlimited claim on our obedience.

There is a long tradition in moral philosophy, from Plato to Kant, according to which such a recognition could never be made by a moral agent. According to this tradition, to be a moral agent is to be autonomous, or self-directed. Unlike the precepts of law or social custom, moral precepts are imposed by the agent upon himself, and the penalty for their violation is, in Kant's words, "self-contempt and inner abhorrence."[11] The virtuous person is therefore identified with the person of integrity, the person who acts according to precepts that she can, on reflection, conscientiously approve in her own heart.

On this view, to deliver oneself over to a moral authority for directions about what to do is simply incompatible with being a moral agent. To say "I will follow so-and-so's directions no matter what they are and no matter what my own conscience would otherwise direct me to do" is to opt out of moral thinking altogether; it is to abandon one's role as a moral agent. And it does not matter whether "so-and-so" is the law, the customs of one's society, or Jehovah. This does not, of course, preclude one from seeking advice on moral matters and even on occasion following that advice blindly, trusting in the good judgment of the adviser. But this is justified by the details of the particular case—for example, that you cannot form any reasonable judgment of your own because of ignorance or inexperience or lack of time. What is precluded is that a person should, while in possession of his wits, adopt this style of decision making (or perhaps we should say this style of abdicating decision making) as a general strategy of living or abandon his own best judgment when he can form a judgment of which he is reasonably confident.

We have, then, a conflict between the role of worshiper, which by its very nature commits one to total subservience to God, and the role of moral agent, which necessarily involves autonomous decision making. The role of worshiper takes precedence over every other role the worshiper has; when there is any conflict, the worshiper's commitment to God has priority over everything. But the first commitment of a moral agent is to do what in his own heart he thinks is right. Thus the following argument might be constructed:

1. If any being is God, he must be a fitting object of worship.
2. No being could possibly be a fitting object of worship, since worship requires the abandonment of one's role as an autonomous moral agent.
3. Therefore, there cannot be any being who is God.

OBJECTIONS AND REPLIES

The concept of moral agency underlying this argument is controversial, and although I think it is sound, I cannot give it here the detailed treatment that it requires. Instead, I will conclude by considering some of the most obvious objections to the argument.

(1) What if God lets us go our own way and issues no commands other than that we should live according to our own consciences? In that case there would be no incompatibility between our commitment to God and our commitments as moral agents, since God would leave us free to direct our own lives. The fact that this supposition is contrary to major religious traditions (such as the Christian tradition) doesn't matter, since these traditions could be mistaken. The answer is that this is a mere contingency, and that even if God did not require obedience to detailed commands, the worshiper would still be committed to the abandonment of his role as a moral agent if God required it.

(2) God is perfectly good; it follows that he would never require us to do anything except what is right. Therefore, in obeying God, we would only be doing what we should do in any case. So there is no incompatibility between obeying him and carrying out our moral responsibilities. Our responsibility as moral agents is to do right, and God's commands are right, so that's that. This objection rests on a misunderstanding of the idea that (necessarily) God is perfectly good. This can be intelligibly asserted only because of the principle that *no being who is not perfectly good may bear the title 'God'*. The catch is that we cannot determine whether some being is God without first checking on whether he is perfectly good;[12] and we cannot decide whether he is perfectly good without knowing (among other things) whether his commands to us are right. Thus, our own judgment that some actions are right and others wrong is logically prior to our recognition of any being as God. The upshot is that we cannot justify the suspension of our own judgment on the grounds that we are deferring to God's command; for if, by our own best judgment, the command is wrong, this gives us good reason to withhold the title 'God' from the commander.

(3) People are sinful; their very consciences are corrupt and unreliable guides. What is taken for conscientiousness is nothing more than self-aggrandizement and arrogance. Therefore, we cannot trust our own judgment; we must trust God and do what he wills. Only then can we be assured of doing what is right.

This is a view that has always had its advocates among theologians. But this Augustinian view suffers from a fundamental inconsistency. It is said that we cannot know for ourselves what is right and what is wrong, because our judgment is corrupt. But how do we know that our judgment is corrupt? Presumably, in order to know that, we would have to know (a) that some actions are morally required of us, and (b) that our own judgment does not reveal that these actions are required. However, (a) is just the sort of thing that we cannot know, according to this view. Now, it may be suggested that while we cannot know (a) by our own judgment, we can know it as a result of God's revelation. But even setting aside the practical difficulties of distinguishing genuine from bogus revelation (a generous concession), there is still this problem: if we learn that God (some being we take to be God) requires us to do a certain action and we conclude on this account that the action is morally right, then we have still made at least one moral judgment of our own, namely, that whatever this being requires is morally right. Therefore, it is impossible to maintain the view that we have moral knowledge and that all of it comes from God's revelation.

(4) Some philosophers have held that the voice of individual conscience is the voice of God speaking to the individual, whether the individual realizes it or not and whether he is a believer or not. This would resolve the conflict, because in following one's conscience, one would at the same time be discharging one's obligation as a worshiper to obey God. However, this maneuver is unsatisfying because if it were taken seriously, it would lead to the conclusion that in speaking to us through our "consciences," God is merely tricking us, for he is giving us the illusion of self-governance while all the time he is manipulating our thoughts from without. Moreover, in acting from conscience, we are acting under the view that our actions are right and not merely that they are decreed by a higher power. Socrates' argument in the *Euthyphro* can be adapted to this point. If in speaking to us through the voice of conscience, God is informing us of what is right, then there is no reason to think that we could not discover this for ourselves—the notion of "God informing us" is eliminable. On the other hand, if God is only giving us arbitrary commands, which cannot be thought of as right independent of his promulgating them, then the whole idea of conscience, as it is normally understood, is a sham.

(5) Finally, it might be objected that the question of whether any being is worthy of worship is different from the question of whether we should worship him. In general, that X is worthy of our doing Y with respect to X does not entail that we should do Y with respect to X. Mrs. Brown, being a fine woman, may be worthy of a marriage proposal, but we ought not to propose to her, since she is already married. Or, Seaman Jones may be worthy of a medal for heroism, but still there could be reasons why we should not award it. Similarly, it may be that there is a being who is worthy of worship and yet we should not worship him since it would interfere with our lives as moral agents. Thus God, who is worthy of worship, may exist; and we should love, respect, and honor him, but not worship him in the full sense of the word. If this is correct, then the Moral Autonomy Argument is fallacious.

But this objection will not work because of a disanalogy between the cases of proposing marriage and awarding the medal, on the one hand, and the case of worship on the other. It may be that Mrs. Brown is worthy of a proposal, yet there are circumstances in which it would be wrong to propose to her. However, these circumstances are contrasted with others in which it would be perfectly all right. The same goes for Seaman Jones's medal: there are some circumstances in which awarding it would be proper. But in the case of worship—if the foregoing arguments have been sound—there are no circumstances under which anyone should worship God. And if one should never worship, then the concept of a fitting object of worship is empty.

The Moral Autonomy Argument will probably not persuade anyone to abandon belief in God—arguments rarely do—and there are certainly many more points that need to be worked out before it can be known whether this argument is even viable. Perhaps it isn't. Yet it does raise an issue that is clear enough. Theologians are already accustomed to speaking of theistic belief and commitment as taking the believer "beyond morality." The question is whether this should not be regarded as a severe embarrassment.

NOTES

1. Charles Hartshorne and Nelson Pike have suggested that St. Anselm's famous definition of God, "that than which none greater can be conceived," should be understood as meaning "that than which none more worthy of worship can be conceived." Charles Hartshorne, *Anselm's Discovery* (LaSalle, Ill.: Open Court, 1966), pp. 25–26; and Nelson Pike, *God and Timelessness* (London: Routledge & Kegan Paul, 1970), pp. 149–60.

2. These phrases are from John Hick, *Philosophy of Religion* (Englewood Cliffs, N.J.: Prentice-Hall, 1963), pp. 13–14.

3. Ludwig Wittgenstein, *Lectures and Conversations on Aesthetics, Psychology, and Religious Belief*, ed. Cyril Barrett, from notes taken by Yorick Smythies, Rush Rhees, and James Taylor (Berkeley: University of California Press, 1967). See also, for example, Rush Rhees, chap. 13 in *Without Answers* (London: Routledge & Kegan Paul, 1969).

4. Wittgenstein, *Lectures*, p. 53.

5. Ibid., pp. 54–55.

6. Isa. 64:6 AV. All biblical citations are to the Authorized (King James) Version.

7. This account of worship, specified here in terms of what it means to worship God, may easily be adapted to the worship of other beings, such as Satan. The only changes required are (a) that we substitute for beliefs about God analogous beliefs about Satan, and (b) that we understand the ritual of worship as committing the Satan-worshiper to a role as Satan's servant in the same way that worshiping God commits theists to the role of his servant.

8. Cf. Nelson Pike, "Omnipotence and God's Ability to Sin," *American Philosophical Quarterly* 6 (1969): 208–9; and C. B. Martin, chap. 4 in *Religious Belief* (Ithaca, N.Y.: Cornell University Press, 1964).

9. Albert Camus, *The Rebel*, trans. Anthony Bower (New York: Vintage, 1956), p. 62.

10. See Kai Nielsen, "Eschatological Verification," *Canadian Journal of Theology* 9 (1963).

11. Immanuel Kant, *Foundations of the Metaphysics of Morals*, trans. Lewis White Beck (Indianapolis: Bobbs-Merrill, 1959), p. 44.

12. In one sense, of course, we could never know for sure that such a being is perfectly good, since that would require an examination of all his actions and commands, which is impossible. However, if we observed many good things about him and no evil ones, we would be justified in accepting the hypothesis that he is perfectly good. The hypothesis would be confirmed or disconfirmed by future observations in the usual way.

PART 2

DEDUCTIVE EVIL DISPROOFS OF THE EXISTENCE OF GOD

INTRODUCTION

This section contains previously published papers and book selections presenting and defending deductive evil disproofs of the existence of God. A deductive evil disproof of God's existence, often called a logical argument from evil for God's nonexistence, is a deductive argument based on a contradiction between the attributes of God and the existence of evil.

A deductive evil disproof of God's existence takes the following general form:

1. If God exists,
    then the attributes of God are consistent with the existence of evil.
2. The attributes of God are not consistent with the existence of evil.
3. Therefore, God does not and cannot exist.

Here are brief summaries of the papers and book selections contained in this section.

J. L. Mackie in a classic 1955 paper "Evil and Omnipotence" presents a deductive evil disproof of God's existence in which it is argued that God, being wholly good, wants to eliminate evil and, being omnipotent, has unlimited power to do so, and thus God eliminates evil completely. However, this is inconsistent with the existence of evil, and therefore God does not and cannot exist. Several possible objections are critiqued. Mackie argues that the free will defense, the best-known objection, makes an assumption that actually strengthens the disproof: if it is possible for

God to create humans who *sometimes* freely choose the good, as assumed in the free will defense, then it should also be possible for God to create humans who *always* freely choose the good, and so there should be no evil, which again is inconsistent with the existence of evil. Further, the free will defense raises the paradox of whether an omnipotent being can make things it cannot control.

In "The Problem of Evil," a chapter taken from *The Miracle of Theism: Arguments For and Against the Existence of God* (1982), Mackie develops the 1955 argument into a stronger deductive evil disproof of the existence of an omnipotent, omniscient, and wholly good God by responding to several possible objections, re-examining the paradox of omnipotence, arguing for the compatibilist over the libertarian (i.e., contracausal) conception of free will, and critiquing a new version of the free will defense devised by Alvin Plantinga that employs possible worlds.

Hugh LaFollette in a 1980 paper "Plantinga on the Free Will Defense" defends Mackie's deductive disproof of God's existence by exposing flaws in Plantinga's possible worlds version of the free will defense, including an inconsistency at its very core: when discussing humans, Plantinga claims that moral good *cannot* be produced without also producing moral evil, but when discussing God, Plantinga assumes that moral good *can* be produced without also producing moral evil.

Quentin Smith in "A Sound Logical Argument from Evil," a selection taken from *Ethical and Religious Thought in Analytic Philosophy of Language* (1997), presents a rigorous deductive evil disproof of God's existence by considering the inconsistency identified by LaFollette in light of three senses of freedom in Plantinga's possible worlds version of the free will defense: external freedom, internal freedom, and logical freedom. Smith argues that an omnipotent, omniscient, and wholly good God could have and thus would have created a world without moral evil, that is, a world containing only rational creatures who, *like God*, are internally and externally free but are logically determined to always choose the good. In short, the existence of God is inconsistent with the existence of moral evil, and therefore God does not and cannot exist.

Richard R. La Croix in a 1974 paper "Unjustified Evil and God's Choice" points out that the problem of evil is not only about whether God had to create a world *with evil* or could have created a world *without evil*, but also about whether God *had to create a world at all*. La Croix argues that if God, in addition to being omnipotent, omniscient, and wholly good, is also wholly free and the greatest possible good, then God would have freely chosen *not* to create a world at all because creating a world, especially one with evil, could not possibly have resulted overall in a greater good than the greatest possible good already in existence. Thus, the existence of God is inconsistent with the creation and existence of a world containing evil, and therefore God does not and cannot exist.

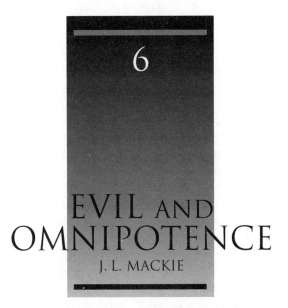

EVIL AND OMNIPOTENCE

J. L. MACKIE

The traditional arguments for the existence of God have been fairly thoroughly criticized by philosophers. But the theologian can, if he wishes, accept this criticism. He can admit that no rational proof of God's existence is possible. And he can still retain all that is essential to his position by holding that God's existence is known in some other, nonrational way. I think, however, that a more telling criticism can be made by way of the traditional problem of evil. Here it can be shown, not that religious beliefs lack rational support, but that they are positively irrational, that the several parts of the essential theological doctrine are inconsistent with one another, so that the theologian can maintain his position as a whole only by a much more extreme rejection of reason than in the former case. He must now be prepared to believe, not merely what cannot be proved, but what can be *disproved* from other beliefs that he also holds.

The problem of evil, in the sense in which I shall be using the phrase, is a problem only for someone who believes that there is a God who is both omnipotent and wholly good. And it is a logical problem, the problem of clarifying and reconciling a number of beliefs: it is not a scientific problem that might be solved by further observations, or a practical problem that might be solved by a decision or an action. These points are obvious; I mention them only because they are sometimes ignored by theologians, who sometimes parry a statement of the problem with such remarks as "Well, can you solve the problem yourself?" or

From *Mind* 64 (1955): 200–12. Copyright © 1955 by Oxford University Press. Reprinted by permission of Oxford University Press.

"This is a mystery which may be revealed to us later" or "Evil is something to be faced and overcome, not to be merely discussed."

In its simplest form the problem is this: God is omnipotent; God is wholly good; and yet evil exists. There seems to be some contradiction between these three propositions, so that if any two of them were true, the third would be false. But at the same time all three are essential parts of most theological positions: the theologian, it seems, at once *must* adhere and *cannot consistently* adhere to all three. (The problem does not arise only for theists, but I shall discuss it in the form in which it presents itself for ordinary theism.)

However, the contradiction does not arise immediately; to show it we need some additional premises, or perhaps some quasi-logical rules connecting the terms 'good', 'evil', and 'omnipotent'. These additional principles are that good is opposed to evil, in such a way that a good thing always eliminates evil as far as it can, and that there are no limits to what an omnipotent thing can do. From these it follows that a good omnipotent thing eliminates evil completely, and then the propositions that a good omnipotent thing exists, and that evil exists, are incompatible.

A. ADEQUATE SOLUTIONS

Now once the problem is fully stated it is clear that it can be solved, in the sense that the problem will not arise if one gives up at least one of the propositions that constitute it. If you are prepared to say that God is not wholly good, or not quite omnipotent, or that evil does not exist, or that good is not opposed to the kind of evil that exists, or that there are limits to what an omnipotent thing can do, then the problem of evil will not arise for you.

There are, then, quite a number of adequate solutions of the problem of evil, and some of these have been adopted, or almost adopted, by various thinkers. For example, a few have been prepared to deny God's omnipotence, and rather more have been prepared to keep the term 'omnipotence' but severely to restrict its meaning, recording quite a number of things that an omnipotent being cannot do. Some have said that evil is an illusion, perhaps because they held that the whole world of temporal, changing things is an illusion, and that what we call evil belongs only to this world, or perhaps because they held that although temporal things *are* much as we see them, those that we call evil are not really evil. Some have said that what we call evil is merely the privation of good, that evil in a positive sense, evil that would really be opposed to good, does not exist. Many have agreed with Alexander Pope that disorder is harmony not understood, and that partial evil is universal good. Whether any of these views is *true* is, of course, another question. But each of them gives an adequate solution of the problem of evil in the sense that if you accept it this problem does not arise for you, though you may, of course, have *other* problems to face.

But often enough these adequate solutions are only *almost* adopted. The thinkers who restrict God's power, but keep the term 'omnipotence', may reasonably be suspected of thinking, in other contexts, that his power is really unlimited. Those who say that evil is an illusion may also be thinking, inconsistently, that this illusion is itself an evil. Those who say that 'evil' is merely privation of good may also be thinking, inconsistently, that privation of good is an evil. (The fallacy here is akin to some forms of the "naturalistic fallacy" in ethics, where some think, for example, that "good" is just what contributes to evolutionary progress, and that evolutionary progress is itself good.) If Pope meant what he said in the first line of his couplet, that "disorder" is only harmony not understood, the "partial evil" of the second line must, for consistency, mean "that which, taken in isolation, falsely appears to be evil," but it would more naturally mean "that which, in isolation, really is evil." The second line, in fact, hesitates between two views, that "partial evil" isn't really evil, since only the universal quality is real, and that "partial evil" is really an evil, but only a little one.

In addition, therefore, to adequate solutions, we must recognize unsatisfactory inconsistent solutions, in which there is only a half-hearted or temporary rejection of one of the propositions which together constitute the problem. In these, one of the constituent propositions is explicitly rejected, but it is covertly re-asserted or assumed elsewhere in the system.

B. FALLACIOUS SOLUTIONS

Besides these half-hearted solutions, which explicitly reject but implicitly assert one of the constituent propositions, there are definitely fallacious solutions which explicitly maintain all the constituent propositions but implicitly reject at least one of them in the course of the argument that explains away the problem of evil.

There are, in fact, many so-called solutions which purport to remove the contradiction without abandoning any of its constituent propositions. These must be fallacious, as we can see from the very statement of the problem, but it is not so easy to see in each case precisely where the fallacy lies. I suggest that in all cases the fallacy has the general form suggested above: in order to solve the problem one (or perhaps more) of its constituent propositions is given up, but in such a way that it appears to have been retained, and can therefore be asserted without qualification in other contexts. Sometimes there is a further complication: the supposed solution moves to and fro between, say, two of the constituent propositions, at one point asserting the first of these but covertly abandoning the second, at another point asserting the second but covertly abandoning the first.

These fallacious solutions often turn upon some equivocation with the words 'good' and 'evil', or upon some vagueness about the way in which good and evil are opposed to one another, or about how much is meant by 'omnipotence'. I propose to examine some of these so-called solutions, and to exhibit their fallacies in detail. Incidentally, I shall also be considering whether an adequate solution could be reached by a minor modification of one or more of the constituent propositions, which would, however, still satisfy all the essential requirements of ordinary theism.

1. *"Good cannot exist without evil"* or *"Evil is necessary as a counterpart to good."*

It is sometimes suggested that evil is necessary as a counterpart to good, that if there were no evil there could be no good either, and that this solves the problem of evil. It is true that it points to an answer to the question "Why should there be evil?" But it does so only by qualifying some of the propositions that constitute the problem.

First, it sets a limit to what God can do, saying that God *cannot* create good without simultaneously creating evil, and this means either that God is not omnipotent or that there are *some* limits to what an omnipotent thing can do. It may be replied that these limits are always presupposed, that omnipotence has never meant the power to do what is logically impossible, and on the present view the existence of good without evil would be a logical impossibility. This interpretation of omnipotence may, indeed, be accepted as a modification of our original account which does not reject anything that is essential to theism, and I shall in general assume it in the subsequent discussion. It is, perhaps, the most common theistic view, but I think that some theists at least have maintained that God can do what is logically impossible. Many theists, at any rate, have held that logic itself is created or laid down by God, that logic is the way in which God arbitrarily chooses to think. (This is, of course, parallel to the ethical view that morally right actions are those which God arbitrarily chooses to command, and the two views encounter similar difficulties.) And *this* account of logic is clearly inconsistent with the view that God is bound by logical necessities—unless it is possible for an omnipotent being to bind himself, an issue which we shall consider later, when we come to the Paradox of Omnipotence. This solution of the problem of evil cannot, therefore, be consistently adopted along with the view that logic is itself created by God.

But, second, this solution denies that evil is opposed to good in our original sense. If good and evil are counterparts, a good thing will not "eliminate evil as far as it can." Indeed, this view suggests that good and evil are not strictly qualities of things at all. Perhaps the suggestion is that good and evil are related in much the same way as great and small. Certainly, when the term 'great' is used relatively as a condensation of 'greater than so-and-so', and 'small' is used correspondingly, greatness and smallness are counterparts and cannot exist without each other. But in this sense greatness is not a quality, not an intrinsic feature of anything; and it would be absurd to think of a movement in favor of greatness and against smallness in this sense. Such a movement would be self-defeating, since relative greatness can be promoted only by a simultaneous promotion of relative smallness. I feel sure that no theists would be content to regard God's goodness as analogous to this—as if what he supports were not the *good* but the *better,* and as if he had the paradoxical aim that all things should be better than other things.

This point is obscured by the fact that 'great' and 'small' seem to have an absolute as well as a relative sense. I cannot discuss here whether there is absolute magnitude or not, but if there is, there could be an absolute sense for 'great', it could mean of at least a certain size, and it would make sense to speak of all things getting bigger, of a universe that was expanding all over, and therefore it would make sense to speak of promoting greatness. But in *this* sense great and small are not logically necessary counterparts: either quality could exist without the other. There would be no logical impossibility in everything's being small or in everything's being great.

Neither in the absolute nor in the relative sense, then, of 'great' and 'small' do these terms provide an analogy of the sort that would be needed to support this solution of the problem of evil. In neither case are greatness and smallness *both* necessary counterparts *and* mutually opposed forces or possible objects for support and attack.

It may be replied that good and evil are necessary counterparts in the same way as any quality and its logical opposite: redness can occur, it is suggested, only if nonredness also occurs. But unless evil is merely the privation of good, they are not logical opposites, and some further argument would be needed to show that they are counterparts in the same way as genuine logical opposites. Let us assume that this could be given. There is still doubt of the correctness of the metaphysical principle that a quality must have a real opposite: I suggest that it is not really impossible that everything should be, say, red, that the truth is merely that if everything were red we should not notice redness, and so we should have no word 'red'; we observe and give names to qualities only if they have real opposites. If so, the principle that a term must have an opposite would belong only to our language or to our thought, and would not be an ontological principle, and, correspondingly, the rule that good cannot exist without evil would not state a logical necessity of a sort that God would just have to put up with. God might have made everything good, though *we* should not have noticed it if he had.

But, finally, even if we concede that this *is* an ontological principle, it will provide a solution for the problem of evil only if one is prepared to say, "Evil exists, but only just enough evil to serve as the counterpart of good." I doubt whether any theist will accept this. After all, the *ontological* requirement that nonredness should occur would be satisfied even if all the universe, except for a minute speck, were red, and, if there were a corresponding requirement for evil as a counterpart to good, a minute dose of evil would presumably do. But theists are not usually willing to say, in all contexts, that all the evil that occurs is a minute and necessary dose.

2. "Evil is necessary as a means to good."

It is sometimes suggested that evil is necessary for good not as a counterpart but as a means. In its simple form this has little plausibility as a solution of the problem of evil, since it obviously implies a severe restriction of God's power. It would be a *causal* law that you cannot have a certain end without a certain means, so that if God has to introduce evil as a means to good, he must be subject to at least some causal laws. This certainly conflicts with what a theist normally means by omnipotence. This view of God as limited by causal laws also conflicts with the view that causal laws are themselves made by God, which is more widely held than the corresponding view about the laws of logic. This conflict would, indeed, be resolved if it were possible for an omnipotent being to bind himself, and this possibility has still to be considered. Unless a favorable answer can be given to this question, the suggestion that evil is necessary as a means to good solves the problem of evil only by denying one of its constituent propositions, either that God is omnipotent or that 'omnipotent' means what it says.

3. "The universe is better with some evil in it than it could be if there were no evil."

Much more important is a solution which at first seems to be a mere variant of the previous one, that evil may contribute to the goodness of a whole in which it is found, so that the universe as a whole is better as it is, with some evil in it, than it would be if there were no evil. This solution may be developed in either of two ways. It may be supported by an aesthetic analogy, by the fact that contrasts heighten beauty, that in a musical work, for example, there may occur discords which somehow add to the beauty of the work as a whole. Alternatively, it may be worked out in connection with the notion of progress, that the best possible organization of the universe will not be static, but progressive, that the gradual overcoming of evil by good is really a finer thing than would be the eternal unchallenged supremacy of good.

In either case, this solution usually starts from the assumption that the evil whose existence gives rise to the problem of evil is primarily what is called physical evil, that is to say, pain. In Hume's rather half-hearted presentation of the problem of evil, the evils that he stresses are pain and disease, and those who reply to him argue that the existence of pain and disease makes possible the existence of sympathy, benevolence, heroism, and the gradually successful struggle of doctors and reformers to overcome these evils. In fact, theists often seize the opportunity to accuse those who stress the problem of evil of taking a low, materialistic view of good and evil, equating these with pleasure and pain, and of ignoring the more spiritual goods which can arise in the struggle against evils.

But let us see exactly what is being done here. Let us call pain and misery 'first-order evil' or 'evil (1)'. What contrasts with this, namely, pleasure and happiness, will be called 'first-order good' or 'good (1)'. Distinct from this is 'second-order good' or 'good (2)', which somehow emerges in a complex situation in which evil (1) is a necessary component—logically, not merely causally, necessary. (Exactly *how* it emerges does not matter: in the crudest version of this solution, good (2) is simply the heightening of happiness by the contrast with misery; in other versions it includes sympathy with suffering, heroism in facing danger, and the gradual decrease of first-order evil and increase of first-order good.) It is also being assumed that second-order good is more important than first-order good or evil, in particular that it more than outweighs the first-order evil it involves.

Now this is a particularly subtle attempt to solve the problem of evil. It defends God's goodness and omnipotence on the ground that (on a sufficiently long view) this is the best of all logically possible worlds, because it includes the important second-order goods, and yet it admits that real evils, namely, first-order evils, exist. But does it still hold that good and evil are opposed? Not, clearly, in the sense that we set out originally: good does not tend to eliminate evil in general. Instead, we have a modified, a more complex pattern. First-order good (e.g., happiness) *contrasts with* first-order evil (e.g., misery): these two are opposed in a fairly mechanical way; some second-order goods (e.g., benevolence) try to maximize first-order good and minimize first-order evil; but God's goodness is not this, it is rather the will to maximize *second*-order good. We might, therefore, call God's goodness an example of a third-order goodness, or good (3). While this account is different from our original one, it might well be held to be an improvement on it, to give a more accurate description of the way in which good is opposed to evil and to be consistent with the essential theist position.

There might, however, be several objections to this solution.

First, some might argue that such qualities as benevolence—and a fortiori the third-order goodness which promotes benevolence—have a merely derivative value, that they are not higher sorts of good, but merely means to good (1), that is, to happiness, so that it would be absurd for God to keep misery in existence in order to make possible the virtues of benevolence, heroism, and so forth. The theist who adopts the present solution must, of course, deny this, but he can do so with some plausibility, so I should not press this objection.

Second, it follows from this solution that God is not in our sense benevolent or sympathetic: he is not concerned to minimize evil (1), but only to promote good (2); and this might be a disturbing conclusion for some theists.

But, third, the fatal objection is this. Our analysis shows clearly the possibility of the existence of a *second*-order evil, an evil (2) contrasting with good (2) as evil (1) contrasts with good (1). This would include malevolence, cruelty, callousness, cowardice, and states in which good (1) is decreasing and evil (1) increasing. And just as good (2) is held to be the important kind of good, the kind that God is concerned to promote, so evil (2) will, by analogy, be the important kind of evil, the kind which God, if he were wholly good and omnipotent, would eliminate. And yet evil (2) plainly exists, and indeed most theists (in other contexts) stress its existence more than that of evil (1). We should, therefore, state the problem of evil in terms of second-order evil, and against this form of the problem the present solution is useless.

An attempt might be made to use this solution again, at a higher level, to explain the occurrence of evil (2): indeed the next main solution that we shall examine does just this, with the help of some new notions. Without any fresh notions, such a solution would have little plausibility: for example, we could hardly say that the really important good was a good (3), such as the increase of benevolence in proportion to cruelty, which logically required for its occurrence the occurrence of some second-order evil. But even if evil (2) could be explained in this way, it is fairly clear that there would be third-order evils contrasting with this third-order good: and we should be well on the way to an infinite regress, where the solution of a problem of evil, stated in terms of evil (*n*), indicated the existence of an evil (*n* + 1), and a further problem to be solved.

4. "Evil is due to human free will."

Perhaps the most important proposed solution of the problem of evil is that evil is not to be ascribed to God at all but to the independent actions of human beings, supposed to have been endowed by God with freedom of the will. This solution may be combined with the preceding one: first-order evil (e.g., pain) may be justified as a logically necessary component in second-order good (e.g., sympathy), while second-order evil (e.g., cruelty) is not *justified*, but is so ascribed to human beings that God cannot be held responsible for it. This combination evades my third criticism of the preceding solution.

The free will solution also involves the preceding solution at a higher level. To explain why a wholly good God gave men free will although it would lead to some important evils, it must be argued that it is better on the whole that men should act freely, and sometimes err, than that they should be innocent automata, acting rightly in a wholly determined way. Freedom, that is to say, is now treated as a third-order good and as being more valuable than second-order goods (such as sympathy and heroism) would be if they were deterministically produced, and it is being assumed that second-order evils, such as cruelty, are logically necessary accompaniments of freedom, just as pain is a logically necessary precondition of sympathy.

I think that this solution is unsatisfactory primarily because of the incoherence of the notion of freedom of the will: but I cannot discuss this topic adequately here, although some of my criticisms will touch upon it.

First, I should query the assumption that second-order evils are logically necessary accompaniments of freedom. I should ask this: if God has made men such that in their free choices they sometimes prefer what is good and sometimes what is evil, why could he not have made men such that they always freely choose the good? If there is no logical impossibility in a man's freely choosing the good on one, or on several, occasions, there cannot be a logical impossibility in his freely choosing the good on every occasion. God was not, then, faced with a choice between making innocent automata and making beings who, in acting freely, would sometimes go wrong: there was open to him the obviously better possibility of making beings who would act freely but always go right. Clearly, his failure to avail himself of this possibility is inconsistent with his being both omnipotent and wholly good.

If it is replied that this objection is absurd, that the making of some wrong choices is logically necessary for freedom, it would seem that 'freedom' must here mean complete randomness or indeterminacy, including randomness with regard to the alternatives good and evil, in other words that men's choices and consequent actions can be 'free' only if they are not determined by their characters. Only on this assumption can God escape the responsibility for men's actions; for if he made them as they are, but did not determine their wrong choices, this can only be because the wrong choices are not determined by men as they are. But then if freedom is randomness, how can it be a characteristic of *will*? And, still more, how can it be the most important good? What value or merit would there be in free choices if these were random actions which were not determined by the nature of the agent?

I conclude that to make this solution plausible two different senses of 'freedom' must be confused: one sense which will justify the view that freedom is a third-order good, more valuable than other goods would be without it, and another sense, sheer randomness, to prevent us from ascribing to God a decision to make men such that they sometimes go wrong when he might have made them such that they would always freely go right.

This criticism is sufficient to dispose of this solution. But besides this there is a fundamental difficulty in the notion of an omnipotent God creating men with free will, for if men's wills are really free, this must mean that even God cannot control them, that is, that God is no longer omnipotent. It may be objected that God's gift of freedom to men does not mean that he *cannot* control their wills, but that he always *refrains* from controlling their wills. But why, we may ask, should God refrain from controlling evil wills? Why should he not leave men free to will rightly, but intervene when he sees them beginning to will wrongly? If God could do this, but does not, and if he is wholly good, the only explanation could be that even a wrong free act of will is not really evil, that its freedom is a value which outweighs its wrongness, so that there would be a loss of value if God took away the wrongness and the freedom together. But this is utterly opposed to what theists say about sin in other contexts. The present solution of the problem of evil, then, can be maintained only in the form that God has made men so free that he *cannot* control their wills.

This leads us to what I call the Paradox of Omnipotence: can an omnipotent being make things which he cannot subsequently control? Or, what is practically equivalent to this, can an omnipotent being make rules which then bind himself? (These are practically equivalent because any such rules could be regarded as setting certain things beyond his control and vice versa.) The second of these formulations is relevant to the suggestions that we have already met, that an omnipotent God creates the rules of logic or causal laws and is then bound by them.

It is clear that this is a paradox: the questions cannot be answered satisfactorily either in the affirmative or in the negative. If we answer yes, it follows that if God actually makes things which he cannot control, or makes rules which bind himself, he is not omnipotent once he has made them: there are *then* things which he cannot do. But if we answer no, we are immediately asserting that there are things which he cannot do, that is to say that he is already not omnipotent.

It cannot be replied that the question which sets this paradox is not a proper question. It would make perfectly good sense to say that a human mechanic has made a machine which he cannot control: if there is any difficulty about the question, it lies in the notion of omnipotence itself.

This, incidentally, shows that although we have approached this paradox from the free will theory, it is equally a problem for a theological determinist. No one thinks that machines have free will, yet they may well be beyond the control of their makers. The determinist might reply that anyone who makes anything determines its ways of acting and so determines its subsequent behavior: even the human mechanic does this by his *choice* of materials and structure for his machine, though he does not know all about either of these: the mechanic thus determines, though he may not foresee, his machine's actions. And since God is omniscient, and since his creation of things is total, he both determines and foresees the ways in which his creatures will act. We may grant this, but it is beside the point. The question is not whether God *originally* determined the future actions of his creatures, but whether he can *subsequently* control their actions, or whether he was able in his original creation to put things beyond his subsequent control. Even on determinist principles the answers yes and no are equally irreconcilable with God's omnipotence.

Before suggesting a solution of this paradox, I would point out that there is a parallel Paradox of Sovereignty. Can a legal sovereign make a law restricting its own future legislative power? For example, could the British parliament make a law forbidding any future parliament to socialize banking and also forbidding the future repeal of this law itself? Or could the British parliament, which was legally sovereign in Australia in, say, 1899, pass a valid law, or series of laws, which made it no longer sovereign in 1933? Again, neither the affirmative nor the negative answer is really satisfactory. If we were to answer yes, we should be admitting the validity of a law which, if it were actually made, would mean that parliament was no longer sovereign. If we were to answer no, we should be admitting that there is a law, not logically absurd, which parliament cannot validly make, that is, that parliament is not now a legal sovereign. This paradox can be solved in the following way. We should distinguish between first-order laws, that is, laws governing the actions of individuals and bodies other than the legislature, and second-order laws, that is, laws about laws, laws governing the actions of the legislature itself. Correspondingly, we should distinguish two orders of sovereignty: first-order sovereignty (sovereignty (1)), which is unlimited authority to make first-order laws, and second-order sovereignty (sovereignty (2)), which is unlimited authority to make second-order laws. If we say that parliament is sovereign, we might mean that any parliament at any time has sovereignty (1), or we might mean that parliament has both sovereignty (1) and sovereignty (2) at present, but we cannot without contradiction mean both that the present parliament has sovereignty (2) and that every parliament at every time has sovereignty (1), for if the present parliament has sovereignty (2) it may use it to take away the sovereignty (1) of later parliaments. What the paradox shows is that we cannot ascribe to any continuing institution legal sovereignty in an inclusive sense.

The analogy between omnipotence and sovereignty shows that the paradox of omnipotence can be solved in a similar way. We must distinguish between first-order omnipotence (omnipotence (1)), that is unlimited power to act, and second-order omnipotence (omnipotence (2)), that is unlimited power to determine what powers to act things shall have. Then we could consistently say that God all the time has omnipotence (1), but if so no beings at any time have powers to act independently of God. Or we could say that God at one time had omnipotence (2) and used it to assign independent powers to act to certain things, so that

God thereafter did not have omnipotence (1). But what the paradox shows is that we cannot consistently ascribe to any continuing being omnipotence in an inclusive sense.

An alternative solution of this paradox would be simply to deny that God is a continuing being, that any times can be assigned to his actions at all. But on this assumption (which also has difficulties of its own) no meaning can be given to the assertion that God made men with wills so free that he could not control them. The paradox of omnipotence can be avoided by putting God outside time, but the free will solution of the problem of evil cannot be saved in this way, and equally it remains impossible to hold that an omnipotent God *binds himself* by causal or logical laws.

CONCLUSION

Of the proposed solutions of the problem of evil which we have examined, none has stood up to criticism. There may be other solutions which require examination, but this study strongly suggests that there is no valid solution of the problem which does not modify at least one of the constituent propositions in a way which would seriously affect the essential core of the theistic position.

Quite apart from the problem of evil, the paradox of omnipotence has shown that God's omnipotence must in any case be restricted in one way or another, that unqualified omnipotence cannot be ascribed to any being that continues through time. And if God and his actions are not in time, can omnipotence, or power of any sort, be meaningfully ascribed to him?

7

THE PROBLEM OF EVIL
J. L. MACKIE

A. SURVEY OF THE PROBLEM

We have examined various arguments for theism. We have found none that is conclusive, nor, indeed, any that has much weight, though we have still to consider whether the cumulative effect of a number of arguments, each quite weak in itself, is to constitute some presumption in favor of theism. Those who are skeptical about traditional religious doctrines can resist all the assaults of the believers; but they need not limit themselves to resistance: they can go over to counterattack. Such a counterattack will naturally start with the posing of the problem of evil. This problem seems to show not merely that traditional theism lacks rational support, but rather that it is positively irrational, in that some of its central doctrines are, as a set, inconsistent with one another.

According to traditional theism, there is a god who is both omnipotent (and omniscient) and wholly good, and yet there is evil in the world. How can this be? It is true that there is no explicit contradiction between the statements that there is an omnipotent and wholly good god and that there is evil. But if we add the at least initially plausible premises that good is opposed to evil in such a way that a being who is wholly good eliminates evil as far as he can, and that there are no limits to what an omnipotent being can do, then we do have a contradiction. A wholly good omnipotent being would eliminate evil completely; if there really are evils, then there cannot be any such being.

The problem of evil, in the sense in which I am using this phrase, is essentially a logical problem: it sets the theist the task of clarifying and if possible reconciling the several beliefs which he holds. It is not a scientific problem that might be solved by further discoveries, nor a practical problem that might be solved by a decision or an action. And the problem in this sense signally does not arise for those whose views of the world are markedly different from traditional theism.

It is plain, therefore, that this problem can be easily solved if one gives up at least one of the propositions that constitute it. Someone who holds that there is in some sense a god, but one who is not wholly good, or, though powerful, not quite omnipotent, will not be embarrassed by this difficulty.[1] Equally, someone who holds that nothing is really evil in the sense in which evil is opposed to the sort of goodness he ascribes to his god, is not faced with *this* problem, though he may have difficulty in explaining the point of his use of the words 'good' and 'evil', and in saying how it is related to more common uses.

Theists who are not prepared to take any of these drastic steps have, nevertheless, tried to solve the problem. The possibility of a solution lies in the fact that either or both of the additional premises suggested above may be modified: the opposition between good and evil may be construed in such a way that a wholly good god would not, after all, eliminate evil as far as he could, and (whether this is so or not) it may be argued that there are limits—and limits that matter in this context—to what even an omnipotent being can do.

For example, it would usually be said that God cannot do what is logically impossible; and this, we can agree, would be no real departure from omnipotence. Then it may be suggested that good cannot exist without evil, that evil is necessary as a counterpart to good. If this counterpart relationship is logically necessary, then a wholly good being would presumably not eliminate evil completely, even if he could do so, since this would logically require the disappearance of goodness also, including, presumably, his own. However, the contrast principle that is being invoked here is very dubious. It is plausible enough to say that if some quality or property were strictly universal, that is, if everything whatever had the property and nothing lacked it, then there would be no need in any language for a predicate that picked out that property; it is also fairly plausible, though not fully persuasive, to say that if a property were thus universal, no one would notice it. But it is not at all plausible to say that if there were nothing that lacked a property, the property itself would not exist, that by being everywhere it would somehow cease to be anywhere. And even if we granted this implausible principle—and, further, neglected the possibility of things' being neither good nor evil—and so admitted that a wholly good god, limited only by logical impossibilities, would have a sufficient reason for not eliminating evil completely, this would explain, compatibly with theistic doctrines, the occurrence of only a minute quantum of evil, just enough to satisfy this odd metaphysical principle and so permit the continuance in existence of the otherwise pervasive goodness of creation and its creator. But it is not in this sense that theists traditionally hold that there are evils in the world: they are not content to regard whatever things they take to be wrong or bad as a minute, necessary, and indeed welcome contrast to goodness which would otherwise efface itself.

Popular theodicies, that is, attempts to justify God in the face of the widespread occurrence of what are at the same time held to be evils, make far more use of the notion that evil is often necessary as a means to good. Of course this way of thinking is entirely natural for human agents in the ordinary circumstances of life. It may well be that children can develop into responsible self-governing adults only by being allowed to make mistakes and to learn from them. Parents, teachers, and statesmen, among others, constantly use, or permit, as means to what they see as good, things which, considered on their own, they regret or deplore. Any sensible person may be ready, though he regards pain in itself as an evil, to put up with painful medical treatment if he is convinced that it is necessary as a means to a lasting improvement in his health, or to endure toil that is in itself undesirable for the sake of commensurate rewards. Also, taking a wider view, it is reasonable to say that though pain, as experienced by animals of many kinds, is bad in itself, it performs a useful warning function: it directs the animal away from what would cause greater injury or death. Even pain which does not itself serve this useful purpose is in general causally connected with that which is beneficial: it would be hardly possible for animals to have nervous systems of the sorts that enable them to be guided by pain away from sources of harm without thereby being liable sometimes to suffer pain that, on these particular occasions, brings no good results. Such truths as these are familiar and obvious; but they are also totally irrelevant. For since they all concern causal relationships, in which something counted as evil is seen to be causally necessary as a means to, or as a result or accompaniment of, something that can be seen as a greater, counterbalancing good, they explain only why agents whose power is limited by independently existing causal laws may reasonably put up with evil for the sake of the associated good. But God, by hypothesis, is not such an agent. If omnipotence means anything at all, it means power over causal laws. If there is an omnipotent creator, then if there are any causal laws he must have made them, and if he is still omnipotent he must be able to override them. If there is a god, then, he does not need to use means to attain his ends. So it is idle to refer, in a theodicy, to any ordinary, factual, means-end, or in general causal, relationships. One would think that so elementary and obvious a point hardly needs to be made; but it does need to be made, and stressed, because it is constantly ignored or slurred over not only in popular but even in philosophical treatments of the problem of evil.[2]

Much more interesting than this is the suggestion that things that are evil in themselves may contribute to the goodness of an 'organic whole' in which they are found, so that the world as a whole is better as it is, with some evils in it, than it could be if there were no evil. This suggestion may be developed in several ways. It may be supported by an aesthetic analogy, by the fact that contrasts heighten beauty, and that in a musical work, for example, there may occur discords which somehow add to the beauty of the work as a whole. Alternatively, the notion of progress may be used: it may be argued that the best possible organization of the world will be not static but progressive, perhaps with what Kant called an endless progress toward perfection: the gradual overcoming of evil by good is really a finer thing than would be the eternal unchallenged sovereignty of good.

In either case, this solution usually starts from the assumption that the evil whose existence constitutes the problem of evil is primarily what is called physical evil, that is, pain, suffering, and disease. If this is taken as the difficulty, the theist can reply that these things make possible the existence of sympathy, kindness, heroism, and the gradually successful struggle of doctors, reformers, and so on to overcome these evils. Indeed, theists often seize the opportunity to accuse those who raise the problem of taking a low, materialist view of good and evil, equating these with pleasure and pain, and of ignoring the more spiritual goods which arise, and can only arise, in the struggle against evils.

To understand this solution, let us call pain, suffering, disease, and the like 'first-order evil'; what contrasts with these, for example, pleasure and happiness, will then count as 'first-order good'. Distinct from this will be 'second-order good', which somehow emerges in an organic whole, a complex situation in which some first-order evil is a necessary component: that is, the first-order evil is logically, not merely causally, necessary for the emergence of the second-order good. Exactly how this emerges will vary from case to case: it may be simply the heightening of happiness by the contrast with misery, or it may include sympathy with suffering, heroism in facing dangers, or the gradual decrease of first-order evil and the gradual increase of first-order good. Then to explain the first-order evils in a theistically satisfactory way, it must be held that the second-order good is greater in magnitude or importance than the first-order evil which is logically necessary for it, that the good outweighs the evil it involves.

This is a particularly subtle attempt to solve the problem. It defends God's goodness and omnipotence on the ground that (on a long-enough view) this is the best of all possible worlds, because it includes the important second-order goods, and yet it admits that real evils, namely, the first-order ones, occur. It reconciles these apparently incompatible theses by, in effect, modifying one of our additional premises. It denies that a wholly good being would eliminate evil as far as he could, but explains this denial by pointing to a reason why a being who is wholly good, in a sense that is thoroughly intelligible to us and coherent with the ordinary concept of goodness, might not eliminate evils, even though it was logically possible to do so and though he was able to do whatever is logically possible, and was limited only by the logical impossibility of having the second-order good without the first-order evil.

Since this defense is formally possible, and its principle involves no real abandonment of our ordinary view of the opposition between good and evil, we can concede that the problem of evil does not, after all, show that the central doctrines of theism are logically inconsistent with one another. But whether this offers a real solution of the problem is another question. Let us call an evil which is explained and justified in the proposed way an *absorbed* evil. For example, some bit of suffering which is actually the object of kindness or sympathy whose goodness outweighs the badness of that suffering itself will be an absorbed evil, as will be miseries or injustices that are in fact progressively overcome by a struggle whose nobility is a higher good which outweighs the evils without which it could not have occurred. What this defense shows, then, is that the existence of completely absorbed evils is compatible with the existence of an omnipotent and wholly good god. But then the vital question is this: can the theist maintain that the only evils that occur in the world are absorbed evils? When this question is squarely put, it is surely plain that he cannot. On the one hand there are surplus first-order evils, suffering and the like, which are not actually used in any good organic whole, and on the other there are second-order evils; these will not be incorporated in second-order goods but will contrast with them: malevolence, cruelty, callousness, cowardice, and states of affairs in which there is not progress but decline, where things get worse rather than better. The problem, therefore, now recurs as the problem of unabsorbed evils, and we have as yet no way of reconciling their existence with that of a god of the traditional sort.

This brings us to the best-known move in theodicy, the free will defense: evils—that is, as we can now say, unabsorbed evils—are due entirely to bad free choices made by human beings and perhaps by other created beings that have free will. But how is this a defense? Why would a wholly good and omnipotent god give to human beings—and also, perhaps, to angels—the freedom which they have misused? The answer must be either that such freedom is itself a higher, third-order, good which outweighs the evils which are either constituted or brought about by its misuse—or, at the very least, which, when the freedom was conferred, outweighed whatever risk of these was even divinely foreseeable—or else that such freedom is logically necessary for some other third-order goods which do the outweighing. Since these (bad) choices are freely made by men or by fallen (or falling) angels, neither they nor their effects can be ascribed to God. All that can be or needs to be ascribed to him is the creation of beings with the freedom to make morally significant choices. But it must also be held that the existence and functioning of such beings either are higher-order goods or are a logically necessary presupposition of higher-order goods, which outweigh (the risk of) such bad choices and their consequences, so that a god might reasonably choose to create such beings and leave them free.

It is plain that this is the only solution of the problem of evil that has any chance of succeeding. This defense alone allows the theist to admit that there are some real and unabsorbed evils, some items which the world would, from however broad and ultimate a perspective, be better without (so that this is *not* the best of all possible worlds), and yet at the same time to detach their occurrence from God, to show them as not having been chosen by God, who none the less seems to have been given a reason, compatible with his complete goodness and omnipotence, and perhaps with his omniscience too, for bringing about the state of affairs from which they arise and for allowing them to occur. We shall, therefore, have to examine this solution with some care. But first I want to glance at some other approaches.

B. ATTEMPTS TO SIDESTEP THE PROBLEM

One of these approaches may be summed up in the phrase "God's goodness is not ours." In other words, when the theist says that God is wholly good, he does not mean that God has anything like the purposes and tendencies that would count as good in a human being. But then why call him good? Is not this description misleading? Or is 'good' here being used simply as an honorific term, without its usual descriptive meaning? Hume appropriately puts this suggestion into the mouth of his skeptic, Philo, who says that "we have no more reason to infer, that the rectitude of the supreme Being resembles human rectitude than that his benevolence resembles the human."[3]

John Stuart Mill, in his *Autobiography,* points out that this approach was implicit in much of the religious teaching of his time. His father, he says, looked upon religion as the greatest enemy of morality, "above all, by radically vitiating the standard of morals; making it consist in doing the will of a being, on whom it lavishes indeed all the phrases of adulation, but whom in sober truth it depicts as eminently hateful." In effect God is being *called* good, while at the same time he is being *described* as bad, that is, as having purposes and acting upon motives which in all ordinary circumstances we would recognize as bad; he is depicted as behaving in some respects like a malevolent demon, in others like a petulant tyrant, and in others again like a mischievous and thoughtless child. Now certainly if such motives as these are ascribed to God, there will be no difficulty in reconciling his omnipotence with the occurrence of what would ordinarily be called evils. But to argue in this way is merely to defend a shadow, while abandoning the substance, of the traditional claim that God is wholly good.[4]

Another approach says that it is a mistake to try to minimize evil or even to see it as a problem for religion. Theists, Rolf Gruner says, "would be wiser still if they not only admitted evil but emphasized it as crucial. For it is no overstatement to say that their faith depends on it. All religious belief is connected with the manner in which men see themselves and the world, and where the 'tragic sense' of life is lacking and the consciousness of indigence, deficiency and transitoriness absent, religion will be unknown. Perfect beings in a perfect universe have no need of it, nor apparently have those for whom evils are avoidable defects to be gradually eliminated by man's growing perfection . . . the strongest believers have usually been those who have had the firmest conviction of the reality of evil, and many or most of them have never made any attempt at theodicy."[5]

There is certainly some truth in this, and it is at least a plausible suggestion that men would not have developed religion in a happier or less frustrating world. Of such a world Bishop Heber might have said,

> All round, with lavish kindness
> God's gifts like manna fall;
> The heathen, in their blindness,
> Do not bow down at all.

But how does this remove or resolve the problem of evil? Gruner clearly thinks it is paradoxical that "Christianity depends on the very fact which is said to disprove it." There is indeed a paradox here, but it lies squarely within orthodox theism. Hume brings this out clearly. While giving the argument for design and the associated task of theodicy to Cleanthes, he puts Gruner's view into the mouth of Demea. What he thus conveys is that both of these represent real and influential, though opposite, trends within orthodox religion. "It is my opinion," Demea says, "that each man feels, in a manner, the truth of religion within his own breast; and from a consciousness of his imbecility and misery, rather than from any reasoning, is led to seek protection from that Being, on whom he and all nature is dependent." And he goes on to stress the miseries of human life. When Cleanthes protests that his experience, at least, does not support this dismal view, Demea replies, "If you feel not human misery yourself . . . I congratulate you on so happy a singularity." Demea's emphasis on the wretchedness of human life is then used by Philo for his presentation of the problem of evil. But Demea, like Gruner, is not disturbed by this problem: "This world is but a point in comparison of the universe: This life but a moment in comparison of eternity. The present evil phenomena, therefore, are rectified in other regions, and in some future period of existence. And the eyes of men, being then opened to larger views of things, see the whole connection of general laws, and trace, with adoration, the benevolence and rectitude of the Deity, through all the mazes and intricacies of his providence."[6]

But, as Cleanthes says, these are "arbitrary suppositions"; we cannot rely on them when the issue whether there is a just, benevolent, and all-powerful deity is still in doubt. And, as Philo says, even if pain and misery in man were *compatible* with infinite power and goodness in the Deity (on the supposition that it will all be put right somehow, somewhere, sometime), this is useless if we are still at the stage of trying to *infer* the existence and the attributes of a god from what we independently know. And even if there were a future life in comparison with which the evils of this one would seem negligible, that still would not explain, compatibly with theism, the occurrence of those evils themselves.

The mere fact, then, that faith often rests upon a tragic sense of the evil in the world does not do away with the need for a theodicy. It means, no doubt, that some of the firmest believers *feel* no need for a theodicy; but one is still needed if their position, and that of theism generally, is to be made rationally defensible. But can a theodicy be, not dispensed with, but rather supplied by this connection between evil and faith? Does God make this world a wretched place so that men will feel the need for religion? Are not only suffering but also sinfulness necessary for the higher goods of redemption and of man's realization of his utter dependence on God?

Two suggestions need to be distinguished here. The notion that God uses evils as a means to such higher goods is, as we have seen, incompatible with the doctrine that he is omnipotent, and therefore does not need to use deplorable means to achieve his ends. It is, of course, understandable that an all-too-human deity might decide to make his creatures miserable so that they would be more abject in their devotion: "I'll make it hot for them, and then they will come crawling back to me." But this account is inconsistent alike with God's goodness and with his power. It would be more coherent to argue that sin, for example, is logically necessary for repentance and redemption, and that "joy shall be in heaven over one sinner that repenteth, more than over ninety and nine just persons, which need no repentance."[7] Sin followed by repentance and redemption would then be an absorbed evil. But, however good the authority for it, this is a very strange view. What the parables plausibly say is that a father may rejoice more over the return of a prodigal son than over another's merely constant good behavior, and that a frugal housewife may be more pleased about recovering a coin she had thought she had lost than about simply not losing several of equal value. But it does not follow that the father prefers on the whole to have a prodigal son who ultimately returns than to have a constantly well-behaved one, or that the housewife would be better pleased on the whole to have lost the coin and found it again than never to have lost it. Perhaps these, odd though they are, would be comprehensible human reactions; even so, it would be hard to transfer them to a supposedly omniscient god, or to endorse the sober evaluation that sin plus repentance is, as an organic whole, better than sinlessness.

Gruner, in fact, does not argue in these ways. He thinks that "the argument from evil . . . cannot be answered at all but only circumvented." The circumvention consists in attacking as incoherent the demand, supposedly implicit in the skeptic's attack on theism, for a world free from all evil. But this is a misleading way of stating the issue. The skeptic is not asking *for* anything: he is merely asking *whether* an apparent inconsistency in the theist's position can be cured. The demand for a world free from all evil is one that seems to be implicit in the set of doctrines that make up orthodox theism—though, as we have seen, such theism *also* stresses and trades upon the fact that the world is *not* free from evil. No doubt a created world—and particularly what Gruner calls "a real, earthly, 'this-worldly' world—as opposed to a realm of pure spirit"—could not be free from what might be seen as mere limitations and deficiencies: it could not, like God, be infinitely perfect; but nothing has been said to show that real, deplorable, unabsorbed evils, such as theists themselves constantly condemn, are logically necessary in an earthly world.

C. THE PARADOX OF OMNIPOTENCE

We shall have to come back, then, to the free will defense as the only hope for a reasoned theodicy. But there is a preliminary problem about the relation between omnipotence and free will. Are men supposed to be free in the sense merely that God *does not* control their choosing, or in the sense that he *cannot* do so? The second alternative poses the paradox of omnipotence: can an omnipotent being make things which he cannot control?

When I originally raised this question, I thought that it was a genuine paradox, that the question could not be answered satisfactorily either in the affirmative or in the negative. I argued that we should distinguish between orders of omnipotence: first-order omnipotence would be unlimited power to act; second-order omnipotence, unlimited power to determine what powers to act things should have. (And so on, if required.) But then if a god had second-order omnipotence, he could use it so as to give certain things a power to act that was independent of his own power to act, so that he would not then have first-order omnipotence. Omnipotences of different orders can thus come into conflict with one another, and I concluded that nothing could have omnipotences of all orders at once.[8]

However, this was a mistake. Clearly, a god might *have* both first- and second-order omnipotence, so long as he did not *exercise* his second-order power in such a way as to limit his first-order power. But, further, it has been argued that the phrase "things which an omnipotent being cannot control" is self-contradictory, so that to make such things is logically impossible, and therefore that God cannot make such things, but that this is no defect in omnipotence of any order, since it has been agreed all along that omnipotence does not include the power to do what is logically impossible. Hence the negative answer to the paradox question is satisfactory after all.[9]

But is there not an equally plausible defense of the affirmative answer? If a being with second-order omnipotence confers on certain beings a power of making uncontrollable choices, then to control their choices would be to control things that are omnipotently made uncontrollable, and *this* is logically impossible. Hence, even a being with (first-order) omnipotence is unable to control such things, and failure to control them does not count against his omnipotence, since, as before, this is admittedly limited by logical impossibilities. Thus, an omnipotent being *can* make things such that he cannot control them.

But if both the affirmative and the negative answers are thus defensible, the paradox is reinstated. We no longer have a contradiction within the notion of unrestricted omnipotence, omnipotence of all orders at once, but we have instead an undecidable question about it.[10]

This problem is related to another question: does omnipotence entail omnificence? If there were an omnipotent (and omniscient) being, would everything that happens be his doing? We might argue as follows: if God can make it to be that not-X, but it is that X, then he has knowingly allowed it to be that X; and is this not equivalent to making it to be that X? Against this, it might be argued that there is a clear everyday distinction between positively bringing something about and merely letting it happen when one could have prevented it. Letting someone die when one could have saved him is not quite the same thing as killing him, though it is a point in dispute among moralists whether the one is as bad as the other. But we must also consider on what this everyday distinction rests. If we bring something about, we exert effort, but if we merely allow it to happen we do not; rather, we spare ourselves the effort it would have cost us to prevent it. There is a passage of force between agent and result when we do something, but not when we merely allow it to happen. Also, merely allowing something to happen, even though we know in some sense that it will, is commonly associated with some degree of inadvertence; bringing something about (intentionally) usually involves some conscious attention. But the more completely the matter is within our power, the less clear does the first ground of distinction become. If it is something that we can either bring about or prevent with negligible effort, allowing it to happen is less clearly differentiated from bringing it about. Similarly, the more completely the matter is within our knowledge and at the focus of our attention, the less clear does the second ground of distinction become. It seems, then, that as power and knowledge increase without limit, this everyday distinction fades out, and for a being with unlimited power and unlimited vision it would not hold at all.

In short, it seems that omnipotence and omniscience together entail omnificence: God does everything. Of course this need not mean that no one else does anything. A man does whatever we ordinarily take him as doing; but if there is a god whose omnipotence means that he is in full control of the man's choices, then he does it too. It would follow that if men sin, then God is also the author of that sin.[11] Consequently the free will defense cannot detach evil from God unless it assumes that the freedom conferred on men is such that God *cannot* (not merely does not) control their choosing. That is, it has to adopt exclusively the affirmative answer to the question in the original paradox of omnipotence, despite the fact that there is nothing in the concept of omnipotence that justifies a preference for this over the negative answer.

Plainly, these are difficulties for theism. But let us suppose (simply in order to complete the discussion) that they can somehow be surmounted, and assume that the freedom invoked in the free will defense is a freedom of choice that even God cannot control.

D. THE FREE WILL DEFENSE

It is customary to distinguish natural evils, such as pain, from moral evils, the various forms of wickedness. Moral evils, it is suggested, consist in the misuse of freedom of choice; they are thus directly covered by the free will defense. Some natural evils are due partly to human wickedness—for example, cruelty— or to human mistakes; but only partly, for something else must have provided the opportunities for cruelty and the conditions in which mistakes can do harm. But the vast majority of natural evils cannot be ascribed to human choices at all, and it seems, therefore, that the free will defense cannot cover them even indirectly. But Alvin Plantinga argues that it can cover them, since they can be ascribed to the malevolent actions of fallen angels.[12] Formally, no doubt, this is possible; but it is another of what Cleanthes called arbitrary suppositions. While we have a direct acquaintance with some wrong human choices—our own—and our everyday understanding extends to the recognition of the like choices of other human beings, we have no such knowledge of the activities of angels, fallen or otherwise: these are at best part of the religious hypothesis which is still in dispute and cannot be relied upon to give it any positive support. This is at most a *possible* explanation of natural evils: it could not be said actually to explain them, even if the free will defense as a whole were in good order.

This fact is all the more important, because the boundary between natural and moral evils is not simple or clear-cut. Even the worst human behavior has a somewhat mixed character. "Here we shall find," says Francis Hutcheson, "that the basest actions are dressed in some tolerable mask. What others call avarice, appears to the agent a prudent care of a family, or friends; fraud, artful conduct;

malice and revenge, a just sense of honor and a vindication of our right in possessions, of fame; fire and sword, and desolation among enemies, a just thorough defense of our country; persecution, a zeal for the truth, and for the eternal happiness of men, which heretics oppose. In all these instances, men generally act from a sense of virtue upon false opinions, and mistaken benevolence; upon wrong or partial views of public good, and the means to promote it; or upon very narrow systems formed by like foolish opinions. It is not a delight in the misery of others, or malice, which occasions the horrid crimes which fill our histories; but generally an injudicious unreasonable enthusiasm for some kind of limited virtue."[13] This is surely right. Hutcheson was writing in 1725, but what he says here applies equally well to the horrors of the twentieth century. Wars, great or small; Stalin's tyrannies and persecutions; the Nazi Holocaust; the unleashing of firestorms on German cities; Hiroshima and Nagasaki; Vietnam; Cambodia; terrorism of all varieties; Islamic fanaticism; in all of these some kind of idealism has played a significant part, providing some justification or excuse, however misguided, that falls under one or more of Hutcheson's headings. Where several parties start with what seems a reasonable pursuit of their legitimate aspirations, they can be and often are trapped in states of conflict where to do terrible things to one another—and, incidentally, to innocent bystanders—appears justifiable or even obligatory. We cannot put this down simply to human failings: a large part of the fault lies in the way these conflict traps arise from human interactions, indeed, but not as the fulfillment of any human intentions. There are *circumstances of injustice:* situations in which people are led to the extremes of inhumanity by steps each of which seems reasonable or even unavoidable. These circumstances of injustice are, therefore, an important variety of *natural* evils which are constantly intertwined with moral ones. There is more than Plantinga may have noticed for which his fallen angels would have to be given the discredit.

If the free will defense is to be of any use to theism, then, it must be extended to cover natural evils, presumably in Plantinga's way, arbitrary though that is. However, I shall leave this extension aside and examine the argument simply with reference to human free will.

Here we must take account of the omniscience that traditional theism ascribes to God. Is he supposed to know in advance, when he creates men with free will, all the uses they will actually make of it? Let us assume, first, that he does know this; we shall come back later to the alternative assumption that he does not. Given that God does know this, anyone who uses this defense must say that it is better on the whole that men should act freely, and sometimes—indeed, quite often—err, as they do, than that they should be innocent automata, acting rightly in a wholly determined way. But he must also say that only these alternatives were open to God, that foreseeable human wrongdoing was an unavoidable accompaniment of freedom of choice—unavoidable even for a being whose powers were limited only by logical impossibilities. But how can this be so? If God has made men such that in their free choices they sometimes prefer what is good and sometimes what is evil, why could he not have made men such that they always freely choose the good?[14] Since there seems to be no reason why an omnipotent, omniscient, and wholly good god would not have preferred this alternative, the theist who maintains that there is such a god, and yet that he did not opt for this—since by his own account human beings make bad free choices —seems to be committed to an inconsistent set of assertions.

For at least some theists this difficulty is made even more acute by some of their further beliefs: I mean those who envisage a happier or more perfect state of affairs than now exists, whether they look forward to the kingdom of God on earth or confine their optimism to the expectation of heaven. In either case they are explicitly recognizing the possibility of a state of affairs in which created beings always freely choose the good. If such a state of affairs is coherent enough to be the object of a reasonable hope or faith, it is hard to explain why it does not obtain already.

Nevertheless, it is often thought that this suggestion, that God could have made men such that they would always freely choose the good, is not coherent. Sometimes this objection rests merely on a confusion. It would, no doubt, be incoherent to say that God makes men freely choose the good: if God had made men choose, that is, forced them to choose one way rather than the other, they would not have been choosing freely. But that is not what was suggested, which was rather that God might have made—that is, created—beings, human or not, *such that* they would always freely choose the good; and there is at least no immediate incoherence or self-contradiction in that.

Again, it may be objected that the notion of beings such that they would always freely choose the good assumes that these beings would be free from temptations, that they would have only innocent inclinations, and so could not exemplify the moral value of resisting and overcoming temptations to do wrong. But it is not for me to make assumptions about this either way. Since I am charging the theist with holding incompatible beliefs, it is *his* conceptions of good, evil, and so on that are in play here. He can take his pick about which he considers to be the better state of affairs, either there being agents with free will but only innocent inclinations—that is, with what Kant calls a holy will—or there being free agents who have a mixture of good and bad inclinations but who always control their bad inclinations, resist temptations, and always act well after all for that reason—that is, who are governed by what Kant calls a sense of duty. The trouble is that, whichever of these he takes to be the ideal state of affairs, he also asserts or admits that it frequently fails to occur.

Having dismissed these two objections, we come the serious question whether it might for some reason have been logically impossible that a god should create beings such that they would always freely choose the good. Let us consider this in a series of steps.[15]

(i) Granted that it is logically possible that one man should on one occasion freely choose the good—which the theist undoubtedly concedes—might it be logically impossible that all men should always do so? Some objectors have thought this, suggesting that whatever is done freely must be sometimes not done. But there is no reason why this should be so, unless 'freedom' is actually defined so as to include or entail variation. And then we have a problem. Freedom, we remember, is supposed to be a higher good which outweighs the badness of the bad actions, and of their results, which it is alleged to bring with it. But in so far as freedom *definitionally* involves variation, it is quite implausible to regard it as such a higher good. What special value could there conceivably be in the variation between good and bad choices as such? This variation aspect of freedom cannot be what makes it so very well worthwhile. And surely whatever the valuable, other, aspects or consequences of freedom may be, it is at least logically possible that they should exist without such variation, that is, without bad choices actually being made. So in any sense of 'freely' that is of use for the free will defense, it must be logically possible that all men should always freely choose the good; and, as we know, it is only logical possibility that matters here.

(ii) Granted this, might it be logically impossible that men should be *such that* they always freely choose the good? If determinism and freedom are compatible, there can be no difficulty about this step. On a determinist view, what agents choose to do results causally from what they antecedently are, and the ascription of freedom denies external constraints which would make their actions depend on something other than their natures; it may also deny certain internal, mental, conditions which would prevent their choices from being proper expressions of their natures. So what a determinist calls free choices flow determinedly from the nature of the agent, and it follows that if it is possible that men should always freely choose the good, it must be equally possible that they should be *such that* they do so. But if compatibilism is rejected, this step becomes controversial. And many thinkers have asserted incompatibilism. Some, accepting determinism, have therefore adopted 'hard determinism', explicitly rejecting what they take to be our ordinary notions of freedom, choice, responsibility, and desert, while others have denied determinism, partly in order to be able to maintain the applicability of these other notions. We must therefore digress to consider this issue.

E. DIGRESSION: THE NATURE OF FREE WILL

For our purposes, it is the second, libertarian, kind of incompatibilist that matters, the thinker who claims that we do indeed have contracausal free will. There are two great difficulties for this position: that of giving any evidence for it, and that of even saying just what contracausal free will would be. The libertarian may try to meet both difficulties at once by appealing to our ordinary belief, or knowledge, that an agent frequently *could have done otherwise* than he did. Now if we can say truly, at time t_2, that although A did X he could have done Y, the following statement must have been true at some earlier time t_1: "A can do X and he can do Y." So let us concentrate on this supposed present situation at t_1, that the agent can do either of these two things. Unfortunately, the word 'can' is indeterminate in meaning. Typically, it denies the presence of obstacles, constraints, or restrictions; but in different contexts it refers to obstacles of different kinds. In this case, it may mean that there are no external barriers to A's doing X or to A's doing Y, and hence that what he does is up to him. It may also mean that there is no abnormal psychological condition from which A is suffering (such as agoraphobia, or having been hypnotized) which would, say, prevent his doing Y or ensure his doing X. Or, again, it may mean that there is nothing at all that excludes either possibility, in particular, no set of antecedent sufficient causes for his doing X rather than Y or vice versa. The causal determinist will in most ordinary cases agree that A can do X and can do Y in the first two senses, but deny this in the third; the libertarian will assert it in the third sense, and therefore also in the other two. But since 'can' and hence also 'could have done otherwise' are systematically indeterminate in meaning between what the determinist accepts and what he rejects but the libertarian asserts, the everyday belief that agents often could have done otherwise does not even begin to settle the issue between them. Even if the libertarian could show that the ordinary use commonly expresses a belief that an agent could have done otherwise in the most comprehensive sense, that there was, antecedently, nothing at all that excluded the doing of Y, it would still be easy for the determinist to argue that this belief may itself rest on a confused transition from the one sense of 'can' and 'could have' to the other.

Perhaps the libertarian will appeal to a 'sense of freedom', to some direct awareness that an agent has that he is choosing between (say) two courses of action that are both open to him in the most comprehensive sense: he knows that he can (without qualification) do X, and equally that he can do Y, that he is not even causally bound to go one way rather than the other. But how could he be aware of this? One can have a pretty direct awareness of external obstacles: one commonly knows, or can easily find out, if one is tied up, locked in, being swept away by a torrent, or indeed if someone is holding a pistol to one's head. Rather less reliably, one may be able to find out if one has been hypnotized or is suffering from some phobia or obsession. By contrast, one can therefore be fairly directly aware that there are, at the moment, no such constraints on one's choice or action. But in normal cases, where there are no such constraints as these, one would not be directly aware of any antecedent causes of one's choosing, and equally, therefore, one could not be directly aware of the absence of antecedent causes. Contracausal freedom, or the lack of it, simply is not the sort of thing of which we could have any 'sense', any immediate introspective evidence. And in fact some of the thinkers who have argued most energetically in favor of contra-causal freedom, such as C. A. Campbell, restrict it to cases where there is a struggle between the (moral) self and its so-far-formed character and do not claim that it occurs in the most obvious everyday situations where people feel free to do one thing or another, for example, in deciding whether to have boiled potatoes or chips.[16]

Campbell argues that the self is conscious, in cases of struggle, of "*combating his formed character*," and therefore "knows very well indeed—from the inner standpoint—what is meant by an act which is the *self's* act and which nevertheless does not follow from the self's *character*." Admittedly one can be aware of struggling against what one takes to be one's character as so far formed; but one cannot be immediately aware that what thus struggles lacks a causal history.

On the other hand, it is true that there is no conclusive evidence or argument for causal determinism about human actions. The most weighty argument on this side relies on the assumption that all mental occurrences are either identical with neurophysiological ones or so closely correlated with their neurophysiological bases that determinism would carry over from the latter to the former and hence to choices and actions. But this argument is somewhat weakened by the indeterminism that is currently accepted in quantum physics, together with the fact that triggering relations would allow an indeterminacy that belongs primarily to microphenomena to carry over into ordinary large-scale affairs. And in any case there would be an ignoratio elenchi involved in relying on a physicalist argument for a fundamental criticism of theism, since a theist would deny the physicalism, being committed to the view that spirit or consciousness is somehow prior to material things. Let us not, therefore, assert that causal determinism holds, but rather leave the possibility of indeterminism open and see whether the libertarian can make any use of it.

Let us grant, then, that human choices and actions may not have antecedent sufficient causes; in what other ways might they come about? They might be purely random, subject to no cause and no explanation. Or there might be some element of randomness within limits set by prior causes. Or they might be brought about by events which are themselves subject only to statistical laws, such as those of quantum physics are supposed to be. But none of these possibilities is of the least use to a libertarian who is hoping to use the free will defense.

For that defense requires that human free will should either be, or be necessary for, something of such great value that it outweighs the badness of such wrong choices as are made, and we can discern no such value in any of these kinds of complete or partial randomness. We can indeed discern value in freedoms of other sorts, for example in doing something because one so wishes, rather than through constraint or duress, or in choosing a pursuit because one values it, or in rationally weighing the merits and demerits of alternative courses of action that are, as far as external constraints are concerned, open to one, and choosing accordingly, or in not being subject to a neurotic compulsion, and so on. But freedoms of all these, and all similar, sorts are entirely compatible with causal determinism, and a fortiori, what matters for our present purpose, with an agent's being antecedently such that he will do one thing rather than another. We can, therefore, shelve the question of what evidence there is for the libertarian's view; it is an even greater problem for him to say clearly what sort of freedom he wants and believes that we have. What could count as a freedom that both is of supreme value (either in itself or in what it makes possible) and is incompatible with an agent's being such that he chooses freely in one way rather than another?

There may be a hint in the account given by John Lucas of why we are reluctant to accept determinism. "If my decision is predictable in this way"—that is, specifically, infallibly, and from temporally antecedent causes—"it is no longer . . . the starting point of action. The action no longer can be said to stem *from* my will, even though it be mediated *through* it. And therefore it seems it is not really mine."[17] But at most this could explain why each agent values his own cause-free status, rather self-centeredly, not how contracausal freedom might be of value from a divine point of view. In any case, the thought that Lucas correctly reports here is confused. The action *does* stem from my will: why would it be *more* mine if I and my will had no causes that would make them predictable (in principle)? In such a line of thought there is often a hint that there is a real *me*, distinct from the one that is believed to have a causal history, and that if determinism held, this real *me* would be helpless, an idle spectator of the course of events. But there is no reason for supposing that there is such an extracausal self, and no account has been offered of how its operation would differ from that of a causal self. We have here a confused reason for disliking determinism, but no positive account of what noncausal action would be like or how it would be of value. The mere deleting of causes and predictability, without some other change in the choosing itself, could not confer a new value upon it.

Does Kant help us here? "Will," he says, "is a kind of causality belonging to living beings so far as they are rational. *Freedom* would then be the property this causality has of being able to work independently of *determination* by alien causes; just as *natural necessity* is a property characterizing the causality of all nonrational beings—the property of being determined to activity by the influence of alien causes."[18] Kant thinks that a will is subject to alien causes if and only if it chooses or acts as it does because of *inducements* of some kind—desired ends, temptations, threats, rewards, and so on—whereas it is not subject to alien causes if it chooses simply in accordance with its own rational ideal of universal law or of humanity (or rational nature generally) as an end in itself. But though Kant himself thought he was asserting the contracausal freedom of some human actions, what he says fails to give any substance to this view. The real distinction he draws is between *alien* causes and the *autonomous* operation of the rational will. But this is entirely compatible with the two suppositions that there are antecedent sufficient causes of a certain agent's having a rational will with a certain strength and that what such a rational will does on any occasion, how it responds to its circumstances and struggles against contrary inclinations, depends causally on its character and its strength. Autonomy as contrasted with heteronomy is completely distinct from contracausal freedom as contrasted with having had a causal history. Though Kant meant to assert both, he succeeded in describing only the former.

These comments apply to the *Groundwork of the Metaphysic of Morals.* In a later work, the *Metaphysic of Morals*, he recognized this distinction. He there contrasted *Wille*, the good, autonomous will, with *Willkür*, the will in the ordinary sense, the faculty of making choices, some right, some wrong, and ascribed contracausal freedom only to the latter. But this emphasizes rather than resolves our present difficulty. The value of freedom has been located in the autonomy, the self-legislative character, of the *Wille*; Kant adds nothing to our vague ordinary views about the value of the *Willkür*'s being uncaused, of the absence of a causal history behind our choices.

In the *Groundwork,* however, he adds a second argument. In the sphere of speculative or theoretical reason, "we cannot possibly conceive of a reason as being consciously directed from outside in regard to its judgments; for in that case the subject would attribute the determination of the power of judgment, not to his reason, but to an impulsion. Reason must look upon itself as the author of its own principles independently of alien influences." Analogously, "as practical reason, or as the will of a rational being, it must be regarded by itself as free; that is, the will of a rational being can be a will of his own only under the Idea of freedom. . . ." This argument has been echoed by many later writers, but it is unsound.[19] The truth is that in the speculative area one cannot make a serious rational judgment, or express a genuine belief, and at the same time see oneself as being *induced* to hold that belief. No one can coherently say "I believe X because I was bribed to do so" or "I believe the quantum theory because otherwise I won't get a degree in physics" or "I believe in God because I might go to hell if I didn't." Equally one cannot have a serious rational belief and at the same time see it as having been caused wholly by irrational causes: for example, no one can coherently combine a serious religious belief with the admission that his own belief is caused wholly by indoctrination in childhood. But what this amounts to is that a rational theoretical judgment cannot be seen by the person who makes it as having been caused *in any of the wrong sorts of way*, that is, in ways irrelevant to the truth or justification of the belief. But there is no difficulty in holding a serious rational belief and at the same time seeing it as having been caused in a proper way. The simplest cases are where the state of affairs which is believed to obtain has caused the belief by affecting the believer's sense organs and interacting with his innate or developed perceptual capacities. It is the presence of a table that has caused my belief that there is a table in front of me. But the same holds for more complicated reasons for belief. Lucas mistakenly assumes that someone who "is open-minded towards the truth, and can be moved by new arguments that occur to him" cannot also see himself as "determined by antecedent physical factors"; but there is no conflict between these, provided that those physical factors are (or will be) the bases or neural counterparts of good arguments. Analogously, a serious rational practical judgment does not need either to be or to see itself as uncaused; it needs merely to see itself as not being *improperly* caused. Exactly what this means will depend upon the rest of the moral theory: for Kant, anything other than pure reason's itself being practical would be improper. But, whatever the proper operation is taken to be, no reason has been given why this should not itself have a causal history.

In short, Kant completely fails to supply any description of contracausally free choosing that might be held to be of high value, nor have his followers been any more successful. A fortiori, we have not been shown any valuable kind of freedom that is incompatible with an agent's being such that he chooses freely in one way rather than another.

F. THE FREE WILL DEFENSE—CONTINUED

We can, then, return from this digression to our main argument, confident that it is *not* logically impossible that men should be such that they always freely choose the good.

(iii) Granted that this is possible, might it not be logically possible that God should create them so? Since the god in question is, by hypothesis, both omnipotent and omniscient, the creation of any contingent natures whatever should be within his power, and he must know exactly what natures he is creating. Might it be objected that to have been created by God with a certain nature would itself destroy an agent's freedom? No doubt 'freedom' might simply be defined as requiring the sheer springing up from nowhere of an agent's nature, and therefore as excluding that nature's having been created, with knowledge of it, by another agent: then for God to create free agents would be for him to create beings without any specific natures, leaving those natures to spring up from nowhere. But once again it is quite obscure what value there could be in freedom thus defined.

There is, then, no incoherence in the proposed alternative, that God should have made men (and perhaps other free agents) such that they would always act well rather than badly; and, if so, the alleged overriding value of freedom provides no explanation of the occurrence of evils in a universe with a supposedly perfect creator.

But would it not be a rather dull world where everyone always acted rightly? Would not I myself find it boring if there were no confused theodicies to refute? Perhaps. But, as I have said before, it is for the theist, not for me, to say what he counts as good. If he says that a fair amount not only of mistake and folly but also of dishonesty, deceit, injustice, cruelty, hatred, malice, treachery, murder, genocide, and so on is all right, that these are appropriate components in what, taken as a whole, is an optimum state of affairs—that is, are wholly absorbed evils—then that is, indeed, for him a solution of the problem. If there are no unabsorbed evils, then theism is in the clear. But the free will defense was an attempt to reconcile theism with the admitted existence of *unabsorbed* evils, and it fails to do this.

However, Alvin Plantinga has restated this defense with the help of his technical apparatus of possible worlds and individual essences. His argument has at its core a criticism of what he calls "Leibniz's lapse." Leibniz thought that if God is omnipotent he could have created any possible world he pleased, provided that it was a world that contained God himself. From the assumption that God is omnipotent in this sense, together with his omniscience and complete goodness, Leibniz inferred that the actual world must be the best of all possible worlds. (Strictly speaking, it would follow only that no possible world is better than this one: there might be others equally good.) This, of course, laid him open to Voltaire's satire in *Candide*. But Plantinga argues that Leibniz need not have got into this trouble: there are possible worlds which even an omnipotent god is not able to create.[20]

He illustrates this thesis with a story about one Curley Smith, a fictional mayor of Boston. Suppose that there is a certain concrete situation in which Curley may be offered a bribe, and he will be free either to take it or to reject it. Perhaps the truth is that if Curley is offered the bribe he will reject it. Then God was not able to create a possible world in which in this situation Curley is offered the bribe and takes it. Less happily, suppose that the truth is that if Curley is offered the bribe he will take it. Then God was not able to create a possible world in which in this situation Curley is offered the bribe and rejects it. Either way, there is at least one possible world which God cannot create, and consideration of other free choices shows that there must be many more. So far so good, and this disposes of Leibniz's lapse. But the crucial step comes next. Plantinga assumes that Curley is so corrupt that "Every world God could have actualized is such that if Curley is significantly free in it, he takes at least one wrong action." Curley Smith suffers from what Plantinga calls "transworld depravity": in whatever world he exists, if he is significantly free he commits some wrong actions; this Plantinga takes to be a fact about Curley's individual essence. Now God, being omniscient, knows all about Curley's essence. There then seems to be a simple answer: whatever persons God creates, he had better not create Curley Smith. But what, asks Plantinga, if it is not only Curley who suffers from transworld depravity, but every other possible created person too? "Now the interesting fact here is this: it is possible that every creaturely essence (i.e., every essence entailing *is created by God*) suffers from transworld depravity," and therefore "it is possible that God could not have created a world containing moral good but no moral evil."

But how is it possible that every creaturely essence suffers from transworld depravity? This possibility would be realized only if God were faced with a limited range of creaturely essences, a limited number of possible people from which he had to make a selection, if he was to create free agents at all. What can be supposed to have presented him with that limited range? As I have argued, it is not logically impossible that even a created person should always act rightly; the supposed limitation of the range of possible persons is therefore logically contingent. But how could there be logically contingent states of affairs, *prior to the creation and existence of any created beings with free will*, which an omnipotent god would have to accept and put up with? This suggestion is simply incoherent. Indeed, by bringing in the notion of individual essences which determine—presumably noncausally—how Curley Smith, Satan, and the rest of us would choose freely or would act in each hypothetical situation, Plantinga has not rescued the free will defense but made its weakness all too clear. The concept of individual essences concedes that even if free actions are not causally determined, even if freedom in the important sense is not compatible with causal determination, a person can still be *such that* he will freely choose this way or that in each specific situation. Given this, and given the unrestricted range of all logically possible creaturely essences from which an omnipotent and omniscient god would be free to select whom to create, it is obvious that my original criticism of the free will defense holds good: had there been such a god, it would have been open to him to create beings such that they would always freely choose the good.

Yet one more attempt may be made to patch up the free will defense.[21] In spite of all that has been said above, let us suppose that there is a concept of a kind of freedom which is of great value and which entails that an agent who is free in this sense chooses one way rather than another, and yet is not antecedently such that he chooses this way rather than that. Let us suppose that, contrary to Plantinga's theory, there are no truths about Curley which entail that if he is offered a bribe in such and such circumstances he will take it, nor any which entail that he will not. Even an omniscient god does not know in advance what Curley would do if the bribe were offered, nor does he know, even when the bribe has been offered, what he will do until he does it. To suppose this is to take sides in the great debate about 'future contingents': God does not know these things, although he knows everything that there is to be known, because until Curley, for example, has made his decision, there *is* no truth about what he will decide to do. When God created free agents—free in this sense—he had to do so without knowing how they would use their freedom.

This development of the defense succeeds better than any other in detaching moral evils, the wrong choices of free agents, from God. But it does so at the price of a very serious invasion of what has commonly been meant by the omniscience ascribed to God. If he does not know future contingents, and, in particular, does not know what free choices human agents will make, it follows that in 1935, for example, he knew little more than we did about the catastrophic events of the twenty years to 1955, and equally that he knows little more than we do now about the next twenty years. And such a limitation of his knowledge carries with it a serious effective limitation of his power. Also, this account forces the theologian to put God very firmly inside time. It could only be *before* God created Adam and Eve that he could not know what they would do if he created them, and the theologian cannot, without contradiction, give God also an extratemporal existence and extratemporal knowledge. This may, indeed, have some advantages: it would make things more interesting for God and eliminate the sheer mystery of extratemporal existence and action. But it abandons important parts of the ordinary religious view.

But even this is not the end of the matter. Although, on this account, God could not have known what Adam and Eve, or Satan, would do if he created them, he could surely know what they *might* do: that is compatible even with this extreme libertarianism. If so, he was taking, literally, a hell of a risk when he created Adam and Eve, no less than when he created Satan. Was the freedom to make unforeseeable choices so great a good that it outweighed this risk? This question must be answered not only with reference to the degree of human wickedness that has actually occurred: men might (strange as it may seem) have been much worse than they are, and God (on this account) was accepting that risk too. He would not then be the author of sin in the sense of having knowingly produced it; he could not be accused of malice aforethought; but he would be open to a charge of gross negligence or recklessness.

But in any case we must withdraw the concession that we made provisionally in introducing this final version of the defense. No concept of freedom has yet been proposed that both requires that free choices should be isolated from the antecedent nature (or essence) of the agent and from the possibility of divine foreknowledge, and at the same time shows this freedom to be, or to be logically necessary for, a good so great that it outweighs the certainty of all the unabsorbed evils that occur, or the risk of all those that might occur. Nor, as we saw at the end of section C, is there any ground for the required assumption that God could confer on men a freedom that put them beyond even his control.

In short, all forms of the free will defense fail, and since this defense alone had any chance of success there is no plausible theodicy on offer. We cannot, indeed, take the problem of evil as a conclusive disproof of traditional theism, because, as we have seen, there is some flexibility in its doctrines, and in particular in the additional premises needed to make the problem explicit. There *may* be some way of adjusting these which avoids an internal contradiction without giving up anything essential to theism. But none has yet been clearly presented, and there is a strong presumption that theism cannot be made coherent without a serious change in at least one of its central doctrines.

This conclusion may seem to be a very modest reward for our labors. It leaves open several possibilities for revised religious views. But it may be of some practical use, not only for its exposure of some typical attempts to escape the problem, but also because each of the changes that would make theism more coherent would also do away with some of its attraction.

NOTES

1. Cf. J. S. Mill, *Three Essays on Religion* (London: Longmans, 1874).

2. E.g., J. Hick in *Evil and the God of Love* (London: Macmillan, 1966) seems to combine an instrumental explanation of evil with the more consistent view that "sin plus redemption is of more value in the sight of God than an innocence that permits neither sin nor redemption."

3. David Hume, *Dialogues Concerning Natural Religion,* part 11.

4. J. S. Mill, chap. 2 in *Autobiography*, ed. Jack Stillinger (Oxford University Press, 1969).

5. R. Gruner, "The Elimination of the Argument from Evil," *Theology* 83 (1980): 416–24.

6. Hume, *Dialogues*, part 10.

7. Luke 15:7.

8. Cf. my "Evil and Omnipotence," *Mind* 64 (1955): 200–12.

9. B. Mayo, "Mr. Keene on Omnipotence," *Mind* 70 (1961): 249–50.

10. This is analogous to the "truth-teller variants" of the liar and other paradoxes; cf.

my *Truth, Probability, and Paradox* (Oxford: Oxford University Press, 1973), pp. 240–41, 260–62.

11. Cf. Hume's *Enquiry Concerning Human Understanding,* section 8, part 2.

12. Alvin Plantinga, *The Nature of Necessity* (Oxford: Oxford University Press, 1974), p. 192. As Richard Swinburne points out in *The Existence of God* (Oxford: Oxford University Press, 1979), p. 202, this is an ad hoc hypothesis the addition of which tends to disconfirm the hypothesis that there is a god.

13. F. Hutcheson, "An Inquiry Concerning Moral Good and Evil," *British Moralists,* ed. L. A. Selby-Bigge (Oxford: Oxford University Press, 1897), vol. 1, pp. 124–25.

14. This was the central thesis of my "Evil and Omnipotence" (see note 8 above) and of A. Flew's "Divine Omnipotence and Human Freedom," *New Essays in Philosophical Theology*, ed. A. Flew and A. C. MacIntyre (London: SCM Press, 1955 and 1963).

15. Cf. my "Theism and Utopia," *Philosophy* 37 (1962): 153–59.

16. C. A. Campbell, *On Selfhood and Godhood* (London: Allen & Unwin, 1957), pp. 167–78, and *In Defense of Free Will* (London: Allen & Unwin, 1967), pp. 41–4.

17. J. R. Lucas, *The Freedom of the Will* (Oxford: Oxford University Press, 1970), p. 28.

18. I. Kant, *Groundwork of the Metaphysic of Morals,* 3d section, and Introduction to the *Metaphysic of Morals*, both in T. K. Abbott, *Kant's Theory of Ethics* (London: Longmans, 1927). Kant's view of freedom is criticized by R. C. S. Walker in Kant (London: Routledge & Kegan Paul, 1978), pp. 147–50.

19. E.g., Lucas, *The Freedom of the Will*, pp. 115–16, where other references are given.

20. Plantinga, *The Nature of Necessity*, pp. 173–89.

21. A. N. Prior develops this view about future contingencies, with many references to earlier, especially medieval, discussions of the issue, but does not use it for a free will defense, in "The Formalities of Omniscience," *Philosophy* 37 (1962): 114–29, reprinted in *Papers on Time and Tense* (Oxford: Oxford University Press, 1968), pp. 26–44.

8

PLANTINGA ON THE FREE WILL DEFENSE
HUGH LaFOLLETTE

I

In his recent book *God, Freedom, and Evil*, Alvin Plantinga formulates an updated version of the Free Will Defense which, he argues, successfully counters all attacks by the atheist. This account, he contends, shows that "it is not within God's power (as an omnipotent being) to create a world containing moral good without creating one containing moral evil."[1] Hence, moral evil must exist, since God has created[2] a world with moral good. Under this interpretation, the presence of moral evil in the world is no longer a problem for the theist—at least not the type of problem which the atheist had attempted to describe. According to this account, evil is not, as the atheist believes, evidence against the existence of God. Since an actualized world with moral goodness must also contain moral evil, then God could not be reprehensible for creating *this* world. The problem of evil thus becomes primarily a religious one: Why am I suffering? How can I deal with this suffering? Will this suffering destroy my faith?

However, I find myself unconvinced by Plantinga's arguments. My intuition is that there are successful responses to this problem—I just don't think Plantinga has provided them. His arguments are too vulnerable to potent criticisms. Accordingly, the task of this paper will be to raise those criticisms against Plantinga. I will begin by briefly setting out his version of the Defense, and then proceed to criticize it.

From *International Journal for Philosophy of Religion* 22 (1980): 123–32. Copyright © 1980 by Kluwer Academic Publishers. Reprinted with kind permission from Kluwer Academic Publishers.

II

Plantinga's treatment of the problem of evil centers around the atheistic claim that an omnipotent, omniscient, and perfectly good God could create a world which contains moral good but no moral evil. This objection, Plantinga contends, is mistaken. Arguments of this sort are clearly erroneous. To consider this general argument, Plantinga selects one particular version offered by J. L. Mackie. Briefly stated, the argument is as follows:

1) God is omnipotent, omniscient, and perfectly good.
2) Any omnipotent God can create any logically possible world.
3) There is at least one logically possible world which contains significantly free creatures who perform only moral actions.
4) A perfectly good God would want to create such a world (3).
5) The actual world contains moral evil.
6) ∴ God, so described, does not exist.

Plantinga readily accepts 1), 3), 4), and 5), but rejects 2). That is, he argues that God would have, if he could have, created a world with only significantly free creatures who always act morally. But, he argues, God cannot create such a world. "What is really characteristic and critical to the Free Will Defense is this claim that God, though omnipotent, could not have actualized just any possible world he pleased."[3]

Plantinga begins his defense by trying to show that there are some possible worlds which God cannot actualize. For example, he argues, if God were a contingent being, that is, did not exist in all possible worlds, then there are obviously possible worlds he could not actualize, namely, those in which he did not exist. Of course, the response to this claim is simple: Plantinga provides it himself in his development of his ontological proof later in the book. A crucial premise of this proof is the claim that God is a necessarily existent being, that is, that he exists in all possible worlds. And, since he strongly endorses this proof, he is unable to consistently hold that God's nonexistence in some possible world(s) is sufficient to show that God could not have actualized those worlds. On the other hand, if he wants to maintain this assertion in his Free Will Defense, he will have to abandon his ontological proof. Yet even if he does maintain this argument by abandoning his ontological proof, the atheist can, as even Plantinga admits, successfully revise 2) to say:

7) An omnipotent God can actualize any possible world in which he exists.

However, since it is apparent that Plantinga wants to hold that God is a necessarily existent being, the atheist does not need 7); he can continue to assert the stronger proposition 2). Plantinga is aware of these responses, so he takes another tack.

He begins this argument by setting forth an example which he contends will establish his claim. Consider, he says, some human, Maurice, who will, at some time t in the near future, be free with respect to some insignificant action—like having oatmeal for breakfast. That is, at time t, he will be free to take oatmeal, but also free to take something else, say, shredded wheat. "Next suppose we consider S′ a state of affairs that is included in the actual world and includes Maurice's being free at time t to take oatmeal and free to reject it."[4] This S′, Plantinga tells us, includes neither Maurice's taking nor rejecting the oatmeal. For the rest, S′ should be considered as much as possible like the actual world. But even though S′ does not include Maurice's taking or not taking the oatmeal, God knows that one of he following conditionals is true:

8) If S′ were to obtain, Maurice will freely take the oatmeal.

or

9) If S′ were to obtain, Maurice will freely reject the oatmeal.

Now, Plantinga says, let us suppose that 8) is true. Then there is a possible world which God, though omnipotent, cannot create.

> For consider a possible world W′ that shares S′ with the actual world (which for ease of reference, I'll call Kronos), and in which Maurice does not take the oatmeal. (We know there is such a world because S′ does not include Maurice's taking the oatmeal.) S′ obtains in W′ just as it is in Kronos. Indeed everything in W′ is just as it is in Kronos up to time t. But whereas in Kronos Maurice takes oatmeal at time t, in W′ he does not. Now W′ is a perfectly possible world; but it is not within God's power to create it or bring it about. For to do so he must actualize S′. But 8) is in fact true. So if God actualizes S′ (as he must to create W′) and leaves Maurice free with respect to the action in question, then he will take the oatmeal; and then, of course, W′ will not be actual. If, on the other hand, God causes Maurice to refrain from taking the oatmeal, then he is not free to take it. That means, once again, that W′ is not actual; for in W′ Maurice is free to take the oatmeal (even if he doesn't do so). So if 8) is true, then this world W′ is one that God can't actualize; it is not within his power to actualize it even though He is omnipotent and it is possible world.[5]

Similarly, Plantinga argues that if 9) is true, then there is a similar result, that is, there are worlds which even an omnipotent God cannot actualize. So since either 8) or 9) is true, then there are possible worlds that God can't create. "If we consider a world in which S' obtains and in which Maurice freely chooses oat-meal at time t, we see that whether or not it is in God's power to actualize it depends upon what Maurice would do if he were free in a certain situation. Accordingly, there are any number of possible worlds such that it is partly up to Maurice whether or not God can actualize them."[6] Thus, concludes Plantinga, there are many possible worlds which God cannot create.

I would contend, however, that Plantinga is mistaken. This, and other similar examples which he forwards, do not support this conclusion. These examples do not specify instances of logically possible worlds which God cannot actualize. Rather, they are, as he has set them up, *not* logically possible at all. Let me explain: Plantinga's Kronos includes the state of affairs S', Maurice's being free with respect to taking the oatmeal, and either 8) or 9) is true. And, he continues, assuming 8) is true, W' includes S' and Maurice's freely rejecting the oatmeal, then God cannot actualize W'. Now I agree with Plantinga: God cannot actualize W'. But the reason he cannot actualize this world is that W', as described, is not a logically possible world—and everyone would agree that God could not actualize something which could not ever be actualized, namely, a world which is not logically possible. That is, if 8) is true in W', S' obtains, and Maurice is free with respect to eating his oat-meal, then he will freely choose to *take* his oatmeal. Or to put it another way, to state that 8) is true in W', S' obtains, and Maurice freely chooses not to take his oatmeal, is to utter nonsense—something which is logically contradictory to utter. There is no way to consistently utter all three statements. And since a logically possible world cannot contain inconsistent propositions, W', so described, is not logically possible. So if 8) is true, and S' obtains in W', then Maurice will freely eat his oatmeal, and if W' includes S' and Maurice freely rejecting his oatmeal, then 8) is *not* true.

Now Plantinga might want to counter this contention by somehow arguing that 8) refers to (is true only of) Kronos, and not to W'. But if that's the case, then God could have actualized W' in which S' obtained and Maurice freely rejected his oatmeal, that is, a world in which 9), not 8), was true. Thus, it appears that Plantinga has still not produced an example of a logically possible world which God cannot create.

III

In section II, I have demonstrated that Plantinga has failed to produce an example of a possible world which God cannot actualize. However, for purposes of more fully examining Plantinga's further arguments in the book I will, for the purposes of this paper, assume that Plantinga can somehow elude my criticisms in the last section. However, even if I do make such an assumption, I think I can demon-strate that his crucial contention is not supported by his arguments.

For example, his Maurice argument only refers to beings with which we are familiar in the actual world, that is, beings who do morally wrong acts—who bring about evil. Such an argument would not be surprising to Mackie; he would certainly agree that the inhabitants of the actual world do evil—that's exactly why he concludes that God doesn't exist. Mackie's contention was that there were possible worlds with *other* people, people other than those who inhabit the actual world. These other people, Mackie contends, would always freely choose to do what is right. So Plantinga's argument, even if successful, would only tell us that (some?) inhabitants of this world can be morally good only if they also produce moral evil. It does not tell us anything about these other possible worlds, nor does it explain why God did not actualize one of these "better" worlds. Plantinga, of course, realizes this problem and attempts to rectify it.

To do so he introduces the notion of transworld depravity. Now for purposes of explaining this notion, let me slightly modify our earlier story about Maurice.[7] Let us assume that Maurice is no longer faced with a morally insignificant decision like eating oatmeal. Instead, he is faced with a decision to take or refuse to take a large bribe. By an argument parallel to that in II, Plantinga asserts that there are worlds which God could not actualize, for example, worlds in which Maurice always freely chooses to not accept the bribe. In fact, Plantinga wants to claim that every world which God can actualize is such that if Maurice is significantly free in it, he takes at least one wrong action. Plantinga calls this malady 'transworld depravity'. Or to put it a little differently, a person A suffers from transworld depravity if in every possible world in which he is significantly free and which God can actualize, he sometimes acts morally wrong.

Plantinga thinks he has clearly demonstrated that Maurice suffers from transworld depravity. He then argues that "if (Maurice) suffers from transworld depravity, then Maurice's essence has this property: God could not have created any world W such that Mauricehood (Maurice's essence) contains the properties *is significantly free in W* and *always does what is right in W*."[8] Hence it is not within God's power to create a world in which Mauricehood is instantiated and in which its instantiation is significantly free and always does what is right.

In light of this "Maurice" argument, Plantinga then moves to the core of his argument:

> And the interesting fact here is this: it is possible that every creaturely essence . . . suffers from transworld depravity. But now suppose that this is true. Now God can create a world containing moral good only by creating significantly free persons. And since every person is the instantiation of an essence, He can create significantly free persons only by instantiating some essences. But if every essence suffers from transworld depravity, then no matter which essences God instantiates, the resulting persons, if free with respect to morally significant actions, would always perform at least some wrong actions. If every essence

suffers from transworld depravity, then it was beyond the power of God Himself to create a world containing moral good but no moral evil. He might have been able to create a world in which moral evil is very considerably outweighed by moral good; but it is not within his power to create worlds containing moral good but no moral evil—and this despite the fact that He is omnipotent. Under these conditions God could have created a world containing no moral evil only by creating one without significantly free persons. But it is possible that every essence suffers from transworld depravity; so it's possible that God could not have created a world containing moral good but no moral evil.[9]

Before I begin examining this account, I would like to make one methodological note: instead of referring to essences, as does Plantinga, I will substitute the term 'possible person'. I think this is warranted since essence is simply a fancy way of speaking of the essential characteristics of any possible person. Hence, if an essence suffers from transworld depravity then every possible person contains some essence, and, in virtue of that containment, would also suffer from transworld depravity. I also chose to make this methodological shift because: 1) eventually I would have to make such a shift since the problem of evil is stated—by both sides of the debate—in terms of possible persons, and 2) I find talk of possible persons both easier and metaphysically more palatable.

Plantinga's claim here is crucial: the Free Will Defense—at least his version of it—turns on this argument. He needs to show that there are no possible worlds which contain moral good but no moral evil—at least not worlds which God could actualize. For even if there is one such possible world, then either God is reprehensible for failing to actualize it, or else he doesn't exist. It is Plantinga's contention that there are no such worlds. The Free Will Defender, however, need not demonstrate that there *are* no such possible worlds, but only that there could possibly be no such possible worlds. That is, since Mackie's atheistic argument is intended to demonstrate that the existence of an omnipotent, omniscient, and perfectly good God is logically inconsistent with the existence of evil, the Free Will Defender only need show that it is logically possible that 1) and 5) are compatible to rebut this strong atheistic argument.

That is Plantinga's intention: to show that it is logically possible that 1) and 5) are compatible. First, he shows, or thinks he shows, that Maurice suffers from transworld depravity, and then concludes that:

10) It is possible that: every possible human being suffers from transworld depravity.

This is where he goes wrong—in asserting that it is possible. True, it is conceivable. But is it logically possible? Given the nature of this claim, I think it is either blatantly false or nondemonstrable. Let me explain.

Plantinga's assertion 10) is not simply a claim about some contingent state of affairs, that is, it is not a claim that it is possible that 10) is true in the actual world or even in worlds sufficiently "similar" to the actual world. He is not making that weak claim, neither would such a weak claim help his argument (see the argument early in this section).

To say something about every possible human is to say something about each possible world. It matters not whether there are possible worlds which do not contain possible people. Even if there are such possible worlds, Plantinga is still asserting a proposition concerning all possible worlds, namely:

11) It is logically possible that: for every possible world Wx, if there are any possible persons in Wx, then all the inhabitants of Wx would suffer from transworld depravity.

Since any assertion about the possibility of some proposition x being true in all possible worlds is, by definition, an assertion that it is logically possible that it is necessarily true that x, then Plantinga is, in essence, claiming:

12) It is logically possible that: it is logically necessary that: all possible humans suffer from transworld depravity.

But now, by 12) and the characteristic S_5 axiom (the axiom of a modal system which Plantinga wholly endorses) we have:

13) It is necessarily true that: all possible persons suffer from transworld depravity.

Plantinga is in a double dilemma, he is unable to support 12)—a claim which he needs to rebut Mackie's argument—without at the same time being plagued by the undesirable consequences of 13).

First, it appears that there is no evidence for 12). For the evidence needed to establish that any proposition is possibly necessary is very stringent indeed. Consider some mathematical conjecture—say, Goldbach's conjecture: every even number is the sum of two primes. Goldbach's conjecture is truly a mathematical *conjecture,* that is, we have no evidence against the theorem, but neither do we have a proof for the conjecture. Each and every even number which has been examined has turned out to be the sum of two prime numbers, yet there appears to be no available mathematical proof to establish the truth of the conjecture. So the status of the conjecture is this: if it is true, then, like all mathematical truths, it is necessarily true. And, like all mathematical truths the knowledge that it is possibly true is sufficient to determine that it is true ($\Diamond\Box p > \Box p$). But if we do not *know* that it *is* true (and hence necessarily true), then we do not, nor cannot, know that it is possibly true. In fact, the only evidence we can have that Goldbach's conjecture is possibly true, is if we can demonstrate that it *is* true.

It appears, in fact, that it is this way with all necessary truths, and Plantinga's claim here appears to be no different. Hence, the only way he can assert that 12) is true is if he already knows that 13) is true. But since: one, he makes no claim to know 13) is true; two, 13) intuitively appears to be false; and three, the best he claimed that he could muster from his Maurice-type examples was that he thought it was possible (conceivable?) that 10) was true, then it appears unlikely either that 13) is true or that he could produce any additional evidence which would lead us to believe that it was true. Now it may be that Plantinga was aware that 10) entails 13) (although it doesn't seem that he was) and believed that his Maurice-type examples were sufficient to establish that 10) was possibly true, but given the above analysis, such a belief is not justified.

It would also seem that even if Plantinga could adequately evidence 12) that he would not want to, that is, that 13) appears to have undesirable consequences for his Defense.

For example, 13) logically entails:

14) It is necessarily true that: no possible human beings can produce moral good without also producing moral evil.

And, since the characteristic which is responsible for moral goodness as well as moral evil is each person's being significantly free,[10] then 14) entails:

15) It is necessarily true that: no significantly free possible human can produce moral good without also producing moral evil.

But 15) seems to generate some problems. Human beings are allegedly significantly free and rational creatures who share these two primary characteristics with God. Yet Plantinga is (or, I would think, should be) committed to saying that God is a significantly free and rational creature who always acts morally, and that it is a necessary truth that humans, who share these same characteristics, cannot produce moral good without also producing moral evil.

Thus, it would appear that Plantinga is guilty of an inconsistency here unless he can produce some general and relevant reason why God would have the ability to act morally without ever acting immorally, while humans can only produce moral good if they also produce moral evil. Now Plantinga might want to try to identify such a difference by appealing to the human 'essence'. But even if that response would allay this criticism, it would produce additional questions, namely, Plantinga would need to explain why it isn't possible that there are other, nonhuman possible creatures who are both rational and significantly free and always choose to do what is morally right. To avoid this criticism he would, it seems, be committed to arguing that:

16) It is necessarily true that: no significantly free possible creatures except God can produce moral good without also producing moral evil.

And such a claim seems clearly undemonstrable (if not preposterous).

However, Plantinga might want to argue that God is not significantly free, and consequently, my immediately preceding argument fails. But such a concession on his part would appear to be disastrous for the Free Will Defender. For if God is not significantly free, yet is perfectly good (in the moral sense), then why cannot God create humans (or nonhuman, rational creatures) who are not significantly free, yet produce only moral good? There is no good answer to this question which is consistent with the main thrust of his argument.

NOTES

1. Alvin Plantinga, *God, Freedom, and Evil* (Grand Rapids, Mich.: Eerdmans, 1974), p. 54.
2. Plantinga prefers using the term 'actualize' here, but for this paper, I, like Plantinga, will loosely use the terms interchangeably.
3. Plantinga, *God, Freedom, and Evil*, p. 34.
4. Ibid., p. 42.
5. Ibid., p. 43.
6. Ibid., p. 44.
7. Plantinga creates a different example to make this point; for simplicity's sake, I will simply modify the earlier example.
8. Plantinga, *God, Freedom, and Evil*, p. 52.
9. Ibid., p. 53.
10. Ibid.

A SOUND LOGICAL ARGUMENT FROM EVIL

QUENTIN SMITH

T he logical argument from evil aims to show that the following two propositions are implicitly self-contradictory:

G. God exists and is omnipotent, omniscient, and wholly good.
E. There is evil.

The argument for a contradiction is similar to the argument for consistency between (G) and (E) in that both aim to produce some third proposition (p). The free will defense and any other argument for consistency aims to produce a third proposition (p) that is consistent with (G) and whose conjunction with (G) entails (E), but the logical argument from evil aims to produce a third proposition (p) that is both a necessary truth and whose conjunction with (G) produces an explicit contradiction. An explicit contradiction is a conjunction of propositions one of which is the negation of the other.

I believe that an explicit contradiction can be produced and that the necessary truth (p′) we need can be discovered by way of a criticism of Plantinga's free will defense. The problem with Plantinga's defense is located in the implicit assumptions he makes. The relevant assumptions are about freedom. Consider the following passage (in which by 'significantly free' Plantinga means freedom

From Quentin Smith, *Ethical and Religious Thought in Analytic Philosophy of Language* (New Haven and London: Yale University Press, 1997), pp. 148–56. Copyright © 1997 by Yale University Press. Reprinted by permission of Yale University Press.

with respect to a moral action): "Now God can create free creatures, but he cannot *cause* or *determine* them to do what is right. For if he does so, then they are not significantly free after all; they do not do what is right *freely*. To create creatures capable of *moral good*, therefore, he must create creatures capable of moral evil."[1] This suggests that by 'free' Plantinga is referring (at least) to what I shall call *external freedom*. A person is externally free with respect to an action A if and only if nothing other than (external to) herself determines either that she perform A or refrain from performing A.

But Plantinga suggests in other passages that by 'free' he also means *internal freedom*: "And a person is free with respect to an action A at a time t only if no causal laws and antecedent conditions determine either that he performs A at t or that he refrains from so doing."[2] A person is internally free with respect to an action A if and only if it is false that his past physical and psychological states, in conjunction with causal laws, determine either that he perform A or refrain from performing A.

Still later, Plantinga implies that he means *logical freedom* as well. This is implied by his claim that it is possible that each free creature chooses to do something wrong in at least one of the possible worlds in which the creature exists. A person is logically free with respect to an action A if and only if there is some possible world in which he performs A and there is another possible world in which he does not perform A. A person is logically free with respect to a wholly good life (a life in which every morally relevant action performed by the person is a good action) if and only if there is some possible world in which he lives this life and another possible world in which he does not.

It is possible to be internally-externally free but logically determined with respect to being morally good. This is the case with God, who is both internally and externally free but who does only good actions in each possible world in which he exists. God's logical determination with respect to moral goodness is entailed by his individual essence, for God's individual essence is *being maximally great,* which entails *being maximally excellent in every possible world.* Maximal excellence, as I noted above, includes the property of being wholly good.

Plantinga's failure to discuss these three senses of 'freedom' *explicitly* has led to confusion among his commentators. Wesley Morriston, for example, conflates logical determinism with internal determinism. He puts forth this criticism of Plantinga:

> As Plantinga defines it, then, significant freedom [freedom with regard to morally relevant actions] is not compatible with determinism. The reason for insisting on this point in the context of a free will defense should be clear. If a compatibilist analysis of freedom and responsibility were acceptable, it would be open to an opponent of the free will defense to argue that God does not have to permit moral evil in order to create significantly free creatures who are capable

of moral goodness. For example, He could instill in each of His creatures an irresistible impulse to do what is right and to refrain from doing evil, without thereby diminishing their freedom and responsibility. . . . [According to Plantinga] God's nature is such that it is logically impossible for Him to perform a wrong action. He is determined—in the strongest possible sense of "determined"—not to perform any wrong actions. Thus it seems to me that, on Plantinga's analysis of significant freedom, God is not significantly free. And since *moral* goodness presupposes significant freedom, it also follows that God is not morally good [which contradicts Plantinga's definition of God as maximally great].[3]

But Morriston's argument is based on a fallacy of equivocation with respect to 'determined'. According to the compatibilist theory of free will, humans are externally free but internally determined; nothing external to the agent causes her actions, but her past psychological or physical states cause her actions. If humans were internally determined, then God could make them so they always do what is right in this sense: he could make them with an "irresistible impulse to do what is right" that causally determines all their morally relevant actions. But, pace Morriston, this is not the sense in which God is determined to do only what is right. God is perfectly free and is not subject to any impulses, cravings, passions, urges, and so forth that causally determine his actions. God is internally free but *logically* determined to do what is right. In each possible world in which he exists, he is externally and internally free to choose what is wrong, but he chooses to do only what is right.

Morriston writes that "God has the power to perform wrong actions—in which case there will be possible worlds in which he does so."[4] This is false because the possession of a power to do something does not entail that one exercises it in some possible world. It is possible that one has the power to do A (that is, is externally-internally free to do A) but chooses not to exercise that power in each possible world in which one exists.

The distinction among these three senses of 'determinism' enables us to reject Morriston's conclusion that God is not morally good. A necessary condition of being morally good, a libertarian may say, is that a person not be externally or internally determined with respect to morally relevant actions. Yet it is not a necessary condition of being morally good that a person not be logically determined with respect to morally relevant actions; a person is morally good if he freely (in the external-internal sense) chooses to do what is right in each possible world in which he exists.

With the distinction among external, internal, and logical freedom in hand, I can begin my evaluation of Plantinga's free will defense. Consider the assumption Plantinga makes at the outset: "A world containing creatures who are sometimes significantly free (and freely perform more good than evil actions) is more valuable, all else being equal, than a world containing no free creatures at all."[5]

Now what does 'free' mean in this quotation? Presumably, it means external
+ internal + logical freedom. But one must ask, does a person who has only
external and internal freedom have less metaphysical worth than a person who is
free in these two respects and also has logical freedom? The answer implied by
Plantinga's own premises must be no, for God has internal-external freedom but
not logical freedom, and God has the greatest possible degree of metaphysical
worth. God does not have logical freedom because God has the property of maximal greatness, which includes the property of being wholly good in each world
in which he exists. Thus, there is a proof that being internally-externally free but
logically determined has greater metaphysical worth than being free in all three
respects, the proof being

1. God possesses the maximally valuable consistent conjunction of great-
   making properties.
2. If it were intrinsically better to be logically free with respect to a morally
   good life than logically determined, and this logical freedom were consistent with God's omnipotence and omniscience, then God would possess this logical freedom.
3. Logical freedom with respect to a morally good life is consistent with
   omnipotence and omniscience.
4. God is logically determined with respect to a morally good life.

Therefore,

5. It is false that it is intrinsically better to be logically free with respect to
   a morally good life than logically determined.

Premise (3) is true because "x knows all truths" does not entail "It is not logically
possible for x to perform a morally wrong action," and "x is all-powerful" does
not entail "It is not logically possible for x to perform a morally wrong action."
Nor does the conjunction of omniscience and omnipotence entail this.

It follows that a possible world W_1 containing N number of persons who
always do what is right and who are logically determined with respect to moral
goodness is (all other things being equal) a more metaphysically valuable world
than a world W_2 containing N number of persons who are logically free with
respect to a morally good way of life. And this suggests that God, if he existed,
would have created W_1 rather than W_2.

Although Plantinga does not address this issue, an unspoken assumption of
his argument is that there are no possible creatures who are internally-externally
free with respect to a morally good life but logically determined. This assumption is false, for "x is an internally-externally free creature with respect to a

morally good life" does not entail "x is logically free with respect to a morally good life." If it did, there would have to be some relevant difference between God and creatures that ensured the entailment goes through in the case of creatures but not God. But what could this difference be? As I have suggested, none of the divine attributes (other than necessary goodness) entails necessary goodness. Nor does a conjunction of two or more of these divine attributes entail it. Further, the relevant nondivine attributes do not entail logical freedom with respect to a morally good life. For example, "x knows many but not all truths" does not entail "x freely chooses to do something wrong in at least one possible world in which x exists." Nor is this entailed by "x has the power to do many but not all things."

Very little by way of argument has been given in the literature for the claim that only God is necessarily good. Morriston attempts to deduce this thesis from the thesis that the divine attributes are necessarily coextensive, that is, that the attributes of omnipotence, omniscience, perfect goodness, and so forth are exemplified by God and only God in each possible world. But then the question reverts to whether there is any reason to believe the thesis of necessary coextensivity. Morriston offers the justification that he has an "intuition" of this necessary coextensivity and that this intuition is justified because it can be traced to a reliable belief-forming mechanism, namely, that if there were a god of this sort, he would have implanted this intuition in us. But we have already seen that this sort of argument fails because the same sort of argument can be used to justify the intuition that there is a god whose attributes are not necessarily coextensive.

Swinburne presents a different sort of argument in *The Coherence of Theism*, namely, that the conjunction of omniscience and perfect freedom entails necessary goodness. This argument, however, even if sound, does nothing to show that if any being is not both omniscient and perfectly free, it is not necessarily good. Swinburne argues that a perfectly free person "cannot do what he does not regard as in some way a good thing"[6] because the only constraint upon doing what one believes is right is a causal influence upon one's choices, and a perfectly free person is causally uninfluenced (as well as causally undetermined). A person other than God can be perfectly free in Swinburne's sense because there can be a finite disembodied mind, for example, an angel, who is not causally influenced by its prior psychological states or anything else. Further, a nonomniscient person can have only true moral beliefs, if only for the reason that it is possible to know all moral truths and not know all mathematical truths. Such a person would be necessarily morally good, given Swinburne's own premises. Indeed, using Swinburne's premises one can prove the possibility of necessarily good persons other than God:

6. It is possible that there is a nonomniscient mind x such that: for each possible world W in which x exists, and for each circumstance in which x is faced with a moral choice, x knows all the factual and moral truths he needs to know to make a correct choice.
7. This mind x is neither causally determined nor causally influenced by any external or internal factors.
8. Necessarily, if a perfectly free mind knows all the moral and factual truths needed to make the morally correct choice in any morally significant circumstance in which he finds himself, then this mind will make the correct choice.

If such persons are possible, worlds containing only such persons and God and no nature (a physical realm) are possible; in these worlds, there is no moral or natural evil. The counterfactual argument that it is possible that if God created these persons in certain circumstances they *would* do something wrong fails because these persons are necessarily good. Accordingly, Plantinga's free will defense cannot be used to show that a world containing these persons is not creatable.

The idea that there are possible creatures who are necessarily good and that God could have created a world containing only them does not depend on the truth of Plantinga's theory of counterfactuals of freedom. At first glance, it might appear there is a dependency because presumably God, if he existed, would have known logically prior to creation counterfactuals about these creatures and made his decision to create a world with them on the basis of this knowledge. For example, God would know prior to creation

9. If the individual essences of some necessarily good creatures were to be instantiated, the instantiations of these essences would always do what is right.

Proposition (9) is true logically prior to creation even if Plantinga's theory is false, for (9) is analytically true and thereby does not require similarity relations among worlds to make it true. Proposition (9) is true because the antecedent entails the consequent. Accordingly, if the Stalnaker-Lewis theory of counterfactuals is true, there are no *logically contingent* counterfactuals of freedom that are true logically prior to creation, but there are logically necessary counterfactuals of freedom that are true logically prior to creation, and the latter are all that God needs to know which world to create.

The fact that necessarily good creatures are possible supplies the missing proposition (p′) that will enable the conjunction of (G), (E), and (p′) to form an explicit contradiction. Statements (G) and (E) we recall are

G.   God exists and is omnipotent, omniscient, and wholly good.
E.   There is evil.

There are several ways to formulate (p′), one being based on a proposition in Plantinga's first discussion of the free will defense in his article "The Free Will Defense."[7] It reads as follows:

10. If God is all-good and the proposition *God creates free humans and the free humans He creates always do what is right* is consistent, then any free humans created by God always do what is right.

If the negation of (E) is to be deduced from (10) and (G), then (10) needs to be a necessary truth. But we need further premises. One is

11. It is consistent that God creates free humans and the free humans he creates always do what is right.

Another is

12. It is possible that: free humans who always do what is right exist without there being any natural evil, and if God creates these humans, he will not create natural evil.

If (10), (11), and (12) are all necessary truths, then the proposition (p′) is the conjunction of (10), (11), and (12) because the conjunction of these three propositions with (G) entails

~E.   There is no evil.

This would give a sound logical argument from evil, for it would show that the theist is committed to a proposition two of whose conjunctions are *there is evil* and *there is no evil.*

In "The Free Will Defense" Plantinga attacks (10). He writes, "There seems to be no reason for supposing that (10) is true at all, let alone necessarily true. Whether the free men created by God would always do what is right would presumably be up to them; for all we know they might sometimes exercise their freedom to do what is wrong."[8]

In one sense Plantinga is right, for humans are logically free with respect to a morally good life and *being logically free* and *being logically determined* are plausibly thought to be essential properties. There is no possible world in which humans are logically determined with respect to a morally good life. But

Plantinga overlooks the possibility that there are possible rational creatures who are internally-externally free but logically determined, and if we take "humans" in (10) in a broad sense as referring to any rational creature, then Plantinga's purported refutation of (10) fails. Thus, the logical argument from evil goes through unscathed by Plantinga's criticism.

The soundness of the logical argument from evil can be seen more clearly if we consider a relevant proposition from Plantinga's *God, Freedom, and Evil*, a proposition that he concedes "for purposes of argument" is a necessary truth (although he subsequently makes no attempt to show it is not a necessary truth). The proposition is

> 13. An omniscient and omnipotent [and wholly] good being eliminates every evil that it can properly eliminate.

A being *properly eliminates* an evil state of affairs if it eliminates that evil without either eliminating an outweighing good or bringing about a greater evil. A good state of affairs g outweighs an evil state of affairs e if the conjunctive state of affairs *g and e* is a good state of affairs. Given these definitions, it is plausible to think that (13) is a necessary truth. If a state of affairs is eliminated by its actualization being prevented, and if a possible world is a state of affairs (a maximal state of affairs), then (13) entails

> 14. God prevents from being actual any world W_1 that contains evil if there is another creatable world W_2 containing at least as much good as W_1 and no evil.

There is no world containing evil that contains more good than a creatable world W_2 that contains no evil and that consists of God and an infinite number of necessarily good and internally-externally free rational creatures who perform an infinite number of good acts. This is true by virtue of the mathematics of infinity, for the addition of more creatures or acts to a world containing an infinite number of them does not increase the amount of good, for infinity plus N for any finite number N equals infinity. Thus, we cannot say that there is a possible world containing evil and infinity-plus-N good acts and that this world contains more good than a world containing an infinite number of good acts and no evil. Of course, we can get *more* good acts if we add to a world with aleph-zero good acts an additional aleph-one acts, where aleph-zero is the number of all finite integers and aleph-one is (by the continuum hypothesis) the number of all real numbers. But this sort of argument can be blocked by supposing there is another world with no evil but with aleph-one good acts. The same holds for any other transfinite cardinal greater than aleph-zero.

The above arguments about necessarily good free rational creatures show that

    15. There is some possible creatable world W_2 containing only God and an infinite number of necessarily good free rational creatures who perform an infinite number of good acts.

This gives us our explicit contradiction, namely, the conjunction of the following propositions:

    G. God exists and is omnipotent, omniscient, and wholly good.
    E. There is evil.
    14. God prevents from being actual any world W_1 that contains evil if there is another creatable world W_2 containing at least as much good as W_1 and no evil.
    15. For any possible creatable world W_1 containing evil and an infinite number of free rational creatures who perform an infinite number of good acts, there is another possible creatable world W_2 containing no evil and an infinite number of necessarily good free rational creatures who perform an infinite number of good acts.
    ~E. There is no evil (from G, [14], and [15]).

The logical argument from evil, then, appears to succeed, or at least Plantinga and nobody else known to me has given a good reason to think it does not. Accordingly, we must relinquish at least for the present the claim that human life has an objective, monotheistic religious meaning. It seems reasonable to believe on the basis of the considerations adduced in this chapter that the presence of evil makes human life religiously meaningless in the monotheistic sense.

    Note that this logical argument from evil is not John Mackie's argument, which Plantinga is commonly credited with refuting. Mackie's argument is, "If God has made men such that in their free choices they sometimes prefer what is good and sometimes what is evil, why could he not have made men such that they always freely choose the good? If there is no logical impossibility in a man's freely choosing the good on one, or on several, occasions, there cannot be a logical impossibility in his freely choosing the good on every occasion."[9]

    In a possible worlds formulation, this may be construed as the claim that there is a logically possible world in which humans always choose what is right. But Plantinga counters this by noting that the existence of such a possible world does not mean that God could have actualized it, for it is possible that if God had created the people in this world and placed them in the relevant circumstances, they would have made wrong choices. In short, Mackie's argument fails because he supposes the logically possible world in which free creatures always do what is right contains *humans* who are *logically free* with respect to living a good life. Mackie's contention is that there is a possible world in which human beings are created by God and always do what is right; he does not argue for the stronger claim that there is a different sort of creature, rational persons who are internally-externally free but logically determined to do what is right, and that there is a possible world containing only them and God. This stronger claim is needed to withstand Plantinga's criticism that it is possible that if God created the persons in question, they would choose to do some wrong acts, even though they might not have.

NOTES

1. Alvin Plantinga, *The Nature of Necessity* (Oxford: Clarendon Press, 1974), pp. 166–67.

2. Ibid., pp. 170–71.

3. Wesley Morriston, "Is God 'Significantly Free'?" *Faith and Philosophy* 2 (1985): 257–64, esp. pp. 257–58.

4. Ibid., p. 262.

5. Plantinga, *The Nature of Necessity*, p. 166.

6. Richard Swinburne, *The Coherence of Theism* (Oxford: Clarendon Press, 1977), p. 146.

7. Alvin Plantinga, "The Free Will Defense," *Philosophy of Religion*, ed. S. Cahn (New York: Harper and Row, 1970). (10) is Plantinga's (6'). This article was originally published in *Philosophy in America*, ed. Max Black (Ithaca, N.Y.: Cornell University Press, 1965).

8. Ibid., pp. 56–57.

9. J. L. Mackie, "Evil and Omnipotence," *Mind* 64 (1955): 209 (reprinted in *Philosophy of Religion*, pp. 7–22).

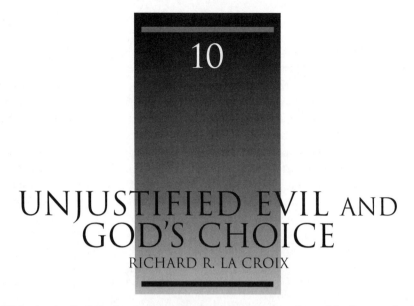

10

UNJUSTIFIED EVIL AND GOD'S CHOICE

RICHARD R. LA CROIX

In chapter 5 of *God and Other Minds,* Alvin Plantinga has critically examined some recent attempts to show that the fact of evil renders traditional theistic belief self-contradictory.[1] He argues that these attempts are unsuccessful and claims that success is more difficult than most atheologians seem to suppose. I want to discuss Plantinga's examination in an attempt to show that the atheologian has not exhausted his arsenal and that the theist needs further defensive weapons in order to sustain his position that theistic belief is not irrational.

Plantinga maintains, and I believe correctly, that in order for the atheologian to show that theistic belief is self-contradictory, it would be necessary to identify a set of propositions which both entails a contradiction and is such that each proposition in the set is either necessarily true, or essential to theism, or a logical consequence of such propositions. Clearly no set of propositions would present a problem for the theist if he were not committed, on some grounds or other, to each proposition in the set or if the set did not entail a contradiction. Furthermore, Plantinga maintains that the atheologians he is criticizing identify the set of propositions, (a) that God exists, (b) that God is omnipotent, (c) that God is omniscient, (d) that God is wholly good, and (e) that evil exists, as the set of propositions which is essential to orthodox theism and which is self-contradictory. But, Plantinga argues, while (a)–(e) is a set of propositions essential to theism, that set does not alone *formally* entail a contradiction.

Plantinga argues that in order to show that theism is self-contradictory, the

From *Sophia* 13, no. 1 (1974): 20–28. Copyright © 1974 by Emory University. Reprinted by permission of *Sophia.*

atheologian must add some further proposition to (a)–(e) and that the additional proposition must also be either necessarily true, or essential to theism, or a logical consequence of such propositions. Now it is quite plain that the additional proposition needed by the atheologian must satisfy a further condition: it must be a proposition which specifies the conditions under which a person can permit evil without forfeiting his claim to moral goodness. After examining several formulations of such a proposition and rejecting them either because they were not adequate for the atheologian's need, or because they failed to satisfy the condition of being necessarily true, or essential to theism, or a logical consequence of such propositions, Plantinga claims that at least part of the proposition the atheologian needs is the proposition that

(f_4) An omnipotent, omniscient person is wholly good only if he eliminates every evil which is such that for every good that entails it, there is a greater good that does not entail it.[2]

But Plantinga finds difficulties with this proposition as well. He points out that the conjunction of (a)–(e) and (f_4) is not a formally contradictory set either, because it does not entail the denial of (e), that is, it does not entail that there is no evil at all. Rather, that set of propositions entails

(g) Every evil E is entailed by some good G such that every good greater than G also entails E.

So, since the conjunction of (a)–(e) and (f_4) does not entail a contradiction, the addition of (f_4) to (a)–(e) is not by itself sufficient to show that theism is self-contradictory. The atheologian must add still another proposition to this set and this new proposition must be either necessarily true, or essential to theism, or a logical consequence of such propositions such that when it is added to the set, the entire set entails the denial of (g):

There is at least one evil state of affairs such that for every good that entails it, there is a greater good that does not.

According to Plantinga, then, the atheologian can convict the theist of inconsistency only if he can deduce the denial of (g) from (a)–(e) and (f_4) together with propositions which are either necessarily true, or essential to theism, or logical consequences of such propositions because since it is (g) and not the denial of (e) which is entailed by (a)–(e) and (f_4), theism can be shown to be self-contradictory only if it is possible to deduce the contradictory conjunction of (g) and the denial of (g) by deducing the denial of (g) in the specified way. Furthermore,

Plantinga indicates that if the atheologian can deduce the denial of (g) and we can say that an evil state of affairs is *justified* just in case it is false that for every good that entails it there is a greater good that does not, then the atheologian will have succeeded in showing that there is unjustified evil because the denial of (g) says that there is at least one evil state of affairs such that for every good that entails it there is a greater good that does not.[3]

Plantinga continues this phase of his examination with an honest but unsuccessful attempt to find a proposition which satisfies the necessary conditions for the deduction of the denial of (g) and concludes by saying, "If this does not show that there is *no* such proposition, it suggests that finding one is much more difficult than most atheologians seem to suppose."[4] Now while Plantinga cannot be faulted for not exploring the entire range of propositions essential to theism, since after all the range is quite enormous, it would seem that he restricted his scope of examination unduly because he thinks that (e) itself is the only likely candidate for the proposition that is both essential to theism and relevant to the deduction of the denial of (g). Plantinga does not say why he thinks that (e) is the only likely candidate out of the enormous number of contenders, and I think that he rejects even this candidate too swiftly because it is not at all clear that his claim that (i) entails (k)[5] is correct, and if it is not, then he himself has produced a plausible candidate for the proposition which will permit the deduction of the denial of (g). However, I do not want to argue this point. What I want to show is that there are other candidates. I want to show that there are three other propositions, and perhaps there are more for all I know, which are essential to theism and which jointly entail the denial of (g) such that when they are added to (a)–(e) and (f_4) the result is a set of propositions which entails the contradictory conjunction of (g) and the denial of (g).

It is quite plain that (a)–(e) does not even approach the limit of exhausting the possible list of propositions essential to orthodox theism. Furthermore, it would seem that

(1) God exists and created everything ex nihilo and in time,

is a proposition essential to theism and that (1) entails both

(2) Prior to creation there was nothing but God

and

(3) Subsequent to creation there is nothing which is not casually dependent upon God,

but the conjunction of (2) and (3) entails

(4) If God had not created there would be nothing but God;

and since another proposition essential to orthodox theism is that

(5) God is the greatest possible good,

then the theist is committed to the proposition that

(6) If God had not created there would be nothing but the greatest possible good,

because (4) and (5) jointly entail (6). Now since the theist also holds that God is wholly free, it would seem that the theist is also committed to the proposition that

(7) God need not have created;

but then (6) and (7) entail

(8) The existence of the greatest possible good does not entail the existence of any other thing;

and (8) entails

(9) The existence of the greatest possible good does not entail the existence of any evil state of affairs.

From (9) it would seem to follow that

(10) Every evil state of affairs is such that for every good that entails it, there is a greater good that does not;

and from (10) it follows that

(11) If there is any evil, then for every good that entails it, there is a greater good that does not.

Now the conjunction of (e), that evil exists, and (11) entails

(12) There is at least one evil state of affairs such that for every good that entails it, there is a greater good that does not;

and since (12) is the denial of (g) and (g) is entailed by the conjunction (a)–(e) and (f_4), the conjunction of (a)–(e) and (f_4) together with (1), (5), and (7) constitutes a set of propositions, let us call it S, which entails the contradictory conjunction of (g) and the denial of (g). So, it would appear that the atheologian can, contrary to what Plantinga believes, identify a set of propositions, (1), (5), and (7), which are essential to theism and entail the denial of (g) such that when these new propositions are added to the others they produce the set S which entails a contradiction.

But even so, Plantinga would reject the claim that S shows that theism is inconsistent and that evil is unjustified because he finds a further difficulty with (f_4). It seems quite clear that (f_4) entails

> (F) An omnipotent, omniscient person who is wholly good can permit an evil state of affairs to exist only if it is entailed by a good which outweighs it.

Now if (F) is false then (f_4) is false, and the theist can reject (f_4) and escape the charge of inconsistency because S would not then show that theism is self-contradictory or that evil is unjustified, and in chapter 6 of *God and Other Minds*, Plantinga says that (F) is by no means self-evident and that apologists for traditional theism have often denied it.[6] These apologists, then, attempt to escape the charge of inconsistency in their theistic belief by claiming that (F) is false. They sustain their claim that an omnipotent, omniscient person can permit evil which is not entailed by some good without forfeiting His claim to moral goodness by arguing that perhaps there are certain good states of affairs that an omnipotent God *cannot* bring about without permitting evil, even though these do not entail any evil at all. An omnipotent God, for example, cannot bring about free will and its attendant moral goods without also bringing about the possibility of evil, even though these goods do not entail any evil. This position, according to Plantinga, is sometimes called the free will defense. The free will argument is an argument intended to sustain the theist's claim that (F) is false and to provide an escape from the charge of inconsistency.

But the free will argument does not get the theist off the hook. While it *may* be adequate to sustain the claim that (F) is false, the free will argument has as one of its essential premises that God is not morally culpable for the evil in the world because God could prevent moral evil only by preventing the possibility of moral good which outweighs it. In Plantinga's formulation of the free will argument he states this premise by saying: "The fact that free creatures sometimes err, however, in no way tells against God's omnipotence or against His goodness; for He could forestall the occurrence of moral evil only by removing the possibility of moral good."[7] In other words, God escapes the charge of moral culpability because preventing evil *entails* preventing the possibility of moral good which outweighs it. So while the theist denies (f_4) he is presumably committed to the claim that

(f_4') An omnipotent, omniscient person is wholly good only if he prevents every evil E which is such that preventing E does not entail preventing the possibility of moral good which outweighs E

and it would seem, then, that we could say that an evil state of affairs is *justified* just in case it is false that preventing it does not entail preventing the possibility of moral good which outweighs it.

Now while (a)–(e) and (f_4') do not entail the denial of (e), they do jointly entail

(g') Every evil E is such that preventing E entails preventing the possibility of moral good which outweighs E.

So the atheologian can still convict the theist of inconsistency and show that evil is unjustified if he can find a set of propositions which is such that each member of the set is either necessarily true, or essential to theism, or a logical consequence of such propositions and which is such that the entire set entails the denial of (g'):

There is at least one evil state of affairs such that preventing it does not entail preventing the possibility of moral good which outweighs it.

The issue, then, is whether or not the atheologian can find a set of propositions which satisfy these conditions. I think that he can and it is not necessary to go very far beyond the set of propositions (1)–(12) in order to produce a set satisfying these conditions.

Since the theist believes not only that God is the greatest possible good but also that His goodness is the highest moral goodness, it would seem that a further claim essential to theism is the claim that

(13) The greatest possible good is moral good which outweighs any possible evil,

and that the theist is committed to the proposition that

(14) If God had not created there would exist moral good which outweighs any possible evil

because (6), from (1)–(12), and (13) jointly entail (14). Furthermore, (4) from (1)–(12) entails

(15) If God had not created there would be no evil;

and (15) together with (7) from (1)–(12) entails

(16) God could prevent evil by not creating.

Now from the conjunction of (14) and (16) it follows that

(17) God could prevent evil without preventing the existence of moral good which outweighs it;

and since it would seem to be necessarily true that

(18) What is actual is possible,

then it would seem that the theist is committed to the proposition that

(19) God could prevent evil without preventing the possibility of moral good which outweighs it,

because (19) follows from the conjunction of (17) and (18). But (19) entails

(20) Every evil state of affairs is such that preventing it does not entail preventing the possibility of moral good which outweighs it;

and from (20) it follows that

(21) If there is any evil, then preventing it does not entail preventing the possibility of moral good which outweighs it.

Now the conjunction of (e), that evil exists, and (21) entails

(22) There is at least one evil state of affairs such that preventing it does not entail preventing the possibility of moral good which outweighs it;

and since (22) is the denial of (g′), and (g′) is entailed by the conjunction of (a)–(e) and (f$_4$′), the conjunction (a)–(e) and (f$_4$′) together with (1), (5), (7), (13), and (18) constitutes a set of propositions—let us call it S'—which entails the contradictory conjunction of (g′) and the denial of (g′). So, it would appear that the atheologian can identify a set of propositions which are either necessarily true or essential to theism and which entail the denial of (g′) such that when these new propositions are added to the others they produce the set S', which both entails a contradiction and which is such that each member of S' is either necessarily true, or essential to theism, or a logical consequence of such propositions. In short, while S may not show that theism is inconsistent or that evil is unjustified, the atheologian can produce S' to convict the theist of inconsistency and to show that evil is unjustified.

Furthermore, since (20) says that every evil state of affairs is such that preventing it does not entail preventing the possibility of moral good which outweighs it, then (20) and (f_4') entail that if there is an omnipotent, omniscient person who is wholly good then he prevents every evil. But (a)–(e) asserts that there is such a person. So, (a)–(e) and (f_4') together with (20) entail that there is no evil, that is, they entail the denial of (e). Not only does S' entail (g′) and the denial of (g′), S' also entails both (e) and the denial of (e).

It is not at all clear how Plantinga would answer the preceding argument because his ingenious proofs in chapter 6 are devoted to a defense of the free will argument against certain specific attacks, and since the preceding argument does not challenge the free will argument, Plantinga's proofs do not speak against it. What the preceding argument shows is that the issue about evil, which the free will argument raises between the theist and the atheologian, is one which really misses the main problem for theism because this issue is usually discussed in such a way as to suggest that God had only two choices with respect to creation: either to create a world with evil or to create a world without evil. The atheologian usually assumes that the theist has a problem just in case God could have created differently, that is, just in case God could have created a world without evil. The theist then counters that there is no problem because, after all, God could not have created differently, that is, God could not have created a world without evil or at least the possibility of evil which as a matter of fact became actualized.

But the question of whether or not God could have created a world without evil misses the point because it is false that theism has a problem *just in case* God could have created differently: the theist has a problem even if God could not have created differently. What the preceding argument shows is that if the theist is right in some of his claims about God, then God is the creator and a wholly free being who did not have just the options of either creating a world with evil or creating a world without evil: He had the further choice of not creating at all. No matter what is accepted about what God could or could not do with a creation, or what God ought or ought not to have done with a creation, it remains that the beliefs of orthodox theism entail both that God need not have created and that if God had not created then there would be no evil at all. On the theist's own view, then, in order to prevent evil God need not have created in a special way.

He could have failed to create altogether and without any loss of free will or moral goodness because the theist also holds that God is wholly free and the highest moral good. Perhaps God could not, for some perfectly plausible reason, create a world without evil, but then it would seem that He ought not to have created at all. If the theist is right in some of his claims about God and evil, then being omniscient and prior to creation God knew that if He created there would be evil, so being wholly good He ought not to have created.

In order to escape this argument, what the theist needs is an apologetic of creation and such an apologetic, it would seem, must come into conflict with at least one of the theist's other claims about God because on the theist's own view prior to creation there was nothing missing from the perfect value of God which would call for creation. One possible approach to a satisfactory apologetic of creation, for example, might be to point out that if God had not created, then there would be no *human* free will or *human* moral good. But this kind of an approach would require a further premise to the effect that a created, hierarchy of value adds to the overall value and, hence, God created. It would follow from this, however, that created value adds to God's value and, hence, that God is not the greatest possible good because His goodness can be increased by the addition of created value. So this approach would not appear to be very promising nor, would it appear, is any other kind of approach because such an apologetic would have to state that God had to create for some reason or other and this would seem to be in direct conflict either with the view that God is wholly free or the view that God has no motives, such as needs or wants, which would adequately explain the alleged creative act. So it would appear that theism is inconsistent and that the theist must give up one or more of his claims about God.

NOTES

1. Alvin Plantinga, *God and Other Minds* (Ithaca, N.Y.: Cornell University Press, 1967), pp. 115–30.

2. Plantinga makes it clear on p. 120 that, to say that one state of affairs entails another state of affairs is to say that the proposition that the one obtains entails the proposition that the other obtains.

3. Plantinga, *God and Other Minds*, p. 122.

4. Ibid., p. 128.

5. Ibid., p. 125 for Plantinga's discussion of (i) and (k).

6. Ibid., p. 131.

7. Ibid., p. 132.

PART 3

DOCTRINAL DISPROOFS
OF THE
EXISTENCE OF GOD

INTRODUCTION

This section contains previously published papers presenting and defending doctrinal disproofs of the existence of God. A doctrinal disproof of God's existence is a deductive argument based on a contradiction between the attributes of God and a particular religious doctrine, story, or teaching about God.

A doctrinal disproof of God's existence takes the following general form:

1. If God exists,
   then the attributes of God are consistent with a particular religious doctrine, story, or teaching about God.
2. The attributes of God are not consistent with that particular religious doctrine, story, or teaching about God.
3. Therefore, God does not and cannot exist.

Here are brief summaries of the papers contained in this section.

Richard R. La Croix in a short 1984 paper "The Paradox of Eden" considers the garden of Eden story in which God issues a command not to eat the fruit of the tree of the knowledge of good and evil. Pointing out that Adam and Eve either *knew* or *did not know* that obeying God is good and disobeying God is evil, La Croix argues that if they *knew*, then God's test of their righteousness was unfair because they had nothing to gain by disobeying God, and if they *did not know*, then God's punishment for wrongdoing was unfair. In either case God was unjust, and therefore a necessarily just God does not and cannot exist.

Raymond D. Bradley in a 2000 paper "A Moral Argument for Atheism" examines the relationship between God's attribute of holiness (or moral perfection) and the doctrine that the Bible is God's revelation with the intention of demonstrating that if there are objective moral truths, then it follows not that God exists, as many theists claim, but rather that God does not exist. Bradley identifies several objective moral truths, cites passages from the Bible in which God violates these truths, argues that it is morally impermissible for God to violate them, and concludes that the divine attribute of holiness is not consistent with the doctrine that the Bible is a divine revelation, and therefore God does not exist.

Christine Overall in a 1985 paper "Miracles as Evidence Against the Existence of God" defines a miracle as a violation of natural law or a permanently inexplicable event, considers some problems with the connection between God and miracles raised by other writers, and then proceeds to identify three inconsistencies between the concept of God and the doctrine of miracles. Overall argues that not only do miracles not provide evidence for the existence of God, but also the doctrine of miracles itself provides a reason to hold that an omnipotent, omniscient, and omnibenevolent God does not and cannot exist.

In a 1997 paper "Miracles and God: A Reply to Robert A. H. Larmer," Overall offers a point-by-point rebuttal to an extensive critique of the 1985 paper.

Richard Schoenig in a 1999 paper "The Argument from Unfairness" begins by proposing a formal definition of unfairness and then considers the four ways that reward/punishment doctrines of salvation handle the postmortem fate of people who die without ever attaining the state of moral accountability. Drawing on these considerations, Schoenig argues that an omnipotent, omniscient, and omnibenevolent God who acts in any one of these ways is unfair, and so is *not* omnibenevolent, and therefore God does not and cannot exist.

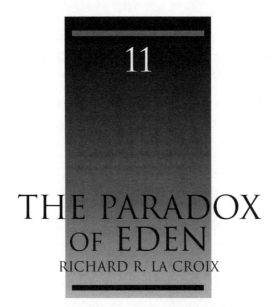

THE PARADOX
OF EDEN
RICHARD R. LA CROIX

In the book of Genesis, we are told that God created Adam and Eve and put them in the garden of Eden. God also placed in the midst of the garden of Eden the tree of the knowledge of good and evil. Adam and Eve were permitted to eat of any of the trees in the garden of Eden, but God commanded them not to eat the fruit of the tree of the knowledge of good and evil. The forbidden fruit was eaten by Adam and Eve, and God punished them for their disobedience (see Gen. 3:16–19).

Notice that there is a difficulty with this story. Before they ate the forbidden fruit, Adam and Eve either knew that obeying God is good and disobeying God is evil, or they did not know this. If they knew it, then Adam and Eve would have already possessed the knowledge of good and evil, and through his omniscience God would know this, and he would also know that Adam and Eve would not very likely be tempted to eat the forbidden fruit because they would have nothing to gain by disobeying God. So, since God's command not to eat the fruit of the tree of the knowledge of good and evil was an inadequate and unfair test of the righteousness of Adam and Eve if they already possessed the knowledge of good and evil, God acted unjustly by making this command if they already had this knowledge.

On the other hand, if Adam and Eve did *not* know that obeying God is good and disobeying God is evil, then they could not have known that it was wrong or evil to eat the fruit of the tree of the knowledge of good and evil. So, since God

From *International Journal for Philosophy of Religion* 15 (1984): 171. Copyright © 1984 by Kluwer Academic Publishers. Reprinted with kind permission of Kluwer Academic Publishers.

punished Adam and Eve for doing something that they could not have known to be wrong or evil, God acted unjustly by punishing them. It would appear to follow that whether or not Adam and Eve knew that obeying God is good and disobeying God is evil, God acted unjustly. But, then, God is just at one time and unjust at another time. Consequently, being just is *not* a necessary or essential property of God.

A MORAL ARGUMENT
FOR ATHEISM
RAYMOND D. BRADLEY

PREAMBLE FOR PHILOSOPHERS

The argument I am about to advance is intended mainly for a nonphilosophical audience.

Nevertheless, I expect some professionally trained philosophers to be present. And some of them may wonder at the fact that I say little about the God of philosophers and much about the God of pulpit and pew.

For them I offer two brief explanations.

First: there is ample precedent for what I am doing. Socrates, for example, examined the religious beliefs of his contemporaries—especially the belief that we ought to do what the gods command—and showed them to be both ill-founded and conceptually confused. I wish to follow in his footsteps though not to share in his fate. A glass of wine, not of poison, would be my preferred reward.

Thus, like Socrates, I take issue with the God of popular belief, not the God of natural theology. And since God, in the minds of most Westerners, is predominantly the God of the Jewish and Christian Scriptures,[1] I have little option other than to quote from the Bible freely so as to confront squarely the theistic beliefs that are my target and preempt charges of having misunderstood or misquoted my sources.

From *The New Zealand Rationalist & Humanist* (spring 2000): 2–12. Copyright © 2000 by Raymond D. Bradley. Reprinted by permission of Raymond D. Bradley.

Second: the fact is that most of the big-name philosophers of religion who publish in academic journals such as *Faith and Philosophy* are themselves believers in the God of the Bible, not just the God of the philosophers. To do a little name-dropping, I have in mind the likes of William Alston, William Craig, Peter van Inwagen, and Alvin Plantinga. All of these are, as Plantinga puts it, "people of the Word [who] take Scripture to be a special revelation from God himself."[2] None is averse to quoting chapter and verse of the Holy Scriptures—the morally palatable ones, anyway—in their publications as well as the pulpit.

Thus, if my philosophical audience still craves the views of some well-regarded philosophers to keep in mind as implicit targets of my criticisms, they could do no better than to consider William Alston's claim that "a large proportion of the scriptures consists of records of divine-human communications," and that God continues to reveal himself to "sincere Christians" of today in ways ranging from answered prayer to thoughts that just pop into one's mind;[3] Peter van Inwagen's statement, "I fully accept the teachings of my denomination that 'the Holy Scriptures of the Old and New Testaments are the revealed Word of God,'"[4] or still again, Alvin Plantinga's paper "When Faith and Reason Clash: Evolution and the Bible" in which he claims, "Scripture is inerrant: the Lord makes no mistakes; what he proposes for our belief is what we ought to believe."[5] These views typify the kind of theism, namely, biblical theism, that I have undertaken to refute.

Now to my argument for atheism.

INTRODUCTION

"If there is no God, all things are permitted." So, according to popular myth, said one of Dostoyevsky's characters in *The Brothers Karamazov*. He was claiming that if God does not exist, then moral values would be a purely subjective matter to be determined by the whims of individuals or by counting heads in the social groups to which they belong; or perhaps even that moral values would be totally illusory and moral nihilism would prevail. In short—the argument goes—if there are objective moral truths, then God must exist.

By way of contrast, I argue that if there are objective moral truths, then God does not exist. I present a moral argument for atheism.

A: Points of agreement with theists.

On four points, two terminological and two substantive, I agree with my theist opponents.

First: I agree with them as to what we mean by the term 'God' when they assert, and I deny, that God exists. We are not talking about just any old god. We are not talking, for instance, about Baal (god of the Canaanites), or Aton (god of the Egyptians), or Zeus (god of the Greeks), or Brahman (god of the Hindus), or Huitzilopochtli (god of the Aztecs). All of these, along with another two hundred or so, named in works on comparative religion, were supreme deities. Each was worshiped and obeyed by millions. Yet, as H. L. Mencken put it in his 1922 essay "Memorial Service," "all are dead."

Although the term 'theism' is sometimes used so broadly as to encompass belief in any sort of supernatural god or gods who reveal themselves to humans, I shall use it—as most philosophers and theologians now do—in a somewhat narrower sense. The theism I will be talking about isn't just the belief in some god or other. It is belief in the god of the orthodox Judaic, Christian, and Islamic traditions. It is belief in a god who is distinguished from these others in two main respects. First, he is holy (that is, morally perfect). Second, he reveals himself to us in Holy Scriptures. It is by virtue of his holiness that he is deemed worthy of worship and obedience. And it is by virtue of his having revealed himself to us in Scriptures that we know about his nature and what he would have us do or forbear from doing.

The God of theism, it should be noted, is a robust supernatural being. He ought not to be identified, therefore, with the metaphysically eviscerated God of liberal theologians like Paul Tillich and Bishop Robinson, for whom God is something like "our deepest concern" and the Bible is only a man-made fable, or at best a quasi-historical novel. Nor should the God of theists be identified with the unknowable God of deists like Voltaire and Thomas Paine for whom God was a hypothetical entity invoked merely to explain the origins and nature of the universe and the Bible a moral and intellectual fraud foisted upon the credulous by prophets, popes, priests, and preachers. In the strict sense of the word, each of these is an atheist. And, in the same sense, so am I. But I see no need for a god of any kind. I see only semantic obfuscation in the liberals' clothing of humanist sentiments (which I applaud) with pietistic God-talk (which I deplore). And I find only fallacious inference in the supposition that we can explain why anything at all exists the way it does by hypothesizing that something else exists the way it does; for that supposition starts one on the path of infinite regress.

Second: I think that theists would agree with me as to what we mean when we talk of objective morality. We mean a set of moral truths that would remain true no matter what any individual or social group thought or desired. The notion of objective morality is to be contrasted with all forms of moral subjectivism. It holds, first, that we have moral beliefs that are either true or false; that they are not mere expressions of emotion, akin to sighs of pleasure or pain. It holds, second, that the truth or falsity of our moral judgments is a function of whether or not the objects of moral appraisal, agents and their actions, have the moral properties that we ascribe to them; that their truth or falsity is not merely a function of the thoughts, feelings, or attitudes of individuals or the conventions of society. And it holds, third, that there may well be moral truths still awaiting our discovery, through revelation (on the theist's account) or through reason and experience—together, perhaps, with our changing biology—(on my account).

Third: I am going to agree with my theistic opponents in holding that at least some moral principles are objectively true. We would allow that disagreements about moral matters—about the permissibility of abortion or capital punishment, for example—often generate strong emotions. But this doesn't mean that such disagreements are nothing more than expressions of emotion. For we take it to be a fact of moral psychology that we have beliefs as well as emotions about such issues. And since nothing counts as a belief unless it is either true or false, we conclude that our moral beliefs—like beliefs about the shape of the earth and the age of the universe—are either true or false. Nor, from the phenomenon of moral disagreement, does it follow that the truth or falsity of moral judgments is to be determined by each individual or by counting heads. For we take it that the relativist view of truth about moral matters is no more defensible than is the relativist view of truth about factual matters.

Fourth: I would expect theists to agree with me when I give some concrete examples of moral principles that I take to be objectively true.

The requirement of objectivity is a strict one: it entails that they should be universal in the sense of being exceptionless—of holding, that is, for all persons, places, and times. Thus, on my view, the principle that it is morally forbidden to kill other persons is not objectively true since—as almost everyone would agree—it admits of exceptions such as killing a would-be murderer in defense of oneself or one's family. As it stands it is false. We may have a prima facie obligation not to kill another person. But sophisticated moral thinkers would allow that there are situations in which this principle should be set aside by virtue of countervailing moral considerations. If we are to provide moral principles that stand in need of no qualification, we need to formulate them in such a way as to make due allowance for these other considerations.

B: Examples of objective moral truths.

Here, now, are a few examples of moral principles that I take to be paradigms of objective moral truths:

P1. It is morally wrong to deliberately and mercilessly slaughter men, women, and children who are innocent of any serious wrongdoing.

A particularly gross violation of this principle is to be found in the genocidal policies of the Nazi SS who, following the orders of Hitler, slaughtered six million Jews, together with countless Gypsies, homosexuals, and other so-called "undesirables." It is no excuse, as I see it, that they believed themselves to be cutting out a cancer from society, or that they were, as Hitler explained in 1933, merely doing to the Jews what Christians had been preaching for two thousand years.[6] Another, more current, violation of this principle is to be found in the genocidal practices of Milosevic and his henchmen for whom it is no excuse to say that they are merely redressing past injustices or, by ethnic cleansing, laying the foundations for a more stable society.

P2. It is morally wrong to provide one's troops with young women captives with the prospect of their being used as sex-slaves.

This principle, or something like it, lies behind our moral revulsion at the policies of the German and Japanese High Commands who selected sexually attractive young women, especially virgins, to give so-called "comfort" to their soldiers. It is irrelevant, I want to say, that most societies, historically, have regarded such comforts as among the accepted spoils of war.

P3. It is morally wrong to make people cannibalize their friends and family.

Perhaps we can imagine situations—such as the plane crash in the Andes—in which cannibalistic acts might be exonerated. But making people eat their own family members—as many Polynesian tribes are reputed to have done—in order to punish them, or to horrify and strike fear into the hearts of their enemies, is unconscionable.

P4. It is morally wrong to practice human sacrifice, by burning or otherwise.

To be sure, human sacrifice was widely accepted by the tribes against whom the children of Israel fought, and—on the other side of the Atlantic—by the Aztecs and Incas. But this—I hope you'll agree—doesn't make the practice acceptable, even if it was done to appease the gods in whom they believed.

P5. It is morally wrong to torture people endlessly for their beliefs.

Perhaps we can think of situations in which it would be permissible to torture someone who is himself a torturer so as to obtain information as to the whereabouts of prisoners who will otherwise die from the injuries he has inflicted on them. But cases like that of Pope Pius V, who watched the Roman Inquisition burn a nonconforming religious scholar in about 1570, fall beyond the moral pale; he can't be exonerated on the grounds that he thought he was thereby saving the dissident's soul from the eternal fires of Hell.

On all of these examples, I would like to think, theists and other morally enlightened persons will agree with me. And I would like to think, further, that theists would agree with me in holding that anyone who committed, caused, commanded, or condoned acts in violation of any of these principles—the five that I will refer to hereafter as "our" principles—is not only evil but should be regarded with abhorrence.

C: God's violations of our moral principles.

But now comes the linchpin of my moral argument against theism. For, as I shall now show, the theist God—as he supposedly reveals himself in the Jewish and Christian Bibles—either himself commits, commands others to commit, or condones acts which violate every one of our five principles.

In violation of P1, for instance, God himself drowned the whole human race except Noah and his family (Gen. 7:23); he punished King David for carrying out a census that he himself had ordered and then complied with David's request that others be punished instead of him by sending a plague to kill 70,000 people (2 Sam. 24:1–15); and he commanded Joshua to kill old and young, little children, maidens, and women (the inhabitants of some thirty-one kingdoms) while pursuing his genocidal practices of ethnic cleansing in the lands that orthodox Jews still regard as part of Greater Israel (see Joshua, chapter 10, in particular). These are just three out of hundreds of examples of God's violations of P1.

In violation of P2, after commanding soldiers to slaughter all the Midianite men, women, and young boys without mercy, God permitted the soldiers to use the 32,000 surviving virgins for themselves (Num. 31:17–18).

In violation of P3, God repeatedly says he has made, or will make, people cannibalize their own children, husbands, wives, parents, and friends because they haven't obeyed him (Lev. 26:29, Deut. 28:53–58, Jer. 19:9, Ezek. 5:10).

In violation of P4, God condoned Jephthah's act in sacrificing his only child as a burnt offering to God (Judg. 11:30–39).

Finally, in violation of P5, God's own sacrificial "Lamb," Jesus, will watch as he tortures most members of the human race for ever and ever, mainly because they haven't believed in him. The book of Revelation tells us that "everyone whose name has not been written from the foundation of the world in the book of life of the Lamb who has been slain" (Rev. 13:8) will go to Hell where they "will be tormented with fire and brimstone in the presence of the holy angels and in the presence of the Lamb; and the smoke of their torment goes up forever and ever: and they have no rest day or night" (Rev. 14:10–11).

D: A logical quandary for theists: an inconsistent tetrad.

These—and countless other—passages from the Bible mean that theists are confronted with a logical quandary which strikes at the very heart of their belief the God of Scripture is holy. They cannot, without contradiction, believe all four of the statements:

(1) Any act that God commits, causes, commands, or condones is morally permissible.
(2) The Bible reveals to us many of the acts that God commits, causes, commands, and condones.
(3) It is morally impermissible for anyone to commit, cause, command, or condone acts that violate our moral principles.
(4) The Bible tells us that God does in fact commit, cause, command, or condone acts that violate our moral principles.

The trouble is that these statements form an inconsistent tetrad such that from any three one can validly infer the falsity of the remaining one. Thus, one can coherently assert (1), (2), and (3) only at the cost of giving up (4); assert (2), (3), and (4) only at the cost of giving up (1); and so on.

The problem for a theist is to decide which of these four statements to give up in order to preserve the minimal requirement of truth and rationality, namely, logical consistency. After all, if someone has contradictory beliefs, then their beliefs can't all be true. And rational discussion with persons who contradict themselves is impossible; if contradictions are allowed, then anything goes.

But which of the four statements will our theist deny?

To deny (1) would be to admit that God sometimes commits, causes, commands, or condones acts that are morally impermissible. But that would mean that God himself is immoral, or even, depending on the enormity of his misdeeds, that he is evil. It would entail denying that he is holy and worthy of worship; and denying, further, that his holiness is the ground of morality.

To deny (2), for the theist, would be to abandon the chief foundation of religious and moral epistemology (ways of obtaining religious and moral knowledge). For if (2) were false, then the question arises as to how we are supposed to know of God's existence let alone look to him for moral guidance. After all, it is a distinguishing feature of theism, as opposed to deism, to hold that God reveals himself to us and, from time to time, intervenes in human history. And the Bible, according to theists, is the principal record of his revelatory interventions. If the Bible, with its stories of Moses and Jesus, is not his revealed and presumptively true word, then how are we to know of him? If God doesn't reveal himself through the Old Testament Moses and the New Testament Jesus, then through whom does he reveal himself? To be sure, a theist could well claim that God also reveals himself through other channels in addition to the Bible: reason, tradition, and religious experience all being cases in point. But to deny that the Bible is his main mode of communication would be to deny that the principal figures in Judaism and Christianity can really be known at all. Apart from the scriptural records, we would know little, if anything, of Moses or Jesus, it being doubtful that secular history has anything reliable to say about either. Apart from the scriptural records, we would know nothing of the so-called Ten Commandments that God supposedly delivered to Moses or of the ethical principles that Jesus supposedly delivered in his sermons and parables.

To deny (3) would be to assert that it is morally permissible to violate our five moral principles. It would be to ally oneself with moral monsters like Genghis Khan, Hitler, Stalin, and Pol Pot. It would be to abandon all pretense to a belief in objective moral values. Indeed, if it is permissible to violate the above principles, then it isn't easy to see what sorts of acts would *not* be permissible. The denial of (3), then, would be tantamount to an embrace of moral nihilism. And no theist who believes in the Ten Commandments or the Sermon on the Mount could assent to that.

That leaves only (4). But to deny (4) would be to fly in the face of facts ascertainable by anyone who takes the care to read: objective facts about what the Bible actually says.

In what follows I will argue that both (3) and (4) are true, thereby confronting theists with the necessity of abandoning either (1) or (2)—the two principal foundations of theistic belief. My arguments will show that if God were to exist, then either he isn't holy or the Scriptures aren't his revealed word.

I shall, however, have to deal with the counterarguments of those who defend God and the Scriptures against criticisms like mine. Theistic apologists have two main strategies. One is to try to show, contrary to (4), that the Bible either doesn't really say what I claim it says or that it doesn't mean what it says. This tactic involves putting some sort of "spin" on the passages at issue so as to render them morally innocuous. The other is to try to show, contrary to (3), that our moral principles are either inapplicable to the situations described in (4) or that they admit of exceptions which would absolve God of violating them.

I will deal with these two apologetic strategies as they arise in connection with my defense of the truth of (4) and (3), in that order.

E: A defense of (4): What the Bible in fact says about God's violations of our moral principles.

P1 and the slaughter of innocents.

First: consider the story, in Genesis, chapters 6 and 7, of the Great Flood and Noah's Ark. It is sufficiently well known not to need retelling in detail. Suffice it to say that because of the wickedness that God saw on earth, he resolved—in his own words—to "blot out man whom I have created from the face of the land, from man to animals to creeping things and to birds of the sky" (Gen. 6:7). The sole human exceptions were Noah and his family.

Second: consider the strange story of God commanding King David to take a census of his people. It is strange for three reasons. As the story is narrated in 2 Samuel, chapter 24, we are told that God issued David with the command "Go, number Israel and Judah"; that after carrying out this command, David comes to the strange conclusion that he had thereby "sinned greatly"; that God then offered David a choice of three punishments: seven years of famine, three days' plague, or three months of being pursued by his enemies; that our noble king chose famine or plague for others rather than peril for himself; and that God complied: "the Lord sent a pestilence upon Israel . . .; and seventy thousand men of the people from Dan to Beersheba died." It is puzzling that a just God would want to punish David for obeying his commands. It is more puzzling that a holy God would vent his wrath on others by killing seventy thousand men (and unspecified numbers of women and children). It is even more puzzling that when the story is retold in 1 Chronicles, chapter 21, we find that it was Satan, not the Lord, who "incited" David to take the census. The inconsistency is bad enough since at least one of these stories must be false. It is worse that, on both accounts, it is the Lord—not Satan—who kills those who had nothing to do with David's apparent sin.

Third: consider the case in which God commands Joshua to slaughter virtually every inhabitant of the land of Canaan. The story commences in chapter 6 of the book of Joshua, telling how the hero and his army conquer the ancient city of Jericho where they "utterly destroyed everything in the city, both man and woman, young and old." Then, in chapters 7 through 12, it treats us to a chilling chronicle of the thirty-one kingdoms, and all the cities therein, that fell victim to Joshua's, and God's, genocidal policies. Time and again we read the phrases "he utterly destroyed every person who was in it," "he left no survivor," and "there was no one left who breathed." And by way of explanation of why only one of the indigenous peoples made peace with the invaders, we are told, "For it was of the Lord to harden their hearts, to meet Israel in battle that he might utterly destroy them, that they might receive no mercy . . ." (Josh. 11:20). The occasion for killing was contrived by God himself.

What is morally troubling about each of these three cases is that God apparently has no compunction about commanding the slaughter of persons who, in any ordinary sense of the words, are "innocent of serious wrong-doing." After all, it is a matter of straightforward empirical fact that newly born children, let alone those as yet unborn, don't have the capacity to do the kinds of things that warrant punishments such as drowning, being put to the sword, ripped from their mothers' wombs,[7] or of dying from a God-sent plague. Yet the Bible unabashedly reports that they, too, were among the countless victims of God's acts or commands.

P2 and giving captive virgins to the troops.

The book of Numbers, chapter 31, commences with the Lord telling Moses, "take full vengeance for the sons of Israel on the Midianites," then tells how—in obedience to God's order—twelve thousand warriors first "killed every male" (verse 7), and "captured all the women of Midian and their little ones" (verse 9). But, we read, "Moses was angry with the officers of the army . . . and said unto them, Have you spared all the women? . . . Now therefore, kill every male among the little ones, and kill every woman that hath known man intimately. But all the girls who have not known man intimately, spare for yourselves" (verses 15–18).

Now it must be admitted that nowhere in this story of mayhem and slave-taking are we told explicitly that the troops in the Lord's armies used the captured virgins for their own sexual pleasure. So it is not surprising that some apologists seize upon this omission in order to argue that P2 wasn't violated after all. One such apologist confidently claims that the soldiers took them only as "wives or servants." After all, he reassures us, "the law of God was that anyone who had sexual relations outside of heterosexual marriage was put to death" and that "any man who committed fornication . . . was forced to marry the woman and never divorce her."[8]

But this won't wash. The Bible recounts numerous instances of so-called "men of God" who bedded the unwedded—and sometimes the already wedded—with impunity from man and God alike. Examples include Abraham's sexual encounters with his Egyptian slave-girl, Hagar; King David's adulterous liaison with Bathsheba; and King Solomon, product of that liaison, and his three hundred concubines.

One would have to be extraordinarily naive to suppose that, of the twelve thousand soldiers, there weren't any who took sexual advantage of the thirty two thousand virgins—more than two apiece—God gave them to use for themselves.

P3 and causing people to cannibalize their relatives.

There are at least five passages in which God tells his people that if they don't obey him they will be punished by being reduced to such straits that they will cannibalize each other: sons, daughters, husbands, wives, fathers, mothers, and brothers, to say nothing of mere friends.[9] The book of Jeremiah is especially telling. There, in chapter 19, verse 9, the Lord himself claims direct responsibility for these horrors when he says: "And I will make them eat the flesh of their sons and the flesh of their daughters. . . ."

For these passages apologists have two main rationalizations to offer. One is that God is merely threatening his chosen people with the fate that will befall them if they don't obey his commandments. A second is that he is merely predicting the fates that will befall them in forthcoming sieges by their enemies. The problem with the threat-hypothesis is that, in each instance, the Children of Israel did not in fact obey his commandments despite the threats. So, if God did not do what he threatened to do, his threats were empty and he repeatedly failed to keep his word. And the problem with the prediction-hypothesis, is that if things hadn't turned out as he predicted, then what he said would have been false. But in any case neither explanation would help with the Jeremiah passage, in which God isn't merely predicting what the Israelites' enemies will cause them to do, but is saying what he himself will cause them to do. There is no gainsaying the fact that if God's word is true, then he causes others to violate P3.

P4 and condoning child sacrifice.

In the book of Judges, chapter 11, we are treated to a cautionary tale about a rash vow and its consequences. Jephthah, we are told, was a mighty man who was used by God to carry on in Joshua's tradition by cleansing the land of another ethnically different people, the sons of Ammon. We read that Jephthah "made a vow to the Lord, and said, If thou wilt indeed give the sons of Ammon into my hand, then it shall be that whatever comes out of the doors of my house to meet me when I return in peace from the sons of Ammon, it shall be the Lord's, and I will offer it up as a burnt offering" (verses 31–32).

The Lord, it seems, found this perfectly acceptable. He kept his part of the bargain by delivering the Ammonites and their twenty cities "with a very great slaughter" into Jephthah's hands. Then came Jephthah's turn to keep his part of the bargain. But sadly it was his daughter who came out of the house to greet him. Jephthah realized that he nevertheless had to keep faith with God. Thus we read: "And it came to pass at the end of two months that she returned unto her father, who did to her according to the vow which he had made. . . ." In other words, Jephthah kept his vow by offering up his beloved daughter as a burnt sacrifice to his unrelenting Lord. Thus did Jephthah earn himself an honorable mention in the Epistle to the Hebrews,[10] where he is listed along with fifteen or so other men of "great faith" such as Noah, Abraham, Moses, Samson, David, and Samuel.

The best spin that can be put on this horrifying story is that it is a sort of Aesop's fable, a man-made tale told with a view to teaching us a lesson about the need for forethought before undertaking commitments to others, especially to a deity. Such a gloss, however, can hardly be acceptable to a Bible-believing theist. But in any case, we shouldn't really be surprised at the Lord's acceptance of Jephthah's sacrifice. After all, God himself—Christian theists believe—offered his own son Jesus as a blood-sacrifice for the mistakes of mankind.

P5 and the eternal torture God has in store for those
who don't believe that Jesus is Lord and Savior.

The fate of Jephthah's daughter pales into insignificance when compared with that which the Christian God has in store for sincere atheists like me; and not only for atheists, but for all those who fail to accept Jesus Christ as their savior. Jesus, who has the dubious distinction of having invented the doctrine of hellfire and damnation, describes their fate vividly. In the Gospel of Matthew alone he characterizes it in terms which evangelists adore: "unquenchable fire," "fiery hell" (twice), "torment," "burned with fire," "furnace of fire" (twice), "weeping and gnashing of teeth" (five times), "eternal fire," and "eternal fire which has been prepared for the devil and his angels."

Assuming that Jesus knew how to say what he meant, the fate of unbelievers is clear. It isn't a clean dispatch into oblivion. It isn't merely the anguish of a soul who is separated from God. It is the torment and agony of a resurrected body, torture differing from that experienced by victims of the Inquisition only in the fact that it lasts not just for minutes but for all eternity. Unlike Auschwitz, Hell offers no finality to those of us who are to fill its ovens. No one will escape its horrors, and its tortures—to be performed before divine spectators—will continue without end.[11]

Were this fiery fate to be reserved for unrepentant mass murderers and the other perpetrators of evil who have blighted human history, such a violation of P5 would be bad enough. But Rev. 13:8 predicts this fate will befall "everyone whose name has not been written from the foundation of the world in the book of life of the Lamb. . . ." And Rev. 20:15 confirms the prediction when it tells us that "if anyone's name was not found written in the book of life, he was thrown into the lake of fire."

Who are they who have not thus been preordained to eternal life? They are all those who—as evangelicals like to put it—aren't "born-again" Christians. According to Luke, the reputed author of the Acts, "there is salvation in no one else; for there is no other name under heaven that has been given among men, by which we must be saved" (Acts 4:12). And St. Paul makes it clearer still when he tells us that "the Lord Jesus Christ shall be revealed from heaven with his mighty angels in flaming fire, dealing out retribution to those who *do not know God* [my emphasis] and to those who do not obey the Gospel of our Lord Jesus Christ. And these will pay the penalty of eternal destruction" (2 Thess. 1:7–9).

At this point, it may occur to some of us that since it is a necessary condition of believing in the name of Jesus that you've both heard the name and understood its significance, no one can be saved from hell if they haven't heard the gospel. Therein, of course, lies the motivation of missionaries. But what of those who have lived in times or places in which the name of Jesus is unknown? Are all those who lived prior to the time of Christ already condemned? How about those who have lived, or still live, in ignorance of the Christian story? Are they—the majority of the human race—condemned for a lack of belief which, for historical or geographical reasons, they are debarred from having?

This harsh conclusion is what the Bible implies. Certainly, Jesus himself seems to have accepted it with equanimity: "The gate [to salvation]," he said, "is narrow and the way is hard . . . and those who find it are few" (Matt. 7:13–14). The exclusion of most human beings—no matter how saintly their lives—for the sole reason that they don't believe in Jesus as Savior, is a consequence of the fact that most of the people who have populated the earth down to the present haven't even heard of him. If we are to take Jesus himself seriously, little comfort can be found in a suggestion by St. Paul that some might find salvation as a result of so-called general revelation. As one of the ablest Christian apologists, William L. Craig, acknowledges, such exceptions to the rule of "salvation through no other name" can at best be rare. This is why Craig makes no pretense of the fact that on his, and Jesus', view even the sincerest believers of other world religions are "lost and dying without Christ."[12]

However, all this talk of the numbers of persons who will be tortured in hell is beside the point. So is the question whether hell's torments are finite or infinite in duration. If there is even one person who suffers the tortures of the damned, then the moral principle we have enshrined as P5 is thereby violated by God himself.

And by virtue of God's violating it—along with our other moral principles—his supposed holiness is clearly compromised. Just as it would be incoherent to say that Hitler was morally perfect despite the fact that he sent people to the gas chambers for the "sin" of lacking the right parentage, so it would be incoherent to suppose that God is morally perfect despite the fact that he will send people to roast in hell for the "sin" of lacking the right beliefs. On the contrary, anyone who is guilty of such atrocities is, not to mince words, simply evil. Little wonder, then, that God says of himself not only "I make peace" but also "I create evil" (Isa. 45:7).[13]

It is worth noting that, compared with God, Satan is depicted throughout the Bible as a relative paragon of virtue. Satan is guilty of just three main misdemeanors.

First, according to a passage which sets the moral tone of the Bible, Satan—in the guise of a serpent—tempts Eve with the forbidden fruit of moral enlightenment, fruit from what is described as "the tree of knowledge of good and evil."[14] One might have thought it a good thing for Satan thus to start her on the path to moral education. But God didn't want her eyes to be "opened," as Gen. 3:5 puts it; he wanted blind obedience. And so God responds in typical fashion. Not only does he punish Eve for an act that she didn't know was wrong until after she'd performed it. He also punishes Adam, and all their descendants, including you and me. He imposes on us all the burden of what theologians call Original Sin: he sees to it that none of us can start life with a clean slate.

Satan appears next in 1 Chronicles where he plays the very same role that was assigned to God in 2 Samuel. So wherein lies his wrong this time? If it is good enough for God to order David's census-taking, can it be evil for Satan to do so?

Satan's third appearance is in the book of Job where he makes life difficult for God's protégé. But that, it should be noted, is only because God had issued him a challenge to do so.

Thereafter, Satan does almost nothing of a dubious nature except for tempting God himself, in the person of Jesus, during his forty days in the desert—an exercise doomed to futility.

What is remarkable, in light of the bad press Satan has subsequently suffered, is that Satan, unlike God, doesn't violate a single one of the important moral principles P1 through P5.

F: A defense of (3): The impermissibility of God's violations of our principles.

The second apologetic strategy is to argue that our principles admit of exceptions which, when they are taken into account, absolve God of guilt.

Chief among the apologetic ploys in this category is what I shall call the Sovereignty Exception. In the words of one apologist, it holds that "God is sovereign over life" and he can therefore do with us as he likes "according to his will."[15] But this argument contains a fatal equivocation on the word 'can'. It is trivially true that if God is—as theists believe—sovereignly omnipotent, then he 'can' do whatever he wants in the sense of having the power or might to do so. But might, we reflect, doesn't confer right. It certainly doesn't follow that God 'can' violate moral principles in the sense of its being morally right for him to do so. If it did, the moral monsters of human history who reigned sovereignly over their empires would equally be innocent of wrongdoing.

A second tactic is to argue that God is exempt from the prohibitions of our principles. It might be said that although these are binding on humans, they are not binding on God. But that would be to introduce a double standard and so compromise the universality of moral principles. It would relativise morality to individuals or times and deprive them of the absolute and objective validity that theists are committed to. Worse still, for the theist's case, it would call into question God's holiness. For holy is as holy does. That is to say, if anyone at all is properly to be described as morally perfect, then their acts of commission, of command, and of permission must also be morally perfect. To say that God is holy despite the evil nature of what he does would be to play with words: it would be to deprive the word 'holy' of its ordinary meaning and make it a synonym for 'evil'.

A third ploy is to argue that in all the cases we have considered God is acting in accordance with what some hold to be the overriding moral principle that sin must be punished. For from this, together with the theological doctrine of Original Sin—the doctrine that every human being, even the newly conceived fetus in its mother's womb, inherits sin or at least the disposition to sin from Eve—it follows that God has the right, not just the might, to punish us as he sees fit. As one apologist put it: "Since the wages of sin is death, God has the right to give and take life."[16] Leave aside the questionable presuppositions of this doctrine: that sin is inherited through our genes or via our supposed souls; and that we can justly be held responsible for inherited or unactualized dispositions to sin. There is a more important objection to this whole apologetic claim. For suppose we grant the implausible claim that it is by virtue of a universal lack of human innocence that God is to be excused for his genocidal practices. Then we shall have to say that there are no circumstances whatever, not even innocence of the victims, in which it is morally wrong to slaughter men, women, and children. We would have to abandon P1 as an objective moral truth since it would be totally vacuous, lacking any application whatever. And that would give us, like God, a license to mercilessly slaughter anyone we liked. All we need to do is to invoke the Punishment for Original Sin Exception. After all, unless we are to adopt the relativism of a double standard, if it is good enough for God, it must be good enough for us.

If even one of the above exceptions to our principles were sound, those principles would not be moral truths but moral falsehoods. At best, they would merely state prima facie moral prohibitions, prohibitions which would—in order to make them objectively binding—have to be qualified in ways that would give a license to some of the most morally abhorrent behavior of which any person could be guilty. In short, if reformulated to accommodate God, they would accommodate the Devil and other personifications of evil as well.

G: Consequences for theism: the falsity of at least one of theism's cornerstones, (1) or (2).

At this point let us return to the inconsistent tetrad which I said posed such problems for theistic belief. I have demonstrated, first, that (4) is true, that is, that the Bible does indeed tell us that God violates our moral principles; and second, that

(3) is true, that is, that it is morally impermissible for anyone—including God—to violate these principles. But if I am right, then theists have no way out of their logical quandary that doesn't destroy the very core of theistic belief.

They have a choice. They must, on pain of contradiction, abandon at least one, if not both, of (1), the belief that all of God's acts are morally permissible, or (2), the belief that the Bible reveals to us what many of these acts are. Yet, as we have seen, if they abandon (1), they therewith abandon the belief in God's holiness; while if they abandon (2), they therewith abandon the belief in the Bible as his revelation.

Here I rest my case against theism: my moral argument for atheism.

H: A corollary of my argument: the falsity of the theistic theory of ethics.

Before finishing, however, I want to draw attention to a corollary of my argument. Consider, once more, the inconsistent tetrad by which the whole edifice of theism is brought to ruin. But this time replace statements (1), (2), (3), and (4) of the original inconsistent tetrad with their respective corollaries:

(1)* Any act that God commands us to perform is morally permissible.

(2)* The Bible reveals to us many of the acts that God commands us to perform.

(3)* It is morally impermissible for anyone to commit acts that violate principle P1.

(4)* The Bible tells us that God commands us to perform acts that violate moral principle P1.

Then a parallel logical quandary arises for the theist's belief that God, as revealed in the Bible, is the source of objective morality or, at the very least, is a reliable guide to what we should and should not do.

Rather than run the argument through again, I will present this additional indictment of theistic belief by first quoting the Bible and then addressing a series of questions to those who, like philosopher Alvin Plantinga, claim that "what [the Lord] proposes for our belief is what we ought to believe." For it should be evident that, if Plantinga and other biblical theists are right, then since the beliefs that the Lord proposes include ones about what we ought to do, if the Lord proposes that we should do so and so, then so and so is what we ought to do.

Consider 1 Sam. 15:3 in which the Lord commands his people:

> Now go and strike Amalek and utterly destroy all that he has, and do not spare him; but put to death both man and woman, child and infant. . . .

Now ask yourself three questions:

(i)   Was "put to death both man and woman, child and infant" the very word of the Lord whom you worship?

(ii) Is it conceivable that your Lord could again issue the same command in our time?

(iii) If you did believe you were so commanded by your Lord, could you and would you obey?

If you answer no to question (i), you deny the authority of God's so-called word, the Bible. If you answer no to question (ii)—perhaps because you think your Lord might have mended his ways—you deny that God's commands have the kind of universal applicability which is a necessary condition of their being in accord with, let alone the source of, moral truths. If you answer no to question (iii), you must think that it is sometimes right, or even obligatory, to disobey God. You thereby admit that moral truths are independent of, and may even conflict with, God's dictates. You admit that ethics is, as most philosophers have long insisted, autonomous; and that we must, therefore, do our moral thinking for ourselves.

But if you answer yes to each question, then I submit that your belief in the God of biblical theism is not just mistaken but morally abhorrent. For, in the words of my friend, John Patrick, who resigned from the Presbyterian ministry here in New Zealand after he discovered how many of his parishioners also answered yes to all three questions: "a doctrine of the Scriptures as containing the Word of God, the supreme ruler of faith and duty, has the power to turn otherwise gentle, thoughtful, and basically loving people into a group prepared to sanction genocide in the name of the Lord they worship."[17]

NOTES

1. For present purposes I say nothing about the God of the Koran. It suffices to say that my argument, if sound, also counts against Islamic theism.

2. Alvin Plantinga, "When Faith and Reason Clash: Evolution and the Bible," *Christian Scholar's Review* 21, no. 1 (September 1991): 8.

3. William Alston, "Divine-Human Dialogue and the Nature of God," *Faith and Philosophy* (January 1985): 6.

4. Peter van Inwagen, "Genesis and Evolution," in *Reasoned Faith*, ed. Eleonore Stump (Ithaca, N.Y.: Cornell University Press, 1993), p. 97.

5. Plantinga, "When Faith and Reason Clash," p. 12.

6. Rod Evans and Irwin Berent, *Fundamentalism: Hazards and Heartbreaks* (La Salle, Ill.: Open Court, 1988), pp. 120–21. Also James A. Haught, *Holy Horrors: An Illustrated History of Religious Murder and Madness* (Amherst, N.Y.: Prometheus Books, 1990), p. 163.

7. See Hos. 13:16: "Samaria will be held guilty, for she has rebelled against her God. They will fall by the sword, Their little ones will be dashed in pieces, And their pregnant women will be ripped open."

8. Brad Warner, "God, Evil, and Professor Bradley" (manuscript circulated privately in response to my debate with Campus Crusade for Christ representative, Dr. Chamberlain, on the topic "Can there be an objective morality without God?"). The debate took place at Simon Fraser University on January 25, 1996.

9. In Lev. 26:29 we read: "You shall eat the flesh of your sons, and the flesh of your daughters you shall eat." In Deut. 28:53–58, after the Lord lists the dozens of evils that will befall his people if they don't observe all his commandments and statutes, he says: "Then you shall eat the offspring of your own body, the flesh of your sons and your daughters. . . . The man who is refined and very delicate among you shall be hostile toward his brother and toward the wife he cherishes, and toward the rest of his children who remain, so that he will not give even one of them any of the flesh of his children which he shall eat." And refined and delicate women, we are further told, will do the same. In Jer. 19:9 the horror show continues when the Lord says: "And I will make them eat the flesh of their sons and the flesh of their daughters. . . ." Finally, in Ezek. 5:10, the divine diet is extended to fathers when God says: "Therefore, fathers will eat their sons among you, and sons will eat their fathers."

10. Of unknown authorship though erroneously attributed to St. Paul.

11. Rev. 14:10–11. To be sure, the verse continues by identifying those who suffer this fate with "those who worship the beast and his image, and whoever receives the mark of his name." But they have already been identified, in Rev. 13:8–18, as those who weren't preordained for salvation.

12. William L. Craig, "No Other Name: A Middle Knowledge Perspective on the Exclusivity of Salvation through Christ," *Faith and Philosophy* (April 1989): 187. In his view, God is justified in sending both witting and unwitting nonbelievers to Hell because he knew—before he created them—that they wouldn't have believed in Jesus as Savior even if they had heard about him.

13. The Hebrew word that is here translated as 'evil' is 'rah'. The New American Standard translators, however, prefer to render it as 'calamity' in the passage from Isaiah and as 'ill' in the passage from Lamentations. But such sanitization of the original doesn't really help. It affords the believer little comfort to be told that God is the source of calamity. And 'ill'—we learn from Webster's *New Collegiate Dictionary*—is just a synonym for 'evil'.

14. Gen. 2:9.

15. Warner, "God, Evil, and Professor Bradley," p. 15.

16. Ibid., p. 14.

17. John Patrick, "By What Authority?" published September 1984, in a newsletter to fellow clergymen in the New Zealand Presbyterian Church explaining why he was resigning. My three questions are derived from ones he had put to his parishioners.

Raymond D. Bradley, professor emeritus of philosophy at Simon Fraser University, originally prepared this paper for oral presentation to the New Zealand Association of Rationalists and Humanists.

13

MIRACLES AS EVIDENCE AGAINST THE EXISTENCE OF GOD

CHRISTINE OVERALL

M ost recent discussions of the concept of miracles have concentrated mainly on the relationship between miracles and scientific laws.[1] As a result, I believe, there has been far too little attention paid to the alleged evidential connections between the existence of miracles and the existence of God.

One reason, presumably, that some philosophers and theologians have traditionally been interested in miracles is that it is assumed that their existence would be evidence—probably conclusive evidence—for the existence of God.[2] (And here, by 'God', I mean the God of Christianity; in John Hick's definition, "the infinite, eternal, uncreated, personal reality, who has created all that exists and who is revealed to human creatures as holy and loving."[3]) Despite this assumption, I would nevertheless like to ask what I think (in light of the epistemic difficulties in providing evidence for the existence of a miracle) may be a sort of counterfactual question: namely, if miracles were to occur, just what would their occurrence really show?

In the context of the type of definition of 'miracle' used recently by some philosophers, it becomes difficult to frame the question in just this way. For they appear to build into the concept of miracle the notion that the event is brought about by a supernatural being. Douglas Odegard, for example, claims,

From *The Southern Journal of Philosophy* 23, no. 3 (1985): 347–53. Copyright © 1985 by the University of Memphis. Reprinted by permission of *The Southern Journal of Philosophy*.

Some who for the sake of argument make the violation of a law a condition of being a miracle would go further and add the condition that the event must have religious significance or be produced by a god. But . . . the notion of violating a law is best understood such that we cannot justifiably claim that an event is a violation unless we have good reason to believe that it is produced by a god.[4]

Similarly, in discussing the concept of miracle, Ian Walker states that

the concept of violations [of natural laws], if it is to be coherent, must have a 'supernatural precondition' built into it. This means that 'violation' miracles can only be characterized on the precondition that they may be the result of a supernatural force at work.[5]

And David Basinger argues that

it would be useful for theologians and philosophers to refrain from defining miracles as violations of natural laws and define them rather as permanently inexplicable or coincidental *direct acts of God.*[6]

Hence, to say that an event x is a miracle is already, by definition, to say that a supernatural being exists, and cannot be used as independent evidence for that being's existence. This concept of miracle, therefore, encourages us to focus on the problem of the identification of a particular event as a miracle rather than on the exploration of the connection between a certain kind of event, called a miracle, and God. To avoid this terminological problem, in what follows I shall mean by 'miracle' simply an event which is a violation of natural law or which (following Basinger[7]) is permanently inexplicable. However, regardless of what definition is adopted, the philosophical question turns out to be the same: What is the connection between, on the one hand, the existence of an event which is a violation of natural law or which is permanently inexplicable (a miracle, in my sense) and, on the other, the existence of God?

Some writers have claimed, at least, that the connection between the existence of miracles and the existence of God is not a straightforward one. Consider the following arguments:

(a) God is thought of as a being existing outside (in of course a nonspatial sense) space and time; he is not a part of the space-time order, but independent of it:

While it makes sense to talk about influence and interference between particular things *within* the universe, this is not the case with the whole. . . . One may ask in a similar vein whether the cause (God) can be otherwise if the effect (the miracle) is spatio-temporal. Moreover, a theist taking this line must explain how

God can hear and answer requests (spatio-temporal events) without being in the space-time sphere himself. Yet, many miracles involve requests and answers.[8]

The point here is that a violation of natural law, or a permanently inexplicable event, occurring within space-time is not the sort of thing which a being outside space-time could produce. The problem here is not, of course, an empirical one, but a logical one. Thus, the argument raises doubts about what the connection between God and miracles could possibly be.

(b) Another problem about making a connection between miracles and God is cited by Alastair McKinnon. He points out that according to "the supernatural account," God is the cause of all events. Hence, says McKinnon, "it makes no sense to say that he is the special cause of one or more particular events."[9] McKinnon is suggesting that the believer in God cannot have it both ways: either all events are caused by God—in which case "it makes no sense to speak of events as *specially caused* by God"—or, if there are special supernatural causes of specific events, God cannot be regarded as "in any sense the cause of regular events."[10] Thus, there is a very real peculiarity in the sort of over-determination which appears to result from trying to maintain that a miracle is caused by God.

(c) George Chryssides presents an ingenious argument according to which, if an event is a miracle, that is, a violation of a scientific law, then it cannot be attributed to an agent of any sort, divine or not; if it can be so attributed, then it is not a miracle. His reason is that "the assignment of agency implies predictability," the subsumption of the act under scientific law, yet this is impossible in the case of a miracle.[11] We assign agency when we have noted that similar actions by other agents in similar circumstances have been followed by similar subsequent events;[12] in the case of a miracle, however, we have a unique event to be assigned to a unique agent. Thus, once again, the question is raised as to how a miracle could possibly be connected with God.

But in spite of these skeptical views, there has not yet been a sufficiently radical questioning of the evidential connection between miracles and God. Odegard, for example, believes that an event identified as a miracle cannot be used as evidence for the existence of a god which is its cause. But his reason is that in order to say that the event is a miracle, we first have to say that it is caused by a god.[13] Similarly, Walker believes that "violation miracles" cannot "form the foundation of any sort of religious polemic," because "any polemic which endeavored to demonstrate the existence of supernatural forces by means of the violation concept of the miraculous would have to assume the very existence of that which was the object of proof in order to maintain consistency in the proof itself."[14]

By contrast, I propose the suggestion that if a miracle in the sense used here were to occur, it in fact would constitute evidence *against* the existence of the Christian God. So, far from its being the case that identifying event x as a miracle would require one first to know that it is caused by God or a god, on the contrary, if one knew that God exists, then probably nothing could be identified as a miracle, and conversely, if event x could be identified as a miracle, one would have good reason to believe that God does not exist. Put simply, my view is that a miracle as an event which is a violation of natural law or which is permanently inexplicable is inconsistent with the concept of God.

I shall now try to give some defense of this suggestion. In so doing I shall perhaps be led into the quagmires of anthropomorphism, but perhaps this is inevitable in dealing with what seems to be an irretrievably anthropomorphic concept.

I propose, first, that we must ask some fundamental questions about the nature of a being which would cause miracles. Douglas K. Erlandson has suggested that the issue here is one of appropriateness: "the believer regards certain acts as appropriate to his God, other acts as inappropriate."[15] But to speak of "appropriateness" suggests, perhaps, a sort of cosmic politeness; so I think that a better word here would be "consistency." Are events which violate natural law, or which are permanently inexplicable, consistent with the nature of God?

In the past, some philosophers and theologians have urged us to consider the supposed order, regularity, and harmony of the universe as evidence of the existence of a benign and omnipotent god. But if order, regularity, and harmony constitute evidence for God, then miracles cannot *also* be accepted as evidence for his existence, for they are, to follow the metaphor, dissonances in the harmony, holes in the patterned fabric of the universe. Hence, a Christian believer cannot have it both ways. A miracle, a violation of natural law or a permanently inexplicable event, is a moment of chaos, a gap in the spatio-temporal structure. If one were to occur, it would therefore have to constitute evidence against the Christian God's existence.

It might, however, be objected that a miracle is not just a meaningless hole in nature's fabric, for after all, it is claimed to have a purpose, a function. As Erlandson remarks, "Inexplicability or mystery *is* an element of the miraculous, but it must be of a certain sort—it must fit a pattern"[16]—not, presumably, a pattern of natural events (for it disrupts them)—but an intelligible pattern of divine activity.

But then the focus of our interest must switch to a consideration of God's supposed purposes and intentions. As Herbert Burhenn remarks, questions about the attribution of miracles are "teleological rather than causal in character."[17] In particular, is a violation of law or an inexplicable event congruent with the purposes of a benevolent God?

I would suggest that it is not. For such an event is misleading to human beings who, as knowledge-seekers, attempt to understand the world by discerning the regularities and patterns in it. The extreme rarity of miracles and the difficulties and controversies in identifying them are an impediment to the growth of scientific and philosophical comprehension. A benevolent God would not mislead his people.

Two related answers to this argument are possible. First, it might be argued that the occurrence of a miracle does not, in fact, have this puzzling effect, because the event itself is part of a *pattern* of the miraculous. Thus, for the religious believer, two very general patterns are discernible: the pattern of natural events, which is studied by science, and the pattern of divine events, consisting of interventions in the natural order.[18] As Erlandson remarks,

> the pattern that the believer perceives extends to many events. Rarely will the believer see only one event as miraculous. Rather, he can point to a series of events which he perceives to be acts of his God. This series presents an overall pattern to the believer, from which he can ascertain the nature of his God, and which provides him justification for deciding that a particular occurrence is a miracle.[19]

Unfortunately, one fact seems to militate against this response, and that is the rarity of miracles. It has a twofold implication. On the one hand, if miracles really do occur infrequently, as they seem to, it will be difficult to discern a pattern of meaning in their occurrence, and there will be controversy as to what the pattern is. On the other hand, if their occurrence were not so rare, then to that degree they would be more disruptive of human efforts to see the world as forming a coherent, unified, consistent pattern. Thus Erlandson is mistaken in supposing that "the believer can hold that some events are to be explained by appeal to the miraculous without in any way impugning scientific autonomy."[20] For, by its very nature, any alleged "pattern" of miraculous occurrences is inconsistent with the pattern of natural events which science seeks to account for, and there is very real epistemic dissonance between the two systems.

A second possible response to the claim that a benevolent God would not mislead his people by causing events which are a violation of natural law or are permanently inexplicable is the following: Some slight confusion in our growing understanding of the world is but a small price to pay for the other goods that a miracle would afford us. For example, "It might accomplish some positive good, such as healing or saving a life. . . . It might aid in the communication of divine teaching. . . . It might serve to revive religious awareness."[21]

But two important questions can be raised about such possible purposes. First, in being accomplished through miracles, they would seem to make use of human weaknesses—for example, fear, suggestibility, ignorance, and awe of the unknown. Second, and more important, this appeal to God's purposes creates an opening for some of the same moves that are made in the argument from evil against God's existence:

> [O]ne could ask why an omnipotent God does not accomplish more and more good miraculously, or why he did not create a better world which would not require miraculous intervention to correct its faults.[22]

If accomplishing good, communicating divine teaching, or reviving religious awareness are divine purposes, miracles seem scarcely adequate to their accomplishment, for few people have been helped, and many remain skeptical. Certainly, if we consider the standard biblical examples of miracles, they reflect a certain caprice—one is cured, another is not; bias—in favor of one group of people over another; and triviality. These events do not appear to be consistent with the sorts of purposes that might be supposed to be held by an omnipotent, omniscient, benevolent being. And even if one were not to use these events as standard examples of miracles, still the very fact that a miracle is an event, and therefore limited in space and time (albeit detached from the natural space-time continuum) means that it is inherently handicapped for conveying the purposes of a limitless God.

I conclude, then, that the reservations of philosophers such as Erlandson, McKinnon, and Chryssides about the connection between miracles and God are a step in the right direction, but that they do not go far enough. For we must question the underlying assumption, ordinarily made by all parties to the debate, that if a miracle, in the sense of a violation of natural law or a permanently inexplicable event, were to occur, then it would be evidence for God's existence. On the contrary, if my arguments are correct, then if a miracle were to occur we would have a very good reason for denying that the Christian God exists. Paul Dietl claims that proving the existence of a being who deserves *some* of the predicates (e.g., sufficient power to cause a violation of scientific law or a permanently inexplicable event) 'God' normally gets would go some way toward proving the existence of God himself.[23] But if I am right, such a being, if it exists, could not have the characteristics we usually attribute to God, and thus could not be the Christian God.[24]

NOTES

1. Herbert Burhenn, "Attributing Miracles to Agents—Reply to George D. Chryssides," *Religious Studies* 13 (1977): 485.

2. Cf. "[I]f we can establish that [an] event is produced by a god, the question of whether the event is a miracle may seem academic, since the ultimate goal is to find evidence of a god's existence. . . . The power to create miracles is often a central feature of

a god, and if the given type of event is not a miracle, the defended god would be stripped of such power, which would be a large conceptual sacrifice." (Douglas Odegard, "Miracles and Good Evidence," *Religious Studies* 18 [1982]: 39.)

3. John Hick, *Philosophy of Religion,* 3d ed. (Englewood Cliffs, N.J.: Prentice-Hall, 1983), p. 14.

4. Odegard, "Miracles and Good Evidence," p. 37; cf. p. 41.

5. Ian Walker, "Miracles and Violations," *International Journal for Philosophy of Religion* 13 (1982): 108.

6. David Basinger, "Miracles as Violations: Some Clarifications," *The Southern Journal of Philosophy* 22 (1984): 7, my emphasis.

7. However, Basinger denies that a nonrepeatable counterinstance to a law, caused by God, would be a violation of natural law, since it does not occur under the exact set of natural conditions presupposed in any set of natural laws (p. 5). But since my argument concerns whether a special event can be linked to God in any way, it seems safe for me to define a miracle as a violation of natural law. For my point is that we cannot start with a definition which assumes God's role in producing the event.

8. Douglas K. Erlandson, "A New Look at Miracles," *Religious Studies* 13 (1977): 421, his emphasis.

9. Alastair McKinnon, "'Miracle' and 'Paradox,'" in *Analytical Philosophy of Religion in Canada,* ed. Mostafa Faghfoury (Ottawa, Ontario: University of Ottawa Press, 1982), p. 162.

10. Ibid., McKinnon's emphasis.

11. George D. Chryssides, "Miracles and Agents," *Religious Studies* 11 (1975): 322.

12. Ibid., pp. 323–24.

13. Odegard, "Miracles and Good Evidence," p. 45.

14. Walker, "Miracles and Violations," p. 108.

15. Erlandson, "A New Look at Miracles," p. 422. However, Erlandson gives as an example what would seem by the standards of most believers to be a most inappropriate example: God's curing a hangnail in response to prayers by a man of faith!

16. Ibid., p. 423, his emphasis.

17. Burhenn, "Attributing Miracles to Agents," p. 489.

18. Cf. Erlandson, "A New Look at Miracles," p. 426.

19. Ibid., p. 424.

20. Ibid., p. 427.

21. Burhenn, "Attributing Miracles to Agents," p. 488.

22. Ibid.

23. Paul Dietl, "On Miracles," *American Philosophical Quarterly* 5 (1968): 133.

24. My thanks are due to Keith Parsons, whose unpublished paper, "Miracles," gave me the impetus to write this paper.

14

MIRACLES AND GOD
A REPLY TO ROBERT A. H. LARMER
CHRISTINE OVERALL

In a paper published ten years ago[1] I argued that, contrary to religious and philosophical orthodoxy, if a miracle were to occur, it would constitute evidence against the existence of the Judæo-Christian God. I defined 'miracle' as an event that violates natural law, or that is permanently inexplicable.

I gave three main reasons for my claim. First, a miracle would be a flaw in the order and regularity of the universe—contrary to what one would expect from an omnipotent God. Second, a miracle would be incongruent with the purposes of a beneficent God, for it would impede the growth of philosophical and scientific knowledge and would at best appeal to human weaknesses—fear, suggestibility, ignorance, and awe of the unknown—an appeal unworthy of a perfect God. Third, events standardly identified as miracles mostly help very few and convert only a handful; if taken as the handiwork of a transcendent agent, they reflect apparent caprice, bias, and triviality, characteristics incompatible with those assigned to God.

In a book devoted to the concept of miracles,[2] Robert A. H. Larmer presents an extensive rebuttal to my arguments. In this article I evaluate Larmer's case against my claims and assess its strength, drawing both on the book and on several of Larmer's published papers.

From *Dialogue* 36 (1997): 741–52. Copyright © 1997 Wilfrid Laurier University Press. Reprinted by permission of *Dialogue: Canadian Philosophical Review*.

METHODOLOGY AND DEFINITIONS

Larmer and I disagree, first, about a fundamental matter of methodology. Before considering what events are properly to be called miracles, he asserts, one must first give an account of what a miracle is. He claims that I reverse the problem: that I assume it is possible to identify miracles as a class, and then attempt to "abstract a definition" of 'miracle' from surveying the class members. I then re-define the term, producing a definition "that has little resemblance to the way the word is actually used." I fail to examine the logically prior question of whether my definitions have "captured what we ordinarily mean by the term *miracle*."[3]

Although I am not sure that I saw abstracting a definition as a major problem of my article, Larmer has correctly identified the different starting points which each of us adopts. He takes as foundational an interpretation that he claims is "what we ordinarily mean by the term *miracle*," and identifies four criteria.[4] A miracle (1) is a physical event beyond the ability of unaided nature to produce, (2) is brought about by a rational agent, (3) is extraordinary, and (4) has religious significance. After setting forth these criteria, which an unidentified reference group ("we") allegedly attributes to the term, he then seeks to identify those events that are accurately describable by the word and argues that such events would constitute good evidence for the existence of the Christian God.

However, it is not self-evident that Larmer's approach is the correct one. It is just as useful to take those events standardly recognized as miracles—in Scripture, ritual, and religious culture generally—as exemplars of the term and then attempt to extract a meaning for the term from observation of the members of the representative set.

Larmer himself does not hesitate to recognize and make use of such exemplars. As a self-identified Christian, he refers to stock biblical examples, including "the Virgin Birth, the feeding of the multitudes, the healing of the sick and the Resurrection." In addition, he creates hypothetical examples, such as "the instantaneous regrowth of a man's withered arm" following prayer for such an event by religious persons of exemplary character. He also provides the fictitious example of a man, also of "exemplary character," who enacts remarkable cures—restoring damaged eyes to sight and reversing supposedly terminal diseases.[5] We are to imagine that this man's healing capacities are not affected by distance, physical screening, or the specific disease or injury of the person needing healing.[6]

The point of these scriptural and fictitious examples is that Larmer has no difficulty providing examples of miracles. In so doing, however, he has no apparent recourse to his own list of criteria but instead relies directly on Christian history and ideology. Indeed, in a paper published in 1989, he acknowledges the significance of "paradigm cases" of miracles,[7] cases that obviate the need for explicit criteria for miracles. My argument is that events such as these, which I readily accept as standard examples of supposed miracles, can be described generally as violating natural laws or as permanently inexplicable (inexplicable, that is, in terms of natural laws). As such, they are incompatible with the existence of the Christian God.

So, not only do Larmer and I disagree about how to begin the investigation of miracles; we also disagree about the appropriate concept of miracle with which to work. I now want to consider the plausibility of Larmer's concept and show that it is unacceptable.

The first problem with his set of criteria is that, for the purposes of arguing for the existence of God, it begs the question of the connection between miraculous events and God, for his concept of miracle includes the concept of supernatural causation. It is trivially true that, if there are events that nature would not produce on its own, that are supernaturally caused, that override nature,[8] and that have religious significance,[9] then there is a god. But to adopt such a concept is to preclude any examination of the possible relationship between God and events that are labeled miraculous. My claim is that this relationship cannot be regarded as straightforward and unproblematic; it must be critically assessed.

Larmer is unperturbed by the circularity of his concept. He concedes that calling an event a miracle presupposes the truth of theism. "But I do not accept the common assumption that it is a consequence of this view that an event we are prepared to call a miracle cannot serve as independent evidence for God's existence." He adds: "we do not need to believe that theism is true before we can decide whether or not we should label an event a miracle."[10]

The problem with these observations is that, if we were ever to identify an event as a miracle in Larmer's sense of the term, then de facto we would have decided that God exists. There could be no *argument* from the existence of a miracle to the existence of God. A miracle, in Larmer's sense, cannot function as evidence for the existence of God, for to call an event a miracle is, by definition, to assert the existence of God.

The second problem with Larmer's definition lies in his inappropriate anthropomorphism with respect to the natural world. He repeatedly describes a miracle as an event that "overrides nature." A miracle is said to be "an overriding of nature that is in accord with God's purposes"; the product of "an agent not bound by nature."[11] In these descriptions, "nature" is implicitly represented as a fallible person, one who is usually in control of what happens in physical reality, but whose will can be overcome or overridden by a being with superior, indeed transcendent, powers.

This inappropriate anthropomorphism sets the stage for the key move in Larmer's defense of the existence of miracles, in his sense: he rejects the standard form of the Law of Conservation of Energy.

NATURALISM, MIRACLES, AND THE
LAW OF CONSERVATION OF ENERGY

A substantial component of Larmer's project is to show that, although miracles overcome or override nature, they do not violate laws of nature. Instead, "a miracle, in the strong sense of an event which nature would not produce on its own, can occur in a world which behaves completely in accordance with the laws of nature."[12] For example, although the laws of nature show that virgins do not conceive "unless nature is overridden in some way," they "do not entail that such an event cannot happen or is antecedently improbable."[13] How is this possible? Larmer explains that, in working a miracle, God creates or annihilates a unit or units of mass/energy. In so doing, he breaks no law of nature but rather changes the material conditions to which the laws of nature apply.[14] In a paper published in 1992, for example, he suggests that God might have enacted the miracle of the loaves and fishes by creating loaves and fishes ex nihilo: "He would not thereby violate any of the laws of nature which apply to the behavior of the matter making up the loaves and fishes."[15]

The latter claim seems puzzling. The matter of fishes develops from other fishes; the matter of loaves is the product of flour, yeast, water, and salt. If loaves and fishes come into existence ex nihilo, such an event appears to violate natural laws governing the origins of loaves and fishes.

In order to overcome such problems, Larmer calls for the rejection of what he calls the "strong form" of the law (or principle) of conservation of energy, namely, that "Energy can neither be created nor destroyed, although its form may change."[16] Given the assumption that energy can be created or destroyed, then it is possible for God to work a miracle without breaking a law of nature.

If one does not reject the strong form of the principle, then, says Larmer, one is ruling out theism a priori.[17] But this assumption is questionable. It is not inconceivable that an all-powerful God could have a created a universe in which the strong form of the law holds.[18] In his book Larmer offers no argument to show that this is impossible. Perhaps he simply assumes that such a universe would be incompatible with an interventionist, miracle-producing God of the sort he is concerned to defend.[19]

Larmer claims that the strong form of the law of conservation of energy is a "defining-postulate" of a belief system or worldview[20] that he calls 'physicalism'.[21] Physicalism is defined as "a species of philosophical monism according to which all that exists and is truly real is physical."[22]

Instead of the strong form of the principle, Larmer advocates acceptance of a weaker form, according to which, "in an isolated system [that is, a system not causally influenced by something other than itself] the total amount of energy remains constant, although its form may change."[23] Larmer claims that it is the weak form of the principle that is directly supported by experimental evidence, and to derive the strong form requires a further inference.[24] However, he adds, there does not and cannot exist any additional body of empirical evidence that permits the derivation of the strong form of the principle.[25] "The most [the physicalist] can ever show by measuring quantities of energy is that it is conserved in a causally isolated system."[26]

Larmer offers no further defense of this latter claim. Perhaps he is implicitly appealing to human beings' finite nature as investigators. If the defender of the strong form of the law of conservation of energy claims to present some evidence to show that, without qualification, energy can neither be created nor destroyed, Larmer might respond that his opponent must temper that claim by acknowledging that it is confined to those portions of the universe we have explored. It is simply not possible for us to move outside our "causally isolated system."[27] As finite, fallible beings, we cannot make a claim that goes beyond our local neighborhood.

If Larmer is relying on this assumption, there are at least two problems with it. First, it begs the question in Larmer's favor. If we must stress our limited knowledge, which is confined only to our local portion of the universe, then human ignorance is put squarely at the forefront of the theory, and the theory opens the door for postulating divine intervention. It makes the leap to the hypothesis of transcendent agency appear to be very easy.

Yet through this move the theory at the same time calls itself into question. For if we must stress the limited nature of human knowledge with respect to one natural law, there seems to be no reason not to similarly qualify other statements of natural law. But if our knowledge of the operations of the natural world is recognized as being limited in all respects, why should we not use this limitation as a reason not to resort to God as an explanation for certain unusual events? Instead of leaping to infer divine intervention as their explanation, let us suspend belief, recognize our human limitations, and await the gathering of further knowledge.

Consider Larmer's own example of the virgin birth. Among the human participants in the drama of Jesus' conception and birth (setting aside, because their existence is controversial, the possible actions of angels), we could have only Mary and Joseph's word that Mary was a virgin. Indeed, Mary's own view of her condition may not have been accurate: it is possible that Joseph could have raped her while she was unconscious; hence, Mary herself would not know that she was not a virgin. It therefore comes down to Joseph's claim that he did not have sexual intercourse with Mary—and that no other man did. Moreover, to preserve the plausibility of the virgin birth, we must assume that no other process—such as a primitive form of artificial insemination—was involved. From this perspective, the number of assumptions that must be made about Mary's sexual and reproductive life and the reliance that must be placed on Mary and Joseph's beliefs and claims about her condition make belief in a virgin birth highly improbable. Rather than believing that Jesus was the result of the divine impregnation of a virgin, it seems more plausible to assume that Jesus was conceived through human sexual intercourse.

Larmer would reject such a move, at least partly because he rejects naturalism. At best, he says, naturalism begs the question of whether nature is an isolated system not subject to outside intrusions. At worst, it "is vulnerable to the charge that it is explanatorily impotent by virtue of the fact that it proves compatible with any conceivable state of affairs or series of events in the world."[28]

But it is impossible to accept that naturalism is explanatorily impotent. The naturalistic hypothesis has an admirable record of gradually enabling human beings to come to understand the regular workings of the world. It is therefore reasonable, in cases of puzzling events, to await explanation through naturalistic mechanisms. Defenders of miracles have not shown that naturalism has any conspicuous record of failure to account for such events. Indeed, Larmer offers no arguments showing that the examples of miracles he cites cannot be explained in naturalistic terms.

Taking the long view of human epistemic progress, with our present awareness of how the human capacity to understand and explain hitherto mysterious events has grown and changed, the naturalistic hypothesis does not look improbable. What would the reaction be if we could, *per impossibile*, convey a television or an airplane back to, say, eighteenth-century England? Some would be inclined to call such devices miraculous—whether in my sense of an event that violates natural law or is permanently inexplicable, or, in Larmer's sense, of an extraordinary physical event beyond the ability of unaided nature to produce, brought about by a rational agent, and possessing religious significance. Such a response is a reaction to unusual events one is not (yet) able to explain.

In 1984 Larmer wrote, "One may endorse the principle of first seeking a natural explanation of an event without thereby being committed to the position that a supernatural explanation of an event can never be legitimately postulated." The logical possibility that revising a scientific law may produce an explanation of an event previously classified as a miracle does not imply that it is always more rational to believe that all events have natural explanations.[29] But naturalism does not merely have logical possibility on its side; it has the accumulated force of centuries of practical accomplishment. Over and over in the history of science, revisions of scientific laws have yielded new explanations of hitherto mysterious phenomena. Resort to explanation by God's intervention, through the creation or annihilation of energy, has no such record of achievement. Hence, the naturalistic hypothesis is more rational than the divine intervention hypothesis.

Given the limits of human knowledge, Larmer provides no independent reasons for making the leap to God as a default position for explaining unusual events. In 1988 he claimed that from the mere fact that one class, such as the class of nonmiracles, contains a great many more members than another, such as the class of miracles, we cannot conclude that "the probability that any particular miracle occurred is low." Instead, to determine whether something exists, we must consider all the evidence.[30] But an analogy will show that this argument is flawed. The class of singleton human births contains a great many more members than the class of quintuplet human births. If a claim were made that a set of quintuplets was born, say, two centuries ago, we could legitimately conclude that the probability of any such birth is low—sufficient, perhaps, to require us to at least suspend belief about claims of its occurrence.

Similarly, the willing if temporary suspension of belief about the explanation of unusual events is a more plausible step than the postulation as their cause of an omnipotent God who both creates and destroys energy. As John Collier notes, "The fact that [miracles] are unusual implies that we have abundant contrary evidence that events of that sort do not happen."[31] The burden of proof—or, rather, the burden of presenting evidence—rests on Larmer to show that the supernatural hypothesis is preferable to an agnostic perspective on such events.

Larmer asserts that, while it is logically possible that a revision of scientific law might provide an explanation for an event previously dubbed a miracle, it is also logically possible that "no revision would enable one to offer a natural explanation of such an event."[32] Were such an extraordinary situation as the latter to prevail, however, it does not follow that a supernatural explanation would be warranted. In fact, if my arguments are correct, such an explanation would be ruled out. One would simply have to say that there is a hole in the explanatory fabric of our knowledge.

LARMER'S RESPONSE TO THE ARGUMENT FROM "COGNITIVE EVIL"

Larmer characterizes arguments such as those I presented in "Miracles as Evidence Against the Existence of God"[33] as claiming that miracles constitute "cognitive evils."[34] He presents a general refutation of such arguments:

> [E]ither the existence of evil in the world proves that God—conceived as being perfectly good and omnipotent—does not exist or it does not. If it proves God does not exist then there is no need to consider the issue of miracles; if it does not then it is hard to see how a lessening of evil in the world—the healing of a child, say—can be seen as intensifying the problem of evil.[35]

The use of the word "proves" in this context seems too strong. Although the history of the philosophy of religion is replete with references to "proofs" both for and against the existence of God, it is more appropriate to the nature of the debate to speak of the accumulation or weight of evidence on either side. Use of the word "proof" implies that the issue is, or at least can be, definitively and uncontroversially settled. Such an implication is out of proportion to the reality of the debate.[36]

But even if we substitute for "proves" the phrase "provides evidence for," Larmer's claim about the significance of the argument from evil misrepresents the issue its various forms raise. The general issue is the weight or significance of evil—primarily in the forms of suffering and injustice—and whether the existence of such evil constitutes strong evidence against the existence of God. My argument with respect to miracles is that claims about the occurrence of miracles greatly *increase* the strength of the argument from evil, by pointing to the botched nature of the existing world, the makeshift and arbitrary solutions in which God is said to engage, and the arbitrary and puzzling nature of allegedly divine acts. If a miracle, in the sense of an event that violates natural law or that is permanently inexplicable, were to occur, it would be incompatible with the kind of being the Judæo-Christian God is said to be.[37]

Larmer states that my claim that any alleged pattern of miraculous occurrences cannot be consistent with the pattern of natural events begs the question of whether nature constitutes the whole of reality or is only a partial system within it.[38] But this response is puzzling. Miracles are, Larmer acknowledges, "explanatory hiatuses."[39] Bearing in mind those events standardly offered as exemplars of miracles, it would seem that part of the point behind miracles is their disruptiveness, their extraordinariness, their failure to blend in. Indeed, Larmer approvingly quotes C. S. Lewis, who says that a miracle is not "interlocked with the previous history of Nature."[40] If miracles are somehow consistent with a greater system, of which nature is only a (small?) part, then the epistemic problem of comprehending that consistency is transferred to understanding the greater system.

Nonetheless, Larmer claims, "To call an event a miracle *is* to explain it; it is to explain it in terms of God's purposes and desires." But such an explanation is at best obscure. On the one hand, Larmer approvingly quotes Richard Swinburne, who says, "Miracles are events with a point in the overall scheme of things and so in a sense very regular." But Larmer also says that an explanation in terms of an agent's—any agent's—intention or purpose need have no close connection to the notion of prediction.[41]

Ordinarily, knowing someone's purposes and intentions provides an indication of what the person is likely to do in the future. Knowing S's purpose gives me an indication of the actions, or range of actions, she is likely to undertake in order to accomplish her purpose. However, if relating an event to a transcendent agent's purposes does *not* help us in any way to predict the agent's future actions, then the notion of "purpose" becomes opaque. Ascribing an anomalous, inexplicable event to God's agency, then, sheds no light on the reason for the event, its intent, or its place within a larger pattern. In other words, ascribing an amazing event to God's agency does nothing to make it comprehensible. Thus, if a miracle were to occur, it would obfuscate human understanding of the world.

Events alleged to be miracles are also often trivial in nature. An excellent example is Jesus' conversion of water into wine[42] to accommodate his mother and other guests at a wedding at Cana. Considering the range of misfortunes and needs in the world, running out of wine at a wedding seems a small problem. According to Larmer, the concept of miracle involves being "brought about by a rational agent,"[43] but the conversion of water to wine does not seem rational. The conversion violates natural laws,[44] does not cohere with anything else known about the substances water and wine, and fails to fit into a larger pattern of divine purpose. Indeed, when first asked to respond to the wineless feast, Jesus himself denied any wish to take action (John 2:4).

As evidence of the incompatibility of miracles and God, I have asserted that miracles reflect caprice and bias.[45] Larmer makes a number of admissions that inadvertently support my claims. "Almost by definition, miracles are nonregular, unpredictable events." Miracles are "not events . . . that most people could expect to observe directly," and "there is no a priori reason to suppose that all ages should be equally endowed with miracles." Miracles "recur when certain relevant antecedent conditions are repeated," yet they are not "of some repeatable type."[46] The reasons for their occurrence in some cultures and not others, to some people and not others, and at some times and not others, are not evident. The theist, admits Larmer, may not be able to explain why God heals a child in one instance but allows nature to "take its course" in another, but this does not imply that God lacks a "morally sufficient reason for performing a miracle in one case and not in another."[47]

Since Larmer provides us with no justification, we must apparently take it on faith that God has a "morally sufficient reason" for favoring some but not others with his miracles. But in the absence of such justification, it seems plausible to conclude that any transcendent being who performs such acts is, indeed, capricious and biased. Larmer gives as examples of miracles the feeding of multitudes and the healing of the sick. Why are some healed and others not? Why are some fed while others starve? Larmer offers no explanation or rationale for these distinctions. Religious skeptics have long argued that the profound injustices and intense suffering experienced by many people are evidence against the existence of an omnipotent, beneficent God. If there are unusual events that seemingly arbitrarily help some of the suffering but not others, these events contribute to the strength of the argument from evil. If God favors some people and not others, then he is capricious and biased. If such miracles occur, they are evidence against the existence of an omnibeneficent being.

Larmer suggests that God's alleged miraculous interventions are a matter of God's adapting himself to "emergent needs." The idea is that, in a world of human beings endowed with free will, God intervenes "in the usual course of events so as to fulfill certain of His purposes which might otherwise be thwarted."[48] The problem with this view is that it is hard to discern what God's purposes might be; to the extent that they *are* discernible, they do not seem to reflect a transcendent being who is omnipotent, omniscient, and beneficent.

It might be argued that some people are more deserving of God's help than others. Larmer states that the conditions for the occurrence of a miracle pertain "not so much to the physical as to the moral realm," and "what determines whether one occurs is not your physical circumstances, but rather the state of your heart before God."[49] But such claims cannot explain God's failure to provide miraculous interventions to help innocent children, about whom it is implausible to claim that they are less deserving of God's assistance. If the healing of a child is "a lessening of evil in the world,"[50] it is nonetheless an arbitrary lessening, which overlooks other equally deserving cases.

The virgin birth is an example of an event that reflects caprice and bias. The idea of an individual's being born of a virgin reflects distaste for human sexual activity. It also subscribes to notions of female purity: women are on a higher level of goodness prior to sexual activity; hence, Mary was "pure" enough to bear the son of God. It is unclear why a perfect being would care about such matters, and Larmer's assurance that God has a "morally sufficient reason" is unfounded.

In conclusion, Robert Larmer does not succeed in defeating my claim that the occurrence of a miracle constitutes good evidence against the existence of the Judæo-Christian God. Larmer's redefinition of 'miracle' is circular. His distinction between violating a natural law and merely overcoming it via God's creation or destruction of energy is specious. And his attempt to show that miracles are the product of a rational, beneficent, omnipotent being, and consistent with that being's purposes, is inadequate.

NOTES

1. Christine Overall, "Miracles as Evidence Against the Existence of God," *The Southern Journal of Philosophy* 23, no. 3 (1985): 347–53.

2. Robert A. H. Larmer, *Water into Wine? An Investigation of the Concept of Miracle* (Montreal: McGill-Queen's University Press, 1988).

3. Ibid., p. 80.

4. Ibid., p. 5.

5. Ibid., pp. 116, 99, 56.

6. Ibid., p. 58.

7. Robert A. H. Larmer, "Miracles and Natural Explanations: A Rejoinder," *Sophia* 28 (October 1989): 11.

8. Larmer, *Water into Wine?* p. 8.

9. Ibid., p. 9.

10. Ibid., p. 113.

11. Ibid., pp. 20, 14, 9.

12. Ibid., p. 79.

13. Ibid., p. 96.

14. Ibid., p. 20.

15. Robert A. H. Larmer, "Miracles and Conservation Laws: A Reply to Professor MacGill," *Sophia* 31, nos. 1–2 (1992): 89.

16. Larmer, *Water into Wine?* p. 24.

17. Ibid., pp. 25, 26.

18. Another possibility is suggested by Neil W. MacGill, who points out that there is no reason to suppose an omnipotent God would choose to enact miracles by creating and annihilating energy rather than, for example, creating a world governed by laws that "do not operate with absolute universality" ("Miracles and Conservation Laws," *Sophia* 31, nos. 1–2 [1992]: 86).

19. In his 1992 paper, Larmer argues that the strong form of the principle of conservation of energy is incompatible with any theory that implies either the creation or the beginning of the universe, whether as events in time or not in time ("Miracles and Conservation Laws," pp. 91, 93). Hence, both the theist who believes that God created all that exists and the skeptic who believes that the universe emerged from something like a "big bang" first cause must reject the strong form of the principle.

20. He defines 'worldview' as "a coherent, or at least apparently coherent, set of basic beliefs about the fundamental character of reality" (Larmer, *Water into Wine?* p. 83).

21. Larmer, *Water into Wine?* p. 61.

22. Ibid., p. 136, n. 1. Throughout much of his book, Larmer discusses physicalism as if it were the only alternative to theism. For example, in Chapter 6, "World-Views and Falsification," he takes the task of the religious believer to be to elaborate and defend "a world-view other than physicalism," namely, theism (p. 75). Only in the last chapter, "Miracles and Apologetics," does Larmer acknowledge the existence of any worldviews other than theism and physicalism: "the rivals to theism are not many. Excluding physicalism, plausible alternative world-views are limited to pantheism and panentheism" (p. 123). (Whereas the pantheist holds that there is no ontological distinction between God and the world [p. 124], the panentheist regards God as not the efficient but the formal cause of the world [p. 125].) What is problematic about this catalogue of "plausible" worldviews is that it omits, without explanation or even acknowledgement, any mention of the possibility of a dualistic metaphysics that employs concepts of the physical and the mental without assuming that one form of the mental is the divine. (However, the possibility of such a worldview is implicitly recognized in Larmer's earlier paper, "Mind-Body Interaction and the Conservation of Energy," *International Philosophical Quarterly* 26 [summer 1986]: 277–85.)

23. Ibid., p. 24.

24. Ibid., p. 61.

25. Larmer, "Miracles and Conservation Laws," p. 90.

26. Larmer, *Water into Wine?* p. 69.

27. Of course, if Larmer is right in believing that miracles, in his sense of the term, occur, then there may be no "causally isolated systems." (He nowhere indicates how systems are individuated and delimited.) God's intervention shows, by definition, that a "system" is not isolated. Larmer believes that God has intervened in the natural world in a variety of ways and circumstances and could intervene elsewhere if he chose. Hence, from this perspective, the weak form of the principle may turn out to be empty.

28. Larmer, *Water into Wine?* p. 59.

29. Robert A. H. Larmer, "Miracles and Criteria," *Sophia* 23 (April 1984): 6.

30. Robert A. H. Larmer, "Against 'Against Miracles,'" *Sophia* 27 (April 1988): 21.

31. John Collier, "Against Miracles," *Dialogue* 25 (1986): 350.

32. Larmer, "Miracles and Criteria," p. 7.

33. See note 1.

34. Larmer, *Water into Wine?* p. 115.

35. Ibid.

36. A similar disproportion is located in Larmer's distinction between confirmation and plausibility. A belief is said to be "plausible" if it is a "reasonable belief to hold on the basis of available evidence" (*Water into Wine?* p. 66). On the other hand, a belief is said to be "confirmed" if "the evidence in some way guarantees that the belief is true" (pp. 66–67). The notion of a guarantee is, presumably, metaphorical, but it implies a much higher level of assurance than that to which we may usually be entitled with respect to debates about God. (Larmer acknowledges that a "physicalist" would say this [p. 67].)

37. In my previous article I claimed that, as an event limited in space and time, a miracle is inherently inadequate to convey God's purposes. Larmer objects that God could *only* convey his purposes to spatio-temporal creatures through a particular event or series of events: "Unless she is prepared to argue that it is logically impossible that God can communicate with spatio-temporal creatures at all, Overall cannot claim that the mere fact that miracles are events limited in time and space entails that they are inadequate vehicles for conveying God's purposes" (*Water into Wine?* p. 82). The issue here, however, is the question of the compatibility of miracles and the concept of God. If God is infinite, omnipotent, and omniscient, then any single event or series of events human beings may witness could not be adequate to convey God to us. At best, only infinite nature in its entirety can begin to reflect God, in the Judæo-Christian concept. This is one reason that the teleological and cosmological arguments for the existence of God are less weak than the argument from miracles.

38. Larmer, *Water into Wine?* p. 81.

39. Ibid., p. 89.

40. Ibid., p. 81.

41. Ibid., pp. 81, 10, 48.

42. Although this example provides the title for Larmer's book, he does not discuss it.

43. Larmer, *Water into Wine?* p. 5.

44. In this supposed miracle it is difficult to see how Larmer's notion that the enactment of a miracle is the result of the creation or destruction of energy applies. For the mir-

acle at Cana involves no creation or destruction, but rather the metamorphosis of one substance into another, contrary to the natural characteristics of both.

45. Overall, "Miracles as Evidence Against the Existence of God," p. 351.

46. Larmer, *Water into Wine?* pp. 43, 99, 107, 51, 52.

47. Ibid., pp. 115–16.

48. Ibid., p. 120.

49. Larmer, "Miracles and Conservation Laws," p. 95.

50. Larmer, *Water into Wine?* p. 115.

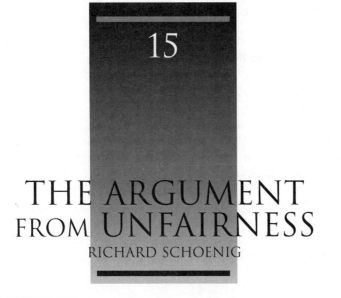

15

THE ARGUMENT
FROM UNFAIRNESS
RICHARD SCHOENIG

1. INTRODUCTION

Following Antony Flew,[1] Michael Martin[2] distinguishes negative from positive
atheism. Negative atheism is the position of not believing that a theistic God[3]
exists;[4] whereas positive atheism is the position of disbelieving that a theistic
God exists. To establish the reasonableness of negative atheism one must show
that the description of, or talk about, God is not meaningful, or that no sound
arguments are sufficient to establish the existence of God.

To establish the reasonableness of positive atheism one must establish the
reasonableness of negative atheism and, in addition, provide sound arguments to
support the conclusion that God does not exist. Atheologians have attempted to
do the latter in a number of ways. They have argued that there are internal inconsistencies in the properties of God, as for example, between His immutability and
His omnipotence.[5] A second approach has been to show a conflict between a
property of God and some indispensable point of logic. For example, J. N.
Findlay claims that theists hold that God's existence is logically necessary.[6]
However, he contends that logical necessity applies only to propositions and not
to the existence of persons. A third approach has attempted to demonstrate inconsistencies between God's properties and indisputable facts about the world. One
interesting illustration of this is what Michael Martin calls the Teleological Disproof for God's existence.[7] Martin, following Wesley Salmon[8] who in turn elab-

From *International Journal for Philosophy of Religion* 45 (1999): 115–28. Copyright © 1999 by
Kluwer Academic Publishers. Reprinted with kind permission from Kluwer Academic Publishers.

orates on Hume, argues that there are good probabilistic reasons to affirm positive atheism. Undoubtedly, the most influential version of this approach is the Argument from Evil, which reasons that there is an inconsistency between God's traditional triad of properties (omnipotence, omniscience, and omnibenevolence) and the fact of the suffering of the innocent.

In this paper I shall present an atheological argument which I call The Argument from Unfairness (AFU), which can be classified as an instance of the last approach just cited. The AFU is intended to demonstrate a conflict between God's omnibenevolence and what the vast majority of theists take to be revealed theological facts. In section 2 of the paper I give a stipulative definition of unfairness which is used in section 4 to help develop the AFU itself. Section 3 describes a number of relevant theological proposals integral to understanding the AFU. Section 5 is a set of objections to the argument and my responses. Finally, section 6 completes the paper with a summary conclusion.

2. A DEFINITION OF UNFAIRNESS

Before I move to a formal definition of unfairness, consider the following three situations which exemplify behavior which most morally sensitive people would classify as unfair.

Situation 1. P is a teacher who without reason gives a certain group of students, A, in her course superlative grades simply on the basis of the fact that they are registered for the course. At the same time, P dictates that the remaining group of students, B, in the same course must satisfactorily complete numerous difficult and burdensome assignments and tests in order to receive the superlative grades that the A group receives automatically and unconditionally. Moreover, there is no guarantee that all the B-students will satisfactorily complete those requirements. In prior offerings of that course, many B-students have not satisfactorily completed those requirements.

Situation 2. Let me now up the ante. Instead of a superlative grade, the outcome here is literally a matter of life or death. Assume that for no apparent reason P unconditionally grants group A a life-saving medical treatment which she grants to group B only if the B-members carry out a long and arduous series of tasks for which a satisfactory completion is not guaranteed. In the past more than a few B-members have, in fact, failed in their attempts.

Situation 3. Now, let me raise the ante infinitely. P arbitrarily and unconditionally grants group A maximal, eternal happiness and dictates that group B will get that same state only if its members negotiate a number of formidable obstacles. There is no guarantee that all B-members will succeed. In the past many have not. In addition, if any B-member does not succeed, he will have to endure maximal, eternal suffering.

The common element of unfairness in these situations is that a person with power uses it arbitrarily to advance, or correlatively to hinder, the interest of one group in contrast to another group with regard to an outcome (grade, life, eternal happiness) which is important to both groups.

Mindful of this common element, I now propose the following formal definition of unfairness (DU). Assume that P, A, and B are persons or groups of persons, and that O is a nonimmoral outcome desired by both A and B.

> **DU**: (1) P acts unfairly toward B in comparison to A with regard to O if and only if, without sufficient reason, either P intentionally treats A in a manner that P knows will assist A in getting O in a way that P does not so assist B, or P intentionally treats B in a manner that P knows will hinder B from getting O in a way that P does not so hinder A. (2) The degree of P's unfairness is commensurate with the degree to which P intentionally and knowingly assists A more than B, or hinders B more than A, in getting O, and also with the importance that O has to the fulfillment of the nonimmoral desires of B and A.

Before formally presenting the AFU, I must first describe a number of important related theological positions.

3. REWARD/PUNISHMENT THEOLOGY (RPT)

God is most prevalently understood as a judgmental deity who reveals one set of standards for salvation for all human beings, although different religious denominations have different and even inconsistent views about the content and interpretation of the standards. If humans adequately adhere to the standards throughout their accountable lives, God will grant them maximal, eternal, postmortem happiness. In common parlance such people are said to have been saved or to have gone to heaven. On the other hand, if people do not adequately satisfy the given standards for salvation, then God will punish them with maximal, eternal, postmortem suffering. They are then said to have been damned or to have gone to hell. I shall refer to this eternal reward/punishment theology as RPT.

An important question is prompted by RPT, namely, what is the postmortem disposition of the large group of humans, call them group A, such as prenatals,[9] neonatals, young children, and the severely mentally handicapped, who die without ever attaining the state of moral accountability? RPT theists have entertained four possible answers.

(1) A-persons are damned. They do not satisfy the revealed requirements for salvation. I call this version of RPT, **RPTD**. This view receives support in the Christian tradition from the doctrine of Original Sin, according to which all persons are conceived and born sharing in the first sin of Adam and Eve. This sin is considered serious enough to send those who die with it to hell. Although it is purportedly forgiven when one is baptized, many A-persons are never baptized and so presumably under RPTD are damned.

(2) A-persons are saved. Although the people in A do not satisfy the requirements for salvation, God knows that they cannot satisfy those requirements because of their physical conditions for which they are clearly not responsible. An omnibenevolent God, therefore, grants all A-persons immediate, unconditional, irrevocable, eternal salvation. I call this version of RPT, **RPTS**.

There are good reasons to argue that this is the most defensible of the four interpretations of RPT. All Christian denominations, for example, affirm that A-persons who are baptized before they die are saved. The fate of unbaptized A-persons, however, is less clear in various Christian circles, but most Christian theists acknowledge that it would seem to be grossly incongruent for an omnibenevolent God to deny A-persons salvation and thereby, in effect, to punish them for something beyond their control. The synoptic Gospels, for example, are supportive on the point of Jesus' concern for infants and young children.

> And they brought unto him also infants, that he would touch them: but when his disciples saw it, they rebuked them. But Jesus called them unto him, and said, "Suffer little children to come unto me, and forbid them not: for of such is the kingdom of God."[10]

There is no reason to think that God would have any less concern for prenatals or the severely mentally handicapped. Thus, one may persuasively argue that A-persons who are never baptized are also treated by God under RPTS and granted unconditional eternal salvation, even in the Christian tradition which includes the doctrine of Original Sin.

(3) A-persons are neither damned nor saved. God grants them an eternal postmortem existence that is considerably less desirable than heaven,

but considerably more desirable than hell. Some Roman Catholic theologians have referred to this state as 'limbo' ("Limbo").[11] This is an admittedly vague position which has never been fully or clearly explicated by theologians. I refer to this version of RPT as **RPTL**.

(4) A-persons are neither damned nor saved. They simply cease to exist after their death. I call this version of RPT, **RPTA** (A = annihilation). This view has not enjoyed wide support since, among other things, it contravenes the generally propounded Christian view that at the moment of conception God unites an *immortal* soul with the fertilized human ovum.

4. THE ARGUMENT FROM UNFAIRNESS (AFU)

In the AFU which follows, 'God' refers to the theistic God (omnipotent, omniscient, and omnibenevolent) who acts in accordance with RPTx theology.

Argument from Unfairness

A = the set of persons who die without ever attaining the state of moral accountability.

B = the set of persons who die only after attaining the state of moral accountability.

O = the gain of postmortem eternal salvation and avoidance of postmortem eternal damnation.

1. If God treats A under RPTD, RPTL, or RPTA, then God acts unfairly toward A in comparison to B with respect to O.
2. If God treats A under RPTS, then God acts unfairly toward B in comparison with A with respect to O.
3. God treats A under RPTD or RPTL or RPTA or RPTS.
4. Therefore, God acts unfairly toward either A or B with respect to O.
5. If a person acts unfairly, then that person is not omnibenevolent.
6. Therefore, God is not omnibenevolent.
7. Therefore, God does not exist.

Premise 1 follows on the basis of the fact that if God were to act under any of RPTD, RPTL, or RPTA, He would act unfairly as described by DU. First, RPTD and RPTA would be clear instances of God, without sufficient reason, intentionally treating A in a manner that He knows will hinder A from getting heavenly salvation in a way that He does not so hinder B. Actually, 'hinder' is too tepid a word to describe God's action toward A under RPTD or RPTA. 'Absolutely prevent' would be the more apt phrase, since under RPTD and RPTA A-persons have absolutely no chance at all to receive heavenly salvation. On the other hand, B-persons can still receive heavenly salvation under RPTD and RPTA by adequately complying with the requirements of salvation. This differential treatment of A and B would clearly be unfair according to DU.

Second, RPTL would also be an instance of unfairness as described by DU, albeit a less severe one than those associated with RPTD or RPTA. It would be another instance of God, without sufficient reason, intentionally treating A in a manner that He knows will hinder A from getting the summum bonum of heaven in a way that He does not so hinder B. Whatever reality the vague notion of limbo is supposed to describe, theists have always strongly affirmed that heavenly salvation is God's most sublime and incomparable reward to human beings. The heavenly Beatific Vision gives the saved the unsurpassable joy associated with the most intimate, intense, fulfilling, and complete union with God (and other heavenly occupants) possible. Given that the maximal ecstasies of heaven are available, the nebulous consolation prize of limbo would be a bland and unfair eternal destiny for those whose destinies were never in their own hands in the first place.

Premise 2 follows on the basis of the fact that if God were to act under RPTS, He would also be acting unfairly as spelled out by DU. Under RPTS God, without sufficient reason, intentionally treats A in a manner that He knows will assist A in getting heavenly salvation in a way that He does not so assist B. That is, God arbitrarily guarantees to A, but not to B, direct, unconditional, eternal, postmortem salvation. As an example, consider God's treatment of Bertrand Russell and an aborted zygote. Russell's postmortem fate was determined by how adequately he conformed to God's standards for salvation throughout his long accountable life. Any time during that life he could have failed to satisfy God's salvific requirements and, as a result, lost eternal salvation and received, instead, eternal damnation. The zygote's postmortem fate under RPTS, on the other hand, is guaranteed by God to be one of immediate, unconditional, irrevocable salvation. God's unaccounted for favoritism toward the zygote is evident in this example.

In the AFU not only is God's treatment of B in comparison to A with respect to O (heavenly salvation) unfair according to DU; it would be the gravest degree of unfairness. Remember that the second part of DU stipulates that the degree of P's unfairness is commensurate with the degree to which P intentionally and knowingly assists A more than B in getting O, and also with the importance that O has to the fulfillment of the nonimmoral desires of B and A. In the AFU where P is an omnipotent God, P will act with maximal effect in assisting A. There would be no possibility that God's intended differential treatment of B and A would be anything but perfectly efficacious. In addition, given that A and B are potentially rational, nothing should be more important to them in terms of satisfying their desires than achieving eternal maximal reward and avoiding eternal maximal suffering.

Premise 3 is based on the fact that RPTD, RPTL, RPTA, and RPTS are the most salient interpretations of RPT that theists have proposed to deal with the question of the postmortem fate of A-persons.

Intermediate Conclusion 4 follows validly from 1 + 2 + 3 by constructive dilemma.

Premise 5 follows from the definitions of omnibenevolence and unfairness. Omnibenevolence obviously precludes acting immorally. As we have seen, acting unfairly, understood along the lines of DU, involves arbitrarily and intentionally assisting or hindering some persons and not others in similar circumstances with respect to achieving an important goal. Assisting/hindering under these conditions amounts to rendering intentional, unwarranted potential or real harm to the unassisted or hindered persons. I take this to be clearly immoral.

Intermediate Conclusion 6 follows from 4 + 5 by modus ponens.

Final Conclusion 7 follows on the basis of the fact that the theistic, RPTx-acting God is by definition omnipotent, omniscient, and omnibenevolent.

5. OBJECTIONS TO THE AFU AND RESPONSES

In appraising the AFU, it should be clear that if the argument is flawed, it is most likely to be so in the first subargument from premises 1, 2, and 3 to intermediate conclusion 4. All but the last of the following objections focus on that subargument.

Objection (1). Premise 3 is false. God does not act toward A according to any of RPTD, RPTL, RPTA, or RPTS. Instead, He has special postmortem salvation/ damnation conditions for A to meet which are comparable to those He has for B in this life.

Response. First, nothing in the theologies of Judaism, Christianity, or Islam has ever held that this is the case. Second, it is very unclear what stipulations and scenarios such postmortem salvation/damnation conditions for A-persons would involve. For example, what knowledge would A-persons have? Do they have free will? In what sense could A-persons be tested in a supernatural environment, especially the numerous, almost bodiless, postmortem zygotes? If beings with bodies are involved, in what place would their testing occur? What sorts of temptations might there be? In what sense would they be comparable to the earthly testing of B-persons? These are challenging questions whose answers, if any, are shrouded in what appears to be impenetrable metaphysical and theological obscurity.

Objection (2). Premises 1 and 2 are incorrect since neither B nor A have any 'right' to eternal salvation. Salvation is a gratuitous gesture from God. Fairness in no way precludes God from setting any particular standards, even arbitrarily different ones for different individuals, for His gift of salvation. To see this point more clearly, imagine a person, M, who finds $75 that is never claimed. She considers distributing it to the needy. In addition, imagine that even before finding the money, she had already donated as much of her means to charity, and perhaps more, than any reasonable moral standard requires. Since she is under no moral obligation to donate *any* of the found money, she would not be acting unfairly if she were either to withhold it all or to donate, say, $50 to one and $25 to another of two needy people in virtually the same circumstances. Regardless of how she donated the money, even as $74/$1, her donations would be supererogatory, and, as such, morality would permit any distribution that she desired. Likewise, God acts supererogatorily in creating humans and endowing them with immortal souls. Any standards He chooses for distributing or withholding the additional gratuity of salvation would also not be bound by the ethics of fairness or unfairness.

   Response. God's action of creating humans and endowing them with immortal souls may be supererogatory, but His subsequent determination of their destinies is not. God is like a parent who, although not morally required to bring offspring into existence, once having done so incurs moral obligations of fairness to the offspring concerning important matters of their well-being that he controls, such as food, shelter, education, and medical care. If the matter concerns the dependent's final eternal destiny, then, a fortiori, the parent/God would have an even stronger moral obligation to avoid acting unfairly to His children. His destiny-determining actions would not be supererogatory.

   The analogy of God's RPTx actions to M's eleemosynary actions cited in the objection is simply too weak. The import of M's actions on those affected by them is infinitesimal in comparison to the import of God's RPTx actions on A and B. While M arbitrarily disperses $25 more to one recipient than to another in order to effect some temporary amelioration of each's condition, an omnipotent God arbitrarily disperses ultimate, eternal destinies to A- and B-persons. Since the stakes have been raised infinitely high, God's RPTx actions are no longer supererogatory as M's actions would be. However, even in M's case if the lives or other serious well-being of the two recipients were at stake, then the dispensation on fairness provided by a supererogatory act would no longer apply. Under these dire particulars fairness would require M to treat the two cases as similarly as the circumstances permitted. Thus, I conclude that God does have firm obligations arising from DU to avoid arbitrary differential determinations of final destinies for His human creatures.

Since most theists, for reasons mentioned earlier, interpret RPT as RPTS rather than RPTD, RPTL, or RPTA, Objections 3–6 concentrate on demonstrating that premise 2 is false.

Objection (3). Premise 2 is false. God does not unfairly disadvantage B in comparison to A with respect to O because the DU phrase, "without sufficient reason," does not characterize God's behavior with respect to B and A. That God's behavior toward B is different than His behavior toward A in RPTS does not, in itself, establish unfairness. There is, after all, an important and relevant difference between B and A that constitutes a sufficient reason for God's differential treatment. B-persons attain the state of moral accountability while A-persons do not. Hence, it is reasonable for God to hold B-persons responsible for their behavior with regard to His revealed standards in a way that it is not with the A's.

Response. This objection does not succeed. For even if there is an obvious difference in the capacity for moral accountability between B and A, that, in itself, does not require God to make salvific standards more difficult for B than for A. Instead, a fair resolution would be for God to remove altogether the physical deprivations of A, or to make the salvific standards for B more akin to those for A, so that postmortem B-persons would also be granted irrevocable eternal salvation.

Theists will object that the latter proposal would conflict with God's characteristic of perfect justice flowing from his omnibenevolence. Justice, they will argue, requires that beings who have the capacity for moral accountability be held accountable for their freely chosen actions in terms of appropriate reward and punishment. This requirement precludes God from guaranteeing eternal reward to all Bs, since they sometimes freely choose to flout the revealed salvific requirements.[12] For example, it would be unjust for God to grant eternal salvation to Adolf Hitler as well as to Anne Frank.

The atheologian can rejoin that, first, within the two most prevalent monotheistic traditions, Christianity and Islam, there are well-known theologies which hold that humans do not and, in fact, cannot earn their eternal rewards or punishments, but that these are predestined by God and are not directly connected with one's earthly behavior.[13] The AFU would be particularly telling against these theologies.

Second, the theist's response only relocates God's unfairness from His differential salvific treatment of A and B in RPTS to His differential salvific treatment of A and B in terms of His arbitrary assignment of persons to those two classes. Why, for example, was Hitler not automatically saved by being naturally aborted? Plainly, membership in those classes is not chosen or merited by the members but rather determined arbitrarily by God. If God chooses not to abolish the two classes, then fairness would require Him to compensate for the arbitrariness of His class membership assignments by equalizing the salvific requirements for the classes. Since none of the RPTx theologies does this, the AFU's charge of unfairness remains on the table.

Objection (4). Premise 2 is false. A quite sufficient reason for God's preferential treatment of A-persons in RPTS is that, in contrast to B-persons, they enjoy few, if any, of the pleasures of bodily earthly existence. They also never have the opportunity to experience the set of empowerment advantages that earthly life brings to Bs. For example, A's miss the opportunity to freely direct their destinies, and to acquire a sense of individuality and self-esteem stemming from freely exercised creativity and effort. Finally, A's also lose the chance to freely develop positive character traits such as heroism, courage, dedication, and compassion.

   Response. First of all, not all Bs enjoy a satisfactory earthly existence. A relatively short and painful life is often the lot of many B-people in this world. Second, considering the stakes involved, namely, everlasting maximal happiness or maximal suffering, if humans were given the opportunity to choose membership in B or A under the rules of RPTS, they would certainly be rational to choose A, since A-members are guaranteed everlasting maximal postmortem happiness and, of course, avoidance of eternal maximal postmortem suffering.[14] The divine partiality toward A envisioned in RPTS is simply too strong. It amounts to an unfair compensation to A's in comparison to Bs. As suggested in the response to the previous objection, a fairer approach would be for God to remove the A handicaps or grant B-persons salvific guarantees comparable to those for A-persons under RPTS.

Objection (5). Premise 2 is false. A perfectly sufficient reason for God's preferential treatment of A-persons in RPTS is that He simply wills it thus. As the most perfect being possible, His will is ipso facto a sufficient reason for whatever is willed. No further reason need be given.

   Response. This objection essentially amounts to an affirmation of what is known as the Divine Command Theory (DCT) of morality; according to which an action is morally justified if God wills it. However, there are serious difficulties with the DCT, including the fact that it makes morality the arbitrary product of God's will. Under the DCT if God were to will the torture of babies, then the torture of babies would be morally acceptable. But surely this is inconceivable. The DCT proponent might counter that God would never will such an action. But the proponent could only know this based on his strong conviction that torturing babies is wrong, and that God would never do what is wrong.[15] But these convictions amount to embracing the alternative (to the DCT) view of morality that "the pious is loved by the gods because it is pious,"[16] which is to say, there is a standard for morality that even God's will cannot trump.

Objection (6). Premises 1 and 2 are questionable. It cannot be logically ruled out that from His omniscient perspective God has a sufficient reason for treating B and A differently with respect to heavenly salvation, O, that the AFU has not identified. So, intermediate conclusion 4, that God acts unfairly toward either A or B with respect to O, has not been deductively demonstrated, nor, therefore, has the final conclusion 7, that the RPTx-acting theistic God does not exist.

Response. I take it that the following two points are not disputed by Objection 6. (1) God treats A and B differently with respect to O; and (2) depending upon which version of RPTx one adopts, A or B is disadvantaged in comparison to the other set with respect to O. What is disputed by Objection 6 is that the AFU has demonstrated that there is no sufficient reason which justifies God's actions described by (1) and (2).

Assume, then, that God has a sufficient reason (SR) for, say, disadvantaging B vis-à-vis A with respect to O as described in RPTS. In addition, bear in mind the following two points: first, according to RPTx theology O is the summum bonum (SB) for all humans;[17] second, a necessary (but not sufficient) condition for justifying a moral agent's disadvantaging one person in comparison to another with respect to experiencing a good, G, is that the disadvantaging is, or produces, a greater good, G+. So, if, as theists claim, God has an SR for disadvantaging B in comparison to A with respect to O, then this proposed SR would have to be, or produce, a good greater than O. But O is the SB. Thus, the SR would have to be, or produce, a good greater than the SB. But it is impossible for there to be a greater good than the SB. Therefore, it is impossible for there to be a sufficient reason for disadvantaging B in comparison to A with respect to O.

In response, the RPTx theist might deny that God's SR has greater value than the SB. She might instead insist that God's SR is part of the SB itself, but an SB construed as more than O alone. This expanded notion of SB (SB+) could be said to consist of O together with what may be termed B-unique conditions associated with B's striving for O. Call the combination of O and these conditions, O+. An example of SB+/O+ might be something like the following: the achievement of O by freely cultivating one's faith in God-as-loving-Father while resisting the temptation to do evil. This sort of an SB+/O+ construal would contain within it the justification for B's apparent disadvantage under the RPTS interpretation. For, if O+ really is the SB+, then B is not being disadvantaged at all in RPTS. In fact, B's treatment under RPTS is a necessary condition for B to experience this SB+.

But no such SB+/O+ construal can ultimately support an SR since any interpretation of the summum bonum which would remove, for example, B's RPTS disadvantage would have to include some sort of B-unique conditions, as it is B's disadvantage, after all, which is being addressed. The B-unique conditions in the SB+, however, would of necessity be inaccessible to A and would, therefore, necessarily produce a correlated disadvantage for A. For if the summum bonum is really SB+, and B's treatment under RPTS is a necessary condition for experiencing SB+, and, constitutionally, A cannot be treated like B under RPTS, then it follows that A is disadvantaged in getting SB+. In short, due to the mutually exclusive descriptions of A and B, a win/lose fairness situation for A/B will always obtain for any SR-as-part-of-SB proposal to justify the RPTx differential treatment of the two sets. Not even God could have an SB-imbedded SR for His differential treatment of A and B that would not end up disadvantaging one of the two sets unfairly (as specified by DU). Nor will it do to respond that O is the summum bonum for A, while O+ is the summum bonum for B. Not only would this do irreparable damage to the RPTx claim of record that the SB is one and the same for all humans, but it would also raise vexing questions about whether it makes conceptual sense to say that there are different SBs for different human beings. For the reasons given, I conclude that there can be no SR for a theistic God to act according to RPTx theology, and that, therefore, the AFU survives Objection 6.

The final objection is a last attempt to limit the potential damage to theism from the AFU, assuming that the preceding objections were not successful.

Objection (7). The AFU does not demonstrate that disbelief in every interpretation of a theistic deity is warranted, but, at best, only that disbelief in the RPTx theistic God is warranted.

Response. This is true, but it is also true that the RPTx theistic God is neither heterodox nor esoteric. It is the God of Paul, the Patristics, Augustine, Muhammad, Anselm, Aquinas, Luther, Wesley and all their many historical and contemporary followers. Today, this interpretation of the deity is officially endorsed in the Roman Catholic, Eastern Orthodox, and a larger majority of Protestant denominations. It is also found in some Jewish and most Islamic theologies. In short, the RPTx theistic God is no mere straw man constructed in order to be torn down by the AFU, but rather the most prevailing, most influential theistic interpretation to be found.

6. CONCLUDING SUMMARY

According to the most prevalent interpretation of the theistic God, the RPT interpretation, God rewards and punishes human beings according to how well they live their lives in conformance with His will. RPT inevitably leads to a question about the postmortem fate of humans who die without reaching the state of moral accountability. Four interpretations of RPT—RPTD, RPTL, RPTA, and RPTS, referred to collectively as RPTx—were discussed as theists' most commonly offered answers to this question. The AFU aimed to demonstrate that, according to a reasonable stipulative definition of unfairness, DU, God would act unfairly in determining the postmortem eternal fate of human beings under any of the four interpretations. This unfairness would ineluctably compromise God's omnibenevolence. Hence, the AFU ultimately concluded that a theistic God who acts in this world according to RPTx cannot exist. This conclusion is significant because the RPTx theistic God represents the most common, most influential interpretation of theism now and in the past.

NOTES

1. Antony Flew, "The Presumption of Atheism," in *God, Freedom, and Immortality* (Amherst, N.Y.: Prometheus, 1984), p. 14.

2. Michael Martin, *Atheism: A Philosophical Justification* (Philadelphia: Temple University Press, 1990), p. 26.

3. The theistic God is taken to be the most perfect being possible. This includes the traditional triad of qualities: omnipotence, omniscience, and omnibenevolence. Henceforth, I shall refer to the theistic God simply as 'God'.

4. This position is frequently also called agnosticism.

5. J. L. Mackie, "Evil and Omnipotence," *Mind* 64 (1955): 211 f.

6. J. N. Findlay, "Can God's Existence Be Disproved?" *Mind* 57 (1948): 176–83 (reprinted in *New Essays in Philosophical Theology*, ed. Antony Flew and Alasdair MacIntyre [New York: Macmillan, 1955], pp. 47–56).

7. Martin, *Atheism: A Philosophical Justification*, pp. 317–33.

8. Wesley C. Salmon, "Religion and Science: A New Look at Hume's *Dialogues*," *Philosophical Studies* 33 (1978): 143–78.

9. For the sake of argument I accept here the belief, widely acknowledged in religious circles, that prenatals are unique persons endowed with an immortal soul from the moment of conception.

10. Luke 19:15–16; see also Matt. 18:1–6; Mark 9:36–39, 10:13–16.

11. *New Catholic Encyclopedia* (1967), Limbo 8: 736.

12. J. L. Mackie and Antony Flew have argued that it is in fact possible for God to have created humans who would never choose to do evil. See Mackie, "Evil and Omnipotence"; J. L. Mackie, chap. 9 in *The Miracle of Theism* (Oxford: Clarendon Press, 1982);

Antony Flew, "Divine Omnipotence and Human Freedom," *New Essays in Philosophical Theology*, pp. 144–69. Philosophic theists such as Alvin Plantinga have argued against this view. See Alvin Plantinga, *God, Freedom, and Evil* (Grand Rapids, Mich.: Eerdmans, 1977), pp. 7–59.

13. This can be read in various passages of the Koran and is characteristic of the Protestant Christian tradition traceable to Martin Luther and John Calvin.

14. I contend in a forthcoming article in *Free Inquiry* titled "Christian Soteriology, Abortion, and Infanticide" that this fact could form the basis for a reductio argument, advocating the practices of abortion and even infanticide as vehicles for guaranteeing eternal salvation.

15. The scriptures of the Judeo-Christian tradition are not completely supportive of this. For example, on numerous occasions in the Old Testament God seems to have endorsed genocide, including infanticide. See, for example, Josh. 6:21 f and 2 Kings 2:23–25.

16. Plato, *Euthyphro*, 10a–e.

17. Thomas Aquinas makes this point at a number of places in *The Summa Contra Gentiles*, Third Book: The End of Man, for example, chap. 37: That Man's Ultimate Happiness Consists in Contemplating God (Anton C. Pegis, *Introduction to Saint Thomas Aquinas* [New York: Random House, 1948], p. 454). "It is therefore evident also by way of induction that man's ultimate happiness consists solely in the contemplation of God, which conclusion was proved above by arguments." Also in the Third Book, chap. 48: That Man's Ultimate Happiness is not in This Life, Thomas says (Pegis, p. 467):

Therefore man's ultimate happiness will consist in that knowledge of God which the human mind possesses after this life, a knowledge similar to that by which separate substances know him. Hence our Lord promises us *a reward . . . in heaven* (Matt. 5:12) and states (Matt. 22:30) that the saints *shall be as the angels,* who always see God in heaven (Matt. 18:10).

PART 4

MULTIPLE ATTRIBUTES DISPROOFS of the EXISTENCE of GOD

INTRODUCTION

This section contains previously published papers and book selections presenting and defending multiple attributes disproofs of the existence of God. A multiple attributes disproof of God's existence is a deductive argument based on a contradiction between two or more of God's attributes.

A multiple attributes disproof of God's existence takes the following general form:

1. If God exists,
   then the attributes of God are consistent with one another.
2. Some attributes of God are not consistent with one another.
3. Therefore, God does not and cannot exist.

Here are brief summaries of the papers and book selections contained in this section.

Theodore M. Drange in a 1998 paper "Incompatible-Properties Arguments: A Survey" lists twenty divine attributes and then presents and briefly discusses ten deductive arguments for the impossibility of God, each based on the incompatibility of a unique pair of attributes from the list. The last of these, the justice-vs.-mercy argument, can also be presented as a single attribute disproof of an omnibenevolent God.

Norman Kretzmann in a 1966 paper "Omniscience and Immutability" argues that an omniscient and immutable being always knows what time it is and is not subject to change, but a being that always knows what time it is *is* subject to change. Since omniscience and immutability are contradictory, a being that is both omniscient and immutable, such as God, does not and cannot exist. Kretzmann considers and replies to seven possible objections, four of which are directed against the statement that a being that always knows what time it is is subject to change.

Anthony Kenny in "Omniscience, Eternity, and Time," a chapter taken from *The God of the Philosophers* (1986), presents a short argument for the incoherence of divine timelessness and then defends Kretzmann's 1966 argument for the nonexistence of an omniscient and immutable being, such as God, by critically examining and replying to the objection that God can know tenselessly all that humans know and express in tensed propositions.

David Blumenfeld in a 1978 paper "On the Compossibility of the Divine Attributes" argues that certain kinds of knowledge cannot be complete unless the concepts involved in that knowledge can be experienced and thus fully understood. For example, it is not possible for a being that believes it is omnipotent to have certain kinds of knowledge involving the concepts of fear, frustration, and despair because such a being cannot experience and thus cannot fully understand these concepts. It follows that a being that is both omniscient and omnipotent, such as God, since it knows that it is omnipotent, cannot have complete knowledge and thus *cannot* be omniscient. In short, omniscience and omnipotence are contradictory, and therefore an omniscient and omnipotent God does not and cannot exist.

Michael Martin in a 1974 paper "A Disproof of the God of the Common Man" observes that the God in whom most ordinary people believe is a being that knows at least as much as and is morally superior to humans. Also, ordinary people suppose that knowledge consists of propositional knowledge (knowledge that), procedural knowledge (knowledge how), and experiential knowledge (knowledge by acquaintance). Martin argues that if God knows at least as much as humans know, then God has at least as much experiential knowledge as humans, but certain experiential knowledge (such as the experiential knowledge of lust and envy) is incompatible with God's moral superiority. Hence the God in whom most ordinary people believe is contradictory, and thus does not and cannot exist.

In "Conflicts Between the Divine Attributes," a selection taken from *Atheism: A Philosophical Justification* (1990), Martin explores the meanings of omniscience, perfect freedom, and omnipotence and argues that these divine attributes are inconsistent with one another and with other divine attributes, such as disembodiedness and moral perfection, and therefore God does not and cannot exist.

Matt McCormick in a 2000 paper "Why God Cannot Think: Kant, Omnipresence, and Consciousness" draws on Kantian ideas to argue that a being with higher consciousness, that is, a being with cognitive abilities to distinguish between an object and its representation and to apply concepts and form judgments about objects must have the ability to discriminate between subject and object, but a being that is omnipresent cannot have this latter ability. Therefore, a God that possesses the attributes of both higher consciousness and omnipresence does not and cannot exist. McCormick replies to several possible objections and ends by briefly discussing some of the implications for other divine attributes if God has either higher consciousness or omnipresence but not both.

Lawrence Resnick in a 1973 paper "God and the Best Possible World" considers a God who exists necessarily; is necessarily omnibenevolent, omniscient, omnipotent, and the sole source of all other existence; and necessarily manifests perfection in all divine works (e.g., creating a world, taking a course of action, exercising moral judgment). Resnick argues that a divine work can only be a manifestation of perfection if there are some possible lesser alternative works to which it can be compared. However, given that God's existence and attributes are logically necessary, *there can be no possible lesser alternative works*, and thus no divine work can be a manifestation of perfection. Since God cannot manifest perfection in any divine works, God does not and cannot exist.

Tomis Kapitan in a 1991 paper "Agency and Omniscience" begins by pointing out that complete faith and confidence in God would seem to be unjustified without the assumption of divine agency and omniscience. Kapitan then explores at length what it means to be an agent, that is, a being capable of intentional action, and reasons that intentional action is, at least in part, caused by the agent's intending, that intending involves taking a particular course of action in a range of open alternatives, and that this is impossible without a presumption of uncertainty about what will transpire in the future. Given this account of agency, and taking omniscience to include complete foreknowledge of the future, it follows that an omniscient being is incapable of intentional action, and thus cannot be an agent. Since omniscience precludes agency, a God possessing both omniscience and agency does not and cannot exist.

In a 1994 paper "The Incompatibility of Omniscience and Intentional Action: A Reply to David P. Hunt," Kapitan responds to several criticisms and in light of these criticisms presents an improved version of the 1991 argument for the nonexistence of an omniscient agent such as God.

Matt McCormick in a paper "The Paradox of Divine Agency," written for this anthology, argues that in addition to the attributes of omnipotence, omniscience, and moral perfection, God must possess the attribute of agency to be worthy of worship. A being with agency conceives goals and acts to achieve them. A goal is a desired state of affairs in the world that a being believes is different from the existing state of affairs, and without this difference between what exists and what is desired there is no ground for action. For an omnipotent, omniscient, and morally perfect God, however, the existing state of affairs in the world is always in perfect conformity with the desired state of affairs, and so it is impossible for God to conceive a goal and act to achieve it. Hence omnipotence, omniscience, and moral perfection are inconsistent with agency, and therefore God does not and cannot exist.

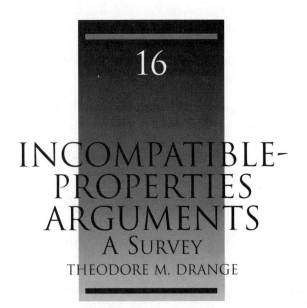

16

INCOMPATIBLE-PROPERTIES ARGUMENTS
A SURVEY
THEODORE M. DRANGE

A theological arguments (arguments for the nonexistence of God) can be divided into two main groups. One group consists of arguments which aim to show an incompatibility between two of God's properties. Let us call those 'incompatible-properties arguments'. The other group consists of arguments which aim to show an incompatibility between God's existence and the nature of the world. They may be called 'God-vs.-world arguments'. A prime example of one of those would be the Evidential Argument from Evil. This paper will survey only arguments in the first group. Arguments in the second group are discussed elsewhere.[1]

To generate incompatible-properties arguments, it would be most helpful to have a list of divine attributes. I suggest the following. God is:

(a) perfect	(g) personal
(b) immutable	(h) free
(c) transcendent	(i) all-loving
(d) nonphysical	(j) all-just
(e) omniscient	(k) all-merciful
(f) omnipresent	(l) the creator of the universe

This is certainly not a complete list, for there are other properties that have been ascribed to God. For example, the list excludes omnipotence. Furthermore,

From *Philo* 1, no. 2 (1998): 49–60. Copyright © 1998 by Western Michigan University. Reprinted by permission of *Philo*.

I am not claiming here that there is any one person who has ascribed all of these properties to God. I would say, though, that each of the properties has been ascribed to God by someone or other.

It would be of interest to consider whether there are pairs of properties from the given list which are incompatible with each other. For each such pair, it would be possible to construct an incompatible-properties argument for God's nonexistence. The present essay aims to study that issue in the style of a survey. It will not go into the relevant philosophical issues in any great depth. Nor will it consider the further matter of whether anyone has actually claimed the existence of a being which possesses any of the incompatible pairs. It is assumed in the background, however, that there are indeed such people. Let us proceed, then, to consider various possible incompatible-properties arguments.

1. THE PERFECTION-VS.-CREATION ARGUMENT

Consider the pair (a)–(l), which takes God to be perfect and also to be the creator of the universe. It seems that those properties might be shown to be incompatible in two different ways. The first way is as follows:

Version 1
1. If God exists, then he is perfect.[2]
2. If God exists, then he is the creator of the universe.
3. A perfect being can have no needs or wants.
4. If any being created the universe, then he must have had some need or want.
5. Therefore, it is impossible for a perfect being to be the creator of the universe (from 3 and 4).
6. Hence, it is impossible for God to exist (from 1, 2, and 5).

Premise 3 might be challenged on the grounds that a perfect being, full of love, could desire to share his love with others. Thus, a perfect being could have a want, which would make premise 3 false. I suppose the only problem with this is that if a being wants something that he does not have, then he cannot be perfect, for he would be in a certain way incomplete. Whether or not this adequately defends premise 3 is hard to say. There is a certain unclarity, and perhaps subjectivity, in the idea of "perfection" which poses an obstacle to any sort of rigorous reasoning about the concept.[3]

Premise 4 might also be challenged. Perhaps God created the universe accidentally. For example, he "slipped and fell," thereby creating a mess, which turned out to be our universe. In that case, God would not have had any need or want in creating the universe, and premise 4 would be false. There are difficulties with this, however. First, almost every theist who takes God to have created the universe takes it to have been done deliberately, not accidentally. And second, if the creation were accidental, then that in itself would imply that God is imperfect (since perfect beings do not have accidents), and that would be another basis for the Perfection-vs.-Creation Argument. Thus, this sort of challenge to premise 4 itself runs into problems.

Version 2
1. If God exists, then he is perfect.
2. If God exists, then he is the creator of the universe.
3. If a being is perfect, then whatever he creates must be perfect.
4. But the universe is not perfect.
5. Therefore, it is impossible for a perfect being to be the creator of the universe (from 3 and 4).
6. Hence, it is impossible for God to exist (from 1, 2, and 5).

The usual reply to this line of thought is that whatever imperfections the universe may contain, they are the fault of mankind, not God. Thus, the universe was indeed perfect when God first created it, but it later became imperfect because of the actions of humans. This could be taken as an attack on the argument's premise 3, construed to imply that what is perfect must remain so indefinitely. I shall not pursue the many twists and turns that this issue might take. It is essentially the same as what is called the "Deductive Argument from Evil," which is a topic beyond the scope of the present survey. Let us instead move on to a new argument.

2. THE IMMUTABILITY-VS.-CREATION ARGUMENT

Let us now consider the pair (b)–(l), which takes God to be immutable (unchangeable) and also the creator of the universe. This argument, too, comes in different versions.[4] However, I shall consider just one of them here:

1. If God exists, then he is immutable.
2. If God exists, then he is the creator of the universe.
3. An immutable being cannot at one time have an intention and then at a later time not have that intention.
4. For any being to create anything, prior to the creation he must have had the intention to create it, but at a later time, after the creation, no longer have the intention to create it.

5. Thus, it is impossible for an immutable being to have created anything (from 3 and 4).
6. Therefore, it is impossible for God to exist (from 1, 2, and 5).

Premise 3 might be challenged on the grounds that the loss of an intention through the satisfaction of it is not a genuine change in a being. If a man wants something, X, and then obtains it, he has not thereby changed his attitude toward X. It is not that he once had a pro-attitude toward X, but now he has a con-attitude toward it. So long as he is satisfied with X, his attitude remains unchanged. This may very well be true, but why claim that the only genuine change there can be in a being is a change in attitude? Why not allow that there can be other sorts of genuine change, and one of them is the loss of an intention through the satisfaction of it? Until some clear answer to this question is given, premise 3 seems to have some merit.

Premise 4 might be attacked in at least two different ways. It has been claimed that both the concept of "prior to the existence of the universe" and the concept of "God existing within time" are bogus. Time is a part or aspect of the universe itself and so there cannot be a time "before the universe." And God is a timeless being, so the idea of God having a certain property at one time but lacking it at a later time is misguided. Since God is not within time, he cannot have properties at particular times.

My response to both objections is that creation is a temporal concept. This is built into the very definition of 'create' as "to cause to come into being." X cannot cause Y to come into being unless X existed temporally prior to Y. Thus, if indeed there was no time prior to the existence of the universe, then it is logically impossible for the universe to have been created. In that case, there could not possibly be a creator of the universe. And, furthermore, if indeed God does not exist within time, then he could not have been the creator of the universe, because, by the very concept of creation, if the universe was created at all, then its creator must have existed temporally prior to it. So if God, being timeless, did not exist temporally prior to anything, then God cannot have been the creator of the universe.

There is another objection to premise 4 which is similar to one we considered in relation to argument 1. It is that 4 would be false if the universe were created unintentionally. Again, it should be mentioned that people who believe that the universe was created also believe that it was created intentionally. But I would like to point out another possible response here. In place of the concept of intention, it would be possible to appeal to some other concept in the construction of argument 2. One candidate for that would be the concept of performing an action. In order for someone to create something, even if it is done unintentionally, the creator must perform an action, and that action must take time. Thus, there must be a time during which a creator is performing a certain action and a later time (after the action has been performed) during which he is no longer performing that action. It could be argued that this, too, represents a *change* in the being who is performing the action. Thus, this would be another reason for maintaining that an immutable being cannot create anything (whether intentionally or not).

3. THE IMMUTABILITY-VS.-OMNISCIENCE ARGUMENT

This argument is based on an alleged incompatibility between attributes (b) and (e) on our list. It, too, comes in different versions, one of which is the following:[5]

1. If God exists, then he is immutable.
2. If God exists, then he is omniscient.
3. An immutable being cannot know different things at different times.
4. To be omniscient, a being would need to know propositions about the past and future.
5. But what is past and what is future keep changing.
6. Thus, in order to know propositions about the past and future, a being would need to know different things at different times (from 5).
7. It follows that, to be omniscient, a being would need to know different things at different times (from 4 and 6).
8. Hence, it is impossible for an immutable being to be omniscient (from 3 and 7).
9. Therefore, it is impossible for God to exist (from 1, 2, and 8).

The usual place at which this argument is attacked is its premise 4. It is claimed that a timeless being can know everything there is to know without knowing propositions about the past and future. Consider the following two propositions as examples:

A. The origin of the planet Earth is in the past.
B. The end (or destruction) of the planet Earth is in the future.

The claim is that a timeless being need not know propositions A and B in order to know everything there is to know, because such a being could know the exact dates of both the origin and the end of the earth and that would suffice for complete knowledge. That is, A and B would be "covered," and so it would not be necessary for the omniscient being to know A and B in addition to those dates.

But, of course, this claim can be challenged. To know the dates of the origin and the end of the earth does not entail knowing propositions A and B. To know

A and B requires being situated within time (somewhere *between* the origin and end of the earth), so they are not anything that a timeless being could know. However, they certainly are things that an omniscient being must know. Thus, the given objection to premise 4 of the argument above is a failure.

It should be noted that a somewhat different incompatible-properties argument could also be constructed using the divine attribute of transcendence instead of immutability. The argument would focus on the point that a transcendent being must be timeless, and a timeless being cannot know propositions about the past and future. However, an omniscient being, as shown above, must know propositions about the past and future. Therefore, it is impossible for a transcendent being to be omniscient. The incompatibility would be between attributes (c) and (e) on our list. Such an argument could be called "the Transcendence-vs.-Omniscience Argument." The same issues would be raised in it as were raised, above, in connection with the Immutability-vs.-Omniscience Argument.

4. THE IMMUTABLE-VS.-ALL-LOVING ARGUMENT

Here the alleged incompatibility is between attributes (b) and (i). The argument may be expressed as follows:

1. If God exists, then he is immutable.
2. If God exists, then he is all-loving.
3. An immutable being cannot be affected by events.
4. To be all-loving, it must be possible for a being to be affected by events.
5. Hence, it is impossible for an immutable being to be all-loving (from 3 and 4).
6. Therefore, it is impossible for God to exist (from 1, 2, and 5).

To be affected is to be changed in some way, so premise 3 is pretty much true by definition. Premise 4 might be challenged, but when the nature of love is contemplated, it is seen that 4 must also be true. The concept of love that is relevant here is that of *agape*, which is the willingness to sacrifice oneself for the sake of others. If events were to call for some sacrifice on God's part, then, to be loving in the relevant sense, he must go ahead and perform the sacrifice. Since that requires being affected, the truth of premise 4 is assured.

This argument is a particularly forceful one. There is another argument which is very similar to it, which pits immutability against the property of being a *person* (property [g] on our list). It could be called the "Immutability-vs.-Personhood Argument." The basic idea behind it would be that in order to genuinely be a person (or personal being), it is necessary that one be capable of being affected by what happens. I think that that one, too, is quite forceful, but I shall not pursue it here. (For a similar argument, see section 6 below.) We have done quite enough with the divine attribute of immutability.

5. THE TRANSCENDENCE-VS.-OMNIPRESENCE ARGUMENT

Here the incompatibility is between properties (c) and (f). The argument may be formulated as follows:

1. If God exists, then he is transcendent (i.e., outside space and time).
2. If God exists, then he is omnipresent.
3. To be transcendent, a being cannot exist anywhere in space.
4. To be omnipresent, a being must exist everywhere in space.
5. Hence, it is impossible for a transcendent being to be omnipresent (from 3 and 4).
6. Therefore, it is impossible for God to exist (from 1, 2, and 5).

The usual place at which this argument is attacked is premise 3. It is claimed that to transcend space does not entail being totally outside space. A being could be partly inside space and partly outside. Consider the Flatland analogy: a three-dimensional object transcends Flatland, and yet it exists within the Flatland dimensions (as well as outside). So, God could be like that. He exists within space (and, indeed, everywhere in space!) but he also exists outside space, the latter feature being what warrants calling him "transcendent."

My only objection here is that the Flatland analogy does not quite make the idea of transcendence intelligible. We understand perfectly well how a three-dimensional object might "transcend" Flatland while still being (partly) within it. However, this is still talking about objects in space. To try to extend the analogy so as to talk about something that is "outside space as well as within it" is unsuccessful. That is something that we are totally unable to comprehend. In the end, the very concept of transcendence that is appealed to here is incoherent. This illustrates the point that defenses against incompatible-properties arguments may very well lead to incoherence or other objections to theism.

6. THE TRANSCENDENCE-VS.-PERSONHOOD ARGUMENT

This is an even better argument for bringing out the relevant incoherence. It pits property (c) against property (g), instead of against (f):

1. If God exists, then he is transcendent (i.e., outside space and time).
2. If God exists, then he is a person (or a personal being).
3. If something is transcendent, then it cannot exist and perform actions within time.
4. But a person (or personal being) must exist and perform actions within time.
5. Therefore, something that is transcendent cannot be a person (or personal being) (from 3 and 4).
6. Hence, it is impossible for God to exist (from 1, 2, and 5).

Again, premise 3 might be challenged on the grounds that a transcendent being could be both partly inside time and partly outside time, with the latter feature being what warrants the label 'transcendent'. That is, God is said to perform actions within time but also to have a part or aspect that extends outside time. However, this notion of "partly inside time and partly outside" is definitely incoherent. No one has a clue what that might mean. To pursue such a line of thought might evade the charge of "incompatible properties," but it leads directly to the charge of incoherence, which is just as bad, if not worse.

Premise 4 might also be challenged. It might be said that its concept of personhood is too limited and that persons (or personal beings) could exist totally outside time. I am inclined to resist this sort of conceptual expansion. If the concept of personhood is extended that far, then it ceases to do the work that it was supposed to do, which was to make God into a more familiar figure. Furthermore, if persons (or personal beings) can exist totally outside of time, then it becomes unclear what it might mean to speak of 'persons' (or 'personal beings') at all. The boundaries of the class become so blurred that the concept becomes vacuous.

Closely related to the concept of personhood is the concept of being free, which is property (h) on our list. An argument similar to 6, above, one which might be called the "Transcendent-vs.-Free Argument," could be constructed, pitting property (c) against property (h). In its corresponding premise 4, the point would be made that, in order for a being to be *free*, it must exist and perform actions within time. Otherwise, there would be no way for any freedom to be manifested. Almost all theists, it should be noted, accept the idea that God is a free agent, and thus are inclined to say of him that he (at least occasionally) performs actions within time. If they call God "transcendent" at all, then they would aim to attack premise 3 of the arguments in question, not premise 4. Of course, as pointed out above, to attack premise 3 leads one to make incoherent statements, so such a maneuver cannot be regarded to be successful.

7. THE NONPHYSICAL-VS.-PERSONAL ARGUMENT

Let us consider pitting property (d) against property (g). Then we get an argument which might be formulated in a very short way, as follows:

1. If God exists, then he is nonphysical.
2. If God exists, then he is a person (or a personal being).
3. A person (or personal being) needs to be physical.
4. Hence, it is impossible for God to exist (from 1–3).

Premise 3 has been advocated by Kai Nielsen, who wrote: "we have no understanding of 'a person' without 'a body' and it is only persons that in the last analysis can act or do things."[6] But not all nontheists would accept 3. One who does not is J. L. Mackie.[7] This argument turns on the issue of whether the idea of a "bodiless person" is consistent and coherent. That is a difficult and highly controversial issue, and I shall not pursue it here in this survey.[8]

It should be noted that the divine attribute of being nonphysical might also be taken to be incompatible with still other divine attributes, such as being free and being all-loving, which would give rise to slightly different incompatible-properties arguments. All such arguments, though, would lead into the same sort of difficult and controversial issues as does the Nonphysical-vs.-Personal Argument, and so should not be regarded to be among the most forceful of the various atheological arguments available.

8. THE OMNIPRESENCE-VS.-PERSONHOOD ARGUMENT

Similar considerations arise when we pit property (f) against property (g). The argument may again be formulated in a brief way, as follows:

1. If God exists, then he is omnipresent.
2. If God exists, then he is a person (or a personal being).
3. Whatever is omnipresent cannot be a person (or a personal being).
4. Hence, it is impossible for God to exist (from 1–3).

The point of premise 3 is similar to that for the previous argument. When we contemplate what it means to be a person (or a personal being), we see that it conflicts with being omnipresent. What sorts of things might be omnipresent, anyway? Perhaps a gravitational field would serve as an example. They would all appear to be items in a different *category* from persons, so to try to assimilate them would be to commit a category mistake. Persons can no more be omnipresent than they can be odd or even (in the mathematical sense).

9. THE OMNISCIENT-VS.-FREE ARGUMENT

We now come to a more complicated argument, which pits property (e) against (h). One way of formulating it is presented by Dan Barker.[9] A slightly different version may be formulated as follows:

1. If God exists, then he is omniscient.
2. If God exists, then he is free.
3. An omniscient being must know exactly what actions he will and will not do in the future.
4. If one knows that he will do an action, then it is impossible for him not to do it, and if one knows that he will not do an action, then it is impossible for him to do it.
5. Thus, whatever an omniscient being does, he must do, and whatever he does not do, he cannot do (from 3 and 4).
6. To be free requires having options open, which means having the ability to act contrary to the way one actually acts.
7. So, if one is free, then he does not have to do what he actually does, and he is able to do things that he does not actually do (from 6).
8. Hence, it is impossible for an omniscient being to be free (from 5 and 7).
9. Therefore, it is impossible for God to exist (from 1, 2, and 8).

Some have denied that omniscience entails knowing all about the future. They say that omniscience only entails knowing what there is to know. But the future actions of free persons are open and not there to be known about. Thus, not even an omniscient being could know about them. This may provide a basis for rejecting premise 3 of the argument.

This sort of objection to 3 can be attacked in many different ways. One way would be to affirm that an omniscient being would indeed need to know all about the future. All propositions about the future are either true or false, and an omniscient being, by definition, must know the truth of any proposition that is in fact true. Furthermore, theists, often following the Bible on this point, commonly attribute unrestricted knowledge of the future to God.[10] Indeed, if God does not know the future actions of any free beings, then there is very little, if any, pertaining to the future about which he can be certain. For no matter what the situation may be, there is always a chance that it will be affected by such actions.

Another way to attack the given objection is to maintain that, even if God does not know about the future actions of *other* free agents, he must know about *his own* future actions. One reason for this is that God's actions are all based on perfect justice and immutable law. There is never any caprice in them. His purposes and intentions have remained steadfast from all eternity, so anyone who totally understands God's purposes and intentions, as he himself does, would be able to infallibly predict his actions. It follows that God must know what he himself will and will not do in the future, which would establish the truth of premise 3 if it is taken to refer to God.

Premise 4 is a consequence of the definition of knowledge. If a proposition is known to be true, then it must be true and cannot be false. So, if X knows that Y will do Z, then it is impossible for Y not to do Z. And this is so even where X and Y are the same person.

Premise 6 says that a free agent can do what he doesn't do. That may sound odd at first, but when it is understood correctly, it seems correct. Suppose we identify what Y does as "act Z." Then in order for Y to be free, prior to doing Z, it must have been possible for Y to do Z and it must also have been possible for Y not to do Z. If it were not possible for Y not to do Z, then Y's doing of Z could not be regarded as a free act. Free acts are avoidable. You can't be free if you *had* *to* do the thing that you did. This seems intuitively right, though some forms of compatibilism might reject it. It is not a totally settled issue in philosophy. I leave it to the reader to ascertain whether or not premise 6 is correct. If it is, then I think the argument goes through.

10. THE JUSTICE-VS.-MERCY ARGUMENT

The last argument to be considered in this survey pits property (j) against property (k). It may be formulated as follows:

1. If God exists, then he is an all-just judge.
2. If God exists, then he is an all-merciful judge.
3. An all-just judge treats every offender with *exactly* the severity that he/she deserves.
4. An all-merciful judge treats every offender with *less* severity than he/she deserves.
5. It is impossible to treat an offender both with exactly the severity that he/she deserves and also with less severity than he/she deserves.
6. Hence, it is impossible for an all-just judge to be an all-merciful judge (from 3–5).
7. Therefore, it is impossible for God to exist (from 1, 2, and 6).

I have heard it said by Christians that the way God judges offenders depends on whether or not they are true believers. If they are, then he is lenient with them, but if they are not, then he treats them with exactly the severity they deserve (which can be pretty bad). By this Christian way of speaking, God is said to be both an all-just and an all-merciful judge. He is all-just in giving everyone an equal opportunity to become a true believer and thereby come to receive leniency, but he is also all-merciful in that every true believer, without exception, receives mercy. This way of viewing matters would be an attack on both premise 3 and premise 4, above.

I would respond by maintaining that premises 3 and 4 come closer to capturing ordinary language than the given Christian way of speaking. According to the latter, God treats some offenders more leniently with regard to what they deserve than he does other offenders. It does not seem that such a judge would (or should) be called "all-just." And similarly, since he does not treat all offenders less severely than they deserve, he would not (and should not) be called "all-merciful" either. Instead of being both all-just and all-merciful, the Christian God, as described, would be neither.

As with many of the previous attacks on the incompatible-properties arguments, this one turns on semantical issues. In a sense, it is all a matter of semantics, for the issue of whether or not certain property ascriptions conflict with certain other property ascriptions depends very much on what exactly they mean. Theists could defend against the arguments by denying that the property terms in question mean what the proponents of the arguments claim they mean. Often such denials lead to still other difficulties for the theist. A full presentation and defense of incompatible-properties arguments should explore such implications and fully pursue the many issues, whether semantical or not. That project is beyond the scope of the present essay.

My aim was simply to survey several of the more common (and a few not so common) incompatible-properties arguments for the nonexistence of God. Just which of those arguments are sound and which of them are most effective in discussions and debates with theists are further issues that are certainly worth pursuing.

NOTES

1. See, especially, Theodore M. Drange, *Nonbelief and Evil: Two Arguments for the Nonexistence of God* (Amherst, N.Y.: Prometheus Books, 1998).

2. Following tradition, and for simplicity, I use the male personal pronoun for God. My apologies to anyone who finds that linguistic practice offensive.

3. This obstacle applies to any version of the Ontological Argument.

4. See, especially, Richard M. Gale, chap. 2 in *On the Nature and Existence of God* (Cambridge: Cambridge University Press, 1991). The versions of the argument discussed by Gale are different from the one taken up in the present essay.

5. Gale, chap. 3 in *On the Nature and Existence of God.*

6. Kai Nielsen, *An Introduction to the Philosophy of Religion* (New York: St. Martin's Press, 1982), p. 36.

7. See J. L. Mackie, *The Miracle of Theism* (Oxford: Clarendon Press, 1982), pp. 1–2.

8. For reasons that support the incoherence of "disembodied persons," see Drange, *Nonbelief and Evil*, appendix E, section 2.

9. Dan Barker, "The Freewill Argument for the Nonexistence of God" [online], www.ffrf.org/fttoday/august97/barker.html [August 1997].

10. For a long list of biblical references to God's knowledge of the future free actions of humans, see Drange, *Nonbelief and Evil*, appendix B, section 2.

17

OMNISCIENCE AND IMMUTABILITY

NORMAN KRETZMANN

It is generally recognized that omniscience and immutability are necessary characteristics of an absolutely perfect being. The fact that they are also incompatible characteristics seems to have gone unnoticed.

In the main body of this paper, I will present first an argument that turns on the incompatibility of omniscience and immutability and, second, several objections to that argument with my replies to the objections.

    (1)   A perfect being is not subject to change.[1]
    (2)   A perfect being knows everything.[2]
    (3)   A being that knows everything always knows what time it is.[3]
    (4)   A being that always knows what time it is, is subject to change.[4]
∴ (5)   A perfect being is subject to change.
∴ (6)   A perfect being is not a perfect being.
         Finally, therefore,
    (7)   There is no perfect being.[5]

In discussing this argument with others,[6] I have come across various objections against one or another of its premises. Considering such objections here helps to clarify the line taken in the argument and provides an opportunity to anticipate and turn aside several natural criticisms of that line.

Because premises (1) and (2) present the widely accepted principles of

From *Journal of Philosophy* 63 (1966): 409–21. Copyright © 1966 by Columbia University. Reprinted by permission from *Journal of Philosophy*.

immutability and omniscience, objections against them are not so much criticisms of the line taken in the argument as they are attempts to modify the concept of a perfect being in the light of the argument. And since premise (3) gives every impression of being an instance of a logical truth, premise (4) is apparently the one most vulnerable to attacks that are genuinely attacks on the argument. The first four of the following seven objections are all directed against premise (4), although Objection D raises a question relevant to premise (3) as well.

Objection A. It must be granted that a being that always knows what time it is knows something that is changing—say, the state of the universe. But change in the object of knowledge does not entail change in the knower.

The denial that a change in the object necessitates a change in the knower depends on imprecise characterizations of the object. For example, I know that the Chrysler Building in Manhattan is 1,046 feet tall. If it is said that the Chrysler Building is the object of my knowledge, then of course many changes in it—in its tenants or in its heating system, for example—do not necessitate changes in the state of my knowledge. If, however, it is more precisely said that the object of my knowledge is the *height* of the Chrysler Building, then of course a change in the object of my knowledge does necessitate a change in me. If a forty-foot television antenna is extended from the present tip of the tower, either I will cease to know the height of the Chrysler Building or I will give up believing that its height is 1,046 feet and begin believing that its height is 1,086 feet. In the case of always knowing what time it is, if we are to speak of an object of knowledge at all it must be characterized not as the state of the universe (which might also be said to be the object of, for example, a cosmologist's knowledge), but as the *changing* of that state. To know the changing of anything is to know first that *p* and then that not-*p* (for some particular instance of *p*), and a knower that knows first one proposition and then another is a knower that changes.

Objection B. The beliefs of a being that always knows what time it is are subject to change, but a change in a being's beliefs need not constitute a change in the being itself. If last year Jones believed the Platonic epistles to be genuine and this year he believes them to be spurious, then Jones has changed his mind; and that sort of change in beliefs may be considered a change in Jones. But if last year Jones believed that it was 1965 and this year he believes that it is 1966, he has not changed his mind, he has merely taken account of a calendar change; and that sort of change in beliefs should not be considered a change in Jones. The change in beliefs entailed by always knowing what time it is, is that taking-account sort of change rather than a change of mind, the sort of change in beliefs that might reasonably be said to have been at least in part initiated by the believer and that might therefore be reasonably attributed to him.

It seems clear, first of all, that the sort of change in beliefs entailed by knowing the changing of anything is the taking-account sort of change rather than a change of mind. But once that much has been allowed, Objection B seems to consist in no more than an expression of disappointment in the *magnitude* of the change necessitated by always knowing what time it is. The entailed change in beliefs is not, it is true, sufficiently radical to qualify as a change of character or of attitude, but it is no less incompatible with immutability for all that. If Jones had been immutable from December 1965 through January 1966, he could no more have taken account of the calendar change than he could have changed his mind.

It may be worth noting that just such small-scale, taking-account changes in beliefs have sometimes been recognized by adherents of the principle of immutability as incompatible with immutability. Ockham, for example, argues at length against the possibility of a change in the state of God's foreknowledge just because God's changelessness could not be preserved through such a change. In Question Five of his *Tractatus de praedestinatione et de praescientia Dei et de futuris contingentibus*, Ockham maintains that "if 'God knows that A' (where A is a future contingent proposition) and 'God does not know that A' *could* be true successively, it *would* follow that God was changeable," and the principle on which Ockham bases that claim is in no way restricted to future contingents. (As an adherent of the principle of immutability Ockham of course proceeds to deny that God could first know that A and then not know that A, but his reasons for doing so involve considerations peculiar to future contingent propositions and need not concern us here.)[7]

Objection C. For an omniscient being always to know what time it is, is to know the state of the universe at every instant, but it is possible for an omniscient being to know the state of the universe at every instant all at once rather than successively. Consequently, it is possible for an omniscient being always to know what time it is without being subject to change.

The superficial flaw in this objection is the ambiguity of the phrase "to know the state of the universe at every instant," but the ambiguity is likely to be overlooked because the phrase is evidently an allusion to a familiar, widely accepted account of omniscience, according to which omniscience regarding contingent events is nothing more nor less than knowledge of the entire scheme of contingent events from beginning to end at once. I see no reason for quarreling here with the ascription of such knowledge to an omniscient being; but the underlying flaw in Objection C is the drastic *incompleteness* of this account of omniscience regarding contingent events.

The kind of knowledge ascribed to an omniscient being in this account is sometimes characterized as "seeing all time at a glance," which suggests that if one sees the entire scheme of contingent events from beginning to end at once, one sees all there is to see of time. The totality of contingent events, we are to suppose, may be known either simultaneously or successively, and an omniscient being will of course know it not successively but simultaneously. In his *Summa contra gentiles* (Book I, chap. 55, sects. [6]–[9]), Aquinas presents a concise version of what seems to be the standard exposition of this claim.

> [T]he intellect of one considering *successively* many things cannot have only one operation. For since operations differ according to their objects, the operation by which the first is considered must be different from the operation by which the second is considered. But the divine intellect has only one operation, namely, the divine essence, as we have proved. Therefore God considers all that he knows not successively, but *together*. Moreover, succession cannot be understood without time nor time without motion. . . . But there can be no motion in God, as may be inferred from what we have said. There is, therefore, no succession in the divine consideration. . . . Every intellect, furthermore, that understands one thing after another is at one time *potentially* understanding and at another time *actually* understanding. For while it understands the first thing actually it understands the second thing potentially. But the divine intellect is never potentially but always actually understanding. Therefore it does not understand things successively but rather understands them together.

On this view an omniscient being's knowledge of contingent events is the knowledge that event *e* occurs at time *t* (for every true instance of that form). Thus an omniscient being knows that my birth occurs at t_n, that my writing these words occurs at t_{n+x}, that my death occurs at t_{n+x+y}. This omniscient being also knows what events occur simultaneously with each of those events—knows, for example, that while I am writing these words my desk calendar lies open at the page bearing the date "Friday, March 4, 1966," and the watch on my wrist shows 10:15. Moreover, since an omniscient being by any account knows all necessary truths, including the truths of arithmetic, this omniscient being knows how much time elapses between my birth and my writing these words and between my writing these words and my death. But I *am* writing these words just *now*, and on this view of omniscience an omniscient being is incapable of knowing that that is what I am now doing, and for all this omniscient being knows I might just as well be dead or as yet unborn. That is what knowing everything amounts to if knowing 'everything' does not include always knowing what time it is. Alternatively, that is what knowing the state of the universe at every instant comes to if that phrase is interpreted in the way required by the claim that it is possible to have that sort of knowledge all at once.

According to this familiar account of omniscience, the knowledge an omniscient being has of the entire scheme of contingent events is in many relevant respects exactly like the knowledge you might have of a movie you had written, directed, produced, starred in, and seen a thousand times. You would know its every scene in flawless detail, and you would have the length of each scene and the sequence of scenes perfectly in mind. You would know, too, that a clock pictured in the first scene shows the time to be 3:45, and that a clock pictured in the fourth scene shows 4:30, and so on. Suppose, however, that your movie is being shown in a distant theater today. You know the movie immeasurably better than do the people in the theater who are now seeing it for the first time, but they know one big thing about it you don't know, namely, what is now going on on the screen.

Thus, the familiar account of omniscience regarding contingent events is drastically incomplete. An omniscient being must know not only the entire scheme of contingent events from beginning to end at once, but also *at what stage of realization that scheme now is*. It is in this sense of knowing what time it is that it is essential to claim in premise (3) that a being that knows everything always knows what time it is, and it is in this sense that always knowing what time it is entails incessant change in the knower, as is claimed in premise (4).

In orthodox Christianity the prevalence of the incomplete account of omniscience regarding contingent events effectively obscures the incompatibility of omniscience and immutability. Aquinas, for example, is not content with proving merely that "it is impossible for God to change in any way." He goes on in the *Summa theologiae* (Book I, Q. 14, art. 15) to argue that "since God's knowledge is his substance, as is clear from the foregoing, just as his substance is altogether immutable, as was shown above, so *his knowledge likewise must be altogether invariable*." What Aquinas, Ockham, and others *have* recognized is that God's knowledge cannot be variable if God is to remain immutable. What has *not* been seen is that God's knowledge cannot be altogether invariable if it is to be perfect, if it is to be genuine omniscience.

Objection D. A perfect being transcends space and time. Such a being is therefore not subject to change, whether as a consequence of knowing what time it is or for any other reason.

The importance of this objection lies in its introduction of the pervasive, mysterious doctrine of the transcendence of space and time, a doctrine often cited by orthodox Christians as if it were both consistent with their theology and explanatory of the notion that God sees all time at a glance. It seems to me to be neither.

In *Proslogium*, chapters 19 and 20, Anselm apostrophizes the being transcendent of space and time as follows:

> Thou wast not, then, yesterday, nor wilt thou be tomorrow; but yesterday and today and tomorrow thou art; or, rather, neither yesterday nor today nor tomorrow thou art, but simply *thou art, outside all time*. For yesterday and

today and tomorrow have no existence except in time, but thou, although nothing exists without thee, nevertheless dost not exist in space or time, but all things exist in thee. For nothing contains thee, but thou containest all.

For present purposes the spatial aspect of this doctrine may be ignored. What is meant by the claim that an entity transcends time? The number two might, I suppose, be said to transcend time in the sense that it does not age, that it is no older now than it was a hundred years ago. I see no reason to quarrel with the doctrine that a perfect being transcends time in *that* sense, since under that interpretation the doctrine is no more than a gloss on the principle of immutability. But under that interpretation the doctrine begs the question of premise (4) rather than providing a basis for objecting to it.

Only one other interpretation of the doctrine of the transcendence of time suggests itself, and that is that from a God's-eye point of view there is no time, that the passage of time is a universal human illusion. (Whatever else may be said of this interpretation, it surely cannot be considered compatible with such essential theses of Christian doctrine as the Incarnation and the Resurrection.) Under this interpretation the doctrine of the transcendence of time does have a devastating effect on the argument, since it implies either that there are no true propositions of the form "it is now t_n," or that there is exactly one (eternally) true proposition of that form. Thus, under this interpretation premise (3) either is vacuous or has a single trivializing instance, and premise (4) is false. But this interpretation preserves the immutability of a perfect being by imposing immutability on everything else, and that is surely an inconceivably high price to pay, in the view of Christians and non-Christians alike.

The remaining three objections are directed against premises (1) or (2) and may, therefore, be considered not so much criticisms of the argument as attempts to revise the principle of immutability or the principle of omniscience in the light of the argument. Objections E and F have to do with premise (2), Objection G with premise (1).

Objection E. Since a perfect being transcends time, it is logically impossible that a perfect being know what time it is and hence logically impossible that such a being know everything. But it is no limitation on a perfect being that it cannot do what is logically impossible. Therefore, its not knowing absolutely everything (in virtue of not knowing what time it is) does not impair its perfection.

Objections E and F are attempts to hedge on omniscience as philosophers and theologians have long since learned to hedge on omnipotence. In Objection E this attempt depends on directly invoking one of the standard limitations on omnipotence, but the attempt does not succeed. Perhaps the easiest way of pointing up its failure is to produce analogous inferences of the same form, such as this: since I am a human being and a human being is a mortal rational animal, it is logically impossible that I should live forever; therefore it is no limitation on me that I must die— or this: since I am a creature of limited power, it is logically impossible that I be capable of doing whatever is logically possible; therefore it is no limitation on me that I cannot do whatever is logically possible. What is wrong with all these inferences is that the crucial limitation is introduced in the initial description of the being in question, after which it does of course make sense to deny that mere consequences of the limiting description are to be introduced as if they constituted additional limitations. It is not an *additional* limitation on a legless man that he cannot walk, or on a mortal being that it must die, or on a creature of limited power that it cannot do whatever it might choose to do. No more is it an *additional* limitation on a being that is *incapable* of knowing what time it is that it *does not* know what time it is. But any claim to perfection that might have been made on behalf of such a being has already been vitiated in the admission that its transcendence of time renders it incapable of omniscience.

Objection F. Just as in explicating the concept of omnipotence we have been forced to abandon the naive formula "a perfect being can do anything" and replace it with "a perfect being can do anything the doing of which does not impair its perfection," so the argument suggests that the naive formula "a perfect being knows everything" must be revised to read "a perfect being knows everything the knowing of which does not impair its perfection." Thus, since the argument does show that knowing what time it is impairs the perfection of the knower, it cannot be a part of the newly explicated omniscience to know what time it is.

Even if Objection F could be sustained, this particular grasping of the nettle would surely impress many as just too painful to bear, for in deciding whether or not to try to evade the conclusion of the argument in this way it is important to remember that in the context of the argument "knowing what time it is" means knowing *what is going on.* Objection F at best thus provides an exceptionally costly defense of absolute perfection, emptying it of much of its content in order to preserve it; for under the newly explicated notion of omniscience Objection F commits one to the view that it is impossible for a *perfect, omniscient* being to know what is going on.

Objection F attempts to draw an analogy between an explication of omnipotence and a proposed explication of omniscience, borrowing strength from the fact that in the case of omnipotence such an explication has long since been recognized as a necessary condition of the coherence of the notion. In evaluating this attempt it is helpful to note that there are at least three types of provisos that may be inserted into formulas of omnipotence for that purpose. The first is relevant to omnipotence generally, the second specifically to eternal omnipotence, and the third specifically to eternal omnipotence as one perfect characteristic of a being possessed of certain other perfect characteristics. (For present purposes it is convenient to say simply that the third is relevant specifically to eternal omnipotence as one aspect of an absolutely perfect being.) These three types of provisos may be exemplified in the following three formulas of omnipotence:

I. A being that is omnipotent (regardless of its other characteristics) can do anything provided that (a) the description of what is to be done does not involve a logical inconsistency.
II. A being that is eternally omnipotent (regardless of its other characteristics) can do anything provided that (a) . . . and (b) the doing of it does not constitute or produce a limitation on its power.
III. A being that is absolutely perfect (and hence eternally omnipotent) can do anything provided that (a) . . . and (b) . . . and (c) the doing of it does not constitute a violation of some aspect of its perfection other than its power.

Provisos of type (c) only are at issue in Objection F, no doubt because provisos of types (a) and (b) have no effective role to play in the explication of omniscience. No being knows anything that *is not* the case; a fortiori no omniscient being knows anything that *cannot be* the case. So much for type (a). As for type (b), since certain things the description of which involves no logical inconsistency would if done incapacitate the doer—committing suicide, for example, or creating another omnipotent being—there is good reason for such a proviso in the explication of eternal omnipotence. It might likewise be claimed that an omniscient being knows everything except things that would if known limit the being's *capacity for knowledge,* the formal justification for this claim being just the same as that for the corresponding omnipotence-claim. The significant difference between these two claims is that the omniscience-claim is evidently vacuous. There is no reason to suspect that there *are* things that would if known limit the knower's capacity for knowledge. More directly to the point at issue in the argument, there is no reason whatever to think that knowing what is going on is a kind of knowing that limits the knower's capacity for knowledge. Thus, although a type (b) proviso is needed in the explication of eternal omnipotence in order to preserve the coherence of the notion of eternal omnipotence, no such proviso need be inserted into the formula of omniscience in order to preserve the coherence of that notion.

The putative analogy in Objection F presupposes that a proviso of type (c) will preserve omniscience as it preserves omnipotence in such a (Cartesian) argument as the following. It is impossible for an absolutely perfect being to lie, for although such a being, as omnipotent, has the power to lie, the exercise of that power would violate the perfect goodness of the being. To say that it is impossible for an absolutely perfect being to lie is not to say that it lacks the power to lie but rather that its absolute perfection in another aspect—perfect goodness—necessitates its refraining from the exercise of that power. Whether or not this line of argument succeeds in doing what it is designed to do, it seems clear that there is no genuine analogue for it in the case of omniscience. Consider the following candidate. It is impossible for an absolutely perfect being to know what is going on, for although such a being, as omniscient, has the power to know what is going on, the exercise of that power would violate the immutability of the being. To say that it is impossible for an absolutely perfect being to know what is going on is not to say that it lacks the power to know what is going on but rather that its absolute perfection in another aspect—immutability—necessitates its refraining from the exercise of that power. A being that has the power to do something that it refrains from doing may not thereby even jeopardize its omnipotence. All the same, a being that has the power to know something that it refrains from knowing does thereby forfeit its omniscience. Omniscience is not the *power to know* everything; it is the *condition of knowing* everything, and that condition cannot be preserved through even a single instance of omitting to exercise the power to know everything.

Therefore, whatever strength Objection F seems to derive from its appeal to the putative analogy between omnipotence and omniscience in this respect is illusory, and this attempted evasion of the argument's conclusion reduces to an arbitrary decision to sacrifice omniscience to immutability.

Objection G. The traditional view of philosophers and theologians that absolute perfection entails absolute immutability is mistaken, founded on the misconception that in a perfect being any change would have to be for the worse. In particular the kind of change entailed by always knowing what time it is, is a kind of change that surely cannot be construed as deterioration, even when it is ascribed to an absolutely perfect being. No doubt an absolutely perfect being must be immutable in most and perhaps in all other respects, but the argument shows that absolute perfection *entails* mutability in at least this one respect.

Objection G proceeds on the assumption that immutability is ascribed to a perfect being for only one reason—namely, that all change in such a being must constitute deterioration. There is, however, a second reason, as has been indicated at several points in the discussion so far—namely, that any change in a "perfect" being must indicate that the being was in some respect not in the requisite state of completion, actualization, fixity. The aspect of absolute completion is no less essential an ingredient in the concept of absolute perfection than is the aspect of absolute excellence. Moreover, those such as Aquinas and Ockham who argue against the mutability of a perfect being's *knowledge* would surely agree that the change they are intent on ruling out would not constitute *deterioration,* since they regularly base their arguments on the inadmissibility of *process* in an absolutely perfect being.

An absolutely perfect being may be described as a being possessing all logically compossible perfections. Thus, if the argument had shown that omniscience and immutability were logically incompossible, it would have called for no more than an adjustment in the concept of absolute perfection, an adjustment of the sort proposed in Objection G. The proposition "things change" is, however, not necessarily but only contingently true. If as a matter of fact nothing else ever did change, an omniscient being could of course remain immutable. In Objection G, however, an absolutely perfect being has been confused with a being possessing all *really* compossible perfections, the best of all *really* possible beings. Perhaps, as the objection implies, the most *nearly* absolutely perfect being in the circumstances that happen to prevail *would* be mutable in the respect necessitated by always knowing what time it is. But that is of no consequence to the argument, which may be taken as showing that the prevailing circumstances do not admit of the existence of an absolutely perfect being.

This concluding section of the paper is in the nature of an appendix. It might be subtitled "Omniscience and Theism"; for it may be shown that the doctrine that God knows everything is incompatible also with theism, the doctrine of a personal God distinct from other persons.[8]

Consider these two statements.

S_1. Jones knows that he is in a hospital.
S_2. Jones knows that Jones is in a hospital.

S_1 and S_2 are logically independent. It may be that Jones is an amnesia case. He knows perfectly well that he is in a hospital, and after reading the morning papers he knows that Jones is in a hospital. An omniscient being surely must know all that Jones knows. Anyone can know what S_2 describes Jones as knowing, but no one other than Jones can know what S_1 describes Jones as knowing. (A case in point: Anyone could have proved that Descartes existed, but that is not what Descartes proved in the Cogito, and what he proved in the Cogito could not have been proved by anyone else.) The kind of knowledge S_1 ascribes to Jones is, moreover, the kind of knowledge characteristic of every self-conscious entity, of every person. Every person knows certain propositions that no *other* person *can* know. Therefore, if God is omniscient, theism is false; and if theism is true, God is not omniscient.

It may fairly be said of God, as it once was said of William Whewell, that "omniscience [is] his foible."

NOTES

1. This principle of immutability is regularly supported by one of two arguments. (I) *From Supreme Excellence:* A perfect being is a supremely excellent being; thus any change in such a being would constitute corruption, deterioration, loss of perfection. (See Plato, *Republic*, II, 381B.) (II) *From Complete Actualization:* A perfect being is a being whose capacities for development are all fully realized. A being subject to change, however, is in that respect and to that extent a being with an unrealized capacity for development, a being merely potential and not fully actualized, a being in a state of process and not complete; hence not perfect. (See Aristotle, *Metaphysics*, XII, 9; 1074b26.) The principle of immutability is a thesis of orthodox Christian theology, drawn from Greek philosophy and having among its credentials such biblical passages as Mal. 3.6 and James 1.17. (See Aquinas, *Summa theologiae*, I, Q. 9, art. 1.)

2. Being incapable of knowing all there is to know or being capable of knowing all there is to know and knowing less than that are conditions evidently incompatible with absolute perfection. Hence (2), which seems even more familiar and less problematic than (1).

3. Part of what is meant by premise (3) is, of course, that a being that knows everything always knows what time it is in every time zone on every planet in every galaxy; but it is not quite in that horological sense that its knowledge of what time it is, is most plainly relevant to considerations of omniscience and immutability. The relevant sense can be brought out more easily in the consideration of objections against the argument.

4. Adopting 'it is now t_n' as a convenient standard form for propositions as to what time it is, we may say of a being that always knows what time it is that the state of its knowledge changes incessantly with respect to propositions of the form 'it is now t_n'. First such a being knows that it is now t_1 (and that it is not now t_2), and then it knows that it is now t_2 (and that it is not now t_1). To say of any being that it knows something different from what it used to know is to say that it has changed; hence (4).

5.   [1f] $(x)(Px \supset \sim Cx)$;

  [2f] $(x)(Px \supset (p)(p \equiv Kxp))$ [K: . . . knows that . . .];

  [3f] $(x)((p)(p \equiv Kxp) \supset (p)(Tp \supset (p \equiv Kxp)))$ [T: . . . is of the form 'it is now t_n'];

  [4f] $(x)((p)(Tp \supset (p \equiv Kxp)) \supset Cx)$;

  [5f] $(x)(Px \supset Cx)$ [entailed by 2f, 3f, 4f];

  [6f] $(x)(Px \supset \sim Px)$ [entailed by 1f, 5f];

  [7f] $(x) \sim Px$ [equivalent to 6f].

The formalization [3f] is an instance of a logical truth; nevertheless, premise (3) is not one of the established principles in philosophical or theological discussions of the nature of a perfect being. Not only is it not explicitly affirmed, but it seems often to be implicitly denied. This circumstance may arouse a suspicion that the formalization [3f] is inaccurate or question-begging. Any such suspicion will, I think, be dissipated in the course of considering the objections to the argument, but it may be helpful in the meantime to point out that the validity of the argument does not depend on this formalization. It is of course possible to adopt less detailed formalizations that would not disclose the special logical status of premise (3) and would nevertheless exhibit the validity of the argument. For example, [2f′] (x)(Px ⊃ Ox); [3f′] (x)(Ox ⊃ Nx) together with a similarly imprecise formalization of premise (4) would serve that purpose.

6. I am indebted especially to Miss Marilyn McCord and to Professors H. N. Castañeda , H. G. Frankfurt, C. Ginet, G. B. Matthews, G. Nakhnikian, W. L. Rowe, S. Shoemaker, and W. Wainwright.

7. The most interesting historical example of this sort that I have seen was called to my attention by Professor Hugh Chandler after I had submitted this paper for publication. It is Problem 13 in the *Tahafut al-Falasifah* of al-Ghazali (d. ca. 1111): "REFUTATION OF THEIR [i.e., the philosophers', but principally Avicenna's] DOCTRINE THAT GOD (MAY HE BE EXALTED ABOVE WHAT THEY SAY) DOES NOT KNOW THE PARTICULARS WHICH ARE DIVISIBLE IN ACCORDANCE WITH THE DIVISION OF TIME INTO 'WILL BE', 'WAS', AND 'IS'" (trans. S. A. Kamali [Lahore: Pakistan Philosophical Congress, 1963], pp. 153–62). This work was not known to medieval Christian philosophers. (See Etienne Gilson, *History of Christian Philosophy* in *the Middle Ages* [New York: Random House, 1955], p. 216.)

8. The following argument was suggested to me by certain observations made by Professor Hector-Neri Castañeda in a paper titled "He," presented at the Wayne State University philosophy colloquium in the fall of 1964.

18

OMNISCIENCE, ETERNITY, AND TIME

ANTHONY KENNY

Thee God of Western theism is an eternal God. The eternity of God is commonly expressed, in the Old Testament and New Testament, as everlasting
duration. God lives forever: he always was and he always will be; there
never was a time when he was not; there never will be a time when there is no
God. Many theologians have taken God to be eternal in rather a different sense,
holding that God's duration is not just an everlasting duration but is strictly
speaking no duration at all. In the sixth century, Boethius defined eternity as the
total and simultaneous possession of unending life and since his time, eternity
has been commonly understood as timelessness.

The timelessness doctrine has appealed to many theologians as seeming to
provide a solution to the problem of the nature of God's knowledge of future contingent events—God's knowledge of human future actions for instance. Thomas
Aquinas[1] makes use of the doctrine of God's timelessness for this purpose.
Future contingents, he maintains, are indeterminate and so cannot be the object
of any kind of knowledge, divine or human. Nevertheless God can know them
because God does not see future contingent facts as being future but as being
present; future contingents are present to God. It is, St. Thomas says, nearer the
truth to say that if God knows a thing then it is than to say that if he knows it then
it will be. I have argued elsewhere that this solution to the problem of future contingents is not satisfactory:

From Anthony Kenny, chap. 4 in *The God of the Philosophers* (Oxford: Clarendon Press, 1986), pp.
38–48. Copyright © 1986 Oxford University Press. Reprinted by permission of Oxford University
Press.

The whole concept of a timeless eternity, the whole of which is simultaneous with every part of time, seems to be radically incoherent. For simultaneity as ordinarily understood is a transitive relation. If A happens at the same time as B, and B happens at the same time as C, then A happens at the same time as C. If the BBC program and the ITV program both start when Big Ben strikes ten, then they both start at the same time. But, on St. Thomas's view, my typing of this paper is simultaneous with the whole of eternity. Again, on this view, the great fire of Rome is simultaneous with the whole of eternity. Therefore, while I type these very words, Nero fiddles heartlessly on.[2]

The difficulties expressed in the above passage were presented long ago in the seventh chapter of Suarez's book *De Scientia Dei Futurorum Contingentium.* Having observed that Aquinas, Augustine, and Boethius think that presence or coexistence is both sufficient and necessary to explain God's knowledge of the future, Suarez insists that though temporal things coexist with the whole of eternity, because eternity coexists with all times, past, present, and future, yet these different times do not coexist with each other. God coexists now with one thing and now with another thing, without changing in Himself; like a tree standing motionless in a river which is successively present or adjacent to different masses of flowing water. The only sense in which things are eternally present to God is as objects of His knowledge. The statement of their presence therefore is a restatement of God's knowledge of the future, and not an explanation of it.

Arthur Prior in a paper called "The Formalities of Omniscience"[3] argued that the effect of treating God's knowledge as timeless would be to restrict God's knowledge to those truths, if any, which are themselves timeless. For example, he says:

God could not, on the view I am considering, know that the 1960 final examinations at Manchester are now over. For this isn't something that he or anyone could know timelessly, because it just isn't true timelessly. It's true now but it wasn't true a year ago (I write this on 29 August 1960) and so far as I can see all that can be said on this subject timelessly is that the finishing date of the 1960 final examinations is an earlier one than the 29th August, and this is not the thing we know when we know that those examinations are over. I cannot think of any better way of showing this than one I've used before, namely the argument that what we know when we know that the 1960 final examinations are over can't be just a timeless relation between dates, because this isn't the thing we're pleased about when we're pleased the examinations are over.

Nelson Pike in his book *God and Timelessness*[4] considers the arguments used by Prior and other philosophers writing in similar vein and claims that they have not in fact identified a range of facts that a timeless being could not know, but only certain forms of words that a timeless individual could not use when formulating or reporting his knowledge. We have not been given a reason for thinking that facts such as that which a temporal being can report by saying "today is the First of May" could not be reported by a timeless being in statements free of temporal indexical expressions.

I shall not try to settle whether a timeless being could or could not know temporal facts. Since, as I have said, I think on independent grounds that the doctrine of a timeless person is an incoherent one, I am not greatly interested in deciding whether a timeless person could be omniscient or not. Moreover, I agree with the general conclusion of Pike's book, which is that the doctrine of the timelessness of God is theologically unimportant and inessential to the tradition of Western theism.

Discarding the doctrine of timelessness, however, does not solve the problems about the relation between time and omniscience. As Norman Kretzmann has shown,[5] problems in this area are generated not only by the doctrine of timelessness, but also by the doctrine of immutability, which is far more deeply entrenched in the tradition of Western theism.

Kretzmann propounds an argument in seven propositions:

(1) A perfect being is not subject to change.
(2) A perfect being knows everything.
(3) A being that knows everything always knows what time it is.
(4) A being that always knows what time it is is subject to change.
(5) A perfect being is therefore subject to change.
(6) A perfect being is therefore not a perfect being.
(7) Ergo there is no perfect being.

A scholastic who had to reply to Kretzmann in a formal disputation might proceed as follows:

> I distinguish your first proposition thus:
> A perfect being is not subject to real change, I agree.
> A perfect being is not subject to apparent change, I deny.
> I counterdistinguish proposition 4:
> A being that always knows what time it is, is subject to real change, I deny.
> A being that always knows what time it is, is subject to apparent change, I agree.
> With the given distinctions I deny your conclusion and reject your proof.

The case for a distinction between real and apparent change has been persuasively argued by Geach:

> The only sharp criterion for a thing's having changed, is what we may call the Cambridge criterion (since it keeps on occurring in Cambridge philosophers of the great days, like Russell and McTaggart): the thing called 'x' has changed if

we have 'F(x) at time t' true, and 'F(x) at time t_1' false, for some interpretation of 'F', 't', and 't_1'. But this account is intuitively quite unsatisfactory. By this account, Socrates would after all change by coming to be shorter than Theaetetus; moreover, Socrates would change posthumously (even if he had no immortal soul) every time a fresh schoolboy came to admire him; and numbers would undergo change whenever e.g. five ceased to be the number of somebody's children.

The changes I have mentioned, we wish to protest, are not 'real' changes; and Socrates, if he has perished, and numbers in any case, cannot undergo 'real' changes. I cannot dismiss from my mind the feeling that there is a difference here. . . . Of course there is a 'Cambridge' change whenever there is a real change, but the converse is not true.[6]

Geach's last two examples are unhappy: surely "Jones minor admires Socrates" and "Five is the number of Smith's children" are not to be regarded as predications about Socrates and five respectively; but his first, venerable example is beyond reproach, and shows that not every change in the truth-value of a predication about an object is a genuine change in it.

The distinction, then, has been made out: we must turn to the counterdistinction. Must a being who knows the time be subject to real change or only to apparent change? Kretzmann considers the objection that change in an object of knowledge does not entail change in the knower. To this he replies that to know a change in anything is to know first that p and then that not p, and this is a change:

Adopting 'it is now t_n' as a convenient standard form for propositions as to what time it is, we may say of a being that always knows what time it is that the state of its knowledge changes incessantly with respect to propositions of the form 'it is now t_n'. First, such a being knows that it is now t_1 (and that it is not now t_2), and then it knows that it is now t_2 (and that it is not now t_1). To say of a being that it knows something different from what it used to know is to say that it has changed.[7]

H. N. Castañeda has replied to Kretzmann in a paper[8] which suggests the following line of argument. "It is now t_1" and "It is not now t_1" are not, despite appearances, related as p and $not\text{-}p$; because the time indicated by "now" is different in each case. There is no more a contradiction here than if I say "I am Kenny" and someone else says "I am not Kenny." What is expressed by these two propositions could be known by someone who is neither of us; and similarly what is expressed by the propositions "It is now t_1" and "It is now t_2" could be known by somebody who was outside either of the times in question.

Kretzmann indeed accepts that to take account of a change, for example, to bear in mind that it is now 1970 and not 1969 is not to change one's mind. It is, however, he claims, still an exception to the doctrine of immutability and sufficient to overturn the traditional doctrine; for that doctrine ruled out not only deterioration-changes, or changes of mind, but anything which was a matter of incomplete actualization.

However, changes in God's knowledge similar to that argued for by Kretzmann were regarded as compatible with divine immutability by Thomas Aquinas. In a passage from which Kretzmann quotes, Aquinas asks whether God's knowledge is changeable.[9] He answers no: his knowledge must be altogether invariable just as his substance is altogether unchangeable. But there is the following difficulty. Once, God knew that Christ was yet to be born. But now he does not know that Christ is yet to be born (*nasciturus*), because Christ is no longer yet to be born. Therefore, God does not now know all that he once knew. And thus his knowledge seems to be changeable.

Aquinas's reply begins by proposing a solution that he considers mistaken: "Nominalists in the past (*antiqui nominales*) said that the propositions 'Christ is being born', 'Christ is yet to be born', and 'Christ has been born' are identical, on the grounds that all three refer to the same thing, namely the birth of Christ, so that it follows that God knows whatever he knew, because he now knows Christ born, which means the same as 'Christ will be born.'"

This position of the old nominalists seems to resemble that of many modern logicians, according to which in a logically perspicuous notation tensed propositions should be replaced by timeless propositions containing an explicit time-reference, so that "It is raining now in Oxford" is replaced by "It is (timelessly) raining at 11:00 a.m. on 18 June 1978 in Oxford." Aquinas goes on to reject it as conflicting with Aristotle's position that the same sentence "Socrates is seated" is true when he is seated, false when he rises:

> It must be granted then that 'Whatever God knew, he knows' is not true if the reference is to propositions (*si ad enuntiabilia referatur*). But it does not follow that God's knowledge is changeable. There is no change in the divine knowledge through his knowing that one and the same thing at one time exists and at another does not; and in the same way, there is no change in the divine knowledge through his knowing that a certain proposition is at one time true, at another time false.

God's knowledge would thereby be changeable only if he knew propositions in the same way as we do.

Aquinas agrees, then, that God is mutable to the extent that if we take the object of knowledge in its propositional expression, then it is false that whatever God knew he knows; that is, we can formulate propositions such that "God knows that *p*" is true at one moment and false at another; as Aquinas's example shows, the propositions are not necessarily about the time, they can be any significantly tensed propositions. But this, Aquinas claims, involves no real change in God because God does not think in propositions as we do. God's knowledge cannot change either by his changing his opinion on a topic or by the truth of the matter changing while his opinion remains unaltered.

Aquinas's solution to the difficulty, like Castañeda's response to Kretzmann considered earlier, depends on the possibility of making a distinction between an item of knowledge and the way in which the knowledge is expressed. Pieces of knowledge are no doubt in general identified and individuated by their expression in language—this is something to which Aquinas would agree, since he believed both that knowledge was a disposition or state of mind (a habitus) and that dispositions were identified by the acts in which they were exercised or manifested.[10] But this does not necessarily mean that each item of knowledge has only one possible expression in language. Can it then be possible for two people A and B to have the same item of knowledge, but for there to be a way of expressing that knowledge which is open to A and not to B?

When we put the question in this way, there is an immediate and obvious answer. If A and B look out of the window at the rain, and A speaks only French and B speaks only English, they both possess the same item of information that it is raining, but A cannot express it by saying "It is raining," and B cannot express it by saying "*Il pleut*." But this answer does not take us very far. Some philosophers make a distinction between sentences and propositions, and say that "It is raining" and "*Il pleut*" are two different sentences but are (or express) only a single proposition, and that in general synonymous sentences in different languages do not add up to more than one proposition. Aquinas's solution to the problem about omniscience demands that a single item of knowledge should be capable of expression not only in different sentences but also in different propositions.[11]

If we count propositions by counting synonymous sentences, then it is clear that "I am tired" and "You are tired" are two different propositions. ("*Je suis fatigué*" would earn poor marks as a translation of "You are tired.") If we understand propositions in this way, it is very natural to say that a single proposition may express two different items of knowledge (when you say "You are tired" to me, and I say "You are tired" to you, we are not each saying the same thing about the same person) and that one and the same item of knowledge can be expressed by two different propositions (as when I say to you "I am tired" and you say to me "You are tired").[12] Moreover, it may be that an item of knowledge which can be expressed by one person in a certain proposition can only be expressed by another in a quite different proposition. For instance, I know, as Boswell knew, that Dr. Johnson was a great lexicographer; but, not having had the pleasure of being acquainted with the doctor, I cannot express that knowledge, as Boswell could, by saying "You are a great lexicographer." This seems to support the suggestion that there can be items of knowledge which an unchanging God can possess which nevertheless cannot be expressed by Him in ways in which a changing temporal being could and would express them.

Now can the distinction between an item of knowledge and the propositions which express it permit a solution to Kretzmann's problem along the lines suggested by Aquinas and Castañeda? If propositions are identified in the way suggested above, then it is clear that many propositions are significantly tensed: "It will rain" is a very different proposition from "It was raining," since one but not the other could be regarded as a translation of '*pluebat*'. If Aquinas's account is correct, then a difference of tenses must be regarded as an instance of a difference of expression involving no difference in the knowledge expressed, so that "It will rain" uttered before a particular shower and "It rained" uttered after can express a single item of information.

Some philosophers believe that all that we now say by the use of tenses could equally well be said in a language which contained no tenses, but whose sentences contained timeless verbs plus an explicit temporal reference or quantification over times. Thus a sentence "It will rain" uttered at time t_1 would on this view have to be understood as expressing a proposition to the following effect: at some time t later than t_1 it rains (timelessly). Prior has argued[13] that this reduction of tenses to times is impossible. For instance, the sense of "It will rain" could only be caught by an analysis such as "At some time later than t_1 it rains, and t_1 *is now*"; and "t_1 is now" cannot in its turn be given a timeless analysis.[14] If tensed sentences could be reduced to tenseless sentences containing quantification over times, then there would of course be no difficulty in admitting that their content could be known by an unchanging, and even a timeless, being. But since they cannot, the difficulty remains.

Neither Castañeda nor Aquinas is committed to the elimination of tensed expressions: nonetheless they claim to have a solution to the difficulty. Castañeda's solution to Kretzmann's problem is well summarized by Richard Swinburne, who accepts it as satisfactory, in the following passage:

A knows on 2 October the proposition 'it is now 2 October'. Surely B on 3 October can know that A knew what he did on 2 October. How can B report his knowledge? By words such as 'I know that A knew yesterday that it was then 2 October'. How can we report B's knowledge? As follows: B knew on 3 October that on the previous day A knew that it was then 2 October. Hence . . . B knows on 3 October what A knew on 2 October, although B will use different words to express the latter knowledge. In reporting B's knowledge of this item, we need a different referring expression to pick out the day of which being 2 October is predicated; but what is known is the same. . . . What A knows on 2 October and B knows on 3 October is that a certain day which can be picked out in many and various ways, according to our location in time, as 'today' or 'yesterday' or 'the day on which A thought that it was 2 October' (or even as '2 October') is 2 October.[15]

If this is correct, then an unchanging being can know the time and date and all that we know and express in tensed propositions.

The essential elements of the solution are these. "Today is Friday" (uttered on Friday) and "Yesterday was Friday" (uttered on Saturday) are indeed two different propositions, but both express the same item of knowledge. God's knowledge is not expressed in propositions, and so he can know the same item of knowledge permanently and unchangingly. It is only because we are temporal changing beings that we have to express the one item of knowledge first in one proposition and then in another.

The solution, however, is not wholly satisfactory. In the first place, it is incorrect to regard "Today" in "Today is Friday" as a referring expression picking out a day; it is no more a referring expression than is the "it" in the synonymous sentence "It is Friday today." Second, and more importantly, "Today is Friday" on Friday does not express the same knowledge as "Yesterday was Friday" on Saturday. This can be proved by the argument used by Prior in the passage quoted at the beginning of this chapter: what I am glad about when I am glad that today is Friday is not at all necessarily the same thing as what I am glad about when I am glad yesterday was Friday. Perhaps Friday is payday, on which I always go out for a massive carouse with my friends: when it is Friday, I am glad today is Friday, but during Saturday's hangover I am not at all glad that yesterday was Friday. Moreover, the power that the knowledge that it is Friday gives me on Friday (e.g., the power to keep engagements made for Friday) is quite different from the very limited power which is given me by Saturday's knowledge that yesterday was Friday if unaccompanied by the realization on Friday that it was indeed Friday.

It was an essential part of Aquinas's reconciliation of omniscience with immutability that God's knowledge was not exercised in thinking of, or uttering, propositions. For if God did indeed think in propositions, then knowledge such as knowledge of the time would undoubtedly involve change: the change, for instance, from thinking the true proposition "Now it is 12:50" to thinking the true proposition "Now it is 12:51." But there can be no general objection to the idea that someone may have a piece of knowledge without uttering, even in the privacy of the imagination, any proposition which expresses that knowledge: the great majority of the things we know at any given time is not, and could not all be, so expressed. What we know we *can* (barring impediments such as aphasia) express in propositions: but we are willing to attribute knowledge even to beings without language, as when we say that a cat knows that there is a mouse in the corner behind the skirting-board. There is not, to be sure, in the case of divine knowledge any obvious analogy to the behavior of animals on the basis of which we attribute animal knowledge; and this lack of analogy is not a trivial matter. But we might indeed imagine God giving even linguistic expression to knowledge of the time. We could perhaps conceive of a cosmic timekeeper on the model of the GPO speaking clock: a voice from the clouds that said, with unfailing regularity, sentences of the form, "Thus saith the Lord: at the third stroke it will be 12:52 precisely" followed by three crashes of thunder.

Even such a fantasy, it seems, would not give substance to the idea that a changeless being might know the time. Merely creating, at the beginning of the world, a cosmic apparatus of the appropriate kind, would not by itself constitute knowledge of the time: the GPO engineers and the voice who recorded the speaking clock are not, by virtue of that very fact, apprised of the correct time at every moment of the day. Whereas if we attribute to God in addition awareness of what the cosmic clock is saying at any given moment, we merely reawaken in fantastic form all the difficulties about changeless awareness of a changing world which we have been considering.

If a changeless being cannot know the time, then it cannot know either what is expressed by tensed propositions. Knowing that "Christ will be born" is true (roughly) throughout the years BC and that "Christ has been born" is true throughout the years AD will not—pace Aquinas—enable one to know which of these two propositions is true *now*, unless one also knows the date. Kretzmann's difficulty, then, is a serious one: it does not simply point to a tiny frivolous exception to an otherwise coherent claim that God knows everything that there is to be known. A believer in divine omniscience must, it seems, give up belief in divine immutability.[16]

NOTES

1. St. Thomas Aquinas, *Summa Theologiae*, Latin and English text, Blackfriars ed. London, 1963 (cited by number of part, question, and article), Ia, 13, 14.

2. Anthony Kenny, *Aquinas: A Collection of Critical Essays* (London, 1969), p. 264.

3. A. N. Prior, "The Formalities of Omniscience," *Philosophy* 37 (1962): 114–29.

4. Nelson Pike, *God and Timelessness* (London: Routledge and Kegan Paul, 1970).

5. Norman Kretzmann, "Omniscience and Immutability," *Journal of Philosophy* 63 (1966): 409–21.

6. P. T. Geach, *God and the Soul* (London: Routledge and Kegan Paul, 1969), p. 71.

7. Kretzmann, "Omniscience and Immutability," note 4.

8. H. N. Castañeda, "Omniscience and Indexical Reference," *Journal of Philosophy* 64 (1967): 203–10.

9. Aquinas, *Summa Theologiae*, Ia, 14, 15.

10. Ibid., Ia, IIae, 54, 2.

11. Aquinas's use of *oratio* versus *enuntiabile* seems to correspond to the distinction between *sentence* and *proposition* sketched above.

12. Some philosophers draw a distinction between propositions and statements. Thus E. J. Lemmon ("Sentences, Statements and Propositions," in *British Analytical Philosophy*, ed. B. A. O. Williams and A. Montefiore [London, 1966], pp. 87 ff.) suggests that we regard two propositions of subject-predicate form as making the same statement if the subject of each proposition has the same reference and the predicate the same extension. A statement, so defined, seems a rather strange entity. For instance the two propositions, "Richard Nixon is a greater philosopher than Plato and Aristotle put together" and "The Republican presidential candidate in the 1972 election was a politician wholly above reproach," would make the same statement, since the subjects refer to the same person and the extension of both predicates is the null class. Certainly my notion of an item of information differs from the notion of a statement, since unlike the latter it is not supposed to be identifiable in any merely extensional manner.

13. A. N. Prior, *Time and Modality* (Oxford, 1957), *Past, Present and Future* (Oxford, 1967), *Papers on Time and Tense* (Oxford, 1968).

14. 'Now' does not mean, e.g., "the time of utterance of this sentence" as is shown by the inscription on the monument in the desert, "Say, O stranger, if thou canst, the time of my inscribing"—an inscription which does not mean "what is the time now?" (I believe I owe this example to Professor P. T. Geach.)

15. Richard Swinburne, *The Coherence of Theism* (Oxford: Clarendon Press, 1977), p. 166.

16. In an interesting appendix, Kretzmann claims that human self-consciousness, as well as knowledge of time, presents a difficulty for omniscience. Each of us knows certain propositions about himself that no other person can know. When I know that Kretzmann is the author of "Omniscience and Immutability," I do not know the same item of knowledge as Kretzmann expresses by saying, "I am the author of 'Omniscience and Immutability'" because Kretzmann, if he became amnesiac, might lose the one piece of information while retaining the other. In his exposition Kretzmann alludes to Descartes: but his argument need not presuppose a Cartesian framework. Writing from a Wittgensteinian background, Professor G. E. M. Anscombe maintains that each of us can utter a genuine proposition 'I am this thing here', pointing to his or her own body ("The First Person," in Guttenplan, *Mind and Language* [London, 1975]). If this is a genuine proposition, it can presumably be known—but by each of us only in his own case. If Anscombe's view of first-person self-consciousness is correct, then Kretzmann's appendix does present another counterinstance to the claim that it is coherent to suppose that there is an omniscient being; but unlike the difficulty about change and time, this seems to me to call for only a trivial restatement of the traditional doctrine.

19

ON THE COMPOSSIBILITY OF THE DIVINE ATTRIBUTES
DAVID BLUMENFELD

Credo quia ineptum
Tertullian

R ecent proponents of the ontological argument have learned an important
lesson from Leibniz: the argument requires the assumption, or premise,
that God is possible. In one form or another, this premise appears in the
versions of the argument endorsed by Hartshorne, Malcolm, and Plantinga.[1] But
Leibniz's lesson has not been taken fully to heart by his modern followers. He
thinks that to bring the argument to a triumphant conclusion one needs to *prove*
that God is possible. For without this proof, we have no assurance that the idea
of God is noncontradictory.[2] So Leibniz struggled—vainly, I think—to produce
two proofs of the possibility of God.[3] His modern followers, however, have on
the whole simply assumed the truth of the critical premise.[4] The fact that there
has been relatively little effort to show that the concept of God is not coherent
probably contributes to whatever plausibility this procedure has.[5] But, plausible
or not, the procedure is mistaken. The concept of God is contradictory—as I shall
argue shortly. Establishing this would have consequences that go beyond the
ontological argument: the entire edifice of orthodox natural theology would fall
at a stroke.[6]

In arguing that the idea of God is contradictory, it is important to be clear
about *what* idea of God I have in mind. My target is the standard Judeo-Chris-

---

From *Philosophical Studies* 34 (1978): 91–103. Copyright © 1978 by Kluwer Academic Publishers.
Reprinted with kind permission from Kluwer Academic Publishers.

tian theological conception of divinity, a being who is by definition absolutely perfect. 'Absolute perfection' is to be taken in a sense strong enough to involve the properties of omniscience, omnipotence, and complete moral goodness. The idea of an absolutely perfect being is that of one who knows all things, has unrestricted power, possesses the maximum amount of virtue, and is free of any sort of defect or limitation. There have been other accounts of deity, and the argument I am going to propose does not apply to all of them. One cannot refute, with a single argument, the existence of such diverse Gods as have been conceived. God has, for example, sometimes been said to be limited in his power or finite in some other way. Those who are content with such a deity need not be concerned with the present argument. God has also sometimes been identified with the universe (or at other times with 'Being Itself'). But it is, of course, not my aim to show that the idea of the universe contains a contradiction. My argument concerns nothing less than the greatest deity which has ever been conceived, and my purpose is to show that this deity has not been conceived coherently.

It will be instructive to ask, initially, what would be required if one were trying to prove the *possibility* of God. To accomplish this, one would need to do two things. First, one would have to show that each perfection has an intrinsic maximum. It is supposed to be essential to divinity to be unsurpassably great. Therefore, to establish God's possibility one would need to show that there is no great-making characteristic which is such that for any amount of it one possessed, it would be logically possible to possess more. Second, one who sought to prove the possibility of God would have to show that all the perfections—in their maximum—are compossible. Not only must there *be* a maximum of knowledge, power, goodness, and so on; there must be no contradiction in the idea of a single being's possessing these properties at once. These requirements suggest two corresponding avenues for proving the impossibility of God. One could show that there is some perfection which has no intrinsic maximum, or one could prove that there are perfections which could not be possessed, in the ultimate degree, by a single being. It is the latter strategy which I shall employ. I shall argue that maximal knowledge and power are not compossible. Since a critical point in the argument turns on the elucidation of the idea of omniscience, let me begin there.

I

Knowledge is a good thing, a perfection. There is no state of knowledge, which, qua knowledge, is bad or merely neutral in value. This is a thesis that has been held by most theological writers, and it is one which makes great sense. Apart from being intuitively appealing, however, it is a view which is basic to the traditional conception of God, and it cannot be given up without relinquishing that concept. If knowledge as such were not a good thing it would not follow from the nature of God as an absolutely perfect being that he is omniscient. But what is an omniscient being? It is one who has unsurpassable knowledge. To have this degree of knowledge one would have to have an utter and complete comprehension of the meaning of every significant proposition. If there were any significant proposition, any part of the meaning of which a being did not comprehend, his knowledge clearly could be greater. To enjoy a state of omniscience, however, one would have to know considerably more than just this. To be *all*-knowing one would have to know of every true proposition that it is true and of every false proposition that it is false. If a being fully understood the meaning of every proposition, but failed to know the truth value of even one of these propositions, his knowledge, again, clearly could be greater. But if there were a being who fully comprehended the meaning of every significant proposition and who also knew of the true that it is true, and the false that it is false, this being would surely possess an understanding unlimited in its scope. He would be omniscient.

The first step in my argument is to show that there are certain concepts for which a full and complete comprehension requires experience. I shall then go on to argue that in the case of at least some of these concepts the experience which is required is of a type which an omnipotent being could not possibly have. Since a being who did not fully comprehend the meaning of every significant proposition would not be omniscient, it will follow that omniscience and omnipotence are not properties which are compossible.

Now it is evident that there are concepts which one could not understand *completely* if he had never had experience of an instance or exemplification of the concept in question. This is a thesis which is sometimes labeled 'concept-empiricism', and it is important to see that I am going to rely on it in an extremely restricted form. The doctrine has been put forward in a variety of different degrees of strength, and I believe that all but the most restricted is false. For example, one would be a concept-empiricist if he held the following view: for every concept, in order to comprehend it, one must have experienced an instance or exemplification of it. This doctrine is palpably false. One can surely understand the concept *aardvark* without having had the pleasure of the acquaintance of the beast. A considerably more plausible version of concept-empiricism is this: for every concept, in order to comprehend it, one must have experienced an instance or exemplification of each of its 'elements'. The idea behind this view is familiar. To have the concept *aardvark* without being acquainted with an actual aardvark, it would be enough to have experienced (separately) something mammalian, something with an extensile tongue, something with sharp claws, a heavy tail, and so on. Or, it would do to have had the experience, not of these things, but of their elements. From the elements one could construct the concept *aardvark* by appropriate mental operations. Now, I am inclined to think that this theory is mistaken, too. But if anyone believes it is correct, that is so much the better for my argument, which requires a view that is considerably weaker than this one.

The thesis I rely on is this: for *some* concepts, in order to *fully* comprehend them, one must have had the experience of an instance or exemplification of them. This version of concept-empiricism seems to me to be as obviously true as it is obvious that the very strong version of it is false. There is a host of concepts which require experience for their complete comprehension. Take the concept of the sensation of red. Surely one could not fully grasp this notion if he had never had an experience of redness. I do not say that he needs to experience a red *object*. He might come to understand the concept by pushing his eyeball and getting the appropriate sensation in that way. But I do say that without any acquaintance with redness, one could not fully comprehend *the sensation of red*. The reason for this is that part of the meaning of the concept consists of a certain subjective experience. One who failed to fully understand what this experience is like would thus lack a perfect grasp of its concept. But there is only one way of fully understanding what an experience of redness is like and that is to have it. There is in principle no access which allows a complete comprehension of an experience except having the experience itself. It is, therefore, a necessary truth that if someone had never experienced redness, there would be at least one concept whose meaning he did not fully understand.

I am not denying that such a person could know a large number of true propositions about the sensation of red. He could know, for example, that it is produced under conditions Q, R, and S; that it is correlated with (or, on some views contingently identical to) brain states of types X, Y, and Z; and so on. Perhaps it could be said that this information would give him a partial grasp of *the sensation of red*. But he could not have an *absolutely complete* grasp of this concept without having had the sensation itself.

Many philosophers would maintain that God does not know by experience and that he does not have an acquaintance with sensuous contents such as red. One argument that has been offered is that God's perfection entails that he is immutable and that, as such, he is not subject to the changes involved in the process of experience. This thesis may be correct and though many have held it, few have been willing to draw from it the conclusion that God is not omniscient.[7] Yet this conclusion does follow from the thesis. For if it is true that God cannot have any experiences, then there are concepts (viz., those that *require* experience) whose full comprehension he is barred from having. But this line of argument would need considerable defense and I shall not rest my case upon it. I use the example of the sensation of red merely to support weak concept-empiricism. For my purposes it can be allowed that God can have this experience and hence that he can also have a full understanding of its concept.

Granting this, however, there are without doubt *some* experiences which God is precluded from having. For certain experiences are possible only if the subject believes that he is limited in power. Since these experiences are required for a full grasp of a number of concepts, it follows that a being who is omnipotent cannot also be omniscient. To make this out, let us first consider some experiences which God could not have. Fear, frustration, and despair are a few examples. The reason I offer for denying that God ever could be subject to these states is not simply that they are experiences. It is rather that their occurrence depends logically on the subject's believing in the limitation of his power. It is important to observe that none of these states is a mere sensation (like an itch or a stinging pain), which could occur in the absence of certain special beliefs that one had. To experience fear, one would have to believe that he was in danger, that he might somehow be harmed. If one did not in any sense believe this, then no sensation he was having—no cold chill, no sinking feeling in the pit of the stomach— would count as fear. One's experiences would be mere sensations—and nothing more. Without the belief in danger these states would have to be described in terms other than those which imply that the person is afraid. A similar account can be given of frustration and of despair. There could be no experience of frustration without the belief that one had been (was being, or might be) thwarted. There could be no sense of despair unless one faced a situation he took to be dire and for which he believed he was very unlikely to find a remedy. Furthermore, one who has not undergone these states would not know what it is like to experience them. Consequently he would not have a full understanding of *fear*, *frustration*, and *despair*. One who had never experienced fear, for example, would lack a complete comprehension of *fear*, just as a man who was blind from birth would lack a full grasp of *the sensation of red*.

My point should now be clear. For what has an omnipotent being to fear? There is no destruction, no harm, nor the slightest diminution of his power that could possibly befall him. In this case (since he knows the extent of his power), he could not believe himself to be endangered, and thus could not have the experience of fear. But if he could not have this experience, he lacks a full appreciation of *fear*. Any proposition involving this concept will be one at least a part of whose meaning he does not comprehend. He is therefore not omniscient.

Similarly, how could an absolutely perfect and omnipotent being experience frustration? He is all-powerful, and so there is no conceivable obstacle to his will. Whatever he wills, he accomplishes. There is nothing which could conceivably thwart him or interfere with his divine plan. Since he knows this, there is nothing which could provide him with the occasion to feel frustration. But then he lacks a full comprehension of *frustration,* and so once again fails of omniscience.

The same can be said of despair. He who is incapable of being thwarted and who possesses the power to remedy any situation is of necessity beyond the experience of despair. And for this reason again there is something he cannot fully understand, something he cannot know.

The concepts I have mentioned are only a few in a large family of notions which an omnipotent being could not entirely understand. In general, for every experience whose occurrence presupposes a person's belief that he is lacking in power, there is a concept of which God cannot have complete comprehension. *Embarrassment, apprehensiveness, forlornness*, and *regret* are all further notions of this type. In view of this, there appears to be a great deal that an omnipotent being could not understand.

II

There are three possible strategies for attempting to refute my argument. First, one might deny that the kind of experience which God is barred from having is required for knowledge of the concepts I have mentioned. Second, he might concede that this experience is required but deny that God must have a full grasp of every concept in order to be absolutely perfect. Third, he might give reasons for supposing God *can* have the kind of experience (and consequently the knowledge) which I have said is not open to him. I will take up each of these strategies in turn.

Let us look at the possibilities for developing the first one. If it were not necessary to have the experience of fear, frustration, and despair to have a full comprehension of the concepts of these states, my argument would fail. But, as I have already tried to show, the experience *is* required. One who had never felt afraid would necessarily lack what might be called an 'existential appreciation' of fear. Yet there is one venerable doctrine which denies that any such existential appreciation is even a partial component of knowledge: platonism. For the platonist, knowledge is purely intellectual (and not sensuous) apprehension. Whatever is known, is known by grasping abstract Ideas or Forms. Experience may stimulate us to recollect these Forms, but that is all. It is in no way essential to knowledge.

I concede that if platonism were true, this would destroy my position. But platonism (or at any rate the extreme version of it required here) is false. Because this theory has long since been reduced to a totally antique system of thought, I shall not treat it as a live option. Should anyone think that it is wrong to dismiss this view so cursorily I cannot attempt to satisfy him now. Ultimately, I should have to repeat arguments which have already been repeated for centuries, and which would be out of place to review in this context.

Not every doctrine which would undercut my position is antique, however. Modern philosophical behaviorism is at odds with it too. According to this theory there is no such thing as the *experience* of fear, frustration, and despair over and above a set of complex dispositions to behave in certain ways. But to fully comprehend a disposition to behave, one need not have had this disposition himself. So, to fully comprehend fear, God need not be afraid. Nor need he ever be frustrated or despairing in order to understand the concepts of these states. If the behaviorist account is correct, one can have a purely intellectual understanding of all psychological concepts.

Now I grant that the behaviorist will not be impressed by my proof of the impossibility of God. But this fact can be of no comfort to the theist, since behaviorism itself provides a proof of the impossibility of God. If this theory were true, then to have any thoughts, or other mental states, God would have to have a body. On the behaviorist view, the notion of a pure spirit is every bit as much an absurdity as the idea of a purely subjective experience. In accepting behaviorism, then, one surrenders the right to believe in the immateriality of God. As traditionally conceived, however, the absolute perfection of God requires that he be immaterial. For God's perfection is taken to exclude even the logical possibility of deterioration—a feature which is essential to material things. Thus, behaviorism provides a way of denying a premise of my argument but not of evading its conclusion. It is not a theory which leaves the concept of God intact.[8]

Another way of trying to get around my argument is through the doctrine of analogy. This theory cautions us not to suppose that God possesses the traits of knowledge, power, and goodness in the same sense as we do. Since God has these traits only in an analogical sense, there is no license to infer that his knowledge has such and such features from the fact that knowledge as we commonly understand it has these features. Yet didn't I make just this sort of inference? I said that in order to understand *despair*, God would have to be despairing. And I based this on the claim that we humans cannot fully comprehend this concept in any other way.

In fact, however, this rebuttal misrepresents my argument. I did not make an inference from the limits of our knowledge to the limits of God's knowledge. I argued, rather, that it is in principle impossible for anyone—human or divine—to fully grasp *despair* without having had an experience of despair. And, I tried to show that God could not have this experience, since he is precluded from having the beliefs on which it is predicated. The theist cannot counter this merely by asserting that God knows things in a way which is different from, but analogous to, ours. To refute my argument he must explicate the analogy, making clear how God can fully appreciate *despair*, and so forth, without ever being despairing.

The first suggestion that comes to mind is that God gains this appreciation by having an experience which is analogous to the ones we are discussing. As we have seen, however, the experience of despair requires the belief that one faces a situation that he cannot remedy. Is it the case that God comprehends despair by having a belief which is analogous to this one? What would such a belief be? If it were of the same sort as ours it would be false: God can remedy any situation. In that case we seem forced to conclude that God has a belief which is analogous to a false one. Yet it is not clear that any sense can be attached to this idea. For what would a belief be which did not have the property *being false* but instead had the property *being analogous to being false*?

Perhaps this is not the correct way of constructing the analogy. Possibly the idea is that God is in a state which is like despair but which involves no beliefs. The concept of despair, however, is so intimately tied to a belief in the hopelessness of one's situation that it is not obvious what to make of this suggestion either. And, even if we could make sense of it, the problem would remain that the experience of despair is a sign of imperfection. We should then apparently have to suppose that God knows *despair* by being in a condition analogous to something imperfect. Yet only pure perfections can be attributed to God, and so it is not evident how this would be possible.

Another alternative is that God does not know *despair* through an experience, but through something analogous to an experience. This suggestion, however, is no easier to understand than the ones that have preceded it. It is altogether obscure how an experience could be analogous to a nonexperience. Although further problems could be enumerated, I think the ones already at hand strongly suggest the unlikelihood of our constructing a clear analogy here at all.

III

The second strategy is to argue that although the experience of states like fear is necessary for a comprehension of their correlative concepts, it is not required that God have the concepts in order to be absolutely perfect. An argument in behalf of this thesis is as follows. I have claimed that one who knows that he is all-powerful cannot be afraid and for that reason cannot have a full grasp of concepts such as *fear*. If this argument is correct, however, it follows that anyone who has a full grasp of *fear,* and so forth, is less than absolutely perfect. But then, it seems, the possession of such concepts cannot be a necessary condition of one's being absolutely perfect. For surely it cannot be a necessary condition of one's *being perfect* that he be in a state which would guarantee that he is less than perfect. Consequently, there is no reason to suppose that God must have a full grasp of the concepts on which I have based my case.

The problem with this argument is that it begs the question. To infer that God need not possess certain concepts because their possession signifies a defect assumes that their possession could not also be required for absolute perfection. It assumes, in other words, that God is possible. After all, if the lack of these concepts signified a defect too, then God would be imperfect in either case. And this is precisely what the argument I gave was designed to show: imperfection of one kind or another follows whether God has concepts like *fear* or lacks them.

What would have to be established to make the present line of response work is that while God's possession of the critical concepts would imply a defect in him, his failure to possess them would not. Within the limits of the current strategy, however, there is no way to argue this effectively. The second strategy—unlike the first—concedes that experience of a sort which God cannot have is required for the full possession of certain concepts. But if knowledge per se is a perfection, then anything less than full comprehension of every concept constitutes an epistemic defect in a being.

Of course, it might conceivably be denied that knowledge per se is a perfection. This would allow one to maintain that a perfect being need not have a complete grasp of every concept, and on this basis one might argue that God's perfection does not require that he fully understand the notions which are in dispute. As I noted earlier, however, this would have the undesirable consequence of robbing God of his essential omniscience. If knowledge per se were not a perfection, God's total and complete knowledge would not follow from his definition as absolutely perfect being.[9]

A remaining option is to argue that a being is *better*, all in all, if he is omnipotent, and thus lacks certain concepts, than he would be if he had a full grasp of every concept but were to some extent impotent. This might be thought to show that the most perfect being does not need to have a full understanding of every concept. Now I do not know what good reason could be offered for ranking power over knowledge in the scale of perfection. But in any case it is clear that this particular ploy is flawed in the same way as the last. Even if power were better than knowledge, the maneuver would divest God of his omniscience, thus leaving us without the traditional notion of deity.

IV

The third way of attacking my position is to argue that God actually can have the sorts of experiences which I have said are precluded by his perfect nature. The reason that I offered for thinking that God could not have the experience of fear, and so on, is that his power is absolute, and knowing this, he would be incapable of having the beliefs on which this experience is founded. One might hope to undo my argument by showing that God is capable of having the requisite beliefs after all. The problem, however, is that the presence of these beliefs is itself indicative of imperfection; if God is omnipotent, the beliefs are *false*. So, there seems to be no way of imagining God's having these beliefs without being tainted by the imperfection that accompanies them.

It might seem more promising to attack the contention that a belief in one's own vulnerability or weakness is required for experiences like fear, frustration, and despair. Perhaps it will be said that, although these experiences are normally accompanied by such beliefs, the beliefs are not logically presupposed by the experiences. Fear might be thought to be a good case in point. Normally, one feels afraid only if he believes himself to be in danger. But occasionally, it seems, one experiences fear even when he does not believe himself to be in danger, when in fact, he knows he is completely safe. For example, I may be terribly afraid when I ride the ferris wheel, though I know perfectly well that there is no real danger. Or, sometimes when I am alone at night, I may feel a sudden uneasiness, a sense of fear without any apparent reason. I know that I am not in danger, for I am at home, snug in bed. The doors are bolted and the neighborhood is a very safe one. I am aware that no harm is imminent, and yet I am afraid. These examples seem to indicate that we can on occasion be afraid without believing in the existence of danger. If this is possible in our case, then an omnipotent being should also be able to experience fear without being subject to the false belief that he is danger.

I do not think this objection is correct. Consider again the examples that were offered in support of the idea that there can be fear without belief in danger. In both of these, the suggestion was made that since I know that I am not in danger, and yet experience fear, there can be fear without a belief in danger. The reasoning is that it follows from the fact that I know that I am not in danger that I believe that I am not in danger. This much is correct. But it does not follow from the fact that I believe that I am not in danger that I do not *also* believe (in some way, or at some level) that I *am* in danger. If someone who rides with me on the ferris wheel tries to calm me with the assurance that there is no danger, I would be very likely to respond, "I know I won't be hurt, but I just can't shake the idea that I might fall." Similarly, my belief in the safety of my home does not rule out the possibility of my having a concurrent belief in my endangered position. Indeed, in both cases, if we do not make the assumption that I harbor such a belief, we will be left without the necessary grounds for describing my experience as fear. My belief in danger may not be my "official" belief, or one which I would take to be well founded. It may not be one which I can easily discern or readily avow. But it is one I must have, if I am to be afraid.

The answer to the objection then is this: we can be afraid even though we know we are in no danger because it is possible for us to have inconsistent beliefs. But obviously there is no similar option for explaining how God can be afraid. A being with an absolutely perfect intellect must be incapable of having any false beliefs. A fortiori, he must be incapable of having inconsistent beliefs.

Another reply to my argument is that an infinite being can experience all of the states which I deny. He has only to become finite, as God did in Christ.

Through the incarnation, God achieved a full grasp of all the concepts involving finitude. This reply, however, presupposes the coherence of faith and does not supply an argument in its behalf. Judged as an answer rather than as a defiant expression of belief, it has no merit. If God is incapable of limitation, then he cannot become finite. To suggest that he *has* done so, without any explanation of the possibility of the miraculous act, is not to advance the case in any way.[10] In response it is sometimes said that while we cannot comprehend how the infinite makes itself finite, we can comprehend that there is no contradiction involved in the idea. But this, again, is assertion without substantiation. Is it the very same being who is at once both finite and infinite, limited in his powers and infinite? Or is it a different being? If it is a different being, the problem is not resolved. If it is the same being, the contradiction is apparent. It is sometimes said that there is no contradiction in the same being's (i.e., substance's) having two natures or essences. Perhaps not, provided that these two natures are logically compatible. But where the natures are such that one entails that the substance is omnipotent and infinite, while the other entails that it is limited in its power and finite, the situation is altogether different.

It seems to me, then, that there is a very strong case for supposing that the traditional concept of God is contradictory. Unless someone can show that there is something wrong with the argument I have given, I think it is fair to say that orthodox theists have a rather serious problem on their hands.[11]

NOTES

1. Charles Hartshorne, chap. 9 in *Man's Vision of God* (Chicago, 1941). Norman Malcolm, "Anselm's Ontological Arguments," *The Philosophical Review* 69 (1960): 41–62. Alvin Plantinga, chap. 10 in *The Nature of Necessity* (Oxford: Clarendon Press, 1974).

2. E.g., G. W. Leibniz, *New Essays Concerning Human Understanding,* trans. A. G. Langley (LaSalle, 1949), p. 504, and *The Philosophical Works of Leibniz,* trans. G. M. Duncan (New Haven, 1890), pp. 50–51 and 140–45.

3. Cf. Leibniz, *New Essays,* p. 714, and *The Philosophical Works,* pp. 145–46.

4. This is true of Malcolm and Plantinga, but not of Hartshorne, who has given an elaborate defense of the coherence of his own conception of God. His notion of deity differs from the one attacked in this essay, however. References listed in note 1.

5. Some exceptions should be noted. For example, see J. N. Findlay, "Can God's Existence Be Disproved?" *Mind* 57 (1948): 176–83, and Norman Kretzmann, "Omniscience and Immutability," *Journal of Philosophy* 63 (1966): 409–21. Charles Hartshorne has also argued at numerous places that the classical conception of God is contradictory.

6. The qualification "orthodox" is important here. Heterodox natural theology—including variants of the ontological argument—would remain possible.

7. Kretzmann, "Omniscience and Immutability," does draw this conclusion, though his reasons are quite different from the ones offered here.

8. It is of interest to note that the platonist and the behaviorist reject my position for opposite reasons. For the behaviorist, subjective experience is too ethereal to be real. For the platonist, it is insufficiently ethereal to be *fully* real or to constitute any part of true knowledge.

9. This maneuver would also place the theist in the following embarrassing position: it would force him to admit that in creating this world—which contains abundant amounts of fear, frustration, and the like—God did not fully understand what he was doing.

10. The present strategy also involves the theist in heresy. If God can only fully comprehend *fear*, etc., by becoming finite, then the incarnation was not an act of grace. It was logically required to secure divine omniscience.

11. This paper is an offshoot of a project, the research for which was supported by a fellowship from the National Endowment for the Humanities. For helpful discussions of the issues dealt with here, I wish to thank Louis Mackey, Laurence BonJour, Jean Beer Blumenfeld, and Charles Hartshorne.

20

A DISPROOF OF THE GOD
OF THE COMMON MAN

MICHAEL MARTIN

In this paper I present a disproof of the existence of the God believed in by many ordinary men. My disproof does not disprove the existence of God in all senses of the ambiguous term 'God'. But no disproof does this. For instance, even if it is sound, what one might call the disproof of God's existence from the problem of evil[1] presumably does not show that God does not exist when 'God' refers to some being that is either not omnipotent or not completely benevolent. Again, the so-called Ontological Disproof of God,[2] even if sound, does not show that God does not exist when 'God' refers to some being that is less than perfect.

In order to tell what relevance such disproofs have for ordinary people's belief in God, one must discern what the ordinary concept of God is. But this is sometimes difficult. We have a good idea of what professional philosophers and theologians mean by 'God' but what the theologically and philosophically unsophisticated mean by 'God' is often not so clear. For instance, it is not so obvious to me that most ordinary people in our culture who believe in God believe that God is a Perfect Being. One suspects that many religious believers have a more limited or modest view of God. If this is so, the above-mentioned disproofs of the existence of God, even if sound, could hardly touch many people's religious convictions.

My disproof of the existence of God does, I believe, refute a belief in God that is based on a common concept of God, a notion of God that many ordinary

From *Question* 7 (1974): 115–24. Copyright © 1974 by the Rationalist Press Association. Reprinted by permission of the Rationalist Press Association, www.rationalist.org.uk.

people hold—although I am willing to admit that this God may not be the God of professional philosophers or theologians. (The concept of God presumed in my disproof is not a Perfect Being and differs from the standard academic notion in other ways.) Thus, I will argue that 'God' in one sense that is widely accepted in nonacademic circles is self-contradictory and that God in this sense cannot therefore exist. I will first give a rather informal exposition of the disproof, then I will give a more formal version. Finally, I will defend the disproof against possible objections.

INFORMAL STATEMENT OF THE DISPROOF

The ordinary man seems to believe that God is the most moral being in the universe. (Whether he believes that God is morally perfect we need not decide.) Part of this belief of the ordinary man is that God does not have certain kinds of feelings. Although God may have the feeling of anger, God does not have the feelings of lust or envy. Moreover, part of this ordinary concept of God is that God knows more than anyone else. (Again, whether the ordinary man believes that God knows everything we leave as an open question.) In particular the ordinary man supposes that God knows (at least) all that men know. However, these two beliefs, once correctly understood, are logically incompatible. Let me explain.

Philosophers in talking about God's knowledge almost invariably equate God's knowledge with what has been called propositional knowledge or knowledge that something is the case. This intellectual view of God does not seem to be shared by the common man. On his view God's knowledge includes other types of knowledge as well. The plain man certainly supposes that God knows how to do many things, and he does not mean by this that God knows that certain things should be done in such and such a way; he believes that God has certain skills (procedural knowledge), that is, at least all those skills that men have.

Moreover, it is not obvious that ordinary people suppose that man's or God's knowledge is exhausted by knowledge that and knowledge how. There is a use of 'know' in ordinary parlance which cannot be reduced to knowledge that or knowledge how. When one says "I know Smith," one does not ordinarily mean merely that one has certain propositional or procedural knowledge concerning Smith. Usually what is at least suggested is that one has met Smith. In other expressions of the form "Person P knows X," the meaning is changed only slightly. When one says "Jones knows sorrow," one does not usually mean only that Jones knows that sorrow results in such and such behavior or that sorrow is caused in such and such a way. One is usually suggesting rather that Jones has had the experience of sorrow. The same thing goes for the expression "He has known lust" or "He has known envy." A person who knows lust and envy has at least had the feeling of lust or envy. Since God has all of men's knowledge and more, He must know lust and envy. But to say God has known lust and envy is to say that God has had the feelings of lust and envy. But this is incompatible with God's moral goodness. Hence God does not exist.

Formal Proof

Premise (1)

If God exists, God has not had the feelings of lust or envy.

Premise (2)

If God exists, God exists as a being who knows at least everything man knows.

Premise (3)

If God exists as a being who knows at least everything man knows, God knows lust and envy.

Premise (4)

If God knows lust and envy, God has had the feelings of lust and envy.

Premise (5)

God exists.
    By hypothesis.

Conclusion (6)

∴God has had and has not had the feelings of lust and envy.
    By (1)–(5).

Conclusion (7)

∴ God does not exist.
    By (5) & (6) QED.

OBJECTIONS TO THE DISPROOF

Objection (1)

God's moral goodness does not concern His feelings; rather it concerns His action and the principle of His action. Thus premise (1) is false.

Answer

Now it is true that sometimes in judging the moral quality of a person, one takes account only of his action and the principle of his action. A person who did good deeds all his life and who acted on moral principles would normally be considered a good person. But still we would consider such a person better if there were not envy or lust in his heart. In any case, it is inconceivable to the ordinary religious believer that God's good action and purpose should hide His feelings of lust and envy. People demand that in God *at least*—who is their moral ideal— the feelings of lust and envy should not exist.

Objection (2)

If God had the feelings of lust and envy and these affected Him, this would indeed detract from His moral goodness. However, God, because of His great powers need not let these feelings affect Him. Thus premise (1) is false.

Answer

It is difficult to know what 'affect Him' means here. Envy and lust are feelings that must affect the person who has them. One need not succumb to such feelings to be affected by them. By definition they do have some effect, that is, these feelings involve certain strivings in the person who has them. Just because God may never be overcome by these feelings is not enough. The mere fact that He has had them would take away from His moral goodness on the common view.

Moreover, unless God sometimes *did* succumb to envy or lust, this would detract from His knowledge and He would know less than some men. To say Jones has known succumbing to lust is presumably to say that Jones once experienced this succumbing himself, that is, he once succumbed. If God lacked this knowledge, He would know less than Jones in one respect at least.

Objection (3)

God's knowledge is only propositional knowledge. Thus premise (3) is false.

Answer

This argument seems to me to be mistaken at least as far as a common view of God goes. Indeed, I would argue that the more personal a view of God one has—and most ordinary people have a very personal view of God—the more mistaken this retort is. People who tend to think of God as a person naturally tend to think of Him as having many characteristics of persons and this includes the sort of knowledge that persons have. And this knowledge includes more than propositional knowledge.

Objection (4)

Since God is all-powerful He can know lust and envy without having the feelings of envy and greed. Thus premise (4) is false.

Answer

As I have already mentioned, I am skeptical that philosophers have adequately characterized the ordinary notion of God and thus I am not sure that omnipotence is a property that most people predicate of God. But, in any case, as I understand the expression "He has known lust," it would be logically impossible for God to have known lust and not have had the feeling of lust. Presumably, even on the academic notion of God, God cannot do what is logically impossible.

Objection (5)

Your argument is in fact a very ancient and well-worn objection and neglects the classical replies that have been made to it. Thus your argument is without merit.

Answer

It is true that an argument similar to mine is found in classical literature. The classical reply to such an argument was usually to point out that God's knowledge of lust and envy need not involve having these feelings. This answer is sufficient in the classical context to refute the argument since the traditional philosophical and theological intellectual notion of God was at issue. In this context only propositional knowledge was relevant. But in the present context such an answer is not sufficient since this traditional philosophical and theological notion of God is not under consideration. We are considering the existence of God of the ordinary man. Here the ordinary sense of 'know' is relevant. And in one ordinary sense of 'know' one does not know lust or envy unless one has experienced lust and envy. Thus, my disproof is not in fact an ancient and well-worn objection that neglects the classical replies.

Objection (6)

This argument, even if sound, refutes the belief in God of the unsophisticated person. But it is hardly surprising that such a person's view of God is inconsistent and that God in *this* sense does not exist. Hence, this argument is philosophically uninteresting.

Answer

I have refuted a belief in God held by many philosophically unsophisticated people, and this view of God may not correspond very well to what philosophers have meant by God. Nevertheless, this does not take away from the interest of the disproof. First of all, it may not be surprising that a common view of God is false. But that such a view is *logically* false is surely surprising—just as surprising as if one showed that people's ordinary view of morality or space was inconsistent. (One does not suppose these concepts are self-contradictory in ordinary thinking, although one may suppose they are unclear, ambiguous, and confused.) Second, it seems to me that part of a philosopher's job (but surely not all) is to analyze and critically evaluate the views of people who are not philosophically sophisticated. This fact has been recognized at least since Socrates. Thus, my disproof of God in the ordinary sense of 'God' does have some philosophical interest.

Objection (7)

There is no reason to suppose your analysis of God captures the ordinary sense of 'God' in our culture. In order to determine this, sociological and anthropological evidence of a certain kind would be necessary. Since you do not produce such evidence, one can well remain skeptical of your disproof of ordinary people's belief in God.

Answer

It is true that I have not appealed to sociological or anthropological evidence to justify my thesis. No such evidence is available at the present time. The evidence that is available to me does suggest that I am correct. More reliable evidence when it is produced may change my mind. Meanwhile, one can at least evaluate the disproof hypothetically. One can ask: if this concept of God is the one implicit in ordinary thinking, is it true that God as is ordinarily conceived does not exist? The answer, as I have tried to show, is yes.

Objection (8)

The argument assumes that there is a fundamental difference in the ordinary concept of God and the theologian's concept of God. Thus, it is maintained in the argument that on the theologian's view God's knowledge is restricted to propositional knowledge, whereas on the ordinary man's view God's knowledge is not so restricted. However, the ordinary man's view of God is a function of what church he belongs to and the theological views of the church. The theological views of the church are in turn a function of the leading theologians associated with the church. Thus the ordinary Catholic holds a view of God influenced by the Catholic Church, which is influenced by the views of leading Catholic theologians; the ordinary Protestant holds a view of God associated with the Protestant Church, which in turn is influenced by famous Protestant theologians and so on. Consequently, a fundamental assumption of the argument is false and the argument is unsound.

Answer

It is no doubt the case that the view of God held by ordinary men is in part a function of the church to which they belong and the views of the theologians associated with that church. But what does not seem to be the case is that the ordinary man's view of God is nothing more or less than the views of the theologians. Simplification and popularization occur in the propagation of abstract theological doctrine to the masses.

The churches themselves sometimes simplify and popularize theological doctrines, and ordinary men, in attempting to understand these views, tend to simplify and popularize them even more. Ordinary men tend to understand God in ways that are familiar to them despite the protests of theologians and intellectual ministers. As a result, God tends to be conceived of in the image of a man—a man much more powerful, moral, knowledgeable, and so on than ordinary men. Thus, there is some reason to suppose that there is a crucial difference between the views of the theologians associated with a particular religion and the views of the common man who is a member of that religion.

Objection (9)

The argument assumes that God, in order to know what man knows, must know envy and lust, that is, He must have the feeling of envy and lust. However, God could know envy and lust empathetically; there is no need for God to be envious or lustful in order to have these feelings. Just as a great writer can create certain emotions in his readers—emotions that are quite alien to the readers by inducing them to identify empathetically with some character in his story—so God, who is free of envy and lust, can create the feeling of envy and lust in Himself by empathetic identification with envious and lustful men without being lustful and envious Himself. Thus God can know envy and lust without moral taint; consequently premise (1) is false.

Answer

The objection assumes that there is a distinction between knowing envy or lust empathetically and knowing envy or lust nonempathetically. The crucial question is what this distinction is. Presumably both ways of knowing lust and envy involve having feelings of lust and envy. What then is the difference?

Now it might be suggested that empathetic feelings are not as strong as nonempathetic ones. It is not clear that this is so. But if it is, it suggests a counter to this objection. One who empathizes with a lustful person will not know lust in its strongest form; consequently, God as an empathizer will not know as much as some men who have strong feelings of lust. On the other hand, if empathetic feelings of lust are as strong as nonempathetic feelings, then why is God not morally tainted by His empathizing?

Another suggestion is that the difference between knowing lust and envy empathetically and nonempathetically lies in the results. When one knows lust nonempathetically, this generally results in one striving for some object. However, when one knows lust empathetically one need not strive for any object. This interpretation of the difference between nonempathetic knowing and empathetic knowing has the following problem however: the empathizer will not know a feeling of lust that results in striving for the object lusted after. Consequently, God as an empathizer will not know as much as someone who does know such feelings. If, on the other hand, empathetic knowledge results in striving for an object, why is God not morally tainted by His empathizing?

A general point can be abstracted from the above two counters to the objection. Either empathetic knowledge of lust and envy is similar in all relevant respects to nonempathetic knowledge or it is not. If it is, then if God knows lust and envy empathetically, He is morally tainted; if it is not, then God does not in His empathetic knowledge know as much as some men do.

Objection (10)

The argument is very misleading. For as the argument is set up, it looks as if certain moral feelings are crucial to it. But this is not so. The argument would work with very trivial and nonmoral examples. For example, God does not know (in the sense at issue in the argument) dirt underneath His fingernails. However, this is hardly interesting. It merely shows that God is not human.

Answer

In my argument I show there is a contradiction between ordinary people's idea of God as a moral ideal and people's idea of what God knows. It is not clear that a contradiction can be shown using the nonmoral example mentioned in the objection. Presumably, the basic idea of the objection is that on the ordinary man's view of God, God does not have a body and consequently He could not know dirt under His fingernails. Thus, He could not know as much as man. But this would conflict with the assumption that God could know as much as man. Consequently, there would be a contradiction in the concept of God. What is not clear, however, is whether the ordinary man's concept of God does exclude the possibility that God has or at least could have a body. (See Objection (11) and the answer to this objection.)

In any case, if the ordinary man's concept of God excludes God's having a body, then by an argument implicit in the objection and sketched out in the last paragraph, another contradiction in the ordinary man's concept of God would be shown; a contradiction different from the one I have indicated. However, this new contradiction would not show that my argument was unsound or that the argument, although sound, was trivial. The idea that God is not human is hardly trivial if His lack of humanity prevents Him from knowing certain things that men know and if on the ordinary view He knows at least as much as men know.

Objection (11)

In the Christian account of God, God became flesh in the person of Jesus Christ. Consequently, Christ, God incarnate, could know envy or lust (as well as dirt underneath His fingernails). Yet Christ is the moral ideal of the ordinary Christian. Consequently, the argument fails.

Answer

This objection seems to assume that having a body is a necessary condition for knowing lust and envy. Now although having a body is surely a necessary condition for knowing dirt under one's fingernails, it is not obvious that it is necessary for knowing lust and envy. In any case such necessity was by no means assumed or denied by the argument. It was assumed merely that knowing lust and envy involves having the feeling of lust and envy, and this is incompatible with God as the moral ideal of mankind. If people believe that Christ, as God incarnate, knows lust and envy, then they cannot consistently think of Christ as the moral ideal of mankind; their moral ideal cannot be logically personified in Christ. On the other hand, unless Christ did know lust and envy, He would know less than ordinary men. Whether the New Testament indicates that Christ did know lust and envy is another question. The Bible does teach that Christ was tempted by the Devil but resisted him. But whether this means that Christ did have, for example, the feeling of lust and resisted the feeling or whether, despite the Devil, He did not even have the feeling of lust is unclear.[3] In any case, no matter what Christianity teaches, the problem still comes to the fore. For if Christ did have the feeling of lust, His status as moral ideal is affected; if He did not, His status as an epistemological ideal is affected. So although Christ may have won His battle with the Devil, Christianity has lost its battle to logic.[4]

NOTES

1. See James W. Cornman and Keith Lehrer, *Philosophical Problems and Arguments* (New York: Macmillan Company, 1968), pp. 340–48.

2. See J. N. Findlay, "Can God's Existence Be Disproved?" *Mind* 57 (1948): 176–83.

3. Matt. 4:3–11; Mark 1:13; Luke 4:2–13.

4. A shorter version of this paper appeared in *Darshana International* 1970 with the title "A Disproof of God's Existence." I would like to thank Professor Frank Coleman for his critical comments on that earlier version of the paper.

21

CONFLICTS BETWEEN THE DIVINE ATTRIBUTES
MICHAEL MARTIN

CONFLICTS INVOLVING DIVINE OMNISCIENCE

One of the defining properties of God is omniscience. What does this mean? In one important sense, to say that God is omniscient is to say that God is all-knowing. To say that God is all-knowing entails that He has all the knowledge there is.

Now, philosophers have usually distinguished three kinds of knowledge: propositional and procedural knowledge and knowledge by acquaintance. Briefly, propositional or factual knowledge is knowledge that something is the case and is analyzable as true belief of a certain kind. In contrast, procedural knowledge or knowledge-how is a type of skill and is not reducible to propositional knowledge.[1] Finally, knowledge by acquaintance is direct acquaintance with some object, person, or phenomenon.[2] For example, to say "I know Smith" implies that one has not only detailed propositional knowledge about Smith but also direct acquaintance with Smith. Similarly, to say "I know war" implies that besides detailed propositional knowledge of war, one has some direct experience of it.

Consider now the following definition of omniscience:

(1) A person P is omniscient = If K is knowledge, then P has K

From Michael Martin, *Atheism: A Philosophical Justification* (Philadelphia: Temple University Press, 1990), pp. 287–92, 297–306, 315. Copyright © 1990 by Temple University Press. Reprinted by permission of Temple University Press.

where K includes propositional knowledge, procedural knowledge, and knowledge by acquaintance. It clearly will not do. For one thing, since there are no restrictions on what P can believe, definition (1) allows P to have false beliefs.[3] But if P has some false belief that ~B, since propositional knowledge consists of true beliefs, P would by definition (1) also believe that B. Thus definition (1) allows P to have inconsistent beliefs.

One must qualify definition (1) to rule out the possibility of inconsistent beliefs. But there is still another problem, for knowledge-how comes in various degrees. For example, one can have only a minimal knowledge of how to solve certain math problems. Definition (1) is compatible with an omniscient being having only minimal knowledge-how, but surely this is an intolerable state for an omniscient being. An all-knowing being must have knowledge-how in the highest degree.

Definition (1) is also compatible with an omniscient being having only superficial knowledge by acquaintance, and again this seems intolerable. An omniscient being must have knowledge by acquaintance of the most detailed kind; it must have direct acquaintance with all aspects of everything.

The following definition avoids these problems:

(2) A person P is omniscient = For every true proposition p, P believes that p, and P believes that p IFF P knows that p, and for every sort of knowledge-how H, P has H to the highest degree, and for every aspect A of every entity O, P has direct acquaintance of A.

The implications of this account for the existence of God have usually not been noticed. God's omniscience conflicts with His disembodiedness. If God is omniscient, then on this definition He would have all knowledge including that of how to do gymnastic exercises on the parallel bars, and He would have this knowledge to the highest degree. Yet only a being with a body can have such knowledge, and by definition God does not have a body. Therefore, God's attributes of being disembodied and of being omniscient are in conflict. Thus if God is both omniscient and disembodied, He does not exist. Since God is both omniscient and disembodied, He does not exist.

The property of being all-knowing conflicts not only with the property of being disembodied but also with certain moral attributes usually attributed to God. By definition (2), if God is omniscient, He has knowledge by acquaintance of all aspects of lust and envy. One aspect of lust and envy is the feeling of lust and envy. However, part of the concept of God is that He is morally perfect, and being morally perfect excludes these feelings. Consequently, there is a contradiction in the concept of God. God, because He is omniscient, must experience feelings of lust and envy. But God, because He is morally perfect, is excluded from doing so. Consequently, God does not exist.[4]

It is important to see that in both of the above arguments it is not necessary to rely on God's omniscience in the sense of definition (2) to derive a contradiction. Indeed, one only needs to assume a concept of God in which God has as much knowledge as some human beings. In the first argument one need merely assume that God knows how to do certain gymnastic exercises; if He does, He cannot exist, since a disembodied spirit cannot know how to do these exercises. In the second argument, it is not necessary to maintain that God is morally perfect, let alone that God is omniscient. If God knows as much as some humans who know lust and envy, and if God, although not morally perfect, could not have the feelings of lust and envy, God could not exist.

In addition, definition (2) conflicts with God's omnipotence. Since God is omnipotent He cannot experience fear, frustration, and despair.[5] For in order to have these experiences, one must believe that one is limited in power. But since God is all-knowing and all-powerful, He knows that He is not limited in power. Consequently, He cannot have complete knowledge by acquaintance of all aspects of fear, frustration, and despair. On the other hand, since God is omniscient, He must have this knowledge.

Various objections to these three arguments can of course be imagined. First, it might be objected that definition (2) is inaccurate. This definition entails that God has all knowledge by acquaintance and all knowledge-how, and it can be argued that this is a mistaken view of God's omniscience. It can be argued that it is not logically possible for God to have all knowledge by acquaintance and all knowledge-how. For God to be omniscient, it is enough that He have in His possession all knowledge that it is logically possible for God to have.[6] This suggests the following definition:

(3) Person P is omniscient = For any true proposition p, if it is logically possible that P could believe that p, then P believes that p, and P believes that p IFF P knows that p, and for any sort of knowledge-how H that it is logically possible for P to have, P has H to the highest degree, and for every aspect A of every entity O that it is logically possible for P to be directly acquainted with, P is directly acquainted with A.

It might be argued that the three arguments given above collapse in the light of this modification of the definition of omniscience. One can admit that God is omniscient and yet, without contradiction, maintain that there is certain knowledge He could not have. The trouble with this reply, however, is that it is logically impossible that God can have knowledge that it is logically possible for humans to have. The result is paradoxical, to say the least. One normally supposes that the following is true:

(a) If person P is omniscient, then P has knowledge that any nonomniscient being has.

Furthermore, omniscience aside, one normally supposes that the following is true:

(b) If God exists, God has all knowledge that humans have.

But both (a) and (b) are false, given definition (3). The definition conflicts with what is normally meant by 'omniscient' and, bracketing omniscience, what one means by 'God'.

In addition, definition (3) does not seem to capture what is meant by omniscience. Consider a being called McNose.[7] His knowledge is of the highest degree, but McNose only knows how to scratch his nose and only has direct experience of all aspects of his nose's itching and being scratched. Let us further suppose that all McNose's beliefs are about his nose's itching and being scratched and that these beliefs constitute knowledge. Absurdly, McNose is omniscient on definition (3).

The problem posed by the example of McNose suggests another modification of the definition of omniscience. McNose's gross lack of knowledge means that he is not epistemologically perfect, whereas an omniscient being must be such. Perhaps then, the concept of epistemological perfection needs to be built into the definition of omniscience. Consider the following:

(4) Person P is omniscient = For any true proposition p, if P's believing that p would increase P's epistemological perfection, then P believes p; and P believes that p IFF P knows that p; and for any piece of knowledge-how H that would increase P's epistemological perfection, then P has H to the highest degree; and for every aspect A of every entity O, if being directly acquainted with A would increase P's epistemological perfection, then P is directly acquainted with A.

One problem with this new account of omniscience is that the notion of epistemological perfection is no clearer than the notion of omniscience. It would seem that unless a being has the knowledge that humans have, it does not have the property of epistemological perfection. But on this interpretation, God does not have epistemological perfection, for, as we have already seen, humans can have certain knowledge-how and knowledge by acquaintance that He cannot have. On the other hand, if one allows God to have the knowledge that humans have, this will conflict with some of God's other characteristics. One can of course define epistemological perfection in such a way that these problems are avoided—for example, by excluding the knowledge-how and knowledge by acquaintance that conflict with God's other attributes. But then "epistemological perfection" will have become a term of art introduced to avoid the problems posed, and the claim that God has epistemological perfection will be trivial.

Another way to deal with the problem of God's seeming not to know what humans know is to argue that God, if He chose, could know how, for example, to do exercises on the parallel bars, for if God chose, He could become incarnate and thus have the requisite skill. Even if one supposes, however, that it makes sense to assume that God can become incarnate, this does not solve the problem. Even if God has the potential to possess this knowledge, He does not have it now. He now lacks some knowledge that some human beings have. Furthermore, if God is omniscient, He is actually, not potentially, omniscient. However, on this account God would merely be potentially omniscient. Moreover, it is not completely clear that it makes sense to suppose that an infinite being can become incarnate.

In addition to these problems, the supposition that God could become incarnate would not solve the problem of knowledge by acquaintance mentioned above. Assuming God became incarnate, as on certain interpretations of Christianity He is supposed to have done, it would still seem that He could not be directly acquainted with lust and envy and yet be the moral ideal of Christians. On the other hand, unless He was directly acquainted with feelings of lust and envy, He would know less than ordinary men, since ordinary men are so acquainted. The teaching of the New Testament on whether Christ was directly acquainted with lust and envy is unclear. This Bible certainly teaches that Christ was tempted by the devil but resisted him. Whether this means that Christ did have feelings of lust and envy but resisted the devil or whether, despite the devil, He did not have feelings of lust and envy is unclear. In any case, whatever Christianity teaches, the problem still comes down to this: If Christ did have feelings of lust and envy, His status as a moral ideal is adversely affected; if He did not, His status as an epistemological ideal is adversely affected.

It might be argued, of course, that God's moral goodness does not concern His feelings but His actions and the principles on which they rest. So the fact that He knows lust and envy does not affect the Christian moral ideal. Now, it is true that in judging the moral quality of a person, one sometimes takes into account only the actions and the principles on which they rest. Thus, one who did good deeds and acted on moral principles throughout life would normally be considered a good person. Still, we would not consider a person morally *perfect,* despite a life of good action, if there was envy and lust in the person's heart. Freedom from such feelings as lust and envy is precisely what religious believers expect of a saint, and it is inconceivable that God would be less morally perfect than a saint.

Various objections might be raised to the argument that there is an inconsistency between omnipotence and omniscience.[8] First, it might be objected that there is no experience of fear or frustration distinct from complex dispositions to behave in certain ways. Consequently, God could have knowledge by acquaintance of fear simply by having knowledge by acquaintance of certain behavior. Obviously, God cannot have knowledge by acquaintance of His own behavior, since He does not have a body. But He can have knowledge by acquaintance of someone else's body. However, if fear is merely a complex behavioral disposition, then belief must be as well. Indeed, the state of fear involves certain beliefs. But then, although God would not have to have a body in order to have knowledge by acquaintance of fear, He would have to have a body in order to have any belief *about* someone else's fear. Since, by definition, God is a pure spirit without a body, He cannot exist if He has any beliefs. But God must have certain beliefs in order to be omniscient.

It might also be objected that, despite the fact that God is omnipotent, He can experience fear and frustration. After all, even humans sometimes experience fear when they know they have nothing to fear. If humans can do this, given their limitations, surely without these limitations God can do so as well. He can experience fear although He knows He has absolutely nothing to fear. However, although in ordinary life we are afraid when we know we having nothing to fear, we *also* have a belief, perhaps an unconscious one, that there *is* something to fear. Indeed, if we did not have such a belief, it would be incorrect to speak of our state as one of fear. Because it is part of the meaning of "P is experiencing fear" that "P believes that P has something to fear," even God must believe He has something to fear if He experiences fear. But He cannot believe He has something to fear if He is omniscient. Furthermore, if someone experiences fear knowing that there is nothing to fear, this fear is by definition irrational. By definition, God cannot be irrational.

Finally, it might be argued that God could experience fear by becoming incarnate, as He did in Jesus Christ. However, this solution to the problem will not do. First, there is the general difficulty of understanding how an infinite God could become incarnate in a human being. Even if this idea does make sense, are we to suppose that Jesus Christ was not all-powerful and not all-knowing? If Christ was all-powerful and all-knowing, the same problem would arise for Him. How could an incarnate all-powerful being experience fear? If He could not, then how could He be all-knowing? If He could experience fear, how could He be all-powerful? If He was not all-powerful and all-knowing, how could Christ be God incarnate? Further, if in order to know fear, God had to become incarnate, then before His incarnation He was not omniscient. But by definition God is *necessarily* omniscient. Hence if He exists, He has always been omniscient.

I must conclude that God's omniscience conflicts with His disembodiedness, His moral perfection, and His omnipotence.

CONFLICTS INVOLVING DIVINE FREEDOM

On one common view, God is completely free. Unlike finite beings, He is not restrained by anything except logic. Human freedom is restricted by the environment and the causal laws operating in it. Even defenders of contracausal freedom admit that to some extent human beings are influenced in their decisions by their culture and their heredity. Richard Swinburne, whose discussion of divine freedom is one of the most developed and sophisticated in recent literature, maintains that God is free in the sense that no agent or natural law or state of the world or other causal factor in any way influences Him to have the intentions on which to act.[9] Given this account of divine freedom, however, God cannot be omniscient in the usual sense. Consider the following definition of omniscience restricted to just propositional knowledge:[10]

> (5) Person P is omniscient = For any true proposition p, P believes that p and believes that p IFF P knows that p.

There are true propositions about the future that God cannot now know. Swinburne argues that if some of God's creatures are free in the contracausal sense, if their choices are not caused, then God cannot know now what they will do in the future. Of course, if God's creatures are not contracausally free, He will know what they will do in the future. However, most theists maintain that humans are contracausally free at least some of the time. Moreover, whatever the case with His creatures, God Himself is completely free in the contracausal sense.[11] Because of this, Swinburne admits that in the usual sense of omniscience, God cannot be omniscient and free since God cannot know what some of His future actions will be.[12] Consequently, a person who is omniscient in the sense specified in definition (5) and free cannot exist.

Although Swinburne is thus committed to the view that because God is free He cannot know certain true propositions, he still chooses to refer to God as omniscient. However, it is clear that his sense of omniscience is weaker than that of definition (5). Swinburne defines 'omniscience' as follows:

> A person P is omniscient at time t IFF P knows, of every true proposition about t or an earlier time, that it is true; *and* P also knows, of every true proposition about a time later than t such that what it reports is physically necessary as a result of some cause at t or earlier, that it is true.

For the reasons cited above, this definition must be modified in the following way:

(6)   A person P is omniscient at time t = For any true proposition p about t
or an earlier time, P believes that p at t and believes that p at t IFF P
knows that p at t, *and* for any true proposition about a time later than t,
such that what it reports is physically necessary as a result of some
cause at t or earlier, P believes p at t and P believes that p at t IFF P
knows p at t.

Let us call one who is omniscient in this sense a person with *limited omniscience* and one who is omniscient in the sense of definition (5) a person with *unlimited omniscience*. On definition (6), God would know about everything "except
those future states and their consequences which are not physically necessitated by
anything in the past; and if he knows that he does not know about those future
states."[13] So according to Swinburne, although God's perfect freedom is incompatible with unlimited omniscience, it is compatible with limited omniscience.

However, Swinburne is mistaken in supposing that God's perfect freedom is
compatible with limited omniscience, for God always has the option of inter-
vening in any natural event and performing a miracle. Swinburne should have
said that God can know that some event in the future, necessitated by physical
laws, will occur *only if* He knows that He will not intervene and perform a miracle. But by Swinburne's own admission, God cannot know now that He will or
will not intervene in some future event. Consequently, He cannot know now
whether *any* particular event will occur in the future. He cannot know what the
future actions of His creatures will be; He cannot know what His own future
actions will be; He cannot know if any event governed by natural laws will occur,
since He cannot know now if He will intervene in the natural course of events.
This seems to cover all possible future events.

God's perfect freedom is thus incompatible with both unlimited and limited
omniscience. A being that by definition has both attributes cannot exist. To be
sure, one can give a still-weaker definition of omniscience to eliminate the incompatibility. However, this move has its price. It seems to conflict radically with
both what is usually meant by 'omniscience' and what is usually meant by 'God'.

There is a further implication of the view that God has limited omniscience
and complete freedom. Given that He cannot know whether any particular future
event will occur, it follows that God cannot know whether His past actions have
been moral. This is because the morality of His past actions and forbearances
depends in part on what will happen in the future, which He cannot know. In
order to know, for example, whether His past decision not to intervene and perform some miracle at some past time t_1 was a correct moral decision, He would
have to know what would have happened after t_1 if He had intervened. In particular, He would have to know what would have been the long-range consequences
if He had intervened.

This is not something that God with His complete freedom can know, for such knowledge depends on knowledge of His creatures' future decisions, which certainly will depend on His own future decisions. But this knowledge He cannot have. God can know, of course, that if His past action or forbearance were to have consequences X, it would be moral. But He cannot know if it will have these consequences, since whether it does or not will depend on His creatures' as yet unknown free choices and His own as yet unknown interventions or forbearances.

The argument to this point suggests one more incoherence in the concept of God. Consider that God is by definition morally perfect. What is meant by 'morally perfect'? A typical account of moral perfection is offered by Swinburne. According to him,[14] to say that God is morally perfect is to say that God never takes any actions that are morally wrong:

> (M) Person P is morally perfect IFF P never does anything morally wrong.

However, as we have just seen, God cannot know whether His past actions or forbearances are morally correct. On (M) this would *not* mean that God could not be morally perfect. It would mean, however, that if God's actions were never morally wrong, it would be by accident. The morally correct outcome would be completely unrelated to God's knowledge. But this suggests that there is something wrong with (M) as an analysis of moral perfection, for a person cannot be morally perfect by accident; the outcome of a morally perfect person's action must be based on the person's knowledge. So although God can be both morally perfect in terms of (M) and completely free, the definition of morally perfect is incorrect. What happens if we attempt to improve (M) to meet the problem? Consider the following revision of (M):

> (M') Person P is morally perfect IFF P never does anything wrong and P's never doing anything wrong is not accidental.

However, on (M') God cannot be morally perfect and completely free. This is because, as we have seen, complete freedom limits God's knowledge in a most radical way, and one cannot be morally perfect and completely ignorant if one is doing what is morally correct. Consequently, God's moral perfection is in conflict with His perfect freedom. Hence God cannot exist.

One can put this point in a slightly different way. God can know that (M') is true since (M') is an analytic truth. But He cannot know that He is morally perfect since He cannot know that He never does anything wrong, let alone if He does, it is not accidental. But God must have knowledge that He is morally perfect to be God. However, this is knowledge that He cannot have. Hence God cannot exist.

The various objections that can be made to the above arguments can all be met. It might be objected that, in our argument that God's freedom is incompatible with His moral perfection, I am assuming some utilitarian theory of morality. It may be said that I must assume that God must know the future consequences of His actions in order to know whether His actions are moral. But it may be maintained that God need not be a utilitarian and, in any case, that utilitarianism is an implausible theory of morality.

My argument does not assume what utilitarianism assumes—namely, that *only* the consequences of one's actions are morally relevant. It simply assumes that the consequences of one's actions are morally relevant and leaves open the question as to whether other factors are also morally relevant. The only moral theory excluded by this argument is an extreme deontological theory such as Kant's, in which the consequences of an action are totally irrelevant to deciding its morality. But this sort of moral theory is almost universally recognized as inadequate.

A critic might also maintain that although God cannot have complete knowledge about the future, He can have probabilistic knowledge. He can know it is unlikely that He will intervene in the working of natural law by performing miracles because He has seldom done so in the past. Given this probabilistic knowledge, God can have probabilistic knowledge as to whether His actions are moral and consequently whether He is morally perfect.

However, inductive inferences about the future presuppose the uniformity of nature, and this in turn assumes not only that nature is governed by natural laws but that these laws are seldom violated by God's intervention. But whether natural laws will continue to operate without God's frequent intervention is precisely what is at issue. Hence this cannot be assumed without begging the question. Furthermore, to suppose that God is likely to continue to intervene infrequently in the workings of natural law seems to limit His freedom. If God is completely free, He is not restrained by this probability. Moreover, even if one could establish that God would seldom intervene to perform miracles without begging the question or limiting His freedom, this would not show that His infrequent intervention in the past was morally justified. Insofar as God's claim to probabilistic knowledge of the morality of His future actions is based on knowledge of His past moral actions, it begs the question of the morality of these past actions. The crucial issue is, can God know whether His past actions are moral? This objection seems to assume in advance that the question has been answered.

One might argue that the logical impossibility that God can know some future events is no limitation on His knowledge. God can be all-knowing in any sense that matters and yet not know the future. In particular, God can be all-knowing and yet not know whether His past actions are moral and, consequently, whether He is morally perfect.

However, the objection seems to assume wrongly that to say some entity is all-knowing means it knows everything that it is logically possible for it to know. However, given that there could be some entity such that it is logically impossible for it to know everything, it would be all-knowing on the account of all-knowing assumed by the objection. But this is absurd. On a more adequate definition of all-knowing—the unlimited sense of omniscience discussed above—an all-knowing being knows all truths and has no false beliefs. However, there are several reasons that God cannot be all-knowing in this sense.[15] Nor can God be all-knowing in the more limited sense suggested by Swinburne. In what sense of all-knowing *is* God supposed to be all-knowing then?

A critic might maintain that God could be completely free and yet know what His future actions would be. Consequently, He could know that He is morally perfect since He could know if His actions are moral. This contention would seem to be supported by the following argument and the analogy to the problem of free will. A person P is said to be free to do A; if P chooses to do A, P will be successful. In this sense of 'free', human action can be both free and determined. But if a future human action is determined, it can be known in advance. And if a human action can be free and predictable, then surely God's action can be as well. Hence God can know what His future actions will be and yet be completely free.

Theists have said this is not an adequate account of human freedom, let alone of divine freedom. Their standard argument against this goes as follows: If a person P's choice to do A is determined, P could not have done otherwise than A. If, on the other hand, P's choice not to do A is determined, P could not have done otherwise than not to do A. In either case, the argument goes, P could not have done otherwise than P did. It is irrelevant that if P had chosen to do A, P would have been successful.

Even if this were an adequate account of human freedom, it does not seem at all plausible as an account of divine freedom. If human action is determined and predictable, this is because it is part of the nexus of natural law. But God is supposed to have created that nexus and to transcend it. He is certainly not supposed to be *part* of the nexus He created.

I must conclude that God's complete freedom conflicts with His omniscience and moral perfection.

CONFLICTS INVOLVING DIVINE OMNIPOTENCE

Another divine attribute is omnipotence. In what follows I consider a sophisticated attempt by Swinburne to define omnipotence, and I argue that it is plagued by serious problems. If omnipotence is defined in the way suggested, then a being that is omnipotent cannot possess other attributes associated with God. But since God is supposed to have these other attributes, God cannot exist.

After rejecting several provisional attempts to define omnipotence, Swinburne[16] comes up with the following definition:

(E) A person P is omnipotent at time t IFF P is able to bring about the existence of any logically contingent state of affairs x after t, the description of the occurrence of which does not entail that P did not bring it about at t, given that P does not believe that P has overriding reasons for refraining from bringing about x.

This definition, according to Swinburne, solves the problems of his earlier provisional definitions and is free of problems of its own. Unfortunately, however, even if this definition avoids the problems of his earlier provisional ones, Swinburne's definition (E) is not free of problems.

In order to understand (E) and its problems, it is necessary to consider its elements as well as Swinburne's rationale for stating the definition as he does.

(1) The first thing to be noted about (E) is that omnipotence is defined in terms of what a being can bring about, not what a being can do. According to Swinburne, a definition in terms of being able to take any logically possible action runs immediately into the problem that certain actions can only be taken by certain kinds of beings. For example, only an embodied being can sit down. So a definition of omnipotence in terms of being able to perform any logically possible action would mean that a disembodied being would not be omnipotent; consequently, God, a disembodied omnipotent being, could not exist.

(2) The temporal qualifications in (E) are introduced to solve another problem. Without such qualifications a being who is omnipotent at t would have to be able to bring about an event *before* t. But according to Swinburne, it is logically impossible to bring about events in the past. Since it is no limitation on an omnipotent being that it cannot bring about what is logically impossible, a temporal qualification is necessary.

(3) (E) requires that the logically possible states of affairs that an omnipotent being brings about be logically contingent. Without this requirement, (E) would entail that P could bring about a logically necessary state of affairs, something that no being can bring about.

(4) The qualification that "the occurrence of which does not entail that P did not bring it about at t" is inserted because otherwise a state of affairs could be described as uncaused or not caused by P. But this description would make it logically impossible for P to bring about the state of affairs. It is no limitation that an omnipotent being cannot bring about a state of affairs that it is logically impossible for it to bring about.

(5) The last qualification, that "P does not believe that P has overriding reasons for refraining from bringing about x," is put in to make omnipotence compatible with being perfectly free. According to Swinburne, a perfectly free being "can only perform an action if he believes that there is no overriding reason for refraining from doing it."[17] If a person had an overriding reason for not performing an action and still performed it, he would be influenced by nonrational factors and consequently not be completely free. Swinburne admits that (E) defines a narrower sense of omnipotence than is sometimes used, but he argues that this limitation is not important. If a being is unable to exercise its power because it judges that, on balance, to do so would be irrational, he says, this does not make the being less worthy of worship.

Thus Swinburne admits that God could *not* be omnipotent in the sense in which the term has often been understood and, consequently, that God, as He is commonly understood, not only does not exist but could not exist. By Swinburne's own admission, then, a common notion of God is incoherent. Swinburne rejects the idea that a different term be used—for example, 'almighty'—and insists on using 'omnipotent' in a narrower sense than it is often understood. But his use should not induce us to suppose he has shown that the common concept of God is coherent. Indeed, just the opposite is true.

He defends himself by saying that theism often understands omnipotence in this narrower sense, although he does not cite any evidence for this contention, and that a being that is omnipotent in this sense is no less worthy of worship. What does he mean by this? Swinburne says that in order to worship a person legitimately, one must show respect toward the person *and* acknowledge this person "as *de facto* and *de iure* lord of all."[18] What properties would a being need to have in order to have lordship of this kind? He says:

> First, in order to be supremely great and the ultimate source of our well-being, he must be perfectly free, for if he is in any way pushed into exercising his power, sovereignty is not fully his. But given this, there must be no limits to his power other than those of logic; otherwise his lordship would not be supreme. This means he must be omnipotent in my sense (E).[19]

The trouble with this justification is that, according to Swinburne's definition (E), there *are* limits to God's power besides logic. Now, as we have seen, in (E) God's power is limited by His freedom. Swinburne is thus incorrect to suppose that if God is omnipotent as defined by (E), He is worthy of worship. In order to be worthy of worship, God must be omnipotent in a stronger sense than (E). For example, if God is omnipotent in the following sense, He is worthy of worship:

(D) A person P is omnipotent at time t IFF P is able to bring about the existence of any logically contingent state of affairs x after t, the description of the occurrence of which does not entail that P did not bring it about at t.

This sense of omnipotence was rejected by Swinburne as incompatible with God's complete freedom. Indeed, sense (E) was generated from sense (D) in order to make God's omnipotence compatible with His complete freedom by adding the qualification "given that P does not believe that P has overriding reasons for refraining from bringing about x." So it would seem that if God is omnipotent in sense (D), He could not exist and be completely free. However, if God is omnipotent in sense (E), He could not exist and be worthy of worship.

There are other problems with Swinburne's definition as well. Richard La Croix has shown that, on Swinburne's definition of omnipotence, God's omnipotence conflicts with God's omniscience.[20] Consider the state of affairs S_1, which has the property of being brought about by a being that has never been omniscient. (E) would seem to entail that in order for P to be omnipotent at t, P would have to be able to bring about S_1 after t. Then the ability of P to bring about S_1 at t entails that P is not omniscient, because it entails that P never had the property of being omniscient. Since Swinburne's definition holds for all existing beings, it holds for God. It follows that if God is omnipotent, He is not omniscient.

A similar argument could be used to show that God is not disembodied, not unchanging, not simple, and so on. In order to avoid these implications, one would have to deny that S_1 is a logically contingent state of affairs after t or say the description of S_1 entails that P did not bring about S_1 at t.

With respect to the first defense, S_1 certainly seems like a logically possible state of affairs in the sense that Swinburne intends: S_1 and not S_1 are both logically possible states of affairs, and S_1 is a state of affairs compatible with everything that happened after t or before t. With respect to the second defense, the description of S_1 would not entail that P did not bring about S_1 if P was omniscient. One might suppose that this entailment would hold if 'God' was substituted for P. However, if 'God' is understood as a proper name, such an entailment would not hold. In particular, 'God' used as a proper name does not entail that someone with this name is omniscient.

But let us suppose that 'God' is not understood as a proper name. Let us suppose rather that 'God' is a short form for a definite description: the being that is omniscient, omnipotent, and all-good. In this case, of course, the entailment would hold and the defense would work. Unfortunately, allowing 'God' to be a short form for this definite description raises another problem. If we allow 'God' to be so understood, consider the expression 'McEar'. Let us understand this expression not as a proper name, but as a short form for a definite description:

the man capable only of scratching his ear. La Croix points out that on (E) McEar is omnipotent. This is because the only states of affairs whose occurrences after t do not entail McEar's not having brought them about are the scratchings of the ear of McEar. Other states of affairs, such as the scratchings of McEar's nose, would entail that McEar did not bring about these states of affairs. Thus, absurdly, McEar is omnipotent on (E).

One objection to La Croix's argument is that God could bring about state of affairs S_1.[21] Let us suppose that S_1 consists of Hidden Valley's being flooded. Suppose this state has been brought about by some being—say, a beaver—that has never been omniscient. It can be argued that an omniscient and powerful being could bring about S_1 indirectly by causing the beaver to build a dam and flood the valley. In order to eliminate this problem, S_1 would have to be stated differently. We would have to say that S_1 is a state of affairs that has the property of not being brought about *directly or indirectly* by an omniscient being. With this small amendment, La Croix's argument is sound; for it is certainly the case that if an omniscient being caused the beaver to build a dam, such a being would indirectly have caused the valley to be flooded.

I must conclude that if God is omnipotent, then He is neither omniscient nor all-good nor disembodied, or else, absurdly, that McEar is also omnipotent. Thus Swinburne's definition fails. However, even if La Croix's argument is wrong, there is our earlier argument that Swinburne's definition of omnipotence is incompatible with his own account of being worthy of worship.

CONCLUSION

We have seen that there is very good reason to suppose that the traditional concept of God is incoherent and, consequently, that God does not and cannot exist. As I have suggested, there are ways of escaping from this conclusion, but these are purchased at a great price. My argument turns, of course, on analyses of the traditional attributes of God which might be rejected by theists. If they do reject my analyses, then the onus is on them to supply an analysis that does not have similar problems.

NOTES

1. For an account of these two types of knowledge, see Israel Scheffler, *Conditions of Knowledge* (Chicago: Scott, Foresman, 1965).

2. See D. W. Hamlyn, *The Theory of Knowledge* (Garden City, N.Y.: Doubleday, 1970), pp. 104–106.

3. See Patrick Grim, "Some Neglected Problems of Omniscience," *American Philosophical Quarterly* 20 (1983): 265–76.

4. This argument was developed in Michael Martin, "A Disproof of the God of the Common Man," *Question* 7 (1974): 115–24.

5. Cf. David Blumenfeld, "On the Compossibility of the Divine Attributes," *Philosophical Studies* 34 (1978): 91–103.

6. For example, Thomas V. Morris in *The Logic of God Incarnate* (Ithaca, N.Y.: Cornell University Press, 1986), pp. 112–15, has argued that our beliefs about the moral perfection of God can be used to limit what we take to be logically possible. On this approach, since experiencing lust and envy would conflict with God's moral perfection, it would be logically impossible for God to know lust and envy. The problem with this is that it has the paradoxical implication that certain things that it is logically impossible for an omniscient being to know, humans can know.

7. Cf. Richard R. La Croix, "Swinburne on Omnipotence," *International Journal for Philosophy of Religion* 6 (1975): 251–55.

8. For a more detailed refutation of these objections, see Blumenfeld, "On the Compossibility of the Divine Attributes."

9. Richard Swinburne, *The Coherence of Theism* (Oxford: Clarendon Press, 1977), p. 145.

10. This definition is due to Grim, "Some Neglected Problems of Omniscience." The usual definition of omniscience (X is omniscient = For any true proposition p, p is true IFF X knows that p) is rejected by Grim for the reason given above.

11. Swinburne is presumably assuming here that there are no counterfactuals of freedom. It seems correct to assume this, for the idea of counterfactuals of freedom makes little sense. See the discussion of counterfactuals of freedom in Michael Martin, chap. 15 in *Atheism: A Philosophical Justification* (Philadelphia: Temple University Press, 1990).

12. Swinburne, *The Coherence of Theism*, p. 172.

13. Ibid., p. 175.

14. Ibid., p. 179.

15. Cf. Patrick Grim, "Against Omniscience: The Case from Essential Indexicals," *Noûs* 19 (1985): 151–80, and "Logic and Limits of Knowledge and Truth," *Noûs* 22 (1988): 341–67, and Roland Puccetti, "Is Omniscience Possible?" *Australasian Journal of Philosophy* 41 (1963): 92–93.

16. Swinburne, chap. 9 in *The Coherence of Theism*; and Richard Swinburne, "Omnipotence," *American Philosophical Quarterly* 10 (1973): 231–37.

17. Swinburne, *The Coherence of Theism*, p. 159.

18. Ibid., p. 288.

19. Ibid.

20. La Croix, "Swinburne on Omnipotence." For a different critique of Swinburne's definition, see Joshua Hoffman and Gary Rosenkrantz, "Swinburne on Omnipotence," *Sophia* 23 (1984): 36–40.

21. Cf. George I. Mavrodes, "Defining Omnipotence," *Philosophical Studies* 32 (1977): 191–202.

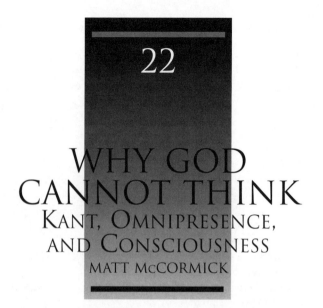

22

WHY GOD CANNOT THINK
KANT, OMNIPRESENCE, AND CONSCIOUSNESS
MATT McCORMICK

The standard theological attributes of God are omniscience, omnipotence, and omnibenevolence. Philosophical discussions have also focused on a set of metaphysical attributes of God that include properties such as perfection, timelessness, immutability, absoluteness, and omnipresence.[1] There is also a set of tertiary attributes that God may have by implication of the other properties or that are implied by classic characterizations. These are consciousness, will, desire, and goals. It is often said that God is aware of your sins, God issues commands, God has a plan, God wants you to do good, and so on.

I believe that a coherent conception of God cannot be formed from the complete set of the theological, metaphysical, and tertiary attributes. Nor can a coherent conception of God be formed from several of the subsets of these attributes because some of the attributes themselves are incoherent, or because combinations of some of the attributes are inconsistent.[2] In this article I will argue that omnipresence is not consistent with having what I will call higher consciousness, which includes the cognitive capacities to recognize and judge objects in the world and to be aware of one's representations as representations. Let us call the combined property of being omnipresent and having higher consciousness, *omniconsciousness*. This article will argue that 1) omniconsciousness is not possible because in order to be conscious a being must be limited in ways that an omnipresent thing is not, and 2) since omnipresence has been attributed to God

From *Philo* 3, no. 1 (2000): 5–19. Copyright © 2000 by Western Michigan University. Reprinted by permission of *Philo*.

by a number of influential theologians and omnipresence is implied by omniscience, omnipotence, and perfection, God cannot have higher consciousness.

The argument turns on some of the powerful insights from Immanuel Kant's arguments in the *Critique of Pure Reason*. In the "Refutation of Idealism" and the "Transcendental Deduction" sections of the *Critique*, Kant argues that self-awareness is not possible without awareness of objects external to one's mind. And unless a being is aware of the self and of external objects as different from self, that being cannot grasp that its mental states are representations of something different from itself. Furthermore, if a being cannot make these fundamental distinctions between self and external objects, that being cannot form judgments about objects. Building from these points in Kant, I will argue that an omnipresent being cannot make object/representation discriminations, so it cannot make a self/other distinction. If it cannot make self/other distinctions, then it cannot apply concepts or form judgments. Without those crucial abilities, an omnipresent being cannot have higher consciousness, so it cannot have a mind.

THE FEATURES OF HIGHER CONSCIOUSNESS

There are two distinguishing and defining characteristics of what we are calling higher consciousness that are precluded by omnipresence.

A. Higher consciousness includes the capacity to recognize one's mental states as representations or draw a distinction between one's representations and the thing being represented.

In order to grasp that a representation is a representation of an object, a being must be able to comprehend several things. First, that being must recognize that there is an object that the representation is a representation of. Humans, for example, are not merely conscious of objects external to them the way a plant can be said to be aware of the sun when it turns its leaves toward the light. Our sensory and mental faculties provide us with representations of things outside of us, and we are aware of those representations *as representations*. To understand that the representation is of something, a being must recognize that the representation is different from the thing represented. That is, the being must grasp that what appears to be the case in the representation may not be the case in the object, and what is the case in the object may not appear to be the case in the representation.[3] When the distant twenty-story building appears to be one inch tall according to the ruler in my hand, I recognize that it is my representation of the building that appears small, not the building itself. I also recognize that there may be things about the building, that it houses a crowd of people, for instance, that are not reflected in my representation. Furthermore, I must be able to see that the divergence or the possibility of error in my representation arises from my use of the representation to stand in for the object; the representation is not the same as the object represented. Understanding the difference between the representation and the object represented also presupposes that the person be able to grasp herself as a distinct object from the one being represented. The representation, understood as a representation of an object, serves as a bridge that connects a being's consciousness with the things that surround it. And to have what we are calling higher consciousness, a being must be able to see itself, the representation, and the object in this three-way relationship. The representation is the means by which a being can have any awareness of objects *as objects* at all.

Kant argues that object/representation discrimination is also a necessary presupposition of self-awareness. A being with higher consciousness must do more than merely recognize or react to objects in the world; it must be able to separate those objects into the one that is the self and the others that are not; it must separate the subjective course of its experience from the objective state of affairs; and it must be able to place itself as an object among the nonself objects. This conceptual difference between the self and others is not possible for a being that does not possess the ability to make object/representation discriminations. The point here is very close to one Kant makes in the "Refutation of Material Idealism" in the *Critique of Pure Reason*. Descartes and Berkeley had maintained that self-awareness is possible prior to knowing or even without the existence of external objects. In contrast, Kant argues that being aware of the self is only possible through the existence and awareness of non-self objects. He says, "The consciousness of my own existence is simultaneously a direct consciousness of the existence of other things outside of me."[4]

Kant also explains the relationship between self-awareness and object awareness this way:

> The *I think* must be *capable* of accompanying all my presentations. For otherwise something would be presented to me that could not be thought of at all—which is equivalent to saying that the presentation either would be impossible, or at least it would be nothing to me.[5]

Kant's "I think" that must be able to accompany a higher consciousness's representations is that being's awareness of itself as a thing among other things in an objective world. A being can recognize the difference between its representations and the objects that they are representations of if and only if that being is also capable of being self-aware.

Let us stipulate that a being that is aware in some sense but is not capable of object/representation discrimination is a being with lower consciousness. Self-awareness of the sort Kant describes is not possible for this being because it necessarily presupposes the capacity to make object/representation discriminations. Many animals fall into the lower consciousness category. The family dog who wags its tail or growls and barks at itself reflected in the mirror is not aware of the image *as an image*. And it is no accident that it fails to recognize the image as an image and it fails to recognize the dog in the mirror as *itself*. Object/representation discrimination cannot be had without self/other awareness because they are two sides of the same ability. Without it, the only sort of interaction with the world that the dog can have is an immediate and instinctual stimulus response.

There are good reasons to think that this capacity is one of the properties that are necessary for having a mind. It is not merely the capacity to have representations that distinguishes the beings with minds from the beings without minds, but the capacity to grasp that those representations are a subjective reflection of an objective state of affairs. A lower consciousness is aware of nothing but the series of representations it has, in the order that they occur. Higher consciousness grasps that its representations are merely one possible subjective course of representations among many that can be had through an objective world. In Kant's famous example, even though I first observed the ship upstream and then downstream, I can conceive of the ship's being downstream first and traveling upstream.[6] The family dog comes to associate the jingle of keys with going somewhere in the car, in that order. We could as easily condition the dog to associate the ringing of a bell with going somewhere in the car. In contrast, we recognize that the keys can jingle or the bell can ring for a number of reasons and that travel in the car may or may not be next. And it is this ability to see that my representations could have been different as well as the ability to causally order my representations that distinguishes higher from lower consciousness. I can separate the cause of an event from objects that are merely accidentally associated with it.

The difference between these two levels of consciousness appears to be a difference in kind, not merely degree. It is also the boundary between beings with minds and beings without because it is the difference between having the capacity for self-reflection, self- and other- awareness, and even freedom, Kant argues. All of these abilities are lacking in lower consciousness. The merely representational and associative consciousness is acted upon by the world, but the being that is aware that its stimuli serve as representations of the world locates itself and its subjective experience in relationship to the world; such a being is aware that objects in the world are acting upon it to generate representations.

A closer look at some beings that are very close to having higher consciousness makes the distinction between higher and lower even sharper. In a recent study on chimpanzees, researchers put a spot of paint on the chimps' foreheads without their knowing it. When the chimps were shown a mirror, they noticed the red spot in the reflection and reached up to *their own* foreheads to remove it.[7]

Their reaction suggests that these chimps both have a higher level of self-awareness than the animals that react to the mirror as if it is another animal, and that they have some rudimentary awareness of the difference between a representation of an object (in the mirror) and the object itself (the paint spot on their own heads). While they may have a partial grasp of the difference between the image and the object, other research suggests that they do not have a conception of what it is for *another* being to share their level of consciousness. In several tests, chimps were just as likely to beg food from a researcher wearing a blindfold or a bucket over her head as from a researcher with her eyes uncovered.[8] These tests suggest that the chimps are not making a distinction between what it is for another being to be aware or not be aware of events around it. So we can modify our account of full self-awareness such that it includes the capacity to make object/representation discriminations, self/other awareness, as well as the capacity to recognize that others possess higher consciousness and self-awareness.

There is another distinctly Kantian mental capacity that we should include in our account of higher consciousness before we examine the implications for God's omnipresence.

B.   Higher consciousness includes the capacity to form judgments about objects, identifying and attributing properties to them.

Some creatures, like ourselves, can identify properties that objects possess, and we can ascribe those properties to the object by means of concepts.[9] Identifying the properties that an object has requires relating it to other similar objects with a general, abstract term that labels the property they have in common. Possessing the concept *brown*, for instance, makes it possible for me to grasp that the trunk of the tree and a dog have something in common. Subsequently, I can form judgments about both: "The tree is brown," and "The dog is brown." But being able to apply the concepts is not enough to form judgments. A being must also be able to recognize the relationships between the different concepts, how and in what order they are connected, which combinations are not syntactically coherent, and so on. Kant refers to this kind of concept employing and judging consciousness as a discursive consciousness in contrast to an intuitive consciousness whose cognitive access to objects is not mediate. It has direct and immediate access to objects as they are in themselves.[10]

So judging requires both the capacity for abstraction, or the ability to recognize the use of one representation to stand in for a group of others, and it requires the ability to employ those concepts within their syntactic system. Again, recent studies on chimps shed light on what these abilities are. Sue Savage-Rumbaugh and Duane Rumbaugh[11] have been able to draw out some remarkably abstract conceptual abilities and even syntactic awareness in chimps with some carefully designed training and trials. The chimps were trained to sort one group of items into two groups of items: food and tools. Then the chimps were trained to associate each of these two groups with abstract symbols that did not resemble the objects in either of the groups. In time, when they were presented with an entirely new food item or tool, the chimps were able to place it with either the symbol for food or tool correctly.

Some of the chimps who had received previous lexical and syntactic training were more successful at the symbol-sorting project than others. These chimps had been trained to use a simple language of two verbs (one for solids and one for liquids) and four nouns (two solid foods and two liquid foods) so that they could form simple requests like, "Give banana." The researchers devised a complicated set of exercises to teach the chimps not only which combinations of the six terms were grammatical and allowable, but also which of the numerous combinations did not form grammatical assertions like "banana juice give."[12] Eventually the chimps were able to make grammatical requests in their simple language with new food items and a corresponding new symbol for that food item. It appears that the chimps had mastered the primitive syntax of their language and had learned to correctly integrate new symbols into the language, although the number of symbols, the syntactical structure, and the abstraction of the symbols were all significantly limited for the chimps. They appear to be poised at the cusp for both of the abilities of higher consciousness that we have singled out.

OMNICONSCIOUSNESS IS IMPOSSIBLE

We are now in a position to see why an omnipresent being cannot have higher consciousness, or why omniconsciousness is impossible. Here is the argument in schematic form:

1. A being with higher consciousness possesses two abilities: A) the ability to discern between the object and a representation of the object, and B) the ability to apply concepts and form judgments about objects.
2. If a being has the ability to discern between the object and a representation of the object, and the ability to apply concepts and form judgments, then that being must be able to grasp the difference between the self and not-self.
3. A being is omnipresent when that being occupies or is present in all places, far or near, in all times, past, present, or future.
4. There is nothing that is not-self for an omnipresent being by definition of omnipresence.
5. So an omnipresent being cannot grasp a difference between the self and not-self.[13]

6. Therefore, an omnipresent being cannot possess higher consciousness.
7. In short, God cannot have a mind because omniconsciousness is impossible.

A brief return to Kant's argument in the "Refutation of Material Idealism" will help clarify the argument that omniconsciousness is impossible. In response to Descartes's skepticism and Berkeley's denial of the existence of external objects, Kant argues first that consciousness (higher consciousness, in our terms) presupposes the capacity to distinguish the self from the nonself, and second, if a being is aware of the self, there must be something in the world that is not that being. Necessarily, for a being to have higher consciousness, there must be something independent or different from that being and that being must be aware of those independent objects as separate. Berkeley thought that the concept of mind-independent objects is incoherent. Descartes thought he could prove the existence of his own mind while the existence of external objects remained in doubt. Kant argues that being aware of one's own existence as a thing with properties (which neither Berkeley nor Descartes denied) is only possible if some mind-independent objects exist and if a being grasps the difference between itself and those objects.

Notice that Kant's conclusion is stronger than the one I have been arguing for. There is an important difference between Kant's antiskeptical conclusion that 1) higher consciousness requires that material objects *exist* in the world, and the claim in this article that 2) higher consciousness requires that a being must *think* of objects in the world as being external. In the "Refutation," Kant is attempting to disprove radical skepticism or idealism about the existence of material objects. Kant's stronger conclusion would support the argument we have been making about omniconsciousness, but it is not necessary to adopt the strong antiskeptical position. The weaker conclusion 2) shows the problem with omniconsciousness just as well, but it makes a more modest claim about the way a conscious mind must think about the objects of its representations, whether there be external, material objects or not. So the success of the argument does not depend upon Kant's strongest antiskeptical argument. Being omnipresent precludes the possibility of there being any objects external to that being as well as the possibility of that being's accurately *thinking of* objects as external.

If there is nothing external to a being or nothing that the being can accurately think of as external, then that being cannot draw a distinction between itself and objects which are not itself. There are no objects that would make such a distinction possible. Without the subject/object distinction, a being cannot possess either of the capacities of higher consciousness. That being cannot recognize that it has representations of objects and that those representations are different from the objects themselves because that being cannot grasp the relationship between itself, its representations, and the objects that it represents. Nor can that being form judgments about objects by attributing properties to them since judging also presupposes the subject/object distinction. In order to judge, "My neighbors are playing loud music," I must be able to distinguish between what the real state of affairs is and what I represent it to be. I assert that the music really is being played loudly, and not merely that I am hallucinating it. When I make a judgment I assert something to be true (rightly or wrongly) about the real state of affairs that I intend my judgment to reflect. If I cannot distinguish between the self and the nonself (which an omnipresent being would not be able to do), I cannot grasp that there is a gap between what I represent to be the case and what is the case.

OMNIPRESENCE

A more careful analysis of omnipresence is needed to complete this argument. There are a number of questions to ask. What reasons do we have for thinking that God is omnipresent? And what exactly does omnipresence entail? If a being is omnipresent, is it true that there is nothing that it can conceive of as separate from itself?

There are several substantial reasons to attribute omnipresence to God. First, a number of important theistic philosophers have insisted that God is omnipresent, and their analyses of the property provide some additional insights into what it is to be omnipresent. On Aquinas's account, God's presence in the world is all pervasive, no matter how far or how many places there may be,

> It belongs therefore to a thing to be everywhere absolutely when, on any supposition, it must be everywhere; and this properly belongs to God alone. For whatever number of places be supposed, even if an infinite number be supposed besides what already exist, it would be necessary that God should be in all of them; for nothing can exist except by Him. Therefore to be everywhere primarily and absolutely belongs to God and is proper to Him: because whatever number of places be supposed to exist, God must be in all of them, not as to a part of Him, but as to His very self.[14]

Aquinas's conception of God's omnipresence is mirrored by John Wesley's, the founder of Methodism, who maintains that, "In a word, there is no point of space, whether within or without the bounds of creation, where God is not."[15]

In Newtonian space, the presence of an object in a certain location in space and time normally precludes the presence of another object in that same time and place. Aquinas argues, however, that God's presence in all locations has a different character that does not prevent the presence of other objects,

> It is written, "I fill heaven and earth" (Jeremiah 23:24). . . . God is in every place; and this is to be everywhere . . . and God fills every place; not, indeed,

like a body, for a body is said to fill place inasmuch as it excludes the co-presence of another body; whereas by God being in a place, others are not thereby excluded from it; indeed, by the very fact that He gives being to the things that fill every place, He Himself fills every place.

Aquinas argues that there is another sense in which God's presence is not like that of other bodies,

God is in all things; not, indeed, as part of their essence, nor as an accident, but as an agent is present to that upon which it works. For an agent must be joined to that wherein it acts immediately and touch it by its power . . . as long as a thing has being, God must be present to it, according to its mode of being.

So God's omnipresence must be a necessary attribute, not a property that is true of God accidentally. And God's presence in every thing is a function of his perfect agency which brings all things into existence and sustains their being. He can be said to be all-present because all things are immediately subject to his power. So on Aquinas's account omnipotence implies omnipresence. Having the power to do anything to any object entails having perfect, immediate presence in all things.

We might also attribute omnipresence to God on the basis of his perfection. A being that does not exist in all times or places would be limited, hence it would lack perfection. Nothing can be separate from a being that is perfect. And as J. N. Findlay has argued, a being that lacks perfection or the other divine attributes is not worthy of the name God; such a being would not be a "proper object of religious reverence."[16] So if there is a thing that is an appropriate religious object, it must be, among other things, omnipresent.

Furthermore, omniscience requires omnipresence. In order to have flawless and complete knowledge of all things, past, present, and future, a being would need to be present in all things at all times. First, an omniscient being must have access to every object to possess all knowledge. And second, that access to each object itself must be perfect. In order to have omniscient access to every truth about every object, there cannot be any object or any part of an object that is not exhaustively present to that being. While it is possible to know some of the truths about an object without being present in that object, exhaustive and perfect knowledge of that thing is not possible for a being that remains separate from it; the mind of the omniscient being must be immediately and completely unified with the objects of its knowledge.

So an omnipresent God occupies or is present in all places, far or near, in all times, past, present, or future. His presence does not preclude other things. God is necessarily omnipresent. Omnipresence is implied by omnipotence, perfection, and by omniscience. Any lesser being would not be deserving of the name *God*.

The argument against omniconsciousness outlined above poses a serious problem for a coherent characterization of God. The objector to the argument might have granted the point and simply given up omnipresence. Without omnipresence, the possibility that God could have higher consciousness remains open but other problems occur. First, a characterization of God that is not omnipresent runs afoul of several classic portrayals like Aquinas's and even God's own claim in Jer. 23:24. And second, there are several reasons to think that God cannot be omniscient, omnipotent, or perfect without omnipresence. So the being in question is either semipresent and undeserving of the name *God* or it is omnipresent and mindless, incapable of judging or doing many of the things that God is commonly thought to be capable of doing.

OBJECTIONS AND RESPONSES

The "Parts of Self" Response

The critic of the argument against omniconsciousness might accept omnipresence as it has been presented and maintain that even if God is everywhere, God would be able to discriminate between parts of himself as being different from each other, and he could thereby possess higher consciousness. My hands, for instance, are part of me, yet I can think about them as objects, form judgments about them, be aware of my representations of them *as representations*. Why is it impossible for an omnipresent God to be conscious of all things the way we are conscious of the parts of our own bodies?

The answer is that even being aware of a part of one's self, like one's hands, requires the capacity to make the subject/object distinction. And an omnipresent being cannot distinguish between subject and object for the reasons discussed above. When I form a judgment like, "This is my right hand," or "My hand hurts," or even that "There are hands" at all, I am judging that there are objects in the world that possess properties. There is a thing, me, that has the property of having hands. I judge that these are my hands and not the person's across the room. And I cannot be aware of these hands as mine, or even as things at all, unless I can distinguish between them and other things in the world that are not me. A necessary condition of being conscious of any object, whether that object be the self, a part of self, or something more distantly external, is being able to judge that the world is occupied with objects, some of which are not me. For an omnipresent being, however, there are no objects in the world that are not the self. So that being cannot make the crucial distinction between itself and other things that makes judgments possible.

The Dualist Response

The theist may present a sort of dualist objection to the way omnipresence has been characterized. God is a spiritual being, according to the objection, composed of spiritual, not material, substance. Spiritual substance, according to Descartes, is not spatial. The Cartesian dualist (and theist) may propose that God's spiritual substance pervades, or is copresent with all things, hence he is omnipresent. But God is not material, so there remains something in the world that is different from God. So God is capable of drawing a distinction between himself and the material world, hence God can have higher consciousness. And since God's spiritual being is present in all things, God is omnipresent as well.

I think a couple of responses can be made to this attempt to reconcile omnipresence and higher consciousness. First, even if we grant the possibility that spiritual, nonspatial substances are possible, a being composed of this substance cannot be omnipresent. By the objection above, at best God is only semi-present, since God is only present in one of the two fundamental categories of substance. If God is not spatial, then there is a class of things, namely spatial things, that God cannot be present in or with. And if there is a class of things that a being cannot be present in or with, it is impossible for that being to be omnipresent. Second, one pays a high price in accepting dualism to solve any philosophical problem. The philosophical community rarely agrees about anything. But one set of issues that is widely agreed upon is the long list of problems and unanswered questions associated with dualism. Mind and body are distinct substances. The latter spatial and temporal, the former temporal only. How does a nonspatial thing control or affect a spatial thing? Where is the locus of their interaction? What are the regularities or laws that govern their interaction? What evidence do we have to think that there are these nonspatial, spiritual substances? What are the other features of these entities? And so on. Unfortunately, satisfactory answers for most of these questions have not been given. Dualism, while often discussed by philosophers, has a number of problems that make it untenable. So proposing a dualist answer to the omniconsciousness problem creates more difficulties for the theist than it solves.

The Anthropomorphism Response

Thus far, I have argued that an omnipresent being cannot have a mind because it would not be capable of making a crucial distinction between itself and the nonself. The critic might reply that the conception of consciousness employed here is too anthropomorphic. If a perfect omnibeing exists, it is unlikely that its consciousness will resemble ours either in the way that it represents objects (if it even has representations) or in the way that it judges objects (if it even judges objects). Proving that God does not have higher consciousness does not prove that God is not conscious.

First, let me point out that this kind of objection to my argument has conceded the point. This response has agreed that an omnipresent God cannot have higher consciousness. Theists may respond that it is not a serious compromise of their position to grant that God does not have a representing and judging consciousness; indeed, an argument for this conclusion can be seen, they respond, as strengthening their conviction that God is something so far beyond us, he is scarcely comprehensible. I believe that conceding the conclusion of my argument is a much more serious breach for classic theism than this response suggests. Reconsider the conclusion being argued. I have said that an omnipresent being cannot make a subject/object distinction, cannot have representations of objects, and cannot judge objects. What has been argued is that an omnipresent being cannot be aware of objects as objects. And the type of consciousness that I have described is not idiosyncratic, inessential, or even anthropomorphic. The sort of consciousness I have been considering is consciousness of objects. If a being cannot be said to be aware of objects and is unable to form thoughts or judgments about their properties, then in what sense of the word can it be said to be conscious at all? There are forms of consciousness, I have conceded, that cannot judge or grasp representations as representations; these beings do not see objects and the self as separate. But the theist will not want to fall back on the position that God's consciousness resembles dog consciousness. The kind of cognitive abilities that we have discussed boost a consciousness from being aware of a mere blind play of representations to being aware of itself, its representations, objects as distinct objects in the world with their own properties, and other beings with higher consciousness. I believe we can side with Kant in saying that this argument describes mental abilities that are no mere accident of human consciousness but are necessary components for a being to think and have a mind. So if theists insist that God possesses some more exotic form of consciousness, the burden of proof is now upon them to explain just what sort of consciousness this is, how it can think about objects, and what reasons they have for believing God's is of this sort.

Kant's distinction between discursive and intuitive consciousness may be useful to the theist here. In contrast to our own, an intuitive mind's awareness of objects is direct, immediate. It is not mediated by representations; it grasps "things as they are in themselves," in Kant's famous phrase. I believe that even Kant is being credulous here, however. As was pointed out in the discussion of omniscience, to grasp something directly and perfectly is essentially to be unified with that object. If there is a separation between the object and the mind of God such that God represents the object to think about it or have knowledge of it, God's knowledge cannot be complete or exhaustive. To know something perfectly is to completely apprehend every facet of its being; to be omniscient is to collapse the distinction between objects and one's representations of objects. And having a mind or being conscious of objects as objects is impossible if this distinction is lost. The substantial burden of proof for the theist is to explain how God can be aware of objects as objects, without God's consciousness being representational. The challenge will be to show how an intuitive and perfect awareness of objects counts as a kind of awareness at all.

There are other problems for the theist's objection that God's consciousness is radically different than the kind we have addressed. Theists in a variety of religious traditions have maintained that God is a being that they can establish and develop a relationship with, a being that is aware of us, who knows our plight, who loves us, who passes judgment on us, and so on. But an omnipresent God can do none of these things. An omnipresent God cannot be aware of itself or us, cannot form thoughts, cannot relate to people as individuals any more than the universe can.

CONCLUDING REMARKS

It has been my purpose to show that the consciousness of an omnipresent being can be neither discursive nor representational. If a being is all-present, it is impossible for that being to distinguish between objects and representations of objects, be aware of the difference between the self and other, recognize that other beings have higher consciousness, apply concepts, and form judgments.

At its foundation, to have higher consciousness of something is to be different from it; to be separated from it somehow, yet have some kind of cognitive access to it. For us, that access is through our mental representations generated by sensations. I have argued that for a being to have a mind, or higher consciousness, that being must be able to form ideas of the object and grasp that those ideas themselves are different than the object being considered. Such a mind is representational by its nature. That is, there is some cognitive content that stands in for or presents the object to the mind, and the mind is aware that there is a difference between the cognition and the thing being thought about. Unless a being can form ideas or have some sort of representations that it is aware of as such, I do not believe that we can plausibly claim that the being has a mind in any substantial sense of the term.

SOME IMPLICATIONS OF THE ARGUMENT
AGAINST OMNICONSCIOUSNESS

An interesting result of the argument that I have presented here is that only semi-present beings can have minds. That is, a being must be limited in time and place in order to be conscious of objects and itself, be aware of its representations of them as representations, and form judgments about them. In many Western theistic traditions, the finite and circumscribed position of the individual in the world is much decried. It is our limitations that are responsible for our sinful ways, our lack of understanding, and our failure to appreciate God, for instance. But if the argument in this article is correct, consciousness is possible *only by means of being a finite creature*. Our finitude is the foundation of selfhood and of having a mind. To eliminate our limitations and become infinite would eliminate the mind we identify as the self.[17]

The impossibility of omniconsciousness also has some serious implications for omniscience. Traditionally, epistemologists have separated kinds of knowledge into knowledge how, propositional knowledge, and knowledge by acquaintance. I know how to ride a bicycle, I know the proposition, "The earth orbits the sun," and I know what Elvis looks like, respectively. Since omnipresence rules out the possibility of higher consciousness, then omnipresence also precludes the possibility of propositional knowledge. If a being is not, never has been, and never will be conscious in the manner described above, then it cannot have propositional knowledge. Whatever it means for a being to have exhaustive and perfect knowledge of all truths, past, present, and future, it cannot mean that it knows them in propositional form. (There are reasons to believe that a perfect being cannot know by means of propositions, since propositions require the use of concepts, as well.[18])

If omniscience requires a presence or access to all things, perhaps the kind of knowledge an omniscient being can have is more akin to knowledge by acquaintance. God might have a direct, immediate, nonpropositional apprehension of all truths that is similar to our immediate recognition of a face, or our intuition that $1 = 1$ simply because it is true. Knowledge by acquaintance is consistent with what we have characterized as lower consciousness. But most theists will not be happy with the result that God's consciousness is more akin to a chicken's than to ours.

The implication of this argument, then, is that in the case that God has higher consciousness, some of the traditional characterizations of God and descriptions of his activities are inconsistent. A God with higher consciousness could love, judge, issue commandments, and so on. God could be the sort of being that we could relate to as another creature with a mind. But such a being cannot be omnipresent. So, it appears that he cannot have all propositional knowledge, or be omnipotent, thus he would fail to have two of the standard theological attributes.

Without those attributes, it is not clear that a being that is only omnibenevolent, if one exists, would be an appropriate object of a religious attitude or worship.

In the case that God is omnipresent, it may still be possible for God to be omniscient. But this being's knowledge could not be propositional, suggesting a fairly serious lack of perfection, that is, God could not know that the proposition "Jupiter is the largest planet in the solar system" is true. Indeed, since this being could not have a mind, there would be nothing to apprehend the truth. It could not be conscious of objects as objects, aware of its own representations as representations, or form thoughts about objects in the world, including itself. Furthermore, without a mind, it is not clear how this being could be said to have all power in any nontrivial sense. The various teleological notions we have of God's having a divine will, or that he exercises his power to bring about a plan, would be difficult to apply nonmetaphorically to a mindless entity. God may still be said to have all power in the sense that the universe can be said to contain all power.

Without higher consciousness, a being could not have the kind of personal relationship with humans that many theistic traditions promise. A God lacking higher consciousness would not be able to love, pass judgment, or issue commandments, among other things. If we are to take Findlay's suggestion seriously, a being that is fitting of the title *God* cannot exist whether omnipresent or not.

NOTES

1. I would like to thank Prof. Jim Feiser, Rebekah Donaldson, Prof. Eric Sotnak, and David Corner for their insightful comments on this article.

2. There may remain some subsets of the list of God's attributes that are logically consistent such that a being possessing them could exist. But those beings would fall short of the title of God, and they would not be worthy objects of worship.

3. And as Kant's boat example from the "Second Analogy" makes clear, what is true of the order of a series of my representations need not be true of the objects I represent. Immanuel Kant, *The Critique of Pure Reason*, trans. Werner Pluhar (Indianapolis: Hackett Publishing Company, 1996), A 192/B 237.

4. Ibid., B 276.

5. Ibid., B 132.

6. Ibid., B 237.

7. Gordon Gallup Jr., "Animal Self-Awareness: A Debate: Can Animals Empathize? Yes," *Scientific American Special Issue: Exploring Intelligence* (winter 1998): 66–71 [online], www.scientificamerican.com/specialissues/1198intelligence/1198debate.html.

8. Daniel Povinelli, "Can Animals Empathize? Maybe Not," *Scientific American Special Issue: Exploring Intelligence* (winter 1998): 67–75 [online], www.scientificamerican.com/specialissues/1198intelligence/1198debate.html.

9. This is a cursory and oversimplified discussion of concepts and their role in thought, but it will suffice for the purposes of this argument.

10. Kant, *The Critique of Pure Reason*, B 93, B 283. This distinction between discursive and intuitive consciousness will be useful later in our discussion.

11. Sue Savage-Rumbaugh, David Rumbaugh, and S. Boysen, "Symbolization, language and chimpanzees: A theoretical reevaluation based on initial language acquisition processes in four young Pan troglodytes," *Brain and Language* 6 (1978): 265; Sue Savage-Rumbaugh, David Rumbaugh, S. T. Smith, and J. Lawson, "Reference: The Linguistic Essential," *Science* 210 (1980): 922–25.

12. Terrence Deacon, *The Symbolic Species: The Coevolution of Language and the Brain* (New York: W. W. Norton and Company, 1997), p. 85.

13. Self-awareness implies the possession of the object/representation discrimination. And the ability to make object/representation discrimination implies the capacity for self-awareness. While the ability to apply concepts and form judgments implies self-awareness, the reverse is not true. A being could be self-aware, at least to the extent that chimps are, and not be able to employ concepts or form judgments.

14. Thomas Aquinas, *Summa Theologiae*, part 1, question 8, articles 1–4, trans. Fathers of the English Dominican Province (New York: Benzinger Brothers Inc., 1947).

15. John Wesley, "On the Omnipresence of God," sermon 111, text from the 1872 edition [online], gbgm-umc.org/umhistory/wesley/sermons/serm-111.stm.

16. J. N. Findlay, "Can God's Existence Be Disproved?" *Mind* 57 (1948): 180

17. The conclusion that the elimination of our limitations would eradicate the self fits nicely with the tenets of Buddhism and a number of Eastern religions. The highest state of enlightenment is achieved when we are able to remove all desire, all that makes us individuals, and reach an infinite expansion of consciousness.

18. While it is not vital to the success of the argument in this paper, there are good reasons to think that an omniscient mind cannot have propositional knowledge by means of concepts. A concept is a general property that we judge different particular objects to share. Propositional knowledge that employs concepts is thus constrained to identify the ways in which unique and particular objects resemble each other. Resemblance can only be recognized by ignoring or failing to recognize the ways different objects are different. That is, resemblance is only possible through lack of resolution and clarity. Propositional information about an object can never be exhaustive and perfect because it can never completely capture the particularity of an object. All propositional information about it must be in terms of properties that the object shares with others. And only a mind that lacks perfect resolution in its apprehension of objects can grasp similarities. A perfect, omniscient apprehension of an object would grasp it directly, as it is in itself, not by means of its crude resemblance to other objects.

23

GOD AND THE
BEST POSSIBLE WORLD
LAWRENCE RESNICK

he God of the Judeo-Christian tradition may be thought of as a combination of different Beings, of which one, the God of Job, for example, is a superhuman monarch in whose image man was created, and another (who might be described as the God of the Ontological Argument) is the necessarily Existing, perfectly Good, Omniscient, Omnipotent, Infinite, Eternal Creator about whose "image" it seems inappropriate even to conjecture. This paper deals with the concept of the latter Being, a concept abstracted from the religious tradition by philosophers and theologians. Specifically, I shall explore the relationship between the claims "God exists" and "This is the best of all possible worlds."

It seems clear that one would have little inclination to say that this is the best of all possible worlds unless one also believed that God exists and that He created this world. In the absence of some such belief, the claim that this is the best of all possible worlds would be virtually inexplicable, that is, it would be difficult to understand why a rational being would believe it to be true. For, on the face of it, no task would put less strain on the imagination than to conceive of improvements in this world. However, given the existence of God, the situation is completely different. If God exists then this must, a priori, be the best of all possible worlds. The problem of *deciding* whether it is best does not exist. The theological problem which does remain is to explain away the appearances which suggest so strongly that better worlds are possible.

Leibniz describes the relationship between God and the world as follows:

From *American Philosophical Quarterly* 10, no. 4 (October 1973): 313–17. Copyright © 1973 by University of Illinois Press. Reprinted by permission of University of Illinois Press.

53. Now, as in the Ideas of God there is an infinite number of possible universes, and as only one of them can be actual, there must be a sufficient reason for the choice of God which leads Him to decide upon one rather than another.
54. And this reason can be found only in the *fitness*, or in the degrees of perfection, that these worlds possess, since each possible thing has the right to aspire to existence in proportion to the amount of perfection it contains in germ.
55. Thus the actual existence of the best that wisdom makes known to God is due to this, that His goodness makes Him choose it, and His power makes Him produce it.[1]

This familiar conception of God and His relation to the universe may also be expressed in these two propositions: (A), "God the Perfect Creator exists of necessity and is the source of all other existence," and (B), "His perfection is manifested in His Works—therefore, it would be contrary to God's goodness to create a world which is not the best of all possible worlds."

Now I shall try to show that these two doctrines are logically inconsistent. I call my argument *The Paradox of Alternative Worlds.*

1. If God exists then this is the best of all possible worlds.
2. If this is the best of all possible worlds, then worlds worse than this one are logically possible.
3. A logically possible world is any world the existence of which is compatible with logical necessity.
4. If "God exists" is necessarily true, then "The world which exists is not the best of all possible worlds" is necessarily false. (That is, if the proposition "God exists" is necessarily true, then any proposition inconsistent with it is necessarily false. But since God's existence, in Leibniz's conception, entails that this is the best of all possible worlds, it also entails that "The world which exists is not the best of all possible worlds" is false. Thus if "God exists" is necessarily true, "The world which exists is not the best of all possible worlds" is necessarily false.)
5. If "The world which exists is not the best of all possible worlds" is necessarily false, then no world which is not the best of all possible worlds is a logically possible world. (That is, if "God exists" is necessarily true and if it is His nature to create only the best of all possible worlds, then it is logically impossible that any lesser world could have come into existence—again, assuming that all things depend for their existence on God.)
6. Given that this world is the one God chose to bring into existence, if no world worse than this one is logically possible, then it is not the case that this is the best of all possible worlds.

Conclusion: If this world was created by a necessarily existing Perfect Creator, then it both is and is not the case that this world is the best of all possible worlds. Therefore, it is not possible that the world was created by a necessarily existing Perfect Creator.

To put the point another way, it is impossible for God to create any world less good than the best of all possible worlds, but since God is the only possible source of existence, worlds less good than the best of all possible worlds cannot possibly come into existence. Therefore, the world God created cannot possibly be better than other possible worlds. (Nothing said thus far rules out the possibility of a number of equally good worlds—about this, more later.)

It is worth emphasizing that all the characteristics or qualities attributed to God in this argument must be thought of as attributable a priori. The concept under consideration is the concept of a Being who exists *necessarily*; is *necessarily* all-Good, Omniscient, and Omnipotent; is *necessarily* the source of the existence of all other things; and *necessarily* manifests His Perfection in His works.[2] That is to say, if there is a being who might conceivably lack any of these characteristics, then that being is not God.

I shall treat the problem raised by my argument as a problem in theory construction. There is a traditional theory about the nature and ultimate origin of the world. The central construct, which, for the purposes of this discussion, will be taken as vital to the theory, is God. My paradox raises a difficulty for this theory which I shall explore ways of avoiding, trying to do the least violence to the concept of the necessarily existing Perfect Creator, but also trying to take account of the general conceptual framework in which the theory appears. By the latter qualification I mean to rule out, for example, the supposition that logical reasoning cannot force us to modify our conception of God and His Powers because that conception is given in revelation, which is superior to logic as a source of truth. It is beyond the scope of this paper to deal with conjectures of this sort, although it is not my purpose to denigrate them. I can imagine a society in which there prevailed some alternative to the scientific rationalism of Western thought. In such a society, the idea that revelation takes precedence over logic might be an appropriate constituent in a successful theology. But in this discussion I am dealing with a problem which could arise only in an extremely rationalistic tradition and, given the context, I shall not consider what might be called non-rationalistic solutions.

It may be useful to begin by setting aside those aspects of the argument which are simply applications of logic from those which are, at least possibly, negotiable. I believe that premises four, five, and six fall into the former category and premises one, two, and three fall into the latter because they contain three crucial notions which bear examination: first, that God's goodness must be manifest in His works; second, that if one world is best, others must be worse; and third, that a logically possible world is one which could conceivably exist. I shall examine these notions in reverse order.

I

Possible worlds. It is usually supposed that if a complete description of a world contains no logical inconsistencies, then the world corresponding to that description might possibly exist. The description, taken as a statement, would be contingent. The leverage in my paradox comes from showing that if there is a necessarily existing Perfect Creator whose goodness is manifest in His works, this cannot be true because it would be contrary to His perfection to create a lesser world. Thus, lesser worlds which can be *described* without contradiction cannot be said, without contradiction, to exist. Or, more accurately, for a statement to qualify as a description of a possible world, it must be both contingent *and* such that it would not be contrary to God's perfection to create a world which corresponds to the description.

To avoid the paradox one might try to *deny* that possible existence is a mark of a possible world. One might stipulate that if a complete description of a world—a description which does not imply that the world exists—is not logically inconsistent, then it is a description of a possible world. On this view, any logically consistent description of a state of affairs would be a description of a possible world, and the question of whether or not its existence is ruled out a priori would be irrelevant. But this solution is patently ad hoc, for, except to escape a paradox, no one would ever suppose that a world which could not possibly exist is a possible world. It seems clear that when Leibniz and others talked about the best of all possible worlds, they meant that of all the possible alternative worlds, God chose this one to bring into existence because it is better than any of the others. Theologians ought to have recognized, but so far as I know, did not, that since it would be contrary to God's perfection to create a lesser world, lesser worlds could not possibly exist.

It is revealing, I think, to delve into what I shall call the phenomenology of overlooking this implication of God's necessary perfection. I mentioned earlier that the God of the Judeo-Christian tradition may be thought of as a combination of different beings. This makes it possible to switch back and forth among the various conceptions without taking account of the variation in their implications. The picture presented by Leibniz appears to be perfectly straightforward. God, the Father Almighty, using His limitless knowledge, inspected all the worlds which lie within the bounds of logical possibility. Drawing on His limitless goodness, He chose one and by means of His limitless power, brought it into existence. My argument shows that if God is conceived to exist necessarily, to be perfect necessarily, and so forth, then this picture has no application. If statements about the Creator's existence and perfection are numbered among the necessary truths, then the existence of what I have called "lesser worlds" is not within the bounds of logical possibility, since their existence would be incompatible with some necessary truths. Only if "God exists" or one of the other relevant statements about God, for example, "He is the one and only Creator," "He is all-good, all-knowing, and all-powerful," or "He manifests His perfection in His works," was either false or not necessarily true, would Leibniz's description be a description of a possible state of affairs.

To some considerable extent, judging from my own case, this conclusion is counterintuitive. God's necessary existence does not "feel" incompatible with the possible existence of lesser worlds. The reason, I conjecture, is that we, atheists and believers alike, think of God as *personified*. A person is, by the nature of the concept, a being who, if he exists at all, exists *in* fact. Insofar as a person is good, powerful, or wise, he is good, powerful, or wise *in fact*. So when we think of God, we usually think we are thinking of a special kind of person, and when we think about a person we are thinking about a being who does not exist necessarily. Thus, when we think about God it does not seem correct to conclude that if God exists no lesser worlds are logically possible. I do not mean to imply that God is sometimes conceived to exist only as a matter of fact. Western theists of whatever persuasion would say, if forced to a decision, that God exists necessarily. But on religious occasions, when people are seeking contact with God, their sense of His existence as an immeasurably good, understanding, and powerful Being to whom one can turn for help may cause to fade into insignificance intellectual questions about His precise ontological status. However, if God *is* taken to be the necessarily existing Perfect Creator who necessarily manifests His perfection in His works, the conclusion is inescapable, so far as I can see, that He cannot create lesser worlds. The "felt inappropriateness" of the conclusion, so I claim, results, not from any error in premise three, but from an assimilation of incompatible elements in our concept of God.

II

The best. Technically, if no lesser worlds are possible, our world cannot be the best. There cannot be a superlative where comparatives are impossible. But one way of reducing the force of my argument may be to admit the consequence that no lesser worlds are possible and turn this admission into an advantage. There cannot be any worlds worse than this one, for that would be contrary to God's goodness. However, it also follows that this is a world than which a better cannot be conceived. From a theological point of view, the phrase, "a world than which a better cannot be conceived" is as fitting in praise of God's works as the more familiar phrase, "the best of all possible worlds." It may be only an historical accident that the one locution is used rather than the other. If this solution is correct, then my argument would still have the merit of showing that lesser worlds are impossible, but it would not cast doubt on the compatibility of the two basic propositions which express the traditional view of God. At the beginning of this paper I put them as follows:

A. God the Perfect Creator exists necessarily and is the source of all other existence.
B. God's perfection is manifest in His works. Therefore, it would be contrary to His goodness to create a world which was not the best of all possible worlds.

Since my argument has shown that if A is true, B, *as explicated,* is false we need only revise B as follows:

B. God's perfection is manifest in His works. Therefore, it would be contrary to His goodness to create a world than which a better could be conceived.

This appears to reconcile traditional theology with the conclusion that if the Perfect Creator exists, necessarily lesser worlds are not logically possible, with one exception. An important advantage of the belief that this is the best of all possible worlds is the certainty in the face of suffering that whatever happens is really for the best. This belief, which has provided solace to many, depends upon the idea that all other possible worlds are worse than this one.

However, despite its apparent promise, the use of the expression, "a world than which a better cannot be conceived" does not help here at all. For although it would be true, if all possible worlds were equally good, that no possible world would be better than this one, it would also be true that no possible world would be worse. The first description, "This is a world than which a better cannot be conceived," cannot be construed to be true in virtue of God's goodness unless the second description, "This is a world than which a worse cannot be conceived," is construed to be true in virtue of God's wickedness, since both descriptions are equally true and equally apt. In fact, of course, if all possible worlds are equally good, then both descriptions are misleading.

The general point, once again, is that in order for God's works to be a manifestation of His perfection, they must at least be better than some possible alternative works. But if God's existence and perfections are logically necessary, then it is impossible for this condition to be met. Thus, so far as I can see, it is self-contradictory to assert that the necessarily existing Perfect Creator necessarily manifests His perfection in His works.

Although I have applied my argument only to the choice among alternative *worlds*, it is easy to see that it applies to any alternatives whatever which God might choose. For if there are two alternatives and one is better, it would be logically impossible for God to choose the other. To put it slightly differently, if God has a genuine choice between X and Y, it follows that they have the precisely equivalent degree of perfection, because if one were worse, it would be logically impossible for God to choose it. To apply here the lesson of the Paradox of Alternative Worlds, we cannot even say that if one alternative is worse than another God could not choose it, but rather that a lesser alternative is not a possible alternative at all. A possible state of affairs is one whose actualization would be consistent with logical necessity. But then no possible state of affairs could be worse than any alternative possible state of affairs because if it were God could not possibly choose to actualize it, and if He could not possibly choose to actualize it, then since He is the only possible source of existence, it could not possibly exist, and if it could not possibly exist, then it is not a possible state of affairs. All lesser alternatives are excluded from possible existence and all remaining alternatives are equally good. Therefore, it is logically impossible for God, as defined, to exercise moral judgment or to make any decision or take any action which reflects His goodness.

III

Manifesting Perfection. If the main body of my argument is correct, then the concept of a necessarily existing Perfect Creator who necessarily manifests His goodness in His works is self-contradictory. Now I shall try to determine whether it is necessarily a characteristic, of God that He manifest His perfection in works. If it is a necessary characteristic, then the concept of God, the necessarily existing Perfect Creator, is self-contradictory.

I shall try to imagine that although God exists necessarily and is necessarily perfect, it is not necessarily true that He manifests His goodness in His works. Assume that He manifests His goodness as a matter of fact. Then it would be logically possible for God to create a lesser world, although, of course, He would not do so, because He is perfectly good. Now the conditions for avoiding the Paradox of Alternative Worlds seem to obtain. Since lesser worlds would be *possible*, the picture drawn by Leibniz appears to have an application. That is, it would make sense to claim that one of the members of the class of possible worlds is better than all the rest; that God in His infinite wisdom knew which one it was; and that because He is perfectly good He used His power to bring it into existence.

Suppose it is granted that the conditions do exist in which God could manifest His goodness by creating the best of all possible worlds. Is it conceivable that an all-good, all-knowing, all-powerful Creator should *not* manifest His goodness when it was open to Him to do so? Clearly not. It makes no sense to say that such a Being might not do what is best. But to say this is to say that it is *necessarily* the case that if He could, God would manifest His Goodness. It is to say that it *cannot* be contingently true that God would do whatever is best. It is to say that if a being could do what is best, but might not, then that being is not God. Thus, we have arrived at a reductio ad absurdum of the supposition that although God is perfect necessarily, He does not necessarily manifest His goodness, but only manifests it in fact.

Therefore, it *is* a necessary characteristic of a necessarily existing Perfect Creator that He manifests His perfection in His works. And as I have already shown, the concept of such a Being is self-contradictory.

One final point: speaking as an outsider, it seems to me that religion has a life of its own, independent of theology. Because religion is not merely the practice for which theology provides the theory, my arguments may challenge a theological conception of God without, so far as I can see, raising any problems for religion.[3]

NOTES

1. G. W. Leibniz, *The Monadology*, trans. R. Latta (London, 1898), pp. 247–48.
2. Unless otherwise specified, I mean by 'God' the Being with all these qualities.
3. I wish to thank the members of the Dartmouth College Philosophy Department for a stimulating discussion of the original version of this paper, which was also read at the American Philosophical Association's Eastern Division Meeting, New York, December 1971.

24

AGENCY AND OMNISCIENCE

TOMIS KAPITAN

I. INTRODUCTION

It is said that faith in a divine agent is partly an attitude of trust; believers typically find assurance in the conception of a divine being's will and cherish confidence in its capacity to implement its intentions and plans. Yet, there would be little point in trusting in the will of any being without assuming its ability to both *act* and *know,* and perhaps it is only by assuming divine omniscience that one can retain the confidence in the efficacy and direction of divine agency that has long been the lure of certain religious traditions.

Is it possible for an *agent* to be omniscient? We think of agents as capable of intentional behavior and, thus, able to prefer, select, and undertake courses of action, abilities typically joined to a capacity for weighing reasons, determining means, evaluating ends, namely, deliberation. While deliberating, however, one's mind is not yet made up, one is in a state of indecision and, as such, there is a sense of uncertainty about what one will eventually do, otherwise there would be no point in deliberating about whether to do it.[1] It follows that a being with complete foreknowledge of the future, specifically, its own future, cannot deliberate, and, seemingly, cannot "make up its mind" or decide among options.

Can an omniscient being nonetheless *intend* to do actions? If intending consists in the mind's being settled upon, or committed to, a particular course of

From *Religious Studies* 27 (1991): 105–20. Copyright © 1991 by Kings College London. Reprinted by permission of Cambridge University Press.

action, must it not be previously *un*settled, not only practically but epistemically as well? What could motivate someone to undertake an action unless he or she sensed both a need for the required effort and a chance that it might succeed, and how could this happen *if* the agent already knew what is to take place? If it is going to occur, no need, and if slated not to occur, no chance. Hence, future-directed uncertainty seems essential to intention, but then, how can an omniscient being will or act intentionally?[2]

There are, of course, a number of ways to deal with these questions within traditional theological frameworks. One might take a cue from proposed solutions to the traditional problem of divine foreknowledge and human freedom, for example, that which repudiates the idea that statements about 'future contingents', say, future free acts, can be foreknown or truth-valued. But this invokes controversial assumptions about free action or truth-conditions for future-tensed sentences and, accordingly, has engendered dissent.[3] A different account solves the problem by appeal to the timeless eternity of the divine being, removing any doubt about its uncertainty *before* formulating intentions. Despite a respectable history, this view raises difficult problems about timelessness and timeless agency.[4] Another position is that divine willing does not involve coming to intend, rather, the divine being's intentions are eternal, contemporaneous with its temporal being and without *prior* indecision. Accordingly, everlasting divine intentions are always in place, and the divine being never has the occasion to either deliberate or choose. The success of this view depends on undermining the argument motivating the uncertainty condition proposed above.[5] A distinct approach circumvents the problem altogether by conceiving divine agency as radically unlike human agency in being devoid of desire, will, intention, or choice in any of the literal senses of these terms.[6]

It is not the concern of this paper to criticize, defend, or develop any of these views. Instead, an independent argument concerning intentional action will be constructed whose conclusion straightforwardly precludes omniscient agency. Whether it poses an insurmountable challenge, provides a new foil for a particular theological gambit, or can be safely diffused, will be left undecided. What will become clear is that a distinct problem for the doctrine of omniscient agency—and, if I am not mistaken, a severe problem—has made its claim for the attention of those taking interest in the merger of divinity with agency.

II. INTENTIONAL ACTION AND INTENDING

If an action or doing is an agent's performance of, or refraining from, an action-type at a time, we distinguish those that are intentional from those that are accidental or instinctual. It is here assumed that agency is exercised only through intentional action, and an action is intentional only if among its causal antecedents is an intending of the agent's—where an *intending* is a state whose content is an *intention*.[7] This does not imply that whatever is intentional is intend*ed*,[8] nor that every intending is deliberative; rather, what one does intentionally is connected, at least causally, to one's being settled upon undertaking a particular course of action. However, the causal connection is not sufficient for intentional action since instinctual and accidental doings can also be caused by intendings, for example, one's inadvertently stepping on a cockroach upon deciding to turn sharply to the right. One must add that the causal link between the intending and the action be of the proper sort, for example, the action is performed as a result of following an intended action-plan.[9] Also, while intentional actions are typically voluntary and under our control, doings which would otherwise be instinctual or habitual can be subjected to conscious control, as when one intentionally avoids blinking or controls a nervous habit for a time despite consequent discomfort.[10]

Yet, talk about 'intending' or 'having an intention' is ambiguous. A distinction between having an intention (being inclined in a certain way) and consciously intending (voliting) is obvious enough. The former is not just a propensity to act; a baby does not intend to suck or to cry, despite evident tendencies to do so. At best, intendings are a subclass of propensities, distinguished by the fact that one must come to intend at some point in time,[11] though this need not be a conscious process of forming an intention.[12] One cannot intend without having *acquired* an intending attitude, otherwise there is no distinguishing intentional states from innate propensities and no demarcating intentional from nonintentional activity. Though there may be genetically based dispositions to have intentions of certain sorts and to engage in corresponding types of behavior, intentional behavior is not innate, and intention-acquisition must always be a modification of behavioral proclivities.

We thereby distinguish having an intention from acquiring an intention, and this, in turn, from rehearsing that intention, namely, consciously affirming an intention already held.[13] Last night, I decided to swim at nine o'clock this morning and upon waking I again thought, in an intending way, of swimming at nine. I did not make up my mind again upon waking; I simply rehearsed an intention already in place. And just as intention-acquisition is not always conscious, it need not involve adopting piecemeal each intentional component of an action-plan one endorses. Finally, while we can distinguish standing inclinations to do certain *types* of acts from intentions to perform their particular instantiates, the former are often causally relevant in the acquisition of the latter.

III. INTENDING, EFFICACY, AND NEED

The perceptive reader might suspect that a significant concession has already been made if one agrees that intending is possible only by the agent *acquiring* an intending attitude. Not only is a strongly temporal dimension to an agent's thought suggested; the specter of antecedent uncertainty is reinvoked. While the position has so far been motivated by the need to distinguish intentional from nonintentional behavior, one might ask whether there are other grounds in its favor.

Recall that conventional wisdom about the origination of intending states accords a role to cognitive factors as well as connative elements.[14] No one acts intentionally from a zero point of view, devoid of antecedent knowledge or beliefs. Every intention is acquired against a background of beliefs, plans, goals, and other intentions, with some idea about the necessary conditions for and probable contribution of the intended action. None of us would intend to swim at the local YMCA without assuming that there is a local YMCA or that it has a pool, nor would we intentionally buy a ticket in order to attend the ballet without believing the purchase to be an appropriate means. In short, because we intend with the aim of realizing our goals, we inevitably consider action-plans by recourse to background presumptions, presumptions that might be tacit, perhaps no more than dispositions to assent to given types of propositions rather than explicitly accepted beliefs. Henceforth, 'presumes' will be used as a generic designation meant to cover this weaker sort of doxastic commitment as well as belief. However vague and inarticulate, these presumptions are the very foundation of rational action and indispensable to the hope that accompanies expenditures of effort.

The linkage of intentional action with the expenditure of effort is helpful in understanding the cognitive context in which intentions are acquired. If we think of coming to intend as the initial phase whereby we attempt to accomplish something, the envisioned background is likely to include tacit assumptions both that intentional effort is needed to effect the desired change and that there is some chance that the environment will cooperate. Intention-acquisition prepares the ground for subsequent exertion by establishing a propensity to expend effort in a certain way, that is, to have volitions or to engage in tryings (if not identical to volitions).[15] And if nature does nothing in vain, an analogous principle of 'least effort' would appear in order: we acquire an intention to do an action only if we presume that we would not be wasting our effort upon undertaking it, that is, intentional effort is something that *needs* to be expended if we are to realize certain ends (the action is not otherwise inevitable) *and* that the action is, as of yet, an *open* alternative for us.[16]

The principle is probably applicable to rational agency only. Despite the 'least effort' label, it should not be confused with a principle of universal laziness, nor with one of efficiency; it claims that rational agents exert themselves with the anticipation of thereby furthering certain of their aims, thus, with a sense of both need and possibility for success. In blending connative with cognitive factors, it requires agents to have a concept of intending, at least under the guise of 'exertion'. Some will find this condition excessive,[17] and although it conveniently divides blind exertion from fully constituted agency, skepticism might only reinforce restriction of the principle to rational agents.

What does such a presumption involve? Apart from being drawn toward a particular course of action, we act intentionally only on the assumption that the action is within our power or under our control, allowing that the appropriate doxastic state be tacit and comparatively lower-level. What does this sense of control include? An obvious candidate is a tacit presumption of *efficacy*; one intends to A only by assuming there is some probability of success, that is,

> (1) If, at t, X acquires an intention to A at t', then X presumes that there is a chance that he would A (would refrain from A-ing) at t' were he to intend to A (to refrain from A-ing) at t'.

Here, the projected time of intending must fall within the interval bounded by t and t', and it is argued in section V that the time of believing must be appropriate prior to t. The weak probability qualifier may be deleted if X believes his effort is guaranteed success, or, alternatively, if the embedded conditionals harbor a tacit ceteris paribus reflecting the improbability of unforeseen intervention.[18] It seems less operative in the distinct, but equally justified,

> (2) If, at t, X acquires an intention to A at t', then X presumes that he would undertake (try) A-ing at t' (or earlier) were he to intend to A at t'.[19]

Satisfying the consequents of (1) and (2) is not sufficient for taking A to be under one's control; the least effort model precludes viewing A-ing as fait accompli, for we must presume that our A-ing would not occur in the absence of our intentional efforts. A state of intending emerges only with a tacit sense of causal requirement, that is, exertion is required:

> (3) If, at t, X acquires an intention to A at t', then X presumes that he would not A at t' unless he intended to A at t'.

To acquire an intention, in short, is to sense its need, to realize, at least tacitly, that what is intended is not otherwise inevitable and that without an appropriate intending some desired state of affairs would not be realized. Even though I might deliberate about something I know I am going to do regardless of what I intend—for example, crash into the concrete barrier that suddenly looms before me—I deliberate only about *how* to do so, at full speed, say, or intentionally, for here is something that remains to be fixed. Similarly, while I might vote for a Republican in the next election fully confident that the Republicans will win, what I intend is that I so vote, not that I bring about a Republican victory.[20]

IV. INTENDING, CONTINGENCY, AND OPEN ALTERNATIVES

There is more to the presumption of openness than revealed in conditions (1)–(3). Sometimes an agent removes a course of action from the range of alternatives by prior commitment. Nathan might think he would drink whiskey were he to try, would not do so unless he intended, yet also believe that he will not so choose. He has ruled out drinking whiskey, perhaps for deep-seated moral reasons, and, having done so, his mind is already settled, and he no longer considers drinking whiskey an *open* alternative, a fact which cannot be explained by the conditional consequents of (1)–(3) alone. Drinking whiskey is taken to be open only if he takes it for granted that he both can so intend and can avoid so intending, that is, only if he presumes that his decision about the matter, whatever it might be, is as yet *contingent*.

An assumed contingency seems vital, but how is the embedded modality to be interpreted? Mere logical or nomological contingency is too weak; one might recognize that there are many things he or she could do in the purely 'theoretical' sense, that is, not being prohibited by the laws of logic or nature alone, but which actual circumstances rule out. Instead, a course of action is taken to be open only by assuming that both it and its complement are possible given circumstances as they now stand. That is, a suitably concrete or relative modality is at stake— where P is contingent relative to a set of conditions S just in case neither P nor not-P is a consequence of S.[21]

The task is now to give a general specification of the set S of conditions relevant to all instances of the contingency presumption. Three candidates are paramount:

- (A) all propositions true at t (including those with reference to the past and future);
- (B) all states of affairs (facts, conditions) obtaining prior to and including t; or,
- (C) all that he or she (the agent) then (at t) believes (or knows).

Each of (A)–(C) has been advocated at one time or another, though it is unimportant for present purposes which is preferred.[22] The doxastic/epistemic contingency of (C) has the advantage of not rendering a decision-making determinist inconsistent and squares nicely with the response of the deliberator who, when asked if he is aware of anything which determines his eventual decision or what that decision will be, reports: "Not at all; *as far as I know* it is entirely up to me which alternative I choose." This minimal type of openness seems integral to decision making, in which case C, at least, is assured. It may also be the key to the implicit ceteris paribus in some readings of (1), insofar as no one deliberates about A-ing unless able to meet the question, "Can you really do A?" with the affirmative, "Yes I can, as far as I can tell." The qualifiers reveal the agent's *cautious* assumption of efficacy; he must take his choice to be efficacious *within* circumstances as he himself understands them, though he might allow that unforeseen factors will prevent success. Relativization to (C) might also explain why explicit inclusion of the probability factor in (1) is unnecessary and the implicit ceteris paribus clause enough.

Still, (C) can be understood in at least two ways depending on whether the phrase "he (she) then believes" occurs outside or inside the scope of belief. The first-person character of our deliberator's responses suggests an internal occurrence, but the two readings are equivalent when the agent in question is omniscient.[23] Of course, for an omniscient agent, (C) is sufficient for (A) and (B), since what it takes itself to know is coextensive with what is the case, so nothing beyond (C) need here be assumed. This in mind, one statement of the minimal contingency presumption is as follows:

(4) If, at t, X acquires an intention to A at t', then X presumes that his intending to A at t' is as yet contingent relative to what he himself then believes (knows).

where 'as yet', falling within the scope of 'believes', expresses X's own representation of time t.

The contingency need not be indexed by all that the agent in fact believes, only by what he *takes* himself to believe or know. Let us refer to the beliefs so described as the agent's *internal* beliefs. The index may be diluted even further; someone might deliberate about acting in a way that is incompatible with what they have previously committed themselves to doing, a commitment accompanied by an internal belief that they will do that thing. Since one can overlook one's commitments during the course of deliberation, it follows that the modal qualifier in (4) must be indexed to *immediately accessible* internal beliefs, a qualification external to the scope of presumption. That is, beliefs can be stratified with respect to retrievability, allowing that one can deliberate about what one already assumes one will not do, so long as this assumption is overridden by a more accessible set of internal beliefs against which contingency remains. While the latter class might be difficult to isolate, it appears indispensable in accounting for such cases of forgetful deliberators.[24]

V. INTENDING AND CHOOSING

Likening intention to an expenditure of effort within the bounds of a least-effort principle effectively equates intention with choice. By conjoining the consequents of (1), (3), and (4) and treating them as constitutive conditions, we obtain a promising analysis of what it is for an agent to take a course of action as an open alternative:

(5) At t, X takes his A-ing at t' to be an open alternative iff, at t, X believes each of the following: (a) there is a chance that he would A (would refrain from A-ing) at t' were he to intend to A (to refrain from A-ing) at t'; (b) he himself would not A at t' *unless* he intended to A at t'; and (c) his intending to A at t' is as yet contingent relative to what he himself then believes.

In the broadest sense, choosing is nothing more than selecting a course of action from a range of presumed open alternatives. If a *minimal range* is the pair composed of X's doing A and X's refraining from A, where A is any action-type, a *minimal choice* is a selection of a course of action from a minimal range. From (4), every intention-acquisition is effectively a minimal choice, not necessarily conscious, inasmuch as the agent takes it for granted that his not A-ing is as open as his A-ing, that is, that each is contingent. This underscores the previous contention that intending emerges from a conception of prevailing circumstances and possibilities as well as from desire, specifically, from a sense of alternatives, however vaguely identified.[25]

VI. THE ANTECEDENT PRESUMPTION OF OPENNESS

The consequents in each of (1)–(4) attribute a belief to the agent, but the *times* of these beliefs remains to be fixed. If (5) is correct, they are simultaneous, but how is their temporal locus to be identified in relation to the times of action and intending?

Undoubtedly, the beliefs can be held no later than the time of intention-acquisition. Can they emerge simultaneously? I think not, at least not for an agent who is minimally rational (locally consistent in the relevant beliefs) and self-reflective enough to realize he or she has intended when he or she in fact has. Let us show this by focusing on the contingency presumption (4), recalling what has been said about the accessibility of beliefs, and confining attention to the case where X is minimally rational and self-reflective.

(6)   If, at t, a minimally rational being X both acquires an intention to A at t′ and believes that he has, then, at some time appropriately prior to t, X presumes that his intending to A at t′ is as yet contingent relative to what he himself then believes.

Proof. Assume the antecedent and suppose that the only time at which X held the belief mentioned in the consequent was simultaneous with t. Realizing that he has at t the intention to A at t′, then relative to his own beliefs at t, his intending to A at t′ is no longer contingent, and, being rational, he could not at t take it to be so. That is, X cannot believe that he will intend to A while at the same time view his intending to A as contingent relative to what he believes. So, the time at which he takes his intending to A to be contingent must be appropriately prior to time t—where a commentary on 'appropriately prior' awaits a more detailed study of the temporal parameters of practical thinking. It follows that X cannot come to intend except by *antecedently* presuming his intending to A to be contingent relative to what he then believes.

Assuming that (5) is correct in ascribing simultaneous presumptions of efficacy, need, and contingency, the following consequence of the principle of least effort is immediate:

(7)   If, at t, a minimally rational agent X both acquires an intention to do A at t′ and believes that he has, then, at some time appropriately prior to t, X presumes that his A-ing at t′ is an open alternative for him.

VII. THE PRESUMPTION OF UNCERTAINTY

It would be wrong to assume that a deliberator cannot know in advance what he will do or choose; as previously indicated, agents can forget what they are already committed to and, therefore, what they already know they will do (see note 2). At the same time, decision does seem to involve passing from a state of uncertainty into a kind of knowledge.[26] Of course, it strains the imagination to speak of deliberating about *whether* to A while occurrently believing that one will A, still more so if the deliberator is occurrently intending to do A; 'whether' suggests a moment of uncertainty and indecision which precludes having one's mind made up modulo occurrent conviction. Perhaps a deliberator's antecedent indecision, ignorance, or lack of doxastic commitment can be restricted to a denial of the relevant occurrent psychological states. But this would be of no help in understanding the state of uncertainty which, like wonder or bewilderment, harbors intentionality. That is, a deliberator is not uncertain in the sense of not knowing what he or she will decide, rather, the agent is cognizant that he or she is not yet settled upon which course of action to undertake in the circumstances. Negation is inside the scope of the agent's uncertainty here, and since conditions that merely prohibit occurrent intendings or believings are expressed with negation having largest scope, then, ascribing no content at all, they are unsuitable as a phenomenological assay of the agent's sense *of* his own indecision and uncertainty. It is the contentual aspect of the latter which demands scrutiny.

A deliberator who responds to a question about what he will choose may very well say: "I don't know, I've not yet made up my mind," implying not indecision, only a *presumption* of such. For a minimally rational agent who takes his A-ing to be consequent upon his so intending, this follows from a further presumption of uncertainty; believing that he himself does not yet know whether he will intend to A at t', then, by (3), he believes he does not yet know that he will A—hence, a presumption *of* indecision. Such uncertainty is, in turn, a result of the presumed contingency sanctioned by (7):

(8) If, at t, a minimally rational being X presumes that his intending to A at t' is contingent relative to what he himself then believes, then, at t, X presumes both that he does not yet believe that he will intend to A at t' and that he does not yet believe that he will not intend to A at t'.

Proof. Suppose X satisfied the antecedent. Then, by taking his intending to A at t' not to be contingent with respect to a set S, he will not regard S as a set of his own beliefs. Given the rationality proviso, he does not suppose his intending to A to be contingent with respect to any set among whose members is the proposition *that he intends to A at t'*. So, he does not view the latter as a set of his own beliefs, that is, he presumes that he himself does not believe he will intend to A at t' and, by a similar argument, that he himself does not believe he will not intend to A at t'. Therefore, he satisfies the consequent.

VIII. SOME CLARIFICATIONS

The preceding principles govern only the *acquisition* of intentions; they fail as principles concerning their *rehearsal*. However, since little has been said about the mechanisms of acquisition and rehearsal, successful counterexamples remain possible pending deeper probes. For one thing, since intention-acquisition is not necessarily a conscious process, it is not necessary to have consciously entertained an intention before rehearsing it, and given its holistic character, the several propensities to act that are established upon endorsing a plan of action need not have been separately formulated.

But this leaves unsettled a problem concerning the rehearsal of indexical intentions. If intending a content of the form "I shall A now" or "I to do A now" is the proximate cause of action, then one could not have adopted *that* intention prior to the indexically designated time, yet one could certainly have known in advance that one would A at the time in question (though not qua 'now'). A counterexample to (8)? I think not; even granting the irreducibility of indexical reference,[27] to *foreknow* that one will A *at t*, is not to foreknow that one will A *now*, and insofar as one knows that one will A now it is only because one is at present cognizant of one's intention to A now. If, on the other hand, one can foreknow that one will endorse an indexical intention to A at t, this is probably due to recognition of an already acquired intention to follow a certain action-plan. The upshot is that the notion of rehearsing an intention must be adjusted in such a way that voliting an indexical intention can still qualify as a 'rehearsal' in virtue of previously adopting a nonindexical counterpart together with certain beliefs linking distinct identifications of the relevant items.

Another problem concerns the presumption of uncertainty (8) and the principles (3), (4), and (6) on which it rests. Some might object to these principles on the grounds that they incorrectly rule out formulating an intention to do something one already knows one will do. For example, at gunpoint you demand that I walk through the door, threatening to force me to do it if I don't do so myself. Hearing this might convince me that I will go through the door. It would seem, however, that I can still formulate an intention to walk through the door even though I already believe that I will do so one way or the other, a result which goes directly against (3), (4), and (6).

The objection can be met in two ways. For one thing, I might already possess a standing conditional intention to walk through the door when so coerced (or, more generally, to go wherever I am commanded to at gunpoint). Then, adopting the intention to walk through the door is concurrent with coming to believe that the relevant circumstance obtains, and it is *hence* that I know (believe) I will walk through the door. But in such a case, knowledge does not antedate intention-adoption, and it remains likely that before I adopted that intention I did not know that I would walk through the door. On the other hand, if I am *deliberating* about whether to comply with the gunman's command, that is, whether to walk through the door or not, then it is unlikely that I already know that I will *walk* through the door. Being forced through the door is not the same as walking through it any more than someone's forcibly raising my arm is an instance of my raising my arm. Thus, my passing through the doorway *is* necessitated, but the distinct content of my possible intention, my walking through the door, is not; the latter, from my perspective, is an open alternative which I can choose to undertake or not, and if I perform it, it qualifies as an intentional action. In short, what I foreknow will occur is not my intentional action but only some event involving me.

Finally, it might seem that I can know (believe) that I will adopt an intention to A at some future point even though I do not now intend to A then. God may have told me that I will intend to A then, or I may be so cognizant of my own incontinence that I unhappily predict what I will intend. Nothing in the preceding principles precludes this; what is required is that at *some* point prior to intention-acquisition there is a moment of sensed (believed) contingency, a state which precludes only a consciously explicit belief that A-ing is already fixed, not a tacit belief to this effect.[28]

IX. THERE IS NO OMNISCIENT AGENCY

Satisfaction of the consequent of (8) does *not* imply that an arbitrary agent X does not know, or have a belief about, what he or she will do, for the attributed belief may well be false. This is not so if X is omniscient. That is, if by 'God' we understand an omniscient being, the following equivalences hold:

(9) For any proposition p and time t, God believes at t that p iff God knows at t that p iff p.[29]

From this and the principle of excluded middle it follows that for each proposition p either God knows that p or God knows that not-p, namely, God's knowledge and belief are negation-complete. Obviously, both are consistent as well.

We now come to the principal result that omniscience precludes the acquisition of an intention, hence, intentional action itself:

(10) If X is omniscient, then there are no times t and t′ and no action type A such that at t X intends to A at t′.

Proof. Suppose, for reductio, the following:

(a) At t, God intends to A at t′ (for times t, t′ and action-type A).

Then, by the description of intending given in section II above, at a time no later than t, God *acquires* an intention to A at t′. So, applying (7),

(b) At some time t″ appropriately prior to t, God presumes that his A-ing at t′ is an open alternative for him.

Then, according to (5), God possesses each of the beliefs attributed in the consequents (1), (3), and (4). Since God is omniscient, it follows from (a) and (9) that,

(c) At t″, God knows that at t he will intend to A at t′.

But, from (a) by (5) and (8), we have,

(d) At t″, God believes that he himself does not yet believe that at t he will intend to A at t′.

and from this, by (9),

(e) At t″, God does not believe that at t he will intend to A at t′.

By (9), again,

(f) At t″, God does not know that at t he will intend to A at t′,

which contradicts (c). Consequently, if God is omniscient, then the reductio supposition (a) cannot be satisfied. It follows that God cannot act intentionally.

X. CONCLUSION

The principle of least effort and its implicate (7) govern the acquisition of intentions, not their rehearsal. Restricted to minimally rational agents, both are limiting principles that might fail to govern all intentional action, yet which apply admirably to an omniscient being whose beliefs are both consistent and closed under implication. If the foregoing account of intention is correct, there is no refuge in the conception that God is a timeless agent or that God's intentions are fixed from eternity. Qua eternal, whether timeless or everlasting, God's propensities to act cannot have been acquired and, therefore, are not intentions at all, rather, inherent dispositions. The latter spawn only instinctual behavior; the 'actions' they induce, if any, cannot be intentional and God's mode of activity can only be something necessary, a consequence of considerable theological significance.

By the same reasoning, we, as finite agents, are able to adopt intentions and act intentionally because of our self-acknowledged limitations in grasping the world in which we find ourselves. Not only is our remarkable ability to forget the past a prerequisite for action, as Nietzsche so aptly observed,[30] so is our imperfect conception of what *will* be, for our efforts to shape the future in accord with our desires are as parasitic upon our ignorance as they are upon our expectations.

Viewed from within the world as we ourselves understand it, each of us is, to a degree, an 'unmoved mover' facing an incomplete and partly unsettled future. For an omniscient being, on the other hand, no state of affairs is epistemically or doxastically contingent and, therefore, it is never presented with options, never enjoys the capacity to acquire intentions, and is unable to act intentionally. Far from being 'free' to choose and act, or unlimited in power, it is, of necessity, omni-impotent.[31]

NOTES

1. That deliberation requires ignorance has been argued by: C. Ginet, "Can The Will Be Caused?" *Philosophical Review* 71 (1962): 49–55; R. Taylor, *Action and Purpose* (Englewood Cliffs: Prentice-Hall, 1966); A. Prior, *Papers on Time and Tense* (Oxford: Clarendon, 1968), pp. 47–48; A. Goldman, *A Theory of Human Action* (Princeton, 1970), p. 195; and N. Denyer, *Time, Action & Necessity: A Proof of Free Will* (London: Duckworth, 1981), p. 48. Doubts are expressed in: P. Quinn, "Divine Foreknowledge and Divine Freedom," *International Journal for Philosophy of Religion* 9 (1978): 219–40; B. Reichenbach, "Omniscience and Deliberation," *International Journal for Philosophy of Religion* 17 (1985): 225–36; and T. Kapitan, "Deliberation and the Presumption of Open Alternatives," *The Philosophical Quarterly* 36 (1986): 230–51. See section VII.

2. That God can neither deliberate not decide has been argued in R. La Croix, "Omniprescience and Divine Determinism," *Religious Studies* 12 (1976): 365–81, disputed in Quinn, "Divine Foreknowledge," and reaffirmed in T. Kapitan, "Can God Make Up His Mind?" *International Journal for Philosophy of Religion* 15 (1984): 37–47; D. Basinger, "Omniscience and Deliberation: A Response to Reichenbach," *International Journal for Philosophy of Religion* 17 (1986): 169–72; and G. Strawson, *Freedom and Belief* (Oxford, 1986), p. 257. R. Swinburne, *The Coherence of Theism* (Oxford, 1977), pp. 172–74, argues that a completely omniscient being could not act freely and thereby supports a weakened sense of omniscience. See also W. Alston ("Divine and Human Action," in *Divine & Human Action*, ed. Thomas Morris [Ithaca, N.Y.: Cornell, 1988], p. 278), who admits that the tension between agency and omniscience is part of a "genuine problem" that remains to be explored. Other recent studies of divine agency include: R. Creel, *Divine Impassibility* (Cambridge, 1986); J. Kvanvig, *The Possibility of an All-Knowing God* (New York: St. Martin's, 1986); T. Talbott, "On the Divine Nature and the Nature of Divine Freedom," *Faith and Philosophy* 5 (1988): 3–24; W. Hasker, *God, Time and Knowledge* (Ithaca, N.Y.: Cornell, 1989); and E. Wierenga, *The Nature of God* (Ithaca, N.Y.: Cornell, 1989).

3. The common exclusion of 'future contingents' from God's knowledge has a long history. Swinburne, *The Coherence of Theism*, pp. 172–78, limits omniscience by allowing that some future contingents may be true but unknowable. J. Runzo ("Omniscience and Freedom for Evil," *International Journal for Philosophy of Religion* 12 [1981]: 139–43) and Denyer (*Time, Action & Necessity*), on the other hand, contend that such propositions are not truth-valued, in which case there is nothing to be known or unknown. They are opposed by L. Zagzebski ("Divine Foreknowledge and Human Free

Will," *Religious Studies* 21 [1985]: 279–98) and Kvanvig (*The Possibility of an All-Knowing God*). I will not argue against the exclusionary view here, save to point out that it must be accompanied by two developments. *First*, reasons must be provided for concluding that there are no causal chains leading up to so-called 'free actions', or that no compatibilist account of free agency suffices, otherwise it begs the question to label such acts 'contingent' (see D. Dennett, *Elbow Room* [Oxford: Clarendon, 1984], and T. Kapitan, "Doxastic Freedom: A Compatibilist Alternative," *American Philosophical Quarterly* 26 [1989]: 31–3). *Second*, as long as propositions about future actions exist—which many do—then it would seem that an omniscient being must know their truth-values. The denial that they have truth-values must be defended on the basis of an independent account of truth-bearers and truth-conditions.

4. N. Kretzmann and E. Stump ("Eternity," *Journal of Philosophy* 78 [1981]: 429–58) champion the Boethian-Thomistic thesis of God as a timeless being, though their solution exacts the stiff price of accommodating timeless agency by allowing *atemporal* activity and will. D. Burrell ("God's Eternity," *Faith and Philosophy* 1 [1984]: 389–406) expresses reservations about their account, particularly, the coherence of their notion of 'atemporal duration', and Q. Smith ("A New Typology of Temporal and Atemporal Permanence," *Noûs* 23 (1989): 322–24) offers an intriguing argument to show that nothing can be eternal or timeless. The timelessness doctrine also confronts a difficult problem about how God can know temporally indexed propositions. See for example: Prior, *Papers on Time and Tense*, pp. 15–44; N. Kretzmann, "Omniscience and Immutability," *Journal of Philosophy* 63 (1966): 409–21; H.-N. Castañeda, "Omniscience and Indexical Reference," *Journal of Philosophy* 64 (1967): 203–10; P. Grim, "Against Omniscience: The Case from Essential Indexicals," *Noûs* 19 (1985): 151–80; and Kvanvig, *The Possibility of an All-Knowing God*. Grim contends that the argument "against omniscience" is conclusive, pp. 173–4, though Wierenga (*The Nature of God*, pp. 52–53) and Hasker (*God, Time and Knowledge*, p. 161) have challenged his reasoning. Misgivings about the timelessness doctrine are voiced in Alston ("Divine and Human Action," p. 279), and Hasker (*God, Time and Knowledge*, pp. 180–81), N. Woltersdorff ("God Everlasting," in *God and the Good*, ed. D. J. Orlebeke and L. B. Smedes [Grand Rapids: Eerdmans, 1975]), and A. Plantinga (*Does God Have a Nature?* [Marquette, 1980]) drop it altogether.

5. This reply is suggested by Quinn, "Divine Foreknowledge," pp. 236–37, and by Creel, *Divine Impassibility*, pp. 21, 112. Creel is uneasy about the Boethian-Aquinas thesis of God's eternity, specifically as concerns God's knowledge, though he retains a sense in which God is not a temporal being (p. 205). Compare Kvanvig, who, while not rejecting the doctrines of timelessness and immutability, finds that of omniscience to be logically independent, thereby allowing an omniscient being to be both temporal and mutable (*The Possibility of an All-Knowing God*, pp. 164–67).

6. The tendency to make a sharp distinction between divine and human agency is characteristic of the Neo-Platonist tradition. Ibn Rushd (Averroes), for example, employs 'will' analogically, arguing that while God does not will as a human does, that is, because of a *lack*, recognition of which brings about an exertion of effort in the willer, he does will each of his 'acts' in that he both knows and approves of its occurrence (see his *Tahafut at-Tahafut*, trans. Simon van der Bergh [London: Luzac & Co., 1954], pp. 157–61, 426–27, 438–39, 449–50).

7. I will speak as if intending is a unique mental state, irreducible to a complex of desires and beliefs, though this is not necessary for the subsequent argument. For strong arguments against the reductionist view see: H.-N. Castañeda, *Thinking and Doing* (Dordrecht: Reidel, 1975); G. Harman, "Practical Reasoning," *Review of Metaphysics* 79 (1976): 431–63; M. Brand, *Intending and Acting* (Cambridge, Mass.: MIT, 1984); D. Gustafson, *Intention and Agency* (Dordrecht: Reidel, 1986); M. Bratman, *Intention, Plans, and Practical Reason* (Cambridge, Mass.: Harvard, 1987); and A. Mele, "Against a Belief/Desire Analysis of Intention," *Philosophia* 18 (1988): 239–42.

8. Bratman, *Intention, Plans, and Practical Reason,* and A. Mele, "Intention, Belief, and Intentional Action," *The American Philosophical Quarterly* 26 (1989): 19–30.

9. Brand, *Intending and Acting,* and A. Mele, "Are Intentions Self-Referential?" *Philosophical Studies* 52 (1987): 309–29, and Mele, "Intention, Belief, and Intentional Action."

10. While an agent might have no control about whether he will perform a certain action during an interval t, he may very well have control whether or not he performs it during a subinterval t', in which case it is partly under his control at t. Let us say that X's A-ing at t is *semi-intentional,* just in case his A-ing at t is not intentional but had he intended not to A at t then he would have refrained from A-ing at t.

11. A. Donagan, chap. 6 in *Choice* (London: Routledge & Kegan Paul, 1987).

12. Mele, "Intention, Belief, and Intentional Action."

13. The contrast between formulating and rehearsing an intention is emphasized by Castañeda, *Thinking and Doing,* pp. 275–78. I will presuppose Castañeda's view that intentions are irreducibly first-personal (pp. 159–72), and will employ 'he himself' and 'she herself' as *quasi-indicators,* namely, pronominal devices used to *attribute* indexical reference (see H.-N. Castañeda, "Indicators and Quasi-Indicators," *American Philosophical Quarterly* 4 [1967]: 85–100, and "Reference, Reality, and Perceptual Fields," *Proceedings and Addresses of the American Philosophical Association* 53 [1980]: 763–822).

14. Brand, *Intending and Acting.*

15. That intendings can be acquired passively, without prior formulation, is argued in Mele, "Are Intentions Self-Referential?" pp. 321–22. The precise relation between volitions and tryings is a difficult matter, as indicated by the discussions in: B. O'Shaughnessy, *The Will: A Dual Aspect Theory* (Cambridge, 1980); H. McCann, "Trying, Paralysis, and Volition," *The Review of Metaphysics* 28 (1975): 423–42, and "Rationality and the Range of Intention," in *Midwest Studies in Philosophy* 10 (Minnesota, 1986), pp. 191–211; and Bratman, *Intention, Plans, and Practical Reason,* though I follow the latter in distinguishing intending, trying, and intentionally doing.

16. A different principle is that if one believed that a state of affairs P is either inevitable or impossible, hence, would occur or not regardless of what one did intentionally, then one would not acquire the intention to bring about P. This principle does not hold given that agents can be irrational or overlook what they already assume is bound to happen.

17. E.g., Donagan, *Choice,* p. 158.

18. In light of the points raised in McCann, "Rationality and the Range of Intention," and Mele, "Intention, Belief, and Intentional Action," the probability in (1) may be weak, i.e., need not be read as "more probable than not."

19. Gustafson, *Intention and Agency*, pp. 167–68, argues that one must believe that he will *undertake* whatever he fully intends. As the notion is here employed, undertaking is no different from what is otherwise called *trying* or *endeavoring* (Bratman, chap. 9 in *Intention, Plans, and Practical Reason*).

20. Compare C. S. Peirce, who wrote: "We can make no effort where we experience no resistance, no reaction. The sense of effort is a two-sided sense, revealing at once a something within and another something without," *The Collected Papers of Charles Sanders Peirce*, ed. P. Weiss, C. Hartshorne, and A. Burks (Cambridge: Harvard, 1935–58), 2: 84.

21. Consequence will be understood generically, with both P and not-P being in no sense consequence of S. This formulation is neutral between construing the modality as a dyadic or a monadic operator (albeit indexed). Relative modality has been discussed by several, e.g., T. Smiley, "Relative Necessity," *Journal of Symbolic Logic* 28 (1963): 113–34, and I. L. Humberstone, "Relative Necessity Revisited," *Reports on Mathematical Logic* 13 (1981): 33–42. In relation to the free will issue, relative modality is treated in: A. Falk, "Some Modal Confusions in Compatibilism," *American Philosophical Quarterly* 18 (1981): 141–8; M. Slote, "Selective Necessity and Free Will," *Journal of Philosophy* 77 (1982): 136–51; and Kapitan, "Doxastic Freedom."

22. With some stylistic variations, (a) is found in Denyer, *Time, Action & Necessity*, (b) in Taylor, *Action and Purpose*, and P. van Inwagen, *An Essay On Free Will* (Oxford: Clarendon, 1983), and variants of (c) in Dennett, *Elbow Room*, and Kapitan, "Doxastic Freedom."

23. See Castañeda, "Reference, Reality, and Perceptual Fields," on the contrast between external and internal occurrences of terms within attitudinal scope. Where x is omniscient we have (u) (x bel [P]) iff x bel [(u)P], regardless of the restriction on u (a point brought to my attention by Professor Paul Spade).

24. See Kapitan, "Doxastic Freedom," pp. 34–5, and A. Munn, *Free Will and Determinism* (Toronto, 1960), pp. 198–203.

25. Kant's language, that rational beings act only "under the idea of freedom" is appropriate here (see part 3 of Kant's *Grundlegung*). A similar requirement is noted by Aristotle, *Nichomacheaen Ethics*, 1112a–1112b, where the alternatives must be within the agent's power, and Thomas Aquinas, *Summa Theologiae* I, Q13, A2, where it is claimed that reference to the range of alternatives is necessary to choice.

26. This is claimed in: S. Hampshire and H. L. A. Hart, "Decision, Intention and Certainty," *Mind* 67 (1958), Ginet, "Can The Will Be Caused?" and O'Shaughnessy, *The Will*, vol. 2, p. 297.

27. Castañeda, "Reference, Reality, and Perceptual Fields," and Grim, "Against Omniscience: The Case from Essential Indexicals."

28. I am grateful to Alfred Mele for having brought this point to my attention. In Kapitan, "Doxastic Freedom," it is argued that the presumption of openness is compatible with tacit beliefs to the contrary, and only in the case of serious, pathological inconsistency will their contraries be equally accessible or 'retrievable'. Expectedly, such inconsistency will not occur in the case of an omniscient being.

29. This principle is set forth and defended in P. Grim, "Some Neglected Problems of Omniscience," *American Philosophical Quarterly* 20 (1983): 265–66. If God does not

know by way of having beliefs (see W. Alston, "Does God Have Beliefs?" *Religious Studies* 22 [1986]: 287–306), the argument can be recast in terms of knowledge alone, assuming, of course, that we can attribute to God knowledge of particular propositions.

30. See F. Nietzsche, *The Use and Abuse of History,* trans. Adrian Collins (Indianapolis: Bobbs-Merrill, 1957), pp. 6–7: "Forgetfulness is a property of all action, just as not only light but darkness is bound up with the life of every organism."

31. I am indebted to Alfred Mele, John Heil, and Richard Creel for helpful comments on previous versions of this paper.

THE INCOMPATIBILITY
OF OMNISCIENCE AND
INTENTIONAL ACTION
A REPLY TO DAVID P. HUNT
TOMIS KAPITAN

I. INTRODUCTION

In "Omniprescient Agency"[1] David P. Hunt challenges an argument against the possibility of an omniscient agent. The argument—my own in "Agency and Omniscience"[2]—assumes that an *agent* is a being capable of intentional action, where, minimally, an action is intentional only if it is caused, in part, by the agent's intending. The latter, I claimed, is governed by a psychological principle of 'least effort', namely, that no one intends without antecedently feeling that (i) deliberate effort is needed to achieve desired goals, (ii) such effort has a chance of success, and (iii) it is yet contingent whether the effort will be expended and the goals realized. The goals can be anything from immediate intentional doings, tryings, or basic actions, to remote and perhaps unlikely consequences of actions, for example, global justice. The thrust of the principle is that it would be impossible for a wholly rational self-aware agent to intend without a background presumption of an *open* future as concerns the desired state and the means to it. But this presumption embodies a sense of *contingency* which, in turn, requires an acknowledged ignorance about what the future holds, otherwise the future would appear closed relative to present knowledge with the desired state presented as either guaranteed (necessary) or ruled out (impossible). Regardless whether this self-directed attitude is accurate, it follows that inten-

From *Religious Studies* 30 (1994): 55–66. Copyright © 1994 Kings College London. Reprinted by permission of Cambridge University Press.

tional action precludes complete knowledge of one's present and future. Consequently, no omniscient or omniprescient being can be an agent.

Hunt's criticisms are directed against the following recasting of the argument:[3]

(1) There is nothing of which God is ignorant. (Divine Omniscience)

(2) God is an agent—that is, there is a Z such that Z is an exercise of agency on the part of God. (Divine Agency)

(3) A is an exercise of agency on the part of X only if there is an action A and times t and t' (t ≤ t') such that X acquires at t an intention to A at t'. (Analysis of Agency)

(4) X acquires at t an intention to A at t' only if X's A-ing at t' is an open alternative for X at t. (Presumption of Openness)

(5) X's A-ing at t' is an open alternative for X at t only if X is ignorant of whether or not he will A at t'. (Presumption of Ignorance)

Therefore,

(6) There is something of which God is ignorant.

(7) (1) and (6) are contradictory.

Therefore,

(8) At least one of the premises (1)–(5) is false.

Attributing to me the view that not both (1) and (2) can be retained, Hunt concludes that I am wedded to the principle:

(P₃) One cannot intentionally do or refrain from doing what one already (prior to intending) knows is going to happen.

He, more anxious to defend traditional theism, rejects (P_3) and targets the premises on which it is based, specifically, (3) and (5).

Before moving to an examination of his criticisms, two things must be clarified. First, the argument Hunt chooses to criticize is not quite the one I presented; not only do (4) and (5) fail to figure into my argument, but (P_3) is not a principle I accept. Nevertheless, the proximity of his to the version I actually gave renders his critical comments relevant, though, rather than issuing in a decisive refutation of my argument against omniscient agency, they pave the way for an improved statement. Second, it suffices if the subsequent principles be restricted to ideally rational agents only, that is, agents whose sets of beliefs are consistent and closed under a suitably broad consequence relation.[4] Since an omniscient being's beliefs would be coextensive with what it knows, it follows immediately that it would be an ideally rational agent.

II. THE ACQUISITION OF INTENTIONS

Hunt singles out the following claim as central to the argument for premise (5):

> (2.4) X intends (something) only if there is an action A and times t and t' (t ≤ t') such that X acquires at t an intention to A at t'.

He then argues that this is based upon the further contentions,

> (C_1) Acquisition at a time is *essential* to intendings.
> (C_2) Acquisition at a time is the *only* difference between intentional and nonintentional propensities.

In "Agency and Omniscience" I favored (C_1) and wrote as if it were sanctioned by (C_2), that is, as though intentions must be acquired in order to distinguish them from innate or instinctual propensities to behave. Of course, (C_2) is an easy target since there are other differences among intentional and nonintentional propensities—content, for one thing (see below). Happily, as Hunt carefully observes,[5] the argument does not depend on (C_2).

Instead, Hunt questions (C_1), claiming that "the dominant account" of intentions cashes them out in terms of some belief-desire complex where "acquisition at a time does not appear to be an essential feature of beliefs or desires in general," nor of "the particular congeries of beliefs and desires which constitute intentions."[6] Suppose I grab an umbrella from the umbrella stand as I go out the door. Were we to explain what makes this action intentional, we might cite beliefs, desires, know-how, goals, plans, rejections of alternatives, and assessments of competing values, but it would seem unnecessary to mention a further requirement of 'acquisition' of an intention as either a sufficient or necessary condition.[7] Intentions usually are acquired, to be sure, but there is no reason for thinking this to be anything more than a contingent feature of human intentionality not automatically extendable to nonhuman agents.

Hunt bolsters the latter point by citing, with favor, Alston's "functionalist" account of the Divine Mind whereby an intention is whatever it is that functionally relates appropriate cognitive and connative factors (inputs) to manifestations of behavior (outputs). There is nothing in this description of an intentional propensity that requires acquisition in time, and so, Hunt concludes,[8] there is no good reason to accept any of (C_1), (2.4), or (3). As a result, there is no barrier to claiming that God's intentions may well have been possessed from all eternity.

Two criticisms of Hunt's strategy arise, one minor, the other significant. On the minor side, attempts to reduce intentions to complexes of beliefs and desires have come under attack within recent years, some arguing that intentional action can only be accounted for by appeal to a separate category of intentions.[9] Their main point is that intending *settles* the mind upon a particular course of action so as to (i) be action-guiding and (ii) provide inputs into subsequent practical reasoning, features not guaranteed by the belief-desire complexes that have so far been identified.[10] Presumably, there is no 'settling' of the mind unless it were previously *un*settled, or, at least, not already committed to a particular course of action. One intends only by becoming *resolved,* even when no antecedent deliberation is present, resolution being a temporal occurrence which results in a *modification* of behavioral proclivities. There would be no need to intend, no occasion for intending, were these proclivities already ensconced within one's motivational system. As such, (C_1) seems inescapable and it is not surprising to find it typically taken for granted.

Perhaps a novel analysis of intentions in terms of a belief-desire complex might be more successful in accounting for these features of intention, though Hunt gives us no reasons to think so. His list of explanatory factors for intentional action—goals, plans, rejections of alternatives, and so forth—employs well-known synonyms for 'intentions' and does little to advance the issue. One is not born with set goals, plans, or rejections of alternatives already in place; these states are acquired over the course of time, consequent upon experience, success, frustration, and the envisionment of alternative actions, states, or modes of life. Any considerations supporting the acquisition of intentions apply mutatis mutandis to the acquisition of goals, plans, and rejections.[11]

Let us suspend these misgivings for the moment, however, and assume with Hunt that (C_1) is false as a general principle, speaking as though each intending is identical to a belief-desire complex. The major difficulty with his argument against (3) is that there remains reason to think that *some* intentions—some belief-desire complexes—must be acquired. Recalling the ill-fated (C_2), note that intendings are 'intentional' in having *contents* whereas the same is not true of the innate propensities to blink or withdraw one's hand from intensely hot surfaces. Intentions are like desires and beliefs in this respect. Yet, we have not secured (C_1); perhaps some desires are innate, say, the desire to live or to satisfy one's hunger, and, similarly, with some intentional propensities, specifically those whose content is purely general, for example, to hit back when struck, or, for an intrinsically good being, to do what is right, to help the needy, to avoid violence, and so on. If such general intentions are instinctual or innate, then (C_1) must be abandoned as a principle governing all instances of intending.

But general intentions are insufficient for fully fledged agency. To *act* is to become related to various *particulars,* be these particular persons, objects, events, places, or times, for example, as when I played billiards with Henry at 4 P.M. yesterday. To act intentionally is to purposely relate oneself to particulars, and intentions—whether reducible to belief-desire complexes or not—are action-guiding only insofar as they serve to direct effort within the spatio-temporal realm of events and objects, that is, within the actual world of particulars. Intentions whose action components—that which is to be done—embody reference to definite particulars may be called *specific intentions,* distinguishing them from intentions whose action component is purely general, say, to help the needy. For example, if I intend to send a paper to *Religious Studies* next week, then *what* I intend is laden with reference to particulars, for example, to a particular agent, myself, to a particular journal, and to a particular interval. Only through this aspect of my intending can I be caused to initiate a chain of events which constitutes my intentionally sending a paper to *Religious Studies.* Even if an intention to help the needy, say, were innate, it would require a further specific intention to help that needy person over there and to do so now, and there could be no innate propensity to expend intentional effort in just *this* direction.

Why not? The reason is twofold. For one thing, to have a specific intention one must possess information about the particulars referred to, information that is itself specific, consisting not merely of knowledge about how members of certain sorts behave or how to behave when in such and such relation to them. It must embody reference to definite objects, events, places, and durations within its content, reference that serves to orientate oneself spatially and temporally to enable the flow of causal energy toward definite space-time regions. Second, such reference is possible only through interaction, presumably causal, with the particulars occupying related regions, in which case there is no way the required information can be obtained except through contact with particulars, though not necessarily those very ones referred to. Even an omniscient creator would have to possess information that it is creating this world rather than that, or just these particulars and not ones of some other sort. The reason that specific intentions must be acquired then is that they are dependent upon acquired information. A reduction of intention to a desire-belief complex does not affect this general point, for if the contents of desires and beliefs are action-guiding as the reductionists claim, then *their* content must also embody reference to definite particulars.

A restricted empiricism underlies this position. While there might be a priori knowledge (belief, thoughts) of a general sort, there is no thinking, belief, or knowledge about specific particulars without some a posteriori input. Such is the insight motivating causal theories of empirical knowledge. Were there an omniprescient being, its foreknowledge would be dependent upon contact with particulars, even if these were its own states, acts, beliefs, powers, and choices.

Specific information must be acquired, and only thus do specific intentions fall into place.

These points are summarized in the following argument:

(a) To act intentionally, an agent must have a specific intention (that is, the agent must intend a content which embodies reference to particular persons, objects, events, times, or places).

(b) To have a specific intention one must have specific information about particulars.

(c) One has specific information about particulars only if one obtains that information through causal interaction with particulars.

Therefore,

(d) Specific information about particulars is not innate.

Therefore,

(e) No specific intention can be innate.

Therefore,

(f) In order to act, an agent must acquire an intention.

Though not equivalent to premise (3) of Hunt's revised argument, (f) is all that is needed for the distinct version set forth in section IV below.

III. INTENTION, IGNORANCE, AND THE PRESUMPTION OF UNCERTAINTY

Hunt is content to retain premise (4),[12] targeting (5) instead. However, because (5) refers to a notion introduced in (4), the *openness* of a course of action, it is necessary to be clear on the interpretation of (4). Obviously an agent can be mistaken about what is or is not open, and consequently, what is required for intention is not so much that the action *be* open as it be *presumed* by the agent as open. Rather than (4), the principle which I proposed in "Agency and Omniscience" is,

(4*) If, at t, a minimally rational agent X both acquires an intention to do A at t′ and believes that he has, then at some time appropriately prior to t, X presumes that his A-ing at t′ is an open alternative for him.

Given this principle—the presumption of openness—I then claimed that to take one's A-ing as open is to assume the following:

(O_1) that there is a chance one would A were one to intend;
(O_2) that one would not A unless one so intended; and
(O_3) that one's intending A is as yet contingent relative to what one believes.[13]

Strictly speaking, the condition of presumed openness provided by (4*) should be modified to allow one's A-ing to be viewed as open even if one's A-ing could only be considered qua component of a larger action-plan, not something singled out as a separate doing.[14] To avoid needless complications, however, it suffices to utilize (4*) alone.

Fortunately, Hunt realizes that the presumption of openness is at stake by the time he scrutinizes (5), and this is brought out in his restatement of that premise:

(5!) X's A-ing at t' is a doxastically open alternative for A at t, that is, X presumes at t that
    (i) there is a chance that he would A (would refrain from A-ing) at t' were he to intend to A (to refrain from A-ing) at t';
    (ii) he would not A at t' unless he intended to A at t'; and
    (iii) his intending to A at t' is as yet contingent, that is,
        (a) it is within his power at t to intend to A (to refrain from A-ing) at t', and
        (b) he does not possess at t a previously acquired intention to A (to refrain from A-ing) at t'
    —only if X is ignorant at t whether or not he will A at t'.[15]

On the assumption that this conditional is essential to my argument, Hunt contends that its antecedent might be satisfied while its consequent not and in the course of his argument raises three critical points. Let us examine them closely, though for reasons of exposition, take up the second and third in reverse order.

Hunt's First Criticism.[16] If we look at (5!) without clause (iiib), Hunt proposes, we can see that it rests on a 'modal fallacy' common to fatalistic arguments for the pointlessness of action:

And on similar grounds, one might claim, it is pointless to intend what (one believes) will happen or what (one believes) will not happen. But the fallacy here is obvious. The fact that X will A at t' only means that X *will not* refrain from A-ing at t': it does not mean that X *cannot* refrain from A-ing at t'. Thus it has no implications for the effectiveness of X's intentions with respect to A-ing at t′, and X (if rational) will not regard it as having such implications.

As a criticism of anything I have said, however, this is off the mark. That X will A at t′, or that X believes he will A at t′, does not imply that X's intentions with respect to not A-ing at t′ would not be efficacious. Nothing I said commits me to saying otherwise, nor does the implied fatalism follow from conditions (i), (ii), and (iiia) alone. Even if we add (iiib) and acknowledge a sense in which a future-tensed truth can be necessary relative to what one now believes, we do not thereby emasculate one's intentions, nor undermine the truth of counterfactuals asserting their efficacy.

Hunt's Third Criticism.[17] Hunt disputes my (O3) construal of the relative contingency in the openness presumption in terms of the set,

(C) all that he or she (the agent) then (at t) believes (knows).

He agrees that an omniscient agent could not take any of its actions as contingent relative to (C), in which case a required sense of openness so construed quickly rules out omniscient agency. Accordingly, he proposes a competitor as the proper index set for relative contingency:

(D) all propositions about times earlier than t that he or she (the agent) then (at t) believes (knows).

Hunt then writes:

Significantly, if doxastic openness were defined in terms of (D) rather than (C), premise (5) would not go through; for then the agent's foreknowledge at t that he will A at t′, since it does not belong to (D), would not count against the relative contingency of his A-ing at t′.[18]

In other words, contingency relative to (D) does not imply contingency relative to all propositions true at t, whereas contingency relative to (C) does. Hence, contingency relative to (D) does not have the same fatalistic consequence that contingency relative to (C) does, in which case it provides a superior account of doxastic openness.

This attempt to salvage omniscient agency fares no better than Hunt's first. For an omniscient being X at time t, set (D) will contain past-tensed propositions about its beliefs and knowledge of future-tensed propositions concerning what it will do or intend at any time t′ later than t. Thus, (D) will include appropriate instances of the schemata,

(1) I (= X) knew that I will do A at t'.

(2) I (= X) knew that I will intend at t to do A at t'.

Since X's beliefs are coextensive with its knowledge, then any such instances will be true. However, from the instance of (1) would follow the correlated instance of,

(3) I (= X) will do A at t'.

and from the instance of (2) follows that of,

(4) I (= X) will intend at t to do A at t'.

Consequently, since the latter are implied by members of set (D), they are necessary relative to set (D), and Hunt is simply wrong to think that (D) avoids the difficulty facing omniscient agency.

One might attempt to escape this consequence by denying truth-values to future contingents, but this is a route that Hunt does not pursue. Alternatively, one could insist that the members of (D) be *purely* about times prior to t, unlike (1) and (2), which contain embedded references to the future. While this move might succeed in blocking the foregoing derivations, it seriously distorts practical thinking. The latter is typically Janus-faced; agents do not face the future with a blank slate, but with a relatively rich set of expectations based on acquaintance with the past. It is in light of *this* set, a set that includes future-tensed expectations, however vague, about the future, that agents deliberate, plan, and commit themselves to various undertakings. The attempt to purify the index set on the presumed contingency, therefore, is committed to an implausible picture of intentional agency.

Hunt's Second Criticism.[19] In his most forceful attack upon (5!), Hunt sets forth what he takes to be the reasoning underlying that principle:

> Any rational agent who (iv) believes that he will perform a certain action and (ii) presumes that he will perform that action only if he intends to perform it must also (v) believe that he intends to perform it. But if in addition he (iiib) presumes that he does not yet possess such an intention, he must (if rational) (vi) believe that he will acquire this intention sometime in the future. But it is impossible (the argument continues) to hold in advance a belief about what one will later decide to do. Since (vi) is necessarily false and is entailed by the conjunction of (i)–(iv), the latter is necessarily false. So if (i)–(iii) are true, (iv) must be false. And this is just what is claimed by (5!).

He then writes that this is the "strongest (if not the only) case that the critic of omniscient agency can make on behalf of (5!)."[20] At its heart is a denial that the following schemata are consistent:

(via) X believes that he will intend to A at t'.
(vib) X believes that he does not yet intend to A at t'.

However, the critic who supports this denial must believe that the only grounds for a belief that one will intend to A is a present commitment to A-ing. That is, the critic must endorse the following conditional:

(H) At t, X believes that he will intend to A at t' only if X already intends at t to A at t' and believes that he so intends.[21]

But this conditional is not true Hunt tells us. For one thing, it places "extraordinary restrictions" on God's foreknowledge, ruling out both "simple foreknowledge" and "middle knowledge." For another, it is falsified by the very possibility of someone's accepting a prediction that he will acquire an intention, say, to commit suicide five years hence (perhaps on the basis of having read this in a "book of life"[22] whose predictions have hitherto come true), even though he does not yet possess that intention. It seems wrong to deny that we can achieve enough understanding of our own character to predict some of our own intentions before actually acquiring those intentions. Hence, (H) is false and (5!) is deprived of support.

Certainly both (5!) and (H) are suspect, but nothing in the argument of "Agency and Omniscience" is committed to them. Nor does it rule out the possibility of simple foreknowledge and middle knowledge; it implies nothing about the mechanisms whereby an omniscient being has knowledge of future acts nor about the nature of 'free' acts. Rather, its claim is that in taking a course of action to be open an agent is disposed toward an avowal *of* ignorance, as would be reflected in the answer of a deliberator who, when interrupted and asked if he now knows what course of action he will pick, replies, "No, not at this stage: I've not yet made up my mind." It is, this *feeling* of one's mind being yet unsettled that underlies the following principle which *was* set forth in "Agency and Omniscience":

(5*) If, at t, a rational being X presumes that his intending to A at t' is contingent relative to what he himself then believes, then at t, X presumes both that he does not yet believe that he will intend to A at t' and that he does not yet believe that he will not intend to A at t' (Presumption of Uncertainty).

For ordinary agents, this presumption might be mistaken, and consequently we allow for the joint satisfiability of (via) and (vib) and insist upon the falsity of (H). In my "Doxastic Freedom: A Compatibilist Alternative,"[23] a case against principles like (5!) was developed by citing the not-infrequent occurrence of forming an intention to A at t, acquiring a corresponding belief that one will A at t, and yet temporarily overlooking or forgetting both in the course of deliberating about an alternative. To overlook an intention or a belief is not to abandon either, though it does suggest that both are submerged beneath a layer of immediately accessed information, including the belief that taking the considered alternative is contingent relative to what one believes. Therefore, one might well have—in some sense of 'have'—a belief that one will intend to A at t while simultaneously possessing a sense of openness about A-ing at t.

The correct way to view (5*) is not as a claim precluding foreknowledge of what one will do intentionally, nor as one ruling out the presumption of an act as open while knowing in advance that one will refrain from it. Rather, the presumption is a crucial aspect of the 'resolution' picture of intention suggested in section II, wherein intentions are acquired against a background milieu of information, information that includes a more or less unarticulated sense that the future is 'open' with respect to a certain intentional effort and, by that very fact, that one is not yet committed or 'settled' upon it. A presumption of openness is at once a presumption *of* indecision and, ipso facto, a presumption *of* uncertainty. Both, in turn, are implied by the agent's sense that the course of action is contingent relative to what he takes himself to believe, or, in the more direct first-person mode, relative to what I take to be the case or, better, "as far as I can tell."[24] Rather than (5!), the incompatibility claim is that an agent cannot, qua rational, simultaneously *access* the beliefs that (i) he will do a certain action A at a future time t and (ii) that his A-ing at t is yet an open alternative. A sense of openness cannot coexist on a par with an equally vivid sense of intentional closure, but here we acknowledge unavoidable epistemic limitations upon agency.

This said, we have an argument for a second premise of the revised argument against omniscient agency. Let X be any ideally rational agent and t_1 and t_2 any times such that $t_1 \leq t_2$:

(g) If at t_1 X acquires an intention to A at t_2, then there is a time t_3, $t_3 \leq t_1$, during which X presumes that his A-ing at t_2 is an open alternative.

(h) If at t_3 X presumes that his A-ing at t_2 is an open alternative, then at t_3 X regards his intending at t_1 to A at t_2 as contingent relative to what he then believes.

(i) If at t_3 X regards his intending at t_1 to A at t_2 as contingent relative to what he then believes, then X at t_3 presumes both that he does not yet believe that he will intend at t_1 to A at t_2 and that he does not yet believe that he will not intend at t_1 to A at t_2.

(j) If at t_3 X presumes both that he does not yet believe that he will intend at t_1 to A at t_2 and that he does not yet believe that he will not intend at t_1 to A at t_2, then at t_3 either X is ignorant of what he will intend or ignorant about what he then believes.

Therefore,

(k) If at t_1 X acquires an intention to A at t_2 then there is a time t_3, $t_3 \leq t_1$, during which X is ignorant of some proposition.

In other words, (k) is the claim that an agent cannot acquire a specific intention unless there is a time during which that agent is ignorant of some proposition.

IV. THE REVISED ARGUMENT AGAINST OMNISCIENT AGENCY

Recall that the argument of section II established the following claim:

(f) To act intentionally presupposes acquiring a specific intention.

In section III we have just shown,

(k) An agent acquires a specific intention only if there is a time during which that agent is ignorant of some proposition.

From these two premises it is but a short step to the major result:

Theorem. There is no omniscient agent.

NOTES

1. David P. Hunt, "Omniprescient Agency," *Religious Studies* 28 (1992): 351–69.
2. Tomis Kapitan, "Agency and Omniscience," *Religious Studies* 27 (1991): 105–20.
3. Hunt, "Omniprescient Agency," pp. 352–53.
4. By a "suitably broad consequence relation" I mean a relation that holds between a set S and a proposition P whenever it is impossible for all the members of S to be true while P is false. The modality is not to be restricted to so-called "logical" necessity. I have discussed nonlogical relations of consequence in T. Kapitan, "On the Concept of Material Consequence," *History and Philosophy of Logic* 3 (1982): 193–211.
5. Hunt, "Omniprescient Agency," p. 356.
6. Ibid., p. 357.
7. Ibid.
8. Ibid., p. 358.
9. E.g.: H.-N. Castañeda, *Thinking and Doing* (Dordrecht: Reidel, 1975); J. Searle, *Intentionality* (Cambridge, 1983): M. Bratman, *Intention, Plans, and Practical Reason*

(Cambridge, Mass.: Harvard, 1987); and A. Mele, "Against a Belief/Desire Analysis of Intention," *Philosophia* 18 (1988): 239–42, and *Springs of Action* (Oxford, 1992).

10. This has been argued by: Searle, chap. 3 in *Intentionality*; Bratman, chap. 2 in *Intention, Plans, and Practical Reason*; and Mele, "Against a Belief/Desire Analysis," and chaps. 8 and 9 in *Springs of Action*.

11. See Castañeda, chap. 10 in *Thinking and Doing*, which argues that intending is the fundamental practical state of mind in terms of which the others may be construed, since each involves propensities to endorse (to intend) specific courses of action.

12. Hunt, "Omniprescient Agency," pp. 359–63.

13. See my "Agency and Omniscience," pp. 111–12, where I claim that a presumption of such relative contingency is constitutive of the principle of least effort.

14. The more accurate view is that A-ing is taken as open by X just in case there is an action-type K such that X believes that his K-ing is open to him in the sense of (4*) and X correctly envisions his A-ing to be a reliable consequence of his K-ing. The notion of reliable consequence is prominent in T. Kapitan, "Ability and Cognition: A Defense of Compatibilism," *Philosophical Studies* 63 (1991): 231–43.

15. Hunt, "Omniprescient Agency," p. 363.

16. Ibid., p. 364.

17. Ibid., pp. 366–68.

18. Ibid., pp. 366–67.

19. Ibid., pp. 364–66.

20. Ibid., p. 365.

21. In a somewhat puzzling pair of paragraphs on the second half of p. 365 in "Omniprescient Agency," Hunt argues that there are *two* grounds for denying the consistency of (via) and (vib), namely, (1) that "X's having already acquired, and believing that he has already acquired, the intention to A at t' is a necessary condition for X's believing that he will intend to A at t'," and (2) that "X's believing that he will intend to A at t' is a (sufficient) condition for X's having already acquired, and believing that he has already acquired, the intention to A at t'." Unless Hunt's text contains a misprint or I simply misconstrue his meaning, these two grounds collapse into the single conditional mentioned.

22. A. Goldman, *A Theory of Human Action* (Princeton, 1970).

23. T. Kapitan, "Doxastic Freedom: A Compatibilist Alternative," *American Philosophical Quarterly* 26 (1989): 31–42.

24. In "Doxastic Freedom," I argued that one might know in advance what he or she will do while still deliberating about it. Crucial to this possibility is that one deliberates against background information; it may well be that some of what one believes fails to be tallied in this backdrop. Forgetting and overlooking do not imply a failure to know what one forgets or overlooks.

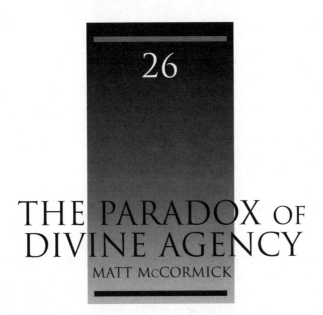

26

THE PARADOX OF DIVINE AGENCY

MATT McCORMICK

If we are to be reasonable about our religious beliefs and attitudes, the label 'God' cannot be attached to just any object. J. N. Findlay says, "our religious object should have an *unsurpassable* supremacy along all avenues, that it should tower *infinitely* above all other objects."[1] To have a religious attitude toward something is to worship it, to view it with profound respect, reverence, awe, fear, devotion, subordination, deference, and love.[2] To have a religious attitude toward anything that falls short of infinite supremacy in any regard would be idolatrous and perverse, or simply foolish. In order for a religious attitude to be appropriate, the being that is its object must possess characteristics that are commensurate to that attitude.

An argument against God's existence can be constructed from this starting point. It has been widely agreed that in order to be God and therefore worthy of a religious attitude, a being must at least be omnipotent, omniscient, and wholly morally good. So, if it is not possible to possess some, one, or all of these properties, or any property that is essential to a religious attitude, then there is nothing befitting a religious attitude, and God does not exist.

I will argue that in addition to those properties listed above, God must be an *agent* who is capable of setting goals and willing and performing actions. I will then defend the central thesis of this paper: when taken together, the divine properties of omnipotence, omniscience, and perfection (moral and otherwise), preclude the possibility of agency. That is, God cannot act. It is impossible for an

Written in 2002 for this anthology.

omnipotent, omniscient, perfect being to act—it cannot exert its will because it can never find the world in a state that does not conform perfectly with its will.[3] In light of this conclusion, the very notion of divine agency, of God's possessing plans and acting to achieve ends in the world, becomes meaningless and must be abandoned. And a God that is incapable of action or agency is not worthy of an attitude of religious reverence. So, since it is not possible for a being to possess all of the necessary properties, God cannot exist.

Let us turn to the argument:

1. It has been widely alleged that God acts or possesses agency.

He is described as planning and creating the world from nothing. He passes judgment and issues punishments or rewards. He has a plan for humankind. He sacrifices his son, sends his prophets, issues commands, causes miracles, and so on. It is God's agency that makes it possible to have the sort of personal relationship to God that is crucial to Christianity, Islam, and Judaism. God has an impact on our lives, it is said, because he interacts with humans, makes choices, expresses his goals and desires. And it is by recognizing his agency in acknowledging his efforts, his commands, his goals, and his desires that we are able to establish a relationship with God and adopt an appropriate religious attitude toward him.

2. A being has *agency* when it has goals, conceives of them, acts on the basis of those goals with the intention of achieving them, and it could have done otherwise had it chosen to.

Thus we can separate agents from other beings that act, and even have goals in a sense, but do not have agency. So speaking loosely, squirrels can be said to act, and we may speak of their burying nuts with the goal of surviving the winter. But we would not attribute agency to them in the sense described in (2) in part because they do not cognize the goal and the means of achieving it. Nor are they free to establish another goal and instigate another action instead.

Not only has God been traditionally portrayed as possessing agency, a stronger case can be made that any object that does not have agency is not worthy of a religious attitude; a being *must* have agency to be worthy of the name of God. A nonagent, no matter how great it is in other respects, is a thing that cannot act to achieve goals, it cannot plan, and it cannot achieve intentional interactions with the world or beings in it. And a being that can do these things is superior to one that cannot. So we should not be religious toward a nonagent because all other things being equal, a nonagent is inferior to an agent.

While it is true that people have had religious attitudes toward a wide variety of objects, including many that were unworthy, we should have a religious attitude toward a thing if and only if we highly value its essential properties and its essential properties make it superior to all other things. It must lack no property that we hold in the highest esteem, and it must possess no negative property. Its properties must render it superior to every other thing, real or imagined. Our worship and admiration would be misplaced if it were directed at one thing while there exists another superior object. And to adopt a religious attitude toward an existing object while it is possible for a superior being to exist would be settling for second best or compromising. A religious attitude toward anything less gives it more respect and esteem than it deserves and would seem to indicate an embarrassing weakness in us, namely, our need to worship something even if it is inferior in some way. Few would dispute the claim that God is unsurpassably great and that only such a being is worthy of worship.

The high value we place on agency in ourselves and in God is evident in a number of ways. Our own agency is not a property that we wish to be rid of. We would not see losing our ability to conceive of and effect change in the world as an improvement. If anything, we strive to better accomplish change in the world and be *more* effective as agents so that we may improve our own situations and the plight of those around us.

Furthermore, there are good reasons to value agency in the God that we worship. We do not and should not adopt a religious attitude toward objects that cannot act because there can be no hope of their establishing a personal relationship with us. Nonagents cannot acknowledge us as minds with goals and the power to achieve them. They cannot act to offer us any moral guidance. They have no telos and no capacity for self-governance because they cannot act to change themselves or anything around them. They cannot respond to our needs or interests, nor can they hear our prayers or do anything about them. A nonagent is not deserving of the religious love that we should have toward a divine being who is capable of loving us in return and who is able to act on that love. To adopt a religious attitude toward objects that are not agents would be idolatrous.

To devote oneself wholly to a thing that cannot act, cannot respond to requests, and is incapable of exerting its will in the world to achieve its goals would be perverse because it would suggest that this being is worthy no matter what it does or does not do. Feeling piety, profound respect, infinite deference, and subordination toward an object that is incapable of acting in any fashion would be self-destructive and absurd because it indicates that we value the inability to act in God despite cherishing the ability so highly in ourselves. So,

3. The possession of agency is a necessary (but not sufficient) property of an appropriate object of a religious attitude.

It should be noted, however, that if the critic takes issue with the claim in (3) that an appropriate religious object *must* possess agency, the argument will still succeed. In what follows, I will show at a minimum that there cannot be a being with the properties of omnipotence, omniscience, moral perfection, and agency. By most accounts, this describes God. So God cannot exist. If the argument for the stronger claim in (3) is successful, I will have also shown that no other being is worthy of a religious attitude or the name 'God'. So both the weaker and the stronger versions of this argument have a profound impact on theism.

Agency has other features that are relevant to my argument. In order for an agent to have goals, a being must acquire a conception, however, rudimentary, of the world *as it is*. If I am not aware that I am fifty pounds overweight, I cannot form the goal of going on a diet in order to lose that fifty pounds. If I do not have a conception of the bus careening toward me at the crosswalk, I cannot form the goal of diving to safety and avoiding it. We can think of the goal that an agent possesses as a conception of the world as the agent would like it to be. So,

4.   In order to have *agency*, a being must recognize some state of affairs in the world (correctly or incorrectly), conceive of another desired state of affairs, and then set about to make the desired/conceived state of affairs real.

It is integral and necessary to the possession and exercise of agency that the agent grasp (in some fashion) that the world is in a state of affairs, P, and through some cognitive activity that being conceives of another state of affairs, ~P, that is not actual (or at least the agent believes it is not actual). More simply put, a being has to see the way things are (rightly or wrongly) and also see the way it wants them to be. Without this *action gap* between what is and what one wants, there can be no ground or opportunity for action at all for an agent. Furthermore, the agent must want that state of affairs to be real. In order to act, the world must be in some sub–optimal condition from the agent's perspective. The state that one wishes to bring about may actually be worse overall, and it may not turn out to be what one wants, or it may already be actual unbeknownst to the agent. But in order to act, the agent must at least think of that state of affairs as being different and better than the one that is actual.

'Conceive' in premises (2) and (4) is being used in a broad and inclusive fashion. There is a wide range of completion or awareness in the agent's conception of the desired state of affairs that leads to action. Sometimes we have a clearer idea of what we want than others; I might go to the grocery store with a specific list of fifteen items, or I might go with only the vague feeling that I am lacking groceries. The actor's awareness of the desired state of affairs can range from lucid to dim. It may even be possible for the actor to be moved to action without *any* conscious awareness of the desired state of affairs that she is moving toward. We should understand 'conception' to cover many cases, but we should also accept that on some occasions we act but we are not acting as agents because our goal is too weakly conceived.

Fallible agents like ourselves need only *believe* that the world is in some state that is different from what we wish it to be. The world may already be in the goal state that we conceive, but we still act on the misconception that it is not. Since an omniscient being will know all truths and believes no falsehoods, God will not have a mistaken belief about the state of the world that leads to his acting. So,

5.   In order for God to exercise agency, the world must actually be in a state of affairs that is different from what God wills or wishes it to be.

So an action gap for God would develop when God accurately comprehends the relevant state of affairs in the world, and there is a divergence between what *actually* is the case in the world and the state of affairs that God has as a goal.

In general,

6.   If there is an action gap for an agent, then a) the being desires to close the gap, but it is not possible for the being to do so; or b) the being has the goal of changing the state of affairs but refrains from doing so because of some other goal; or c) the being possesses the nonactual state as a goal and acts to make it actual.

When an action gap occurs for an agent, any number of things can intervene that might interfere with that being's closing the gap, thus creating the situation in (6.a). For humans, the list of factors that keep us from getting what we want is long. Obstacles to closing the gap can be internal or external. Internally, we may have X as a goal, but we want Y more and X precludes Y. I may want to buy a new car, but my need and desire to have food to eat is greater, so my desire for a new car goes unfulfilled. So in some cases, something is within our power to obtain, but we choose not to act to obtain it in favor of an alternative action. An internal obstacle to closing the action gap is imposed by the will of the agent. In these cases, an agent does not have a unified or singular will; the agent possesses multiple goals, and achieving them all is not possible because they are not all compatible with each other or the agent's abilities or resources do not allow it.

When the obstacle to closing the action gap does not arise from the exercise of the agent's will, then it is external. In some cases, we have goals or objects of desire that are not within our power to obtain. I may dearly wish to be a brain surgeon, but I do not and will not ever have the intellectual aptitude to achieve it. It is not naturally possible for me to become one. External obstacles to closing the action gap are involuntary because the interference does not arise from any willed choice of my own.

Let us call a *natural* obstacle to acting one that arises as the direct result of the laws of nature and not as the result of another agent's actions. An *artificial* obstacle is one that arises from another agent's actions, for example, a prejudicial admissions officer who prevents me from getting into medical school to become a brain surgeon. An agent may have its goals thwarted because what he wants is not logically possible as well. My intense desire to be the first married bachelor will forever remain unfulfilled. So in sum, there can at least be internal, external, natural, artificial, logical, voluntary, and involuntary restrictions to an agent's closing the action gap.

With the possible exception of logical restraints, there can be no obstacles to God's actions that fall into any of these categories. First, in virtue of being omnipotent, there will be no external obstacles to God's getting what he wants. Since God has all power, no other being or object will prevent God's actions. Should he choose to act, no force, phenomena, being, or thing will prevent that action from having the desired outcome.

Similarly, there can be no natural restrictions on God's actions. The laws of nature which are ultimately behind a finite creature's lack of strength, intelligence, or ability will not confine God's agency. Being omnipotent gives God the power to control the laws of nature. Indeed, this is how miracles are commonly characterized.

Furthermore, there can be no artificial restraints on God's actions. Since God is perfect, and since there is only one God according to classical theism, there is no other free agent who is up to the task of restraining God's will. And no other imperfect or inferior being has enough power or knowledge to interfere with the exercise of God's agency.[4]

Could logical restraints help to create a gap between what God wants in the world and what is actually the case? If omnipotence is the capacity to do anything that is logically possible, as many philosophers have argued, then there could be a state of affairs that God desires but that God cannot acquire, namely, a logically impossible state of affairs. God could wish to create a square circle or some other impossible feat.

God's other attributes, however, would prevent him from having any logically contradictory goals. Omniscience would include the knowledge that God cannot do that which is logically impossible, so it cannot be that God continues to desire the unobtainable because he does not know any better. And it cannot be that God cannot obtain it because he does not know how to get it. Rather, the only reasons that would lead God to set logically impossible goals would imply God's imperfection. A perfect being would have goals that are perfectly aligned between what is desired and what is possible and what that being is capable of accomplishing. Perfection would require that the agent not have internal conflicts between its various properties.

So the situation in (6.a) cannot occur for God. There are no limits on what God can do with his power except perhaps logical limits, and God would not have a logically contradictory state of affairs as a goal.

Can the situation in (6.b) occur for God? That is, does God ever internally, voluntarily restrain his power to achieve one goal because he subordinates that goal to another one?

No, God never foregoes one goal for the sake of another because God's will must be *singular* and *unified*. When there is an internal, voluntary restriction of the behavior of finite creatures like ourselves, when we want something but choose not to pursue it, we do so because of competing, conflicting, or overriding goals. That is, agents for whom there is an action gap that they voluntarily choose not to close must have multiple and diverse goals or motives. In our case, more often than not, our actions are the result of the combination of a variety of impulses, reasons, goals, and desires. I barely endure the excruciating discomfort of a root canal in the dentist's chair by weighing a long-term and broader goal of having good health against my aversion to pain and my intense desire to avoid the drill. Biological factors, evolutionary traits, base impulses, rational insight, personality traits, and other factors dramatically complicate the decision and action process for human agents. As a result, we often find ourselves acting to achieve one thing while still possessing a strong desire that we were doing something else or that some other state of affairs would be the result of our action, such as when we must do expensive repairs on a car. Even when we act voluntarily and achieve the intended goal, a gap often persists between what is the case and what goals we have. In short, inferiority leads to goal subordination because a lack of knowledge, power, or perfection renders a goal unobtainable or forces one to settle for less.

But multiple, incompatible goals and action gaps that persist because of subordinated goals in an inferior agent do not occur for God. The nagging doubts that put our motives in conflict do not occur for an omniscient being who perfectly apprehends every facet and every implication of his actions. God knows perfectly what the results of his actions will be; he knows how to achieve the perfect or optimal results for any situation, no matter how complex; and he perfectly and unerringly assesses and chooses the goals he sets. Once chosen, those goals cannot be of mixed value to God the way the root canal is a mixed blessing for us. God does not grudgingly or disappointedly admit that employing means X is the least unhappy way to achieve end Y the way we do when we use chemotherapy to cure cancer, or when we sell a car rather than do costly repairs on it. First, an omnipotent being will not make use of imperfect or crude means to achieve his ends as we do in the dentist's office. And second, God has no lack of power or knowledge, so he is never forced to settle for a means or an end that satisfies some but not all of his goals. And third, his perfection would prevent him from possessing goals that are not or cannot be satisfied by the actions that are available to him. Unfulfilled longing is the product of imperfection and/or a lack of power. God's perfection and the resulting alignment of his faculties would prevent any lingering discontent with the best possible resolution of an action gap. A perfect, rational, omniscient, and omnipotent being assesses the situation, recognizes the best possible solution, and then has the confidence, knowledge, and unification of will to be satisfied with the results.

So the decision process, if it can be called that, for God must be of a radically different nature. The perfect alignment and balance of God's attributes means that there will be no internal conflict of motives. What he knows combined with perfect rationality form a singular, unerring will behind the exercise of power. There can be no overzealous emotional impulses, rash judgments that one regrets later, floods of passion, or unfulfilled longing. Nor does God have the biological, physical, or evolutionary impulses that we do that sometimes run counter to what reason tells us we should do.

So God's will must be singular and unified. Therefore, the situation in (6.b) will never occur for God because God will never internally, voluntarily restrain his power to achieve one goal in order to achieve another.

But since, as we have seen, there can be no external factors forcing an omnipotent, perfect agent to refrain from doing something,

> 7.   There can be no restraints, internal or external, on the actions of an omnipotent, omniscient, perfect agent's will.

So, if a perfect divine agent does not change some state of affairs, then that state of affairs is in perfect accord with that being's will. Another way to put the point is that if the being wills to restrain itself and does not change some state of affairs, then that being is actually willing that state of affairs. If God accepts a state of affairs and there is no obstacle to his changing it, then he is willing that state of affairs to be.

Now we arrive at the heart of the argument that God cannot act. If God chooses not to act, then the state of affairs in the world is in perfect accord with God's will. God does not have mixed motives about the choice not to act; he recognizes exactly what is the best and nothing can interfere with his achieving it. So if he chooses not to act, the world must be exactly as God wishes.

In order for God to choose to act, on the other hand, something impossible has to occur. In order to act, the state of affairs in the world has to diverge at some point from what God wills. Unless there is a gap between what is the case and what God wants to be the case, no action to close that gap is possible. Hence, there will be no opportunity for action.

So the question is, how could the world get out of alignment with God's will, thus creating the opportunity for him to act? How could (6.c) happen for God where there is an action gap, he possesses the nonactual state as a goal and then, on the basis of that nonactual state, sets out to make it actual? The answer is that such a situation cannot occur. God's omniscience includes perfect knowledge of every fact in the world, so something could not have diverged from his will without his knowledge. And nothing is beyond his power, so it cannot be that some state of affairs occurred that God does not have the power to alter. And since God's will is singular and unified, he never acts in one way while some other dissatisfying state of affairs persists. So everything that occurs must be in perfect accordance with a divine being's will. No suboptimal state (from God's perspective) can occur because for it to occur, God must have willed it. And if God willed it, then it is not contrary to God's will, and it is not suboptimal. There is simply no way for things to become different from what God wants which would create the opportunity to act.

8.   Therefore, it is impossible for there to be a state of affairs in the world that does not accord perfectly with an omnipotent, omniscient, perfect agent's will. The world always conforms perfectly with God's will.

9.   And since action requires that there be some state of affairs that is different from what an agent wills, God cannot act.

Conclusion: I have argued that God, in order to be worthy of the label, must have certain properties. In addition to the standard theistic properties of omnipotence, omniscience, and moral perfection, God must also be an agent in order to be worthy of worship. God must be able to devise goals and act to achieve them. But now we have seen that a being with the divine properties cannot act. Given God's properties, no occasion for action can ever develop. The divine attributes preclude the possibility of conceiving of some desired outcome, devising a plan to achieve it, then willing to bring it about. But a being that cannot act is not worthy of a religious attitude. So, it is not possible for any being to have the properties that would warrant a religious attitude. So, God cannot exist.[5]

NOTES

1. J. N. Findlay, "Can God's Existence Be Disproved?" *Mind* 57 (1948): 179.
2. Again, Findlay's argument is quite powerful and eloquent on this point: "A religious attitude was one in which we tended to abase ourselves before some object, to defer

to it wholly, to devote ourselves to it with unquestioning enthusiasm, to bend the knee before it, whether literally or metaphorically" (Ibid., p. 177).

3. Tomis Kapitan has argued a related thesis in "Agency and Omniscience," *Religious Studies* 27 (1991): 105–20. Kapitan argues that God's omniscience makes it impossible for him to act because "a being with complete foreknowledge of the future, specifically, its own future, cannot deliberate, and seemingly, cannot make up its mind or decide among options" (p. 105). My argument shows that the opportunities for action never occur for a divine being.

4. The critic might suggest that the devil could thwart God's plans. By most accounts, however, Satan is subordinate to God's power. But even if we grant the point, God would know if and when his efforts to achieve his ends would be thwarted by Satan. And if he is perfect and omniscient, God would know better than to try to obtain some end that he cannot achieve. The perfect alignment of all his attributes would lead God to apply himself only to those tasks that he could achieve and not to be in conflict with himself or anyone else for those that he cannot.

5. I must thank Ricki Monnier, Michael Martin, and Rebekah Donaldson for many helpful comments on drafts of this article.

PART 5

SINGLE ATTRIBUTE DISPROOFS OF THE EXISTENCE OF GOD

INTRODUCTION

This section contains previously published papers presenting and defending single attribute disproofs of the existence of God. A single attribute disproof of God's existence is a deductive argument based on a self-contradiction within just one attribute of God.

A single attribute disproof of God's existence takes the following general form:

1. If God exists,
   then every attribute of God is self-consistent.
2. A particular attribute of God is not self-consistent.
3. Therefore, God does not and cannot exist.

Here are brief summaries of the papers contained in this section.

Gilbert Fulmer in a 1977 paper "The Concept of the Supernatural" considers a God who possesses the attribute of creator of the universe, including creator of all natural laws. Fulmer argues that God's creation of the universe, including all natural laws, presupposes the natural law that whatever God wills to be created is created (a fact of nature independent of God's will). Since God's creation of *all* natural laws presupposes *one* of them, the single attribute of creator of the universe is self-contradictory, and therefore a God who is creator of the universe, including all natural laws, does not and cannot exist.

J. L. Cowan in a 1965 paper titled "The Paradox of Omnipotence" considers the concept of omnipotence, that is, the power to do anything that is logically possible, and argues that there are certain logically possible abilities that are mutually contradictory, even prior to being exercised. Since the concept of omnipotence involves all logically possible abilities, and since some of these are mutually contradictory, even prior to being exercised, it follows that the concept of omnipotence is self-contradictory, and therefore an omnipotent being such as God does not and cannot exist.

In a 1974 paper "The Paradox of Omnipotence Revisited," Cowan develops the 1965 argument further by applying it to the well-known stone paradox, clarifying some key points, and replying to several objections.

Patrick Grim in a 1985 paper "Against Omniscience: The Case from Essential Indexicals" formulates two arguments from essential indexicals for the nonexistence of God. In the first, a disproof of an omniscient being from the essential indexical 'I', Grim argues that no other being can know what I know in knowing certain propositions essentially indexed to me, and therefore, since I am not omniscient, a being who knows all that can be known is impossible. Grim also presents a multiple attributes disproof of an omniscient and timeless being from the essential indexical 'now'. It is argued that there are different things that can be known only at different times, and therefore a God who is omniscient and timeless does not and cannot exist.

Roland Puccetti in a 1963 paper "Is Omniscience Possible?" argues that an omniscient being must have knowledge of the totality of facts, including surely the fact that it itself is omniscient. To know this fact, however, it must know the truth of the statement "There are no facts unknown to me." Since this statement is a universal (uncircumscribed) negative, an omniscient being can know its truth only by knowing that its denial is contradictory. Given that there is no way of knowing this, an omniscient being, such as God, does not and cannot exist.

Patrick Grim in a 1988 paper "Logic and Limits of Knowledge and Truth" presents three deductive disproofs of an omniscient God. In the argument from expressive incompleteness, Grim employs Cantor's power set theorem to argue that any system of expression or language that models omniscience must satisfy certain conditions that simultaneously render that system incomplete, that is, fail to express some truth. Thus, no system of expression or language is adequate to encompass all knowledge. In the argument from internal incompleteness, Grim employs Gödel's incompleteness theorem to make out a case that even if all truths are expressible in some language, then the requirement that the knowledge of these truths be consistent will still leave some truths unknown. Finally, again using Cantor's power set theorem, Grim argues that there are always more truths than can be contained in any set of truths, including even the set of all truths. The concept of a set of all truths, like the concept of the largest possible natural number, is self-contradictory, and thus a complete body of knowledge of all truths is ruled out. It follows from each of these three arguments that an omniscient God does not and cannot exist.

In a 2000 paper "The Being That Knew Too Much," Grim defends the preceding arguments against an omniscient God by clarifying some points, exploring some complications, and replying to some objections. For example, the Cantorian argument against a set of all truths can be directed against an infinite set of all truths of any cardinality, against a "class" or "collection" of all truths, or against simply "many" truths without reference to a set, class, or collection. In short, every body of knowledge leaves out some truth, and therefore an omniscient God does not and cannot exist.

27

THE CONCEPT OF THE SUPERNATURAL

GILBERT FULMER

Traditional theism holds that the universe is dependent on a Creator who is supernatural, since he created ex nihilo the natural order, which is sustained only by his will. It has sometimes been thought that the existence of this being could be demonstrated by the teleological, the cosmological, and the ontological arguments. I will argue, however, that all these notions are undermined by a common logical incoherence. In the end, I suggest, it is evident that the universe cannot be dependent on a personal Creator and is ultimately impersonal.

1. R. G. Swinburne has attempted to revive the teleological argument.[1] It is impossible to explain all natural laws scientifically, he argues, for we must eventually come to "the most fundamental regularities," for which no explanation is known. At this point we have progressed as far as possible in explaining events naturalistically, he claims; so if we are to continue our explanatory efforts, we must entertain a different kind of hypothesis: that all natural laws result from the will of a god. If confirmed this hypothesis would greatly simplify our system of explanations, for then everything would ultimately be explained by reference to the will of this god. (Swinburne does not discuss the possibility that the most fundamental facts of nature might be statistical; nor shall I, since nothing in the present argument hinges on that issue.)

But even if Swinburne's god hypothesis were correct, it could not provide the ultimate explanation which was its goal. The purpose of the hypothesis is to explain all natural laws in terms of something *other* than natural law. The expla-

From *Analysis* 37 (1976/77): 113–16. Copyright © 1976 by Blackwell Publishing. Reprinted by permission of Blackwell Publishing.

nation is not to be based on regularities of events at all, but on the free decisions of a supernatural rational agent. Obviously, then, this god must not himself depend on natural laws. That is, the god's actions must not presuppose any facts of the natural universe; for if they did, his choices would be logically less funda-mental than these facts—and would not, after all, be the ultimate explanation. But explanations in terms of Swinburne's god *do* involve an appeal to a natural law. For if the god can impose his will on the world, it is a natural law that what-ever he wills, occurs. That is, it is a fact of the universe that if the god wills x, then x is the case; for example, if he wills that $E=mc^2$, it is so. And this fact cannot itself be the product of the god's will; for if it were not a fact, his will could produce no effects whatever—and to make his will effective would be to produce an effect. The fact that events occur as he wills them cannot be the result of his will. Thus, this fact is logically more fundamental than the god's choices: his acts presuppose this fact, but not the converse.

The fact that the god's will is effective is natural in exactly the same sense that any other fact is natural: it occurs independently of any agent's choice. (Of course, it would be pointless to say that this law is due to the fiat of yet another rational agent, since it would then be a natural fact that *his* will was done.) This fact is, on Swinburne's god hypothesis, the ultimate available explanation. It is therefore impossible to explain all natural laws in animistic terms, since the very fact that a mind can effect its choices is a further law. So Swinburne's god hypothesis cannot achieve the final explanation which was to justify our enter-taining it. And the reformulated design argument is as powerless as the original to establish a supernatural architect.

(A widely accepted argument for the autonomy of ethics holds that moral obligations cannot originate with divine command. For if there were no obliga-tion to obey God's command, there would be no obligation to obey his command to obey his command; so there must be at least one obligation which does not acquire its force from divine command, namely, the obligation to obey such com-mands. The present argument is parallel. If a being had no power to make events conform to his will, his decision could not create this power; so there must be at least one fact of nature which does not result from his will, namely, the fact that his will is effective.)

2. All the elements of this argument are to be found in section 7 of Hume's *En-quiry Concerning Human Understanding*. And J. S. Mill stated it in so many words:

> The power of volitions over phenomena is itself a law, and one of the earliest known and acknowledged laws of nature. . . . There is, therefore, no more a suppo-sition of violation of law in supposing that events are produced, prevented, or mod-ified by God's actions, than in the supposition of their being produced, prevented, or modified by man's actions. Both are equally in the course of nature, both equally consistent with what we know of the government of all things by law.[2]

But its implications have not, it seems to me, received the attention they merit. Animism cannot provide an alternative to explanation by natural laws, because the power of a mind to bring about its choices is itself such a law. All that can be said, in the end, is that these are facts of nature. Failure to see this may stem in part from a lingering notion that natural laws are prescriptive rather than descriptive. It would be unfair to charge supporters of supernaturalism with believing, *simpliciter*, that a law requires a lawgiver. But it is a similar mistake to imagine that explanations in terms of personal agency can ultimately account for natural laws. If a rational agent's will is always or sometimes effective, that regularity is an impersonal fact about the universe which cannot be the result of his will.

3. This has implications for the cosmological argument as well. Like the design argument, it claims that a divine artificer is required to account for observed phenomena. But, while the former argues that a designer is necessary to explain particular features of the cosmos, the latter proposes an explanation for the natural order as a whole. It is widely agreed, however, that if this argument is to succeed, it must do more than merely identify a god as one more member in a causal sequence. In that case his status would be no different from that of any other cause, and it would be necessary to ask what caused the god. The only promising version of the cosmological argument, therefore, is the one which holds that the natural universe cannot be a self-supporting system of merely contingent facts but must depend on something beyond itself: a supernatural being. It is only in this form that the argument offers a God who is the all-sustaining Creator and the ultimate explanation of the universe.

But even if there were a bodiless rational agent who created the familiar objects and laws of nature, it would remain a natural fact that the will of that being is fulfilled. So the power of the being on which the universe is said to depend would itself be a fact of that universe. The natural order would therefore *not* have been explained in supernaturalistic terms, since there would remain a natural fact which was independent of the decision of the posited being. Thus even the strongest form of the cosmological argument cannot explain nature by reference to something which is not natural. But to do so was the only justification for introducing the idea of the creating being in the first place; so the cosmological argument can give no reason to suppose that such a being exists.

4. The present argument further shows that the doctrine of creation ex nihilo cannot be correct. It could not be the case that a supernatural agent created the universe including *all* the laws that govern it. For the fact that he can create would be a law of the universe, independent of his will.

5. The ontological argument can now be seen to fail for the same reason. It has been frequently argued that God's existence is either logically necessary or logically impossible. Many skeptics grant that if God existed, his existence would be logically necessary; but they insist that, because of the characteristics

ascribed to him, it is logically impossible that he exists. And if the argument being urged here is sound, this must be true. For even if there were a being who created all the universe we know, it would still be a fact of nature, independent of his will, that he could put his decisions into effect. It is logically impossible that any agent could stand above and control the whole of nature, because his very power to act would be a fact which was not the result of personal agency and hence natural. Therefore, the being himself would be a part of nature: he would be subject, as are we all, to natural law. Thus, the animistic belief that nature could be the work of a supernatural Creator cannot be correct; the concept of such a being is incoherent. Whatever else the ontological argument may prove, it cannot show the existence of the God of theism.

6. So the concept of supernatural agency can provide no alternative to explanation in terms of natural facts. There must be at least one fundamental fact of the universe which is not the result of any agent's choice. And so, whatever the role of human or other personality in the universe, the universe itself must be ultimately impersonal. We must recognize this if we are to understand the world and our place in it.

NOTES

1. R. G. Swinburne, "The Argument from Design," *Philosophy* 43 (1968): 199–212.

2. J. S. Mill, "Theism," in *Three Essays on Religion* (1874; repr., New York: Greenwood Press, 1969), pp. 226–27.

28

THE PARADOX OF OMNIPOTENCE

J. L. COWAN

The claim that God is omnipotent is presumably the claim that He can do anything. The most direct way of arguing against such a claim is therefore to attempt to show that there is something God cannot do. Thus, it has been argued that even God cannot do self-contradictory things. He cannot, for example, draw a square circle.

That this sort of objection will not really do the job, however, seems clear. The reasons why it will not are essentially those advanced by Aquinas.[1] To put Aquinas's point in a more contemporary jargon, the only thing which gives this sort of objection any plausibility is the frequently convenient but often misleading material mode expression "self-contradictory things." Actually, there are no self-contradictory things. It is expressions, statements, phrases, descriptions, or predicates which are self-contradictory or not. Those which are self-contradictory are so constituted that they are logically vacuous; they cannot, as a matter of logic, truly be applied to anything. Thus, when we have noted that God cannot draw a square circle, we have still not noted any *thing* which God cannot draw. We have still not produced anything which God cannot do. Therefore, we have still not provided any valid objection to the doctrine that God can do anything, the doctrine of God's omnipotence.

There are, however, other predicates, predicates which are not self-contradictory and which are thus not logically vacuous as are those we have so far been considering, predicates which, indeed, are not vacuous at all, which not only can

From *Analysis* 25 (1965/supplement): 102–108. Copyright © 1965 by Blackwell Publishing. Reprinted by permission of Blackwell Publishing.

be but are truly applied, and which yet raise difficulties for the concept of omnipotence. Consider the old question of whether God can create a stone too heavy for Him to lift. There does not seem to be any inconsistency here. The expression "making something too heavy for the maker to lift" is not, like "drawing a square circle," one which we must refuse to apply to any activity whatsoever, but is, rather, one which we readily and correctly apply to many quite simple, homely, everyday activities. I myself have performed such and know many others who have. Can God perform such activities? Can He do what even I have done? Can He make something too heavy for the maker to lift? If He cannot, then He is not omnipotent since there is something (namely, this) which He cannot do. If, on the other hand, He can do this, He is not omnipotent since there is something else (namely, lift everything) which He cannot do. So in any case He cannot, it would seem, be omnipotent.

It may be argued, however, that in spite of the apparent differences between the present sort of objection to God's omnipotence and that first considered, the sort of response given by Aquinas to the original objection is actually applicable here as well. One might reason that even though a predicate may not itself be self-contradictory, its *predication* of an omnipotent being might be so. This in fact has been the conclusion reached in a series of recent discussions of this ancient (more accurately medieval) paradox.

J. L. Mackie began the series, in a paper on omnipotence and evil, by arguing that even apart from the problem of evil the present paradox poses formidable obstacles for those who would accept the concept of an omnipotent God.[2] Mackie then suggested two "solutions" of the paradox. The first of these would in effect eliminate the concept of omnipotence. The second would in effect eliminate the concept of God. G. B. Keene next suggested a simpler "solution."[3] Keene's idea was that the paradox when suitably phrased proves not to be a paradox at all. B. Mayo then showed that Keene's translation was inadequate and so that his proposed solution would not do the job.[4] Mayo concluded, however, by pointing out that the statement of the paradox contains a self-contradiction and suggesting that it was therefore resoluble along the same lines as that about round squares. Finally, G. I. Mavrodes argued to the same effect in greater detail.[5]

Mavrodes's formulation is the more elaborate. If, he argues, we assume that God is not omnipotent, we can, of course, "prove" that He is not omnipotent. But if we assume that God is omnipotent, then presumably the statement that God can make something too heavy for Him to lift becomes, on analysis, the statement that a being who can lift anything can make something too heavy for Him to lift. But since this statement is self-contradictory and thus vacuous in the sense explained above, God's "inability" to perform the pseudotask described by the statement can constitute no more objection to His omnipotence than his "inability" to draw a square circle. To ask that God be both omnipotent (as for the purposes of the argument we must assume Him to be) *and* able to make something too heavy for Him to lift is exactly comparable to asking our friend Smith to be a married bachelor or a teetotaller who drinks Scotch.

This Mayo-Mavrodes argument is an ingenious one, yet it leaves me unhappy. The argument shows that the statement that God is both omnipotent and can make something He cannot lift is self-contradictory and thus does not constitute the description of something God could be expected to do. But the argument does not thereby show that the concept of omnipotence is *itself* self-contradictory and that it therefore constitutes *in itself* something not to be expected of God. But since it is just this which is the real point of the objection to God's omnipotence now under consideration, the present argument, and indeed any argument along the lines taken by Aquinas in response to the sort of objection initially considered, might be taken to support rather than to rebut this second kind of objection to the doctrine of God's omnipotence. I shall argue in this paper that this is in fact the case, that Mayo and Mavrodes are quite correct in holding that the paradox contains a self-contradiction, but that the paradox still constitutes a valid objection to the doctrine of omnipotence since that contradiction stems from the concept of omnipotence itself.

The crux of the entire issue lies in one simple fact. Because of its central importance I shall state this in three ways, in the formal mode as (1a), in the material mode as (1b), and in a simple logical notation as (1c). These are quite equivalent, however, and I shall refer to them indiscriminately as '(1)'.

(1a)   There are perfectly respectable, non-self-contradictory predicates, predicates meaningfully and even truly predicable even of such lowly beings as you and me, predicates which, however, are such that the capacity to have them truly predicated of one logically excludes the capacity to have *other* similarly non-self-contradictory predicates truly predicated of one.

(1b)   Some capacities imply limitations; there are things one can do only if one cannot do certain other things.

(1c) $(\exists F)(\exists G)(x)(pFx \supset \sim pGx)$. Here 'pFx' means 'x can (do or be) F', and the other symbols are as usual except that to rule out all suspicion of having cheated the Mayo-Mavrodes objections, we might limit the range of the Fs and Gs to the non-self-contradictory.

One example of the sort of thing referred to in (1) is the manufacturing ability we have been considering. If one can make something one cannot lift, one cannot lift everything (collectively or distributively) that one can make. It is important to note, moreover, that the existence of such mutually exclusive predicates is a matter of logic. If we did not have them already, we could define some.

Thus (1) is not merely true, it is a logical truth in the sense of being true by (following logically from) definitions.

But since there are such mutually exclusive predicates the assumption that God (or anything else) is omnipotent becomes, on analysis, self-contradictory. That God is omnipotent presumably means that He can do anything the description of which is not self-contradictory. He can do F, which is not self-contradictory; He can do G, which is also not self-contradictory; and so on. But since the ability to do F will in some cases logically imply the inability to do G, the claim that God is omnipotent will implicate both the claim that God can do G and the claim that He cannot do G. More formally:

(1)	$(\exists F)(\exists G)(x)(pFx \supset \sim pGx)$	By definition.
(2)	$(F)pFg$	Assumption that God is omnipotent. 'F' again restricted to the non-self-contradictory.
(3)	$pFg \supset \sim pGg$	From (1) by instantiation.
(4)	pFg	From (2) by instantiation.
(5)	$\sim pGg$	From (3) and (4) by modus ponens.
(6)	pGg	From (2) by instantiation.

For example, since God is omnipotent and thus can make any kind of thing, He can make something He cannot lift; but since He is omnipotent and thus can lift any kind of thing, He cannot make something He cannot lift.

The same point may be put in a way which confronts even more directly the line of reasoning represented by Mavrodes's argument. This may be done by challenging the basic premise of this kind of argument. It is *not* necessary to begin a proof that God is not omnipotent either with the assumption that He is not omnipotent or with the assumption that He is. To prove that neither God nor anything else is omnipotent, one need assume nothing more than (1). Since there are things one can do only if one cannot do certain other things, it follows that there will be, for everyone (everything), *something* he (it) cannot do. Formally:

(1)	$(\exists F)(\exists G)(x)(pFx \supset \sim pGx)$	By definition.
(2)	$pFx \supset \sim pGx$	By existential instantiation on F and G, and universal instantiation on x.
(3)	pFx	Conditional proof assumption.
(4)	$\sim pGx$	By modus ponens from (2) and (3).
(5)	$(\exists F)\sim pFx$	Existential generalization from (4).
(6)	$pFx \supset (\exists F)\sim pFx$	Conditional proof from (3)–(5).
(7)	$\sim pFx$	Conditional proof assumption.
(8)	$(\exists F)\sim pFx$	Existential generalization from (7).
(9)	$\sim pFx \supset (\exists F)\sim pFx$	Conditional proof from (7)–(8).

(10)	$pFx \lor {\sim}pFx$	Tautology. Horns between which we cannot slip by the Mayo-Mavrodes gambit since no omnipotent being is mentioned.
(11)	$(\exists F){\sim}pFx$	By constructive dilemma from (6), (9), and (10).
(12)	${\sim}(F)pFx$	By quantifier negation from (11).
(13)	$(x){\sim}(F)pFx$	Universal generalization from (12).
(14)	${\sim}(\exists x)(F)pFx$	By quantifier negation from (13).
or (14a)	$(x)(\exists F){\sim}pFx$	By quantifier negation from (13).

Since no one can make something he cannot lift unless he cannot lift everything, everyone (including God) will be limited either with respect to his making or with respect to his lifting or both.

Moreover, since (1) is a logical truth, since the existence of mutually exclusive predicates is assured by definition, and since the nonexistence of anything omnipotent follows directly from (1) without any further premise being necessary, that nothing is omnipotent is not merely true, it is a logical truth exactly comparable to the truth that nothing is a square circle. Our concepts of being able to do (or be) things are simply not such that they will all fit together on any one subject. Since being able to do some perfectly legitimate, non-self-contradictory things involves (logically) being unable to do others, nothing can (logically) be able to do everything non-self-contradictory. We would therefore seem to have no choice but to abandon as irrevocably vacuous the concept of omnipotence, to admit that neither God nor anything else can be omnipotent.

I suspect, however, that, clear and cogent as this argument seems, the proponents of the line of reasoning I have been criticizing will not yet be quite satisfied, for I have not yet confronted quite directly enough what must be the basic points at which they are driving, or, as I should prefer to put it, the basic sources of their confusion. Surely, such a proponent might argue, the only things we can show a priori, by logic alone, that God cannot do are self-contradictory "things." From this it would seem to follow that we cannot, by logic alone, show that there is any non-self-contradictory thing God cannot do. This in turn would seem to mean that we cannot, after all, show, by logic alone, that God is not omnipotent.

There are two confusions in this short line of reasoning. In the first place, even if we restrict God's omnipotence to the ability to do anything the description of which is not self-contradictory, there is *one* thing which, even if its description *is* self-contradictory, is still relevant to the question of God's omnipotence. That thing is omnipotence itself. Since the concept of being able to do anything not self-contradictory is *itself* self-contradictory, one can indeed, by showing that there is "something" self-contradictory which God cannot do, show that there is something *not* self-contradictory which God cannot do.

A second confusion turns on an ambiguity in the phrase "show that there is something non-self-contradictory which God cannot do." It is true that the only definite, specific things we can logically prove God cannot do are self-contradictory "things." We can, however, still by logic alone, prove that there is *something* non-self-contradictory that God cannot do. We cannot by logic alone say specifically *what* that thing is, but simply proving that it exists is enough to prove that God cannot do everything non-self-contradictory, that He is not omnipotent.

I shall put this point in concrete form once again. There is a perfectly simple, straightforward, entirely non-self-contradictory task which I, who am fairly skillful at making things but not much on muscles, can do. I can make something too heavy for the maker to lift. Our friend Smith, on the other hand, who is quite strong but incredibly inept at making things, can perform another, equally straightforward and non-self-contradictory task. He can lift anything the lifter can make. But no one, not even God, can do *both* what I can do *and* what Smith can do. To ask God, or anyone else, to be able so to do would be to ask for something self-contradictory and thus vacuous, a pseudosomething. So either Smith or I, although we cannot by logic alone say which, can do something even God cannot do. Thus God cannot be omnipotent.

So much for the argument. What does it really establish? After all, whatever I could make, God could make still better; whatever Smith could lift, God could lift this and more. Mavrodes, indeed, feels that the argument, even if accepted, would establish nothing at all. Even if God's ability to make were "limited" by His ability to lift, he reasons, since God's ability to lift would still be infinite, His ability to make would likewise be infinite.

But surely this line of reasoning confuses finitude with limitation and one limitation with another. One might just as well argue that puppy A which cannot catch its own tail is really no more limited than puppy B which, being somewhat more flexible, *can* catch its own tail. After all, one may reason, this places no limitation on how far puppy A may run or how fast. Puppy A might still be able to catch B's tail and might indeed be able to do so even more easily than puppy B can. All this is quite true, but it is also quite irrelevant. The fact remains that puppy A, however splendid his other qualities, lacks a capacity possessed by puppy B.

Perhaps part of the difficulty of grasping the force of this conclusion stems from having, thus far, kept our examples so simple. But consider two possible (theologically interesting) conceptions of a limited God: (a) a God who cannot completely control the development of every universe he can create, and (b) a God who cannot create a universe he cannot completely control. Our argument then shows that the actual God, if there is one, must possess either limitation (a) or limitation (b). He cannot escape both.

The argument also has applications beyond theology. In the United States the founding documents of colleges and universities usually state that their governing boards shall have the power to hire and fire "at pleasure," or "whenever, in the judgment of the board, the interests of the university shall require," or something to this effect. These documents state, in brief, that within this area the governing board is to be omnipotent. Thus the courts have traditionally maintained that any contract for employment at such an institution not terminable at will (let alone a tenure arrangement) was invalid as constituting a limitation on the power to discharge. More recently, however, as the value of contracts and tenure systems has become more apparent, courts have upheld such contracts on the grounds that to deny governing boards the power to enter into them would constitute a limitation on their power to employ. Despite their contradictory conclusions both arguments are, of course, quite correct. The original documents granting omnipotence even within such a limited area are, if interpreted straightforwardly, self-contradictory. The power to hire (for a fixed term, for example) cannot be unlimited unless the power to fire can be limited and conversely.[6]

The same argument, moreover, is applicable to other omniconcepts. It is applicable, for example, to omniscience.[7] Does God know how to create a universe the potentialities of which He does not know?

The final upshot of our argument, then, would seem to be that there is more work to be done than some have thought. In the area of law, for example, such blanket empowerings as we have considered, since they are ruled out by logic, will have to be replaced by more specific grantings and withholdings whether by statute or by the courts. In theology it would seem that those theologians or philosophers of religion who have explored various conceptions of a limited God have been taking the only consistent course. Rather than trying to cut the Gordian knot of God's nature with impossible concepts like omnipotence and omniscience, we must try to unpuzzle it strand by strand. We cannot have everything, but must be content with the best of all *possible* gods.

NOTES

1. Thomas Aquinas, *Summa Theologiae,* part I, Q. 25, art. 3.
2. J. L. Mackie, "Evil and Omnipotence," *Mind* 64 (1955): 200–12.
3. G. B. Keene, "A Simpler Solution to the Paradox of Omnipotence," *Mind* 69 (1960): 74–75.
4. Bernard Mayo, "Mr. Keene on Omnipotence," *Mind* 70 (1961): 249–50.
5. George I. Mavrodes, "Some Puzzles Concerning Omnipotence," *The Philosophical Review* 72 (1963): 221–23.
6. For references see W. P. Murphy, "Educational Freedom in the Courts," *A.A.U.P. Bulletin* 49 (1963): 309–327.
7. As was pointed out to me by my colleagues R. L. Caldwell and R. D. Milo.

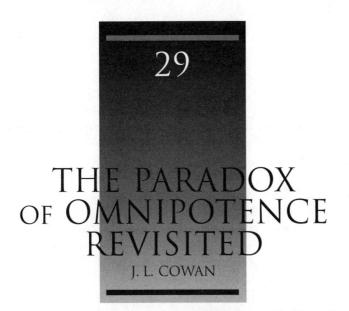

THE PARADOX OF OMNIPOTENCE REVISITED

J. L. COWAN

A.   (1)   Either God can create a stone which He cannot lift, or He cannot create a stone which He cannot lift.

      (2)   If God can create a stone which He cannot lift, then He is not omnipotent (since He cannot lift the stone in question).

      (3)   If God cannot create a stone which He cannot lift, then He is not omnipotent (since He cannot create the stone in question).

      (4)   Therefore, God is not omnipotent.

In a paper published in *Analysis*,[1] I tried to show (a) that any attempt to find something wrong with all arguments of the general form of A above, any attempt to resolve the "paradox," must fail, (b) that the reason these attempts must fail is that at least some arguments of this form are essentially sound, and (c) that the only thing which makes these arguments seem paradoxical, their conclusion to the effect that God is not omnipotent, is, like at least some versions of the arguments to this conclusion, quite correct.

Subsequent correspondence with George I. Mavrodes and the publication of articles by C. Wade Savage[2] and Julian Wolfe[3] have convinced me, however, that my earlier paper did not deal adequately with certain key points. I should thus like further to develop these points here.

From *Canadian Journal of Philosophy* 3, no. 3 (March 1974): 435–45. Copyright © 1974 by University of Calgary Press. Reprinted by permission of University of Calgary Press.

I

In order to circumvent an objection to arguments of form A which had been raised by Bernard Mayo[4] and developed by Mavrodes,[5] Savage reformulated the argument, as I had done in my paper, in a manner not requiring reference to God:

Where x is any being:

B. (1) Either x can create a stone which x cannot lift, or x cannot create a stone which x cannot lift.

(2) If x can create a stone which x cannot lift, then, necessarily, there is at least one task which x cannot perform (namely, lift the stone in question).

(3) If x cannot create a stone which x cannot lift, then, necessarily, there is at least one task which x cannot perform (namely, create the stone in question).

(4) Hence, there is at least one task which x cannot perform.

(5) If x is an omnipotent being, then x can perform any task.

(6) Therefore, x is not omnipotent.

Savage then suggested the following "schematic representation" of B(1)–(3) where Sx = x is a stone, Cxy = x can create y, Lxy = x can lift y, x is any being, and the universe of discourse is limited to conceivable entities:

C. (1) $(\exists y)(Sy \cdot Cxy \cdot -Lxy) \vee -(\exists y)(Sy \cdot Cxy \cdot -Lxy)$.

(2) $(\exists y)(Sy \cdot Cxy \cdot -Lxy) \supset (\exists y)(Sy \cdot -Lxy)$.

(3) $-(\exists y)(Sy \cdot Cxy \cdot -Lxy) \supset (\exists y)(Sy \cdot -Cxy)$.

Savage then claimed that since C(3) is not logically true, the argument falls through.

But surely Savage's C formulation must seem just a bit too "schematic." He was perhaps misled by the surface similarity of B(2) and B(3), and especially by the phrase "the stone in question," which occurs in both. In spite of this surface resemblance the logical structures of B(2) and B(3) are clearly very different. B(2) does involve the assertion of the existence of a stone of given characteristics, but B(3) involves rather the denial of the existence of a stone with those characteristics, or, equivalently, the assertion that any stone which does exist lacks them. This confusion might be avoided entirely simply by substituting for B(3) the following:

B(3)′ If x cannot create a stone which x cannot lift, then, necessarily, there is at least one task x cannot perform (namely, create a stone x cannot lift).

An even more fundamental flaw in C, however, is its allowing the consequents of C(2) and C(3) to refer basically to stones at all, when the consequents of B(2) and B(3) refer rather to tasks. Let us therefore try a somewhat more literal translation, D, using the same conventions as in C but with the addition of Tz = z is a task, Pxz = x can perform z, and Ox = x is omnipotent.

D. (1) $(\exists y)(Sy \bullet Cxy \bullet -Lxy)$ v $-(\exists y)(Sy \bullet Cxy \bullet -Lxy)$.

To get a proper (2) and (3), let us introduce two tasks, *a* and *b*:

(1') $Ta \bullet \{Pxa \equiv (y)[(Sy \bullet Cxy) \supset Lxy]\}$, i.e., x can perform task *a* means that x can lift any stone he can create, and

(1") $Tb \bullet [Pxb \equiv (\exists y)(Sy \bullet Cxy \bullet -Lxy)]$, i.e., x can perform task *b* means that x can create a stone he cannot lift.

Then from (1') follows

(2) $(\exists y)(Sy \bullet Cxy \bullet -Lxy) \supset (\exists z)(Tz \bullet -Pxz)$,

while from (1") in the same manner follows

(3) $-(\exists y)(Sy \bullet Cxy \bullet -Lxy) \supset (\exists z)(Tz \bullet -Pxz)$.

From (1), (2), and (3) by constructive dilemma we obtain

(4) $(\exists z)(Tz \bullet -Pxz)$

while

(5) $Ox \supset (z)(Tz \supset Pxz)$

would seem to be required by any adequate definition of omnipotence. But from (4) and (5) we obtain

(6) $-Ox$.

Since x is any being, this form of the argument would indeed seem to prove that the existence of an omnipotent being, God or any other, is impossible.

As is usually the case, a suitable formalization does not resolve the philosophical problems, but it does help us to locate those problems more precisely. In D (1) is a logical truth; (2), (3), (4), and (6) follow by completely uncontentious formal moves from preceding steps. The only remaining points to which relevant exception might possibly be taken will thus be (1'), (1"), and (5).

Now (5) simply as it stands might seem open to objection. Someone might maintain, for example, that in the Creeds, not only *Pantocrator* but also *omnipotens* means that God is the ruler of all things rather than that He can do anything. But so far as I am aware, the only grounds for such a distinction are simply the beliefs that God cannot do anything contrary to reason or morality. If "acts contrary to reason" means "self-contradictory acts," then I should certainly accept their exclusion since, as I shall argue below, there cannot be any such thing. Immoral acts, as well as "acts contrary to reason" in the sense of "unwise," there certainly can be and are, but as neither is necessary to my argument I shall be happy to exclude them as well. Wolfe's distinction between capacities and powers may be an extension of the same sort of objection. At any rate I shall render (5) as innocuous as possible by limiting the range of the task predicate "T" to genuine tasks, not self-contradictory, neither immoral nor unwise and such that capacity to perform them is a genuine power. It is hard to see how any further restriction would be compatible even with actually ruling over all things rather than merely reigning somewhat in the manner of a modern British monarch, or could be consistent with, still less implied by, infinitude. If and insofar as there are alternative conceptions of omnipotence the present, one should at any rate have sufficient relevance to them to be of interest in that respect as well as intrinsically. These restrictions should then allow me to concentrate on premises of the sort represented by (1') and (1") as the only possible remaining source of difficulty for the argument.

II

What the sort of challenge to the conception of omnipotence here represented thus boils down to is simply an example of the most decisive method of challenging any universal generalization, the finding of a counterexample. What one who would challenge the concept of omnipotence along these lines must do, in short, is to find a genuine bona fide task God could not perform, and thus a power to perform He could not have.

In trying to develop such a counterexample, to discover a task God could not perform, we are presumably limited to the resources provided by logic. We are scarcely in a position actually to put to God, somewhat as Eurystheus did to Heracles, a series of tasks of increasing difficulty in order to test His capacities. Our only hope of success in such a search must lie in ruling out some task and correlative power as somehow involving self-contradiction. The real issue, then, is whether or not it is possible to find an appropriately genuine task which can be so ruled out.

Given this limitation the simplest and most straightforward approach is certainly that of just specifying a "task" the specification of which is itself internally self-contradictory. "Drawing a round square" is the stock medieval example. But Aquinas already showed that, and essentially why, this approach will not do the job.[6] It is not things or genuine tasks which are self-contradictory. It is rather statements, or descriptions, or predicates which are or are not so. Those which are so preclude by their own structure their successful application to anything. Thus a self-contradictory description such as "round square" does not and cannot apply to anything, and "drawing a round square" does not specify a genuine task which God or anyone else could be faulted for failing to be able to do.

Other purported tasks fail on the same ground even though less obviously so. Thus it might even seem that we do not need logic at all. Consider an example suggested by Mavrodes, the task description "finding a fatter man than the fattest man in Ann Arbor." There is surely nothing self-contradictory about this. One can readily imagine finding such a man, in Detroit perhaps. Yet suppose that as a matter not of logic but of mere empirical fact there just happens to be no fatter man, in Detroit or anywhere else, than the fattest man in Ann Arbor. Then presumably even God could not accomplish the task described by the straightforward non-self-contradictory task description "finding a fatter man than the fattest man in Ann Arbor."

The trouble with such cases as this arises when one begins to think about *why* God could not accomplish this "task." Such reflections soon reveal that while there is indeed nothing contradictory about the task description "finding a fatter man than the fattest man in Ann Arbor," there is also nothing inherently impossible about performing the task simply so described. The task specified by the initial noncontradictory task description is impossible only if and in so far as conditions are such that the explicitly self-contradictory task description "finding a man fatter than the fattest man" is *also* applicable to that "task." But, as shown by the preceding considerations, a "task" to which a description such as that is applicable is no genuine task at all, and thus does not provide us with a genuine counterexample.

The ingenuity of the argument of the stone, as in A, B, and D above, lies in its attempt to use self-contradiction to eliminate a power, yet to do so in a manner which does not involve self-contradiction in any description of the power eliminated. The strategy is simply to find two (or more) powers such that no description of either is inconsistent in itself, but so related that the ascription of both powers to the same individual would be self-contradictory. Success in this strategy would then enable us to say that for any being there is some task it cannot perform, some power it must lack, and that omnipotence is therefore a self-contradictory concept.

It is essential to see just how this approach attains the aims of its more simplistic predecessors by using their methods while at the same time avoiding their fatal flaws. Otherwise one might be tempted to reason erroneously as follows. The kind of situation required for the paradox is precisely analogous to that of finding a man fatter than the fattest man in Ann Arbor. There we had a task description which was not in itself contradictory. But circumstances were such that the "task" it singled out was also describable by a description which was self-contradictory. The "task" described was thus really no task at all, and the "inability" to perform it no real limitation of power. Suppose then that we were to grant that "making something the maker cannot lift" is, in general, a perfectly legitimate task specification. But consider a being which can lift anything. With such a being, just as with the fat man, we would have an external circumstance which would logically deprive the intrinsically noncontradictory task specification of an object. To ask a being which can lift anything to make something it cannot lift would again be to ask for something self-contradictory, thus no task at all, and thus nothing such that the "inability" to perform it would constitute a genuine limitation of power.

There is truth in this line of reasoning. To ask a being which can lift anything to create something it cannot lift would be to ask for something self-contradictory. That is exactly why we can say that a being which can lift anything cannot create something it cannot lift. Where the reasoning errs is in its failure to see that in addition to this point of positive analogy with the case of the fat man, the paradox situation possesses vital points of negative analogy.

The circumstance of there being no fatter man than the fattest man in Ann Arbor universally deprives the task specification "finding a man fatter than the fattest man in Ann Arbor" of application. In that circumstance it can have no instantiation. You cannot find such a man, I cannot find such a man, Jones cannot find such a man, no one can find such a man—for there is no such a man to find. But the circumstance of there existing a being which can lift anything does not universally deprive the task specification "making something the maker cannot lift" of application. I can make such a thing, you can, Jones can. That this task description has instances of its successful accomplishment proves that neither it nor any other description identical in extension is self-contradictory and that the task specified is thus far genuine.

The reasoning I have been criticizing is essentially the same as the following. Suppose Jones has a red chair while Smith has none. To ask Smith to have a red chair when he has none would be to ask for something self-contradictory. Therefore, Smith does not really lack anything Jones has. The sophistry is less masked in this example, but it is the same sophistry. The real thing Smith is not doing is not, of course, having a red chair and *also* having none, but is rather having a red chair *instead of* having none. Just so the real thing a being who is able to lift anything is not able to do is not, to be able to create something it cannot lift *while* being able to lift anything, but is rather being able to create something it cannot lift *instead of* being able to lift anything. That having a red chair and having none are logically incompatible does not mean that each is not a genuine state but only that nothing can simultaneously occupy both. So too that being able to make something one cannot lift and being able to lift anything one can make are logically incompatible does not mean that each is not a genuine power, but only that nothing can simultaneously possess both, and that nothing can therefore be omnipotent.

Even with the basic structure of the "paradox" thus grasped and defended, however, objections remain. Tasks suitable for the purposes of such an argument will clearly have to be complex tasks having two characteristics. They must, first, be reflexive. The same agent must be carried through the different parts of the complex. Second, the powers involved must be such as to limit each other. Critics of the argument have been bothered by both of these characteristics.

III

One ground for objecting to the argument appears to be the suspicion that the whole procedure is simply a verbal trick based on the use of token reflexives and revealed as a sophistry simply by the easily accomplished elimination of such reflexives.

Let us see how this line of attack proceeds. Consider an expression containing token reflexives such as "being able to make something the maker cannot lift." This phrase is truly applicable to many people, to Jones for one. But assuming that God can lift anything conceivable, then the phrase is not truly applicable to Him. Thus it would seem that Jones has creative powers God lacks. But, my critics reason, this is surely absurd. The source of the absurdity, they continue, must lie in the use of token reflexives in the original expression. If we reformulate this in terms of its specific substitution instances, we get "Jones's being able to make something Jones cannot lift," "God's being able to make something God cannot lift," and so on. But then, the critics conclude, the entire illusion of Jones's creative powers being superior to God's vanishes, and the balance is restored. For God can also make things Jones cannot lift, while Jones most assuredly cannot make anything God cannot lift either. Thus, it is revealed that Jones does not actually possess powers not possessed in still greater abundance by God.

The only trouble with this line of reasoning is that it completely begs the entire question. For the powers God and Jones have triumphantly been shown to have and lack were never a matter of contention in the original argument, while that power which alone was there at issue has been entirely ignored. The power at issue is not that of making something Jones could not lift, nor is it that of making something God could not lift. It is the power of making something that the maker could not lift.

In order to see more clearly what my critics are driving at here, let us consider a more complex example, again suggested by Mavrodes. Suppose each of two men, Smith and Jones, has built a boat. Now both are given an additional task. Each man is to load his own boat onto a truck. Smith accomplishes this with ease, while Jones fails miserably. Has Smith demonstrated a power Jones lacks? Were we so to conclude Jones might quite properly object along the following lines. "Smith's boat is much smaller and lighter than mine. The task assigned me was thus actually a very different and much more formidable one than that assigned him. This difference is not altered in the slightest by the mere fact that both tasks could be described by the same form of words, 'loading your own boat onto a truck,' containing as it does the token reflexive, 'your own.' My inability to perform my task therefore reflects not at all on my boat loading powers relative to those of Smith."

Surely, Jones would be correct here, and with him Mavrodes, Savage, and Wolfe. The reason they would be correct here, however, has nothing to do with any inherent and ineradicable defect in token reflexives as task specifiers. It is rather merely that token reflexives fail us with the particular type of task in question simply because that type of task, boat loading, is not itself inherently and essentially reflexive. What Mavrodes, Savage, and Wolfe, as opposed to Jones, have to show in order to establish their position, however, is not that this or that task is not essentially reflexive, but that none is, or at least none of the sort needed for pairing with its contradictory, in the "paradox." That sort of showing is in itself a task of substantially greater difficulty.

Consider another story. We are operating a wilderness survival training school. One skill we are endeavoring to get each of our trainees to master is that of building, alone, without aid, and utilizing only native materials, a boat which not only can carry its builder but which, to negotiate the inevitable portages, he in turn can carry. Smith and Brown succeed. Jones fails; his boat can carry him, but not he it. Have Smith and Brown not demonstrated an ability, capacity, or power Jones lacks?

In this case the sort of arguments Jones previously and successfully used to the contrary would seem to be of no avail. "Surely the task assigned me was a very different and much more formidable one than those assigned Smith and Brown," he might aver. "Surely you cannot fault my building powers, since my boat is even lighter than Smith's nor yet my carrying powers since I can carry even more than Brown." What can or need we reply to Jones here except that he has misunderstood the task at issue. Successful accomplishment of that task undoubtedly called for more building capacity on the part of Jones than on that of Smith, since the carrying capacity of the latter was greater. Such success also called for more carrying capacity on the part of Jones than on that of Brown since the latter has an advantage in building capacity. But it was neither building nor carrying capacity alone which here constituted capacity or power successfully to accomplish the task assigned. It was rather a relative combination or coordination of the two on the part of the *same* person which was required here. *That* ability or power Smith and Brown possessed and Jones lacked in spite of Jones's superiority to each of the others in *different* respects. And with *that* ability or power, as opposed to those different ones, there is nothing misleading about token reflexives, since *that* ability or power, as opposed to those different ones, is itself essentially reflexive although a genuine power or ability nonetheless—and to one alone in the wilderness even a potentially lifesaving power or ability.

Certainly all genuine tasks and correlated powers to perform them are not of this essentially reflexive kind. But just as certainly many others are, even when not so obviously or explicitly such. Take maintaining an equable disposition. Suppose you get angry rather more often than do I, and in even less intrinsically upsetting circumstances. It will not avail you a whit to say that you are still better at controlling tempers than I am only yours is harder to control, and that if you but had as compliant a one as I do, you would never get upset at all. The task in question is again essentially reflexive. It is to control your own temper, however unruly it might be. Or take running the one-hundred-yard dash. You surely cannot argue that, even though it takes you considerably longer to do it, you are better at running the one hundred than I am since you weigh 210 pounds and I, a mere 150. That is simply irrelevant to the task we call "running the one-hundred-yard dash," since this involves moving down the course in a given time one's *own* body whatever weight, shape, or size that body might happen to be.

Let me consider only one more example. In the primary school attended by my children grades were formerly awarded simply on the basis of level of attainment in, for example, reading, writing, and arithmetic. It was later decided that, while these were important, the learning of a different sort of skill was perhaps even more important. What is now graded is the extent of the accomplishment in each field on the part of each individual student of the task of working up to the highest level permitted by that student's own individual capacities.

Students, and even parents, have some difficulty in understanding this new system. "Jimmy can read better than Johnny," they will exclaim. "Why then did Johnny get the better grade?" We might even put their objection in a form identical with that used by my critics above. "Learning to read as well as the learner could learn to read" is an example of the sort of task now in question. If we eliminate the token reflexive, we get something like "Johnny's learning to read as well as Johnny could learn to read," "Jimmy's learning to read as well as Jimmy could learn to read," and so on. Then we find, of course, that Jimmy learned to read even better than Johnny could learn to read, while Johnny most assuredly did not learn to read as well as Jimmy could learn to read. But the "illusion" of Johnny's having accomplished something Jimmy did not most certainly does not vanish with the token reflexive expressions. Johnny has an IQ of 75, Jimmy of 150. Johnny learned to make the most of his meager resources while Jimmy remained capable only of squandering his abundant ones. It is the accomplishment or lack of it of *that* task which is here in question, a task essentially reflexive, yet not only perfectly legitimate but even extremely important for all of that.

Finally, we have expressions having a general form like "creating a stone which cannot be lifted." But these forms imply as subalterns the forms involving explicit token reflexives. If x can create a stone which cannot be lifted, x can create a stone which x cannot lift. Thus, anyone accepting the general forms as genuine task specifiers must on pain of contradiction accept the token reflexive forms as doing likewise. Should someone reject such general expressions, on the other hand, it is hard to see what portion of our linguistic-conceptual structure he could accept.

IV

I hope, then, that the preceding remarks will have sufficiently allayed general suspicions about sophistry in the use of token reflexives and the genuineness of essentially reflexive acts and powers to perform them. There remains, however, an additional problem, or apparent problem, in the application of these considerations to God.

Suppose we admit that the expression "making a stone the maker cannot lift" defines, in general, a perfectly legitimate act. Suppose, further, that we assume God can lift anything and therefore cannot create a stone He cannot lift. Have we, even by these suppositions, indicated any real limitation on God's powers to create?

The problem seems to arise because our hypotheses, which "limit" God's power to create solely by His power to lift, leave the latter infinite. Thus take all the dimensions of a stone increasing values of which might make it harder to lift, say size, shape, texture, and weight. Consider specific values for each of these dimensions. However large these values are, God's power to lift, since infinite, will still exceed them, and a stone having them will therefore remain within His power to create. What, then, are the values of the appropriate dimensions of the stone God cannot create?

I think that the appearance of a problem here stems basically from the same confusion of reflexive tasks with other irrelevant tasks against which I argued above. Suppose we have a mathematical system with two variables, m and n, ranging over the integers. The statement "m is greater than n" would still be significant even though it does not mean that there is some value n may not take, but only that whatever value it takes, m will take a greater. The system in question will thus be quite different than it would be if "n is greater than m" were true of it instead, and of no system will both these statements be true. All this in spite of the infinite range of the two variables.

This is just the point Savage missed in his attempt to reformulate B. The argument is not that there is some stone that a being who can lift anything cannot create, but rather that, unlike most of the rest of us, there is no stone such a being can make but not lift. The being in question would thus lack a power to create that most of us possess even though having innumerable other powers perfectly splendid in their own ways.

Just so too to say that a puppy cannot catch its own tail is not to limit how far it can run or how fast or how many other puppies' tails it can catch, but only its ability to catch its own tail—which is still *something* even though it is not *everything*.

Should such examples as the stone still bother anyone, however, they can too be dispensed with, as, like acts immoral or unwise they too are not essential to the "paradox." Pointing out that some tasks even if specified with token reflexives are not essentially reflexive was not sufficient for the purposes of the opponents of the argument of the stone, since there remain other tasks which are essentially reflexive. But so too pointing out that the inability to perform some types of essentially reflexive tasks generates problematic limitations is not enough for those opponents, since there remain other types of essentially reflexive tasks completely free of such problems.

The peculiarity of the type of example we have been considering is that it involves two powers which are directly correlated, which increase or decrease together. The dependent variable, the power to create, is limited solely by the independent variable, the power to lift. In ordinary cases some external limit on the independent variable will obtain and thus another on the dependent variable as well. In the case of God, where the independent variable is allowed to range without limit, the dependent variable will in effect do likewise.

But this particular kind of relationship between powers is of course by no means the only one possible. The most obvious among alternatives is that in which the powers, rather than being directly correlated, are inversely so. Thus an increase in one, rather than leading to an increase in the other as in our original example, leads to a decrease in it. The condition which leads some to imagine problems on the original type of case is thus completely eliminated. For with powers inversely correlated, increasing one without limit, rather than likewise increasing the second, will in general eliminate the second completely.

Tasks, and powers to accomplish them, having the requisite inversely correlated relation are not difficult to find. As I pointed out in my *Analysis* paper, the founding documents of colleges and universities in the United States often state that their governing boards shall have the power to hire and fire "at pleasure" or "whenever, in the judgment of the board, the interests of the university shall require," or something to this effect. These documents state, in brief, that within this area the governing board is to be omnipotent. Thus, the courts have traditionally maintained that any contract for employment at such an institution not terminable at will, let alone a tenure arrangement, was invalid as constituting a limitation of the power to discharge. More recently, however, as the value of contracts and tenure systems has become more apparent, courts have upheld such contracts on the grounds that to deny the governing board the power to enter into them would constitute a limitation on its power to employ.[7] Despite their conflicting conclusions both arguments are, or course, quite correct. The original documents granting omnipotence even within such a limited area are self-contradictory. The power to hire, for a fixed term, for example, is most certainly a genuine, bona fide power. If it is not, it is certainly most difficult to think of one which is. So too is the power to fire. But the former cannot be unlimited unless the latter is limited and conversely. This is, again, simply a matter of logic. Were God Himself a member of the Board of Regents (ex-officio perhaps), the situation could not be otherwise.

This same example, moreover, has the advantage of easy translatability into indubitably theological contexts. Is it that God cannot completely control every universe He can create, or that He cannot create a universe He cannot completely control? It must be the one or the other. Put more specifically this question might be: Can God create men who are genuinely free, beyond His control, or can He not?

When Job says, "How should a man be just with God? . . . For he is not a man, as I am, that I should answer him, and we should come together in judgment. Neither is there any daysman betwixt us, that might lay his hand upon us both," or "Thine hands have made me and fashioned me together round about; yet thou dost destroy me," we may consider that the latter alternative is being explored. But when he says, "Thou knowest that I am not wicked. . . . Though he slay me, yet will I trust in him: but I will maintain mine own ways before him . . . I know that I shall be justified . . . till I die I will not remove mine integrity from me," it may be the former alternative which is under examination.

But these are genuine mutually exclusive alternatives. This is one of the things which makes their exploration by the author or authors of Job such splendid philosophical theology. And it is at the same stroke one of the things which makes the concept of omnipotence as useless in theology as in law or morals or anywhere else.

NOTES

1. J. L. Cowan, "The Paradox of Omnipotence," *Analysis* 25 (1965/supplement): 102–108.

2. C. Wade Savage, "The Paradox of the Stone," *The Philosophical Review* 76 (1967): 74–79.

3. Julian Wolfe, "Omnipotence," *Canadian Journal of Philosophy* 1, no. 2 (December 1971): 245–47.

4. Bernard Mayo, "Mr. Keene on Omnipotence," *Mind* 70 (1961): 249–50.

5. George I. Mavrodes, "Some Puzzles Concerning Omnipotence," *The Philosophical Review* 72 (1963): 221–23.

6. Thomas Aquinas, *Summa Theologiae,* part I, Q. 25, art. 3.

7. For references, see W. P. Murphy, "Educational Freedom in the Courts," *A.A.U.P. Bulletin* 49 (1963): 309–27.

AGAINST OMNISCIENCE
THE CASE FROM ESSENTIAL INDEXICALS
PATRICK GRIM

N o one else—no one other than me—knows what I know in knowing that:

1. I am making a mess.

Or so the argument goes.[1] Since an omniscient being would be a being that knows all that is known, since only I know what I know in knowing (1), and since I am not omniscient, there is no omniscient being.

In what follows I want to present and ponder this and similar arguments against omniscience, each of which turns on the issue of knowledge expressed by means of indexicals: 'I', 'here', 'now', and the like. Consider also the following argument, for example: No one knows at any time other than now—no one has known at any time in the past and no one will know at any time in the future—what I know in knowing that:

2. The meeting is starting now.

Or so the argument goes.[2] But if an immutable being must know at any one time just what that being knows at any other time, and if what is known in knowing (2) can only be known now, it appears that no immutable being of any decent

From *Noûs* 19 (1985): 151–80. Copyright © 1985 by Blackwell Publishing. Reprinted by permission of Blackwell Publishing.

duration can know what is known in knowing (2) —and thus no immutable being can also be omniscient. Similar problems would seem to arise concerning any being conceived as both *timeless* and omniscient.

In the end, and with some qualifications, I want to claim that arguments such as these really *do* show that some attributes standardly assigned to God are not compossible with omniscience and really do cast serious doubt on the existence of an omniscient being. In the first three sections of the paper, I present the positive case from indexicals against omniscience, first in terms of 'I' and then in terms of 'now'. But the full argument requires more. In section IV, I address objections raised against similar arguments in the past, including most importantly objections raised by Nelson Pike and Hector-Neri Castañeda against earlier arguments by A. N. Prior and Norman Kretzmann.[3] In section V, I consider recent work by John Perry, David Lewis, and Roderick Chisholm, which creates some important complications for the case against omniscience.[4]

The positive argument against omniscience presented in the first three sections is I think a strong one. Buttressed and expanded by the work of the later sections, I think, it proves conclusive.

The checkered history of attacks on omniscience by means of indexicals is as follows. Prior first posed temporal indexicals as a problem for the notion of a being both timeless and omniscient in 1962,[5] and it is basically Prior's argument that is used against the compossibility of omniscience and immutability in Kretzmann's 1966 article. Kretzmann also offers an argument against omniscience based on what might now be called knowledge *de se*, however, drawing on work by Castañeda,[6] which was in turn first anticipated by P. T. Geach in 1957.[7] Kretzmann's piece was subjected to a very strong reply by Castañeda,[8] however, which has generally been taken to be decisive.[9]

The strong influence of Castañeda's earlier work[10] is also clearly evident in recent work on indexicals by Perry, Lewis, and Chisholm.[11] Despite critical comments later in the paper, I rely heavily on each of these in constructing a case against omniscience in the tradition of Kretzmann and Prior.

I. OMNISCIENCE AND KNOWLEDGE *DE SE*

Consider a case borrowed from Perry[12]:

I follow a trail of spilled sugar around and around a tall aisle in the supermarket, in search of the shopper who is making a mess. Suddenly I realize that the trail of sugar that I have been following is spilling from a torn sack in *my* cart, and that *I* am the culprit—*I* am making a mess.

What it is that I come to know at that point—what I know when I come to know that

1. I am making a mess

is traditionally regarded as the *proposition* that I am making a mess. The proposition thus known, moreover, is traditionally regarded as the same proposition as that expressed by:

3. Patrick Grim is making a mess.

There *is* the following difference between (1) and (3) on the traditional view. *I* can express the proposition at issue in (1) and (3) by using (1), with its indexical 'I'. Others cannot and are forced instead to use some mode of reference such as the 'Patrick Grim' of (3). But this is not much of a difference. On the traditional view, the same proposition is expressed in each case, and what I know or express in knowing or expressing (1) is just what others know or express in knowing or expressing (3).

As Perry, Lewis, and Chisholm have argued, however—in large part following Castañeda[13]—this seems much too simple an account of objects of knowledge in general and of what is known in cases such as (1) in particular. Contrary to the traditional view, what is known or expressed in terms of (1) and (3) is *not* the same. For the 'I' of (1) is an *essential* indexical—essential to what it is I know or express in knowing or expressing (1).

The argument is as follows.[14] When I stop myself short in the supermarket, gather up my broken sack, and start to tidy up, this may be quite fully explained by saying that I realize (or come to believe, or come to know) that I am making a mess—what I express by (1). But it cannot be fully explained, or at least as fully explained, by saying that I realize that Patrick Grim is making a mess— what is expressed by (3). In order to give a realization on my part that Patrick Grim is making a mess the full explanatory force of my realization that *I* am making a mess, in fact, we would have to add that I know that *I* am Patrick Grim. And that, of course, is to reintroduce the indexical.

At this point we might also bring in an argument adapted from Prior.[15] The most that can be said impersonally of me and my mess, in a certain sense, is that Patrick Grim is making a mess—what is expressed by (3). But what I realize when I realize that *I* am making a mess can't be merely this impersonal matter of a named individual making a mess, because that is not what I am suddenly *ashamed* of or what I suddenly feel *guilty* about in being ashamed or feeling guilty that I am making a mess. Others might be embarrassed by the fact that Patrick Grim is making a mess—Grim's friends and relatives might quite often be embarrassed by his antics. But only I can feel the shame and mortification of knowing that those antics are *mine.*

What is known or expressed in terms of (1), then—that *I* am making a mess—is not merely what is known or expressed without the indexical in terms of (3).[16]

Let us apply all this to the issue of omniscience.

In order to qualify as omniscient or all-knowing, a being must know at least all that is known. Such a being must, then, know what I know in knowing (1):

1. I am making a mess.

But what I know in such a case, it appears, is known by no omniscient being. The indexical 'I', as argued above, is *essential* to what I know in knowing (1). But only I can use that 'I' to index me—no being distinct from me can do so. *I* am not omniscient. But there is something that I know that no being distinct from me can know. Neither I nor any being distinct from me, then, is omniscient: there is no omniscient being.

A being distinct from me *could,* of course, know (3):

3. Patrick Grim is making a mess.

But as argued above this does not amount to what I know in knowing (1).

Would an appeal to belief *de re* be of any help to omniscience here? No.[17] For what I know, or come to know, in knowing (1),

1. I am making a mess,

is not what I or others know in knowing, say, (4) *de re* of me:

4. *He* is making a mess.

For consider a case in which I see myself and my messy trail of sugar in a fish-eye mirror at the end of the aisle. I might then come to believe (4) *de re* of the man in the mirror—of myself, as it happens—just as anyone else might come to believe (4) *de re* of me. But I would not thereby know what I know in knowing (1), for I still might not realize that it is *me* in the mirror. A knowledge *de re* of me and my mess, then, still falls short of what I know in knowing (1) *de se.*[18]

Essential indexicals of this type seem to pose quite serious difficulties for any doctrine of omniscience or of an omniscient God. In any world such as ours, it seems, inhabited by a plurality of distinct self-conscious beings, there can be no omniscient or all-knowing being. For surely each distinct self-conscious being will have *something* that it knows *de se* and which thus cannot be known by others.

In later sections I want to strengthen the case against omniscience by also defending the arguments above against important objections. But let me first offer a similar argument regarding time.

II. KNOWLEDGE AND 'NOW'

Consider a case patterned on that of the preceding section, but in which it is 'now' rather than 'I' that is the crucial indexical: Just a moment ago, let us suppose, I was working placidly at my desk, happily scribbling away. "Plenty of time to work a bit yet," I was thinking to myself, "the meeting won't be starting for quite a while." At this point I calmly stop to listen for those reassuring meeting-hasn't-started-yet noises of my colleagues bustling about in their offices. But what I hear instead is a tomblike and ominous silence, and now the faint sound, so very far off, of laughing voices and of chairs being rearranged. With sudden panic I realize that the meeting is starting *now*.

What it is that I have realized or come to know—that

2. The meeting is starting now

—is traditionally regarded as the *proposition* that the meeting is starting now. The proposition thus known, moreover, is traditionally regarded as the same proposition as that expressed at the time of the meeting by

5. The meeting is starting at noon,

assuming that it is noon at which the events of the story take place. On the traditional view, moreover, the proposition at issue might be expressed at any time or timelessly by means of (5) with a tenseless interpretation of 'is starting'. It might have been expressed earlier by means of (6),

6. The meeting will be starting at noon,

or later by means of (7):

7. The meeting was starting at noon.

Clearly 'now' functions with respect to times, on the traditional view, much as 'I' functions with respect to people. Given this similarity, it should not be too surprising that a traditional treatment of 'now' also raises many of the same difficulties.

As I jump from my chair and scurry panic-stricken down the hall, my behavior can be quite fully explained by saying that I realize that the meeting is starting now—what is expressed by (2). But it cannot adequately be explained by saying that I know in some timeless sense that the meeting starts at noon—what is expressed by (5) on a tenseless interpretation. Nor can it adequately be explained by saying that I know what is supposedly expressed at different times by (6) and (7)—that the meeting was-or-will-be starting at noon. I may well know throughout the day, after all, that we meet at noon; "meeting at noon" may be written boldly in my date book and etched deep into my brain. But no such timeless or tenseless knowledge will suffice to explain why I am scurrying to the conference room *now*. In order satisfactorily to explain *that* we need to point out that I realize that the meeting is starting *now*—what is expressed by (2). At the very least we need to indicate that I know that it is *now* noon, once again introducing the indexical.

Prior argues that "what we know when we know that the 1960 final exams are over can't be just a timeless relation between dates because this isn't what we're *pleased* about when we're pleased that the exams are over."[19] Here we might argue along similar lines that what I know in knowing that the meeting is starting now cannot be merely some tenseless or timeless relation between the meeting and noon, because that is not what I am worried or upset about as I scurry toward the conference room. What worries and upsets me is that the meeting is starting *now*.

'Now', it appears, is an *essential* indexical: essential to what is known in knowing (2)—that the meeting is starting *now*—just as 'I' is essential to what is known in knowing (1)—that *I* am making a mess.

In the case of 'I' and knowledge *de se*, it appears that what is known in knowing (1) *de se* is something that cannot be known by another person. In the case of 'now' and what we might term knowledge *de presenti* it appears that what is known in knowing (2) *de presenti* is something that cannot be known at another *time*. The indexical 'now', as argued above, is essential to what is known in such a case. But only *now* can we use 'now' to index the appropriate time. What is expressed by (6) or (7), of course, or by a timeless reading of (5), *can* be known or expressed at another time. But as argued above, none of these amounts to what is known or expressed in knowing or expressing (2)—that the meeting is starting *now*.

What of belief or knowledge *de re,* however? Might it not be that what we have termed belief and knowledge *de presenti* are simply forms of belief *de re* in which the *rem* at issue are *times*?

What is known at one time in knowing (2), on this proposal, might be expressed later not by (7),

7. The meeting was starting at noon,

but by (8) *de re* of a time:

8. The meeting was starting then.

In the story with which we began, on this account, what I realized when I suddenly leapt from my desk and started for the conference room was that the meeting was starting *then*.

I want to argue that this does *not* capture what is known or expressed in knowing or expressing (2), and that belief or knowledge *de presenti* is no more merely belief or knowledge *de re* with respect to a time than belief *de se* is merely belief *de re* with respect to a person. It must be admitted, however, that this is not easy to show. A distinction between belief *de se* and belief *de re* regarding oneself is hard enough to show, since we are almost always well aware of who, *de re*, is us—hence the resort to fish-eye mirrors in the example of the preceding section. The distinction between belief *de presenti* and belief *de re* regarding a particular time is even more difficult to establish, because we so invariably know whether a particular time is *now*. I beg the reader's patience, then, in presenting a necessarily complex and peculiar example.

Consider a video camera which runs all day every day in the conference room, recording the passing scene on tape. And consider Professor Q, a colleague of mine, who has a time machine—or at least a time machine of sorts. What Professor Q has is a device that delivers each day's complete conference room videotape, like a morning newspaper, at the *beginning* of the day.

Here objection might be raised, I think quite rightly, against an appeal to anything so logically suspect as a time machine. I will address that objection in a moment, but for now I ask that you temporarily suspend disbelief.

At 11:55, to return to our story, Professor Q puts today's tape on his video machine. With his thumb on fast forward he skips quickly past the boring morning activities, but slows down the tape when he sees people gathering and arranging their chairs. The clock shown in the background says twelve o'clock. "Ahh," says Professor Q, settling back to watch the fun, "the meeting is starting," or perhaps "Ahh, here the meeting is starting."

Professor Q has come to believe, *de re* of that time shown or indicated on his screen, that the meeting is starting *then*. But what Professor Q does not know is that the tape he is watching is at this point running simultaneously, as it happens, with the events that it records. So although Q knows *de re* of the time shown on his screen that the meeting is starting *then*, he does not know (*de presenti*) that the meeting is starting *now*.

If this example goes through, it does clearly seem to show that belief or knowledge *de re* with respect to times does not amount to belief or knowledge *de presenti*—what is known in knowing (2), for example. But the example may fail to carry conviction because it relies so centrally on something so logically suspect and conceptually dubious as a time machine. This is at least something of an embarrassment. Can we do without it?

Yes. In the case above, Professor Q actually owns a time machine. But since it is for the most part only Q's *beliefs* that are at issue, we can construct an example equally satisfactory for our purposes by supposing only that Q *believes* that he owns a time machine.

Let us suppose that we, the rest of the faculty, have perpetrated an elaborate hoax on poor Q. At some appropriate ceremony we presented him with a video machine and fed him a pack of atrocious lies about how each morning a tape of that day's events would be delivered to his office. Q believes every word of it, and we maintain this deceitful charade by delivering to Q's office each morning a tape of the *previous* day's activities. One day is much like another in this department, and Q never catches on.

Each day that Q thinks that he is watching that day's events on his time machine, then, he is actually watching the previous day's events on an ordinary video machine. Except today. For some reason we neglected to record yesterday's activities, so today Q's machine is being fed instead a tape of today's events as they happen.

At 11:55, Q turns on the set and begins to review the day's events. Q thinks, of course, as always, that it is today's events that he is watching—and today, unlike other days, he's right. He runs quickly past the boring morning events, already recorded, then slows down the machine when he sees a quorum gathering and arranging their chairs. At this point, unbeknownst to Q of course, we have run out of prerecorded tape and his set is operating live from the conference room.[20] As far as Q knows, however, he is simply watching today's meeting as he watches every day's meeting, shown after or before it occurs as the case may be. "Ahh," says Q, as he settles back to watch the fun, "here the meeting is starting."

Q believes, and perhaps even knows, *de re* of the time shown on the screen—of *that* time—that the meeting is starting *then*. What he doesn't know is what we know in knowing (2) *de presenti*—that the meeting is starting *now*. And this time around we have rewritten the strange case of Professor Q without recourse to any device as logically questionable as a time machine.

Belief *de presenti* no more amounts to merely belief *de re* regarding a particular time, then, than belief *de se* amounts to merely belief *de re* regarding a particular person.

The consequences of belief *de se* for omniscience were considered in the preceding section. Does belief *de presenti* have similar consequences?

III. OMNISCIENCE AND KNOWLEDGE *DE PRESENTI*

There are things known at particular times, it seems, such as what I know in knowing that

2. The meeting is starting now,

which cannot be known at other times.

Does this pose a threat to doctrines of omniscience? Not as *direct* a threat, I think, as that posed by knowledge *de se*. But it does call for some care in specifying what omniscience is to be and does raise serious difficulties regarding the compatibility of omniscience with other traditional attributes of God.

Consider first the issue of specification. To be omniscient or all-knowing, of course, is to know all that is or could be known. But this is still a bit unclear. Must an omniscient being know, at every moment of omniscience, all that is or could be known at any moment whatever?

If omniscience *is* so specified, there is and can be no omniscient being. For as argued above, there are different things that can be known only at different times. There is thus no time at which all such things might be known, and thus no time at which any being could satisfy the requirements, so stipulated, of omniscience.

If omniscience is to be possible at all, then, we will have to specify it along something like the following lines:

Df. 1. x is omniscient at $t =_{df.} x$ knows at t all that is and all that can be known at t.[21]

This is not, perhaps, the standard image of omniscience, in which an omniscient being possesses a single timeless volume of all truths. The argument of the preceding section, however, is precisely that all truths are *not* timeless truths, and thus omniscience, if possible at all, must instead be a dynamic characteristic involving a knowledge of different truths at different times.

So understood, at least, omniscience is not directly threatened by knowledge *de presenti*. Nor does there seem to be any particular difficulty raised by the notion of a being both omniscient in this sense and eternal. Knowledge *de presenti* appears to pose a more serious threat, however, with regard to the compatibility of omniscience with two other attributes commonly ascribed to God: timelessness and immutability.

A *timeless* being is one which at no time exists at that time to the exclusion of any other time. The God of Boethius, Anselm, and Aquinas is apparently intended to transcend time in this sense. Anselm writes:

> Thou wast not, then, yesterday, nor wilt thou be to-morrow; but yesterday and to-day and to-morrow thou art; or, rather, neither yesterday nor to-day nor to-morrow thou art; but simply thou art, outside all time.[22]

Nelson Pike has pointed out that a timeless being would have neither duration— any *spread* in time—nor any temporal location: "God did not exist *before* Columbus discovered America nor will He exist *after* the turn of the century."[23]

Anthony Kenny, following Suarez, has argued that such a notion of timelessness is simply incoherent.[24] But even if this is not so, and there *could* be a timeless being, it appears that no being could be *both* timeless and omniscient.

A timeless being, as Pike emphasizes, has no temporal location. But it appears that there are things which can be known only at a particular temporal location—what I know in knowing that the meeting is starting *now,* for example. If this cannot be known by a being at any other time—at any other temporal location—then it surely cannot be known by any being which has no temporal location at all. No timeless being can know what I know in knowing such timely truths, and thus no timeless being can qualify as omniscient. As Prior puts the point regarding a God conceived as timeless:

> God could not, on the view I am considering, know that the 1960 final examinations at Manchester are over. For it isn't something that he or anyone else could know timelessly, because it just isn't true timelessly.[25]

The traditional attribute of immutability may raise similar difficulties. Could any being be both omniscient and *immutable?*[26]

If immutability requires that everything true of a being at any one time also be true of that being at any other time, knowledge *de presenti* would indeed seem to pose a serious difficulty here. For if there are different things that can be known only at different times, a being lastingly omniscient in the sense of Df. 1 must know different things at different times. That he knows what I know in knowing (2), then—that the meeting is starting now—will be true of him, as of me, at one time and not another. An omniscient being of this sort, then, cannot also be immutable.

Immutability in *this* sense, however, may be too much to ask of any being. Intuitively, I think, we would want to distinguish real from merely apparent or Cambridge changes and would want to require of an immutable being only that he undergo no *real* change.[27] Might a being be both immutable in *this* sense and omniscient?

That clearly depends on where we choose to draw the line between real and apparent change. This much, however, might still be said against the compossibility of omniscience and immutability: a being omniscient in the sense at issue does believe different things at different times and so adopts new beliefs and abandons old ones as time passes. This has at least some claim to being a *real* change, and if it *is* a real change no omniscient being of the sort at issue could also be immutable in even this revised sense.

We might adopt a still-weaker sense of immutability, however, which clearly *would* be compatible with omniscience. Nothing said above indicates that a being who holds different beliefs at different times must be said to *change his mind* over time, and nothing indicates that such a being will be changeable in character, inconstant in general purpose, or in any way fickle. Were we to limit the requirements of immutability to *this* type of constancy and reliability, knowledge *de presenti* would seem to pose no particular difficulty in the supposition of a being both omniscient and immutable.

The theological difficulties posed by 'now' and knowledge *de presenti*, although important, are not nearly so direct as those posed by 'I' and knowledge *de se*. Neither omniscience alone, at least if carefully stipulated relative to times, nor omniscience and eternity together, seem threatened. Omniscience and immutability, however, may be consistent only on a fairly weak construal of 'immutability', and it does not appear that the standard attributes of omniscience and timelessness are compatible at all.

Here I have considered only 'I' and 'now', knowledge *de se* and *de presenti*. Other indexicals may pose other theological problems. What is known in knowing (*de hoc loco*) that the test site is *here*, for example, would seem to raise similar issues regarding omniscience and ubiquity or regarding omniscience and transcendence of space. Nor should it be assumed, I think, that the role of indexicals has been exhausted once 'I', 'now', and 'here' have been considered.[28]

IV. SOME OBJECTIONS: PIKE AND CASTAÑEDA

In the preceding sections I have attempted to present the positive case from indexicals against omniscience—an argument in the tradition of Prior and Kretzmann. Prior and Kretzmann's work has not gone uncriticized, however, and so in defense of my arguments above some reply to their critics is called for. Noteworthy among the critics are Nelson Pike and Hector-Neri Castañeda.

In *God and Timelessness*, Pike maintains that all that is shown by arguments such as those in the preceding section is not that there is any range of facts that a timeless being could not know, but only that there are "certain forms of words that a timeless individual could not use in formulating or reporting his knowledge"[29]:

[The timeless individual] says: 'At 3.47 p.m. on the sixth of September—the moment at which Pike said "the first scene is now on the screen"—the first scene was on the screen.' Would the timeless individual have reported the same fact as I reported when [at 3.47 on the sixth of September] I said: 'The first scene is now on the screen?' . . . I can find no reason for thinking that I and the timeless individual have not reported the same fact.[30]

This is not much of an argument, however. There is, moreover, ample reason —or the same sort offered with regard to other examples above—for thinking that whatever a timeless being might know in such a case, it would *not* be what I know in knowing that the first scene is now on the screen. The impatience with which I quickly grab my popcorn and the haste with which I scamper in to find a seat, for example, are quite fully explained by saying that I realize that the first scene is now on the screen. But these are *not* explained, or at least not as fully explained, by saying that I realize that the first scene was-is-or-will-be on the screen at 3:47 p.m. on the sixth of September—what is known by a timeless being. Nor are these as fully explained by saying that I realize that the first scene did-does-or-will appear at the moment that Grim says "the first scene is now on the screen"—not without adding, at least, that I realize that I am *now* saying that, and that *I* am Grim, thereby reintroducing the indexical with a vengeance.

Pike does offer one further consideration in behalf of the identity of what is known now and what is known timelessly in such a case:

> If called upon later to justify my original comment, I would point to the fact that at 3.47 p.m. on the sixth of September—the moment at which I said: 'The first scene is now on the screen'—the first scene was on the screen. This is precisely what the timeless being would point to if challenged to justify his report.[31]

This will not do, however. For consider the case in which the claims at issue are to be justified *at 3:47.* At that time, even if I establish all that a timeless being could ever establish—that at 3:47 p.m. on the sixth of September, and so on—I will still not have established that the first scene is *now* on the screen. In order to establish *that* I would in addition have to establish some claim in which the indexical reappears—that it is *now* 3:47 p.m., for example, or that Grim is *now* saying, "The first scene is now on the screen."

Pike is right, I think, to consider patterns of justification here. But the *differences* in justification noted above support the claims of the preceding sections— that what is known in terms of 'now' is *not* something that might be known timelessly—rather than Pike's claims to the contrary.

In an intricate reply to Kretzmann, Castañeda notes that arguments such as those in the preceding sections rely on the claim that a person cannot "believe, know, consider, or in general, apprehend and formulate for himself and by himself a proposition that contains an indexical reference by another person."[32] Castañeda challenges this claim directly:

it seems to me that there is a perfectly accessible way of, so to speak, capturing another person's indexical statements qua indexical. This way consists of what I have elsewhere called "quasi-indicators."[33]

In order to capture the indexical 'now' at other times, however, the quasi-indicator that Castañeda offers is 'then'. What this *suggests* is that what is known or expressed in knowing or saying that the meeting is starting now might later be known or expressed in knowing or saying that the meeting was starting *then*. Both Swinburne and Kenny have taken this to be Castañeda's view.[34]

As argued above using Professor Q and the video machine, however, what is known in knowing *de re* of a time that the meeting was starting *then* does *not* amount to what is known in knowing *de presenti* that the meeting is starting *now*. If this *were* Castañeda's position, then, his view would seem to be fairly easily disposed of.

But this is not in fact Castañeda's position. What he actually holds can perhaps most clearly be indicated in two steps: First, Castañeda holds that the *fact* that someone knows something that he might express using an indexical is a *fact* that can be expressed by others or at another time using a quasi-indicator in *oratio obliqua*. That someone X knows at t_1 what he might express by "The meeting is starting now," for example, is a fact that can later be expressed by "At t_1, X knew that the meeting was starting then." This is clearly quite different from the claim above that *what* is expressed at one time using an indexical can *itself* be expressed at another time using a quasi-indicator in *oratio recta*.[35]

Second, Castañeda proposes a principle (P):

> (P) If a sentence of the form 'X knows that a person Y knows that . . .' formulates a true statement, then the person X knows the statement formulated by the clause filling the blank '. . .'.[36]

Together, these two steps clearly do entail that one can know what is known in terms of indexicals by others or at other times. If X knows now—at t_1—that the meeting is starting now, then by the first step Y can know at some later time that at t_1, X knew that the meeting was starting *then*. By principle (P), Y thereby knows what X then knew.[37]

None of this, however, gives us any *expression* of what it is that Y knows in (supposedly) knowing what X then knew, other than perhaps as "what X knew . . ." or "what X expressed by. . . ." It does not, in particular, allow us to say that what Y knows is that "The meeting was starting then," for Castañeda is quite careful to emphasize that (P) does not license detachment of this type.[38]

Castañeda in fact never even *attempts* to enunciate precisely *what* it is that one knows in (supposedly) knowing what is known by others or at other times in terms of indexicals. This might seem to leave him open to the following argument: What *could* be known by others that would count as what I know in knowing I am making a mess, and what *could* be known at some other time that would count as what is *now* known in knowing that the meeting is starting *now*? Knowing that "Patrick Grim is making a mess," or that "The meeting starts at noon" clearly will *not* suffice, for reasons given in preceding sections. Nor will knowledge *de re* suffice, no matter how intimate. But if what supposedly can be known by others or at other times is *not* one of these, what could it possibly *be*? If Castañeda can supply no further candidate for what it is that is supposedly known in such cases, it might be argued, we may have at least some grounds for doubting that there *is* anything so known.

What this argument demands, however, is that Castañeda offer an expression in *oratio recta* of what is known by others or at other times in terms of indexicals. But this might simply be shrugged off as a further misunderstanding, for Castañeda nowhere claims that what is so known *can* be known or expressed in *oratio recta*.[39] Castañeda does maintain that one can know or express what is known or expressed by others or at other times in terms of indexicals, but maintains only that what is so known can be known or expressed using quasi-indicators in *oratio obliqua*. The proposition that I know or express by "I am making a mess," on Castañeda's view, is also known or expressed *in situ* in terms of the subordinate clause "he (himself) is making a mess" in "Patrick Grim knows that he (himself) is making a mess."[40] What a person K knows or expresses by "The meeting is starting now," by the same token, can later be known or expressed *in situ* in terms of the subordinate clause "the meeting was starting then" of "At t_1, K knew that the meeting was starting then." It might also be expressed tenselessly, on Castañeda's view, by the subordinate clause "the meeting is (tenselessly) starting then" of "At t_1, K knows (tenselessly) that the meeting is (tenselessly) starting then."[41]

When finally disentangled from various misinterpretations, however, it is clear that Castañeda's position is open to a quite crucial objection.

Consider first a case in which an individual McQ knows, on quite general grounds, that:

9. The shortest spy knows that he (himself) is a spy.

Genuine spying, after all, would require at least some measure of premeditation. Suppose also, however, that *I* am a spy, and—unbeknownst even to me, perhaps—I am the shortest in my profession.

On Castañeda's view, it appears that McQ would know in virtue of knowing (9) what I know in virtue of knowing (10):

10. I am a spy.

For what I know in knowing that I am a spy, Castañeda maintains, is captured *in situ* by the subordinate clause "he (himself) is a spy" of (9). By principle (P), McQ knows what is expressed in that clause in virtue of knowing (9).

But this is at least strongly counterintuitive. For McQ may well know that

9. The shortest spy knows that he (himself) is a spy,

and yet not know what I know. What I know, after all, is that I am a spy. McQ, although fully cognizant of (9), may not know that—he may not know that I am a spy—just as he may not know that I am the shortest spy. McQ, then, although he knows (9), does not know what I know in knowing (10). I am safe in my deception.

As Robert Merrihew Adams notes with respect to two related examples by Adams and Rogers Albritton:

> it is clear that the problem arises because the person who knows the complex proposition ascribing an *oratio obliqua* fails in some way or respect to know who the person is to whom the *oratio obliqua* is ascribed—although of course he does know something that he could give as an answer to the question to whom he is ascribing the *oratio obliqua*. . . . The person to whom it is ascribed could not fail to grasp it in the same way, however.[42]

A similar example might be constructed using names. Consider a case in which intentional mess-making is a capital crime and in which officer McQ, on the basis of a single teletyped message from the FBI, knows that:

11. Patrick Grim knows that he (himself) is making a mess.

Unbeknownst to McQ, however, I am perpetrating my nefarious deeds using an alias and a disguise, posing as a tidy and law-abiding fellow officer.

On Castañeda's view, McQ in knowing (11) would know what I know in knowing (1):

1. I am making a mess.

For what I know in knowing that I am making a mess, Castañeda maintains, is captured *in situ* by the subordinate clause "he (himself) is making a mess" of (11), and by principle (P) McQ knows what is expressed in that clause in virtue of knowing (11).

But this is surely incorrect. McQ may well know that

11. Patrick Grim knows that he (himself) is making a mess,

and yet not know what I know. What I know, after all, is that I am making a mess. McQ, although fully cognizant of (11), may not know that—he may not know that I am making a mess—simply because he may not know that I am Patrick Grim. My ruse is a success.

In knowing (11) McQ does *not* necessarily know what I know in knowing that I am making a mess. At least one part of Castañeda's two-part position, then, must be incorrect. Either what I know or express by "I am making a mess" is *not* captured by the relevant subordinate clause, or someone does *not* know what I know solely in virtue of knowing that I know it.

Such a case is also possible concerning time. It is 10:00, let us suppose, and I know that:

2. The meeting is starting now.

McQ, on the other hand, knows that:

12. At 10:00 Patrick Grim knows (tenselessly) that the meeting is (tense-lessly) starting then.

On the view at issue, what I know in knowing (2) is also something that McQ would know in virtue of knowing (12). For what I know, Castañeda main-tains, is captured *in situ* by the subordinate clause "the meeting is (tenselessly) starting then" of (12), and McQ knows what is expressed in that clause in virtue of knowing (12).

But this is again clearly incorrect. For McQ may well know that

12. At 10:00 Patrick Grim knows (tenselessly) that the meeting is (tense-lessly) starting then,

and yet not know what I know. What I know, after all, is that the meeting is starting now. McQ, although fully cognizant of (12), may not know that—he may not know that the meeting is starting now—simply because McQ may not know that it is now 10:00.[43]

Someone who knows (12), then, does not necessarily know what I know in knowing (2)—that the meeting is starting now. At least part of Castañeda's posi-tion must be incorrect: either what I know or express by "The meeting is starting now" is *not* captured by the relevant subordinate clause, or someone does *not* know what I know solely in virtue of knowing that I know it.

Castañeda's position will not do, then, despite its sophistication, as a reply to the arguments presented in the preceding sections. It falls victim, in fact, to the same general difficulty encountered above with regard to other attempts to capture ephemeral or nontransferable indexical knowledge by means of some permanent or transferable nonindexical equivalent: knowledge of the supposed equivalent amounts to what is known in terms of indexicals only on the assumption of some further indexical knowledge.

Knowledge *de se* and *de presenti,* then, still pose a crucial difficulty for doctrines of omniscience.

V. SOME COMPLICATIONS: PERRY, LEWIS, AND CHISHOLM

As noted in the introduction and at various points throughout, I have borrowed freely in preceding sections from arguments offered by John Perry, David Lewis, and Roderick Chisholm. What has not been noted above is that each of these authors also presents a positive account of knowledge and its objects, which creates complications for the case against omniscience.

It is these complications that I want to consider here. In one case—that of Perry—I will argue directly against the account proposed. With regard to Lewis and Chisholm, on the other hand, I want merely to show that the accounts proposed offer little consolation for standard doctrines of omniscience.

Perry's is a two-pronged account which relies on a crucial distinction between *objects* of belief and belief *states*.[44] *What* I know in knowing that I am making a mess, Perry proposes—the *object* of my belief—*is* what is known by others in knowing *de re* of me that I am making a mess. Knowledge *de re* and *de se* do not differ in their objects, and thus "anyone can at any time have access to any proposition."[45]

Knowledge *de re* and *de se* do differ, however, as Perry's examples of spilt sugar in the supermarket and of mirrors at the ends of aisles clearly indicate. But this difference, Perry maintains, is a difference of belief *state* rather than of what is believed. In believing *de se* that I am making a mess I believe *what* others believe in believing *de re* that I am making a mess. But I am not in their belief *state*—I am instead in the belief state of all those who believe *themselves* to be making a mess, whoever they might be.

Neither what I believe, on such a view, nor my belief state, is unique to me. What is unique to me is their combination:

> Anyone can believe of John Perry that he is making a mess. And anyone can be in the belief state classified by the sentence 'I am making a mess.' But only I can have that belief by being in that state.[46]

Perry's position, if adequate, *would* offer a way in which doctrines of omniscience might escape the difficulties noted above. For nothing has been said to indicate that some other being might not know *de re* of me that I am making a mess, and nothing has been said to indicate that a being at some other time, or a timeless being, could not know *de re* of a time that the meeting is starting *then*. If what is known in terms of indexicals—that *I* am making a mess, or that the meeting is starting *now*—were in this way captured by knowledge *de re*, then, indexicals would pose no particular problem for omniscience. On this view, of course, no other being could know what I know in knowing that I am making a mess, and no timeless being could know what I know in knowing that the meeting is starting now, *by* being in the same belief state. Other beings or time-less beings *could* know *what* I know, however, and that would seem to be all that omniscience demands.

Perry's account is not in the end a very plausible account, however, and must I think be rejected in light of precisely the type of case that Perry presents. For con-sider again an example in which I see, in a fish-eye mirror at the end of the aisle, a man with a broken sack in his shopping cart and a trail of sugar behind him.

At this point in the story I know, *de re* of the man in the mirror, that:

4. *He* is making a mess.

But there is also quite clearly something that I *haven't* yet realized and that I *don't* yet know: that it is *me* in the mirror, and that *I* am making a mess. That *I* am the culprit is something that I realize only a moment later and with a sudden shock of guilty recognition.

Were Perry's account correct, however, this would not be the case. For on Perry's account, once I know (4) *de re* of the man I see in the mirror—of myself, as it happens—I know all I ever know. On this account there *is* nothing more that is known in knowing *de se* that *I* am making a mess, and thus there is nothing more that I suddenly realize or recognize or come to know in discovering that *I* am the culprit. Perry does maintain that my belief *state* will change, but that is quite sharply distinguished from my beliefs; there will be nothing I come to believe that I did not believe before, and nothing I come to know that I did not already know.

Because this is so drastically counterintuitive, I think, both Perry's account and any hope it might have seemed to offer for doctrines of omniscience must be abandoned. Here we might borrow again an argument from Prior. What I know in knowing *de se* that I am making a mess cannot be merely what I know in knowing *de re* that *he* is making a mess, because that is not what I am *ashamed* of, or what I feel *guilty* about, in being ashamed or feeling guilty that I am making a mess. Nor, of course, am I suddenly ashamed of being in a particular belief state. What I am ashamed of is what I suddenly realize, above and beyond the fact that *he* is making a mess—that it is *me* in the mirror, and that *I* am making a mess.

A quite different type of account has been proposed by David Lewis and

Roderick Chisholm in considering indexicals. Each proposes an account of belief as the self-ascription of *properties*. For Lewis,

> I say that *all* belief is 'self-locating belief.' Belief *de dicto* is self-locating belief with respect to logical space; belief irreducibly *de se* is self-locating belief at least partly with respect to ordinary time and space, or with respect to the population. I propose that any kind of self-locating belief should be understood as self-ascription of properties.[47]

For Chisholm,

> Believing must be construed as a relation between a believer and *some* other thing; this much is essential to *any* theory of belief. What kind of thing, then? ... The simplest conception, I suggest, is one which construes believing as a relation involving a believer and a property—a property which he may be said to attribute to himself.[48]

Here, for the sake of simplicity, I will concentrate on Lewis's account. Differences in Chisholm will be noted in due course.

What I self-attribute in knowing or believing *de se* that I am making a mess, on such an account, is of course the property of making a mess. What I self-attribute in knowing that

3. Patrick Grim is making a mess,

on the other hand, is something quite different: the property of being in a world in which Patrick Grim is making a mess.[49] This distinction clearly allows a property account to avoid some of the major pitfalls of a traditional propositional account, in which what is known is in each case the same.

A property account also suggests, however, that what is known in terms of indexicals—that I am making a mess, or that the meeting is starting now—*is* something that can be known by others or at other times. For if belief and knowledge are matters of the self-attribution of properties, and if others can attribute to themselves the same properties that I attribute to myself, it would appear that they can then know or believe what I know or believe. What I know in knowing that I am making a mess, on such a view, would be what others know in knowing themselves to be making a mess.[50]

Lewis accepts this quite stalwartly as a consequence of his account. Lewis notes with regard to the mad Heimson, who believes himself to be Hume:

> There are two ways out. (1) Heimson does not, after all, believe what Hume did. Or (2) Heimson does believe what Hume did, but Heimson believes falsely what Hume believed truly. ...

> If we can agree that beliefs are in the head, so that Heimson and Hume may indeed believe alike, then the first way out is shut. We must take the second. Heimson's belief and Hume's have the same object, but Heimson is wrong and Hume is right . . . the object of their shared belief . . . is a property: the property of being Hume. Hume self-ascribes this property; he has it; he is right. Heimson, believing just what Hume does, self-ascribes the very same property; he lacks it; he is wrong.[51]

What are the consequences of such a view for the possibility of omniscience? At first glance, it might seem to offer an escape for omniscience from indexical difficulties, since on such a view what is known in terms of indexicals *can* be known by others or at other times. Any such sanguine hopes will be disappointed, however. On an account such as Lewis's, at least, omniscience is in *worse* shape than before.

One of the things I know now, let us say, is that I am making a mess. Another is that:

13. I have made some terrible mistakes in my time.

On Lewis's account, what I know in each case *can* be known by some other being. But can it be known by *God*? Certainly not, at least if God's other attributes are what they are traditionally reputed to be. In order for God to know what I know, on Lewis's account, he must self-attribute truly the properties of making a mess and of having made some terrible mistakes. But God *cannot* self-attribute such properties truly, for God makes neither messes nor mistakes. God does not, then, know what I know. God is not omniscient.

Here we need not appeal to other divine attributes, however. For consider a case in which I know that I am making a mess, but in which McK, sweeping up spilt sugar in the supermarket, knows what he would express by "I am *not* now making a mess." A being which knows all that is known, on a view such as Lewis's, would have to self-attribute truly all that is self-attributed truly. But clearly no being could self-attribute truly both what I and McK self-attribute. Given two beings of two minds, in such a sense, no being is omniscient.

Finally, and perhaps most simply, consider what I know in knowing that:

14. I am not omniscient.

Clearly what I self-attribute in knowing (14) could not be self-attributed truly by any omniscient being. Given any being self-conscious of its own *lack* of omniscience, on a view such as Lewis's, no being is omniscient.

Lewis's account, then, offers little or no room for doctrines of omniscience. Chisholm's account, although in many respects the same as Lewis's, also differs in some important ways. But it does not differ in any ways that would seem to offer significant hope for traditional notions of omniscience.

Chisholm and Lewis agree on at least the following points. For each, belief is to be treated in terms of the self-attribution of properties.[52] Belief *de re* and *de dicto*, moreover, are given very similar subsidiary accounts.[53] Conditions for truth in self-attribution, and hence for knowledge, appear to be the same as well.[54]

There are also points of disagreement in the two accounts, however. Although each offers a property account, for example, it is not clear that Lewis and Chisholm agree as to *what* properties are at issue. For Lewis, "the property of being Hume is a perfectly possible property." For Chisholm, it may not be a property at all—Chisholm finds a "demonstrative sense" in proper names, and considers it problematic whether "terms and predicates containing demonstratives . . . will have properties as their senses."[55]

There might also be a more important point of disagreement, however. Lewis, as noted above, treats the properties self-attributed as the *objects* of belief or knowledge, and so treats identity of property self-attributed as sufficient for identity of what is known or believed. Sydney Shoemaker has characterized Chisholm as well as holding that "the objects of belief are properties."[56] But this may not be Chisholm's view:

> In the case of direct attribution as well as attribution generally, we shall say that the property attributed is the *content* of the attribution and that the thing *to* which the property is attributed is the *object* of the attribution. But there is no reason to suppose that there is still *another* thing, somehow involving both the individual thing and the property of being wise, which is properly called '*the* object' of direct attribution, this despite the fact that in such a case one can ask: 'And *what* is it that he believes?' For we have rejected the view that explicates attribution by reference to the acceptance of propositions.[57]

Chisholm is not an easy man to interpret. But perhaps Chisholm is here proposing a more radical rejection of "objects of knowledge" in a traditional sense, and of talk of "*what* is believed," than either Lewis offers or that Shoemaker credits him with. The passage above might be interpreted as suggesting not that Chisholm replaces propositions with properties as the objects of belief or knowledge, or as *what* is known or believed, but that he rejects any notion of objects of belief in this sense, or of *what* is known or believed, altogether.

This more radical view, if it *is* Chisholm's, would clearly distinguish his position importantly from Lewis's. But it is not clear that it would offer any consolation for standard notions of omniscience. The traditional characterization of a being as all-knowing or omniscient seems to demand that we quantify over objects of knowledge or over what is known: to be omniscient is to know all *x,* where *x* is something known. To abandon altogether any notion of what is known or of objects of knowledge, of course, would be to abandon any traditional notion of omniscience of this sort as well.

VI. CONCLUSION

I have tried to present as strong a case as possible against omniscience, in terms of both positive argument from essential indexicals and critical consideration of complications and objections. With as much modest dogmatism as is justified in any such attempt, I consider the case against omniscience to be conclusive. Considerations of what is known in terms of temporal indexicals such as 'now' *do* show that no being can be both timeless and omniscient. Considerations of what is known in terms of the indexical 'I' *do* show that there is no omniscient being.

Does this leave *no* option for doctrines of omniscience of *any* sort? That would of course be too strong. I see two possible options:

One option would be to declare by fiat that what is known in terms of indexicals is a special case of some sort and to weaken the requirements of omniscience accordingly. Indexical knowledge might be declared 'nonpropositional' in some suitably defined sense, for example, and 'omniscience' redefined so as to demand merely knowledge of all things *propositional*.

Another option would be to follow the example of those who have tried to save *omnipotence* from logical difficulties. We might propose, for example, that a being is omniscient if it knows all that it is *logically possible* for such a being to know. If stubborn difficulties in the case of omnipotence are any indication, however, a satisfactory account of this sort would not be easy.[58]

Each of these options, of course, calls for an understanding of omniscience in something other than the traditional sense of being literally all-knowing: of knowing all that is or could be known. The case against omniscience in the traditional sense, I think, is closed.[59]

NOTES

1. This argument is not presented fully until section I. Those familiar with John Perry, "Frege On Demonstratives," *Philosophical Review* 86 (1977): 474–97, however, will undoubtedly guess the form it will take.

2. *This* argument is not fully presented until sections II and III. I do not in fact argue that no immutable being can also be omniscient, however. I do argue that no timeless being can also be omniscient.

3. Nelson Pike, *God and Timelessness* (London: Routledge and Kegan Paul, 1970); Hector-Neri Castañeda, "Omniscience and Indexical Reference," *Journal of Philosophy* 64 (1967): 203–10; A. N. Prior, "The Formalities of Omniscience," *Philosophy* 37 (1962):

114–29 (repr. in *Papers on Time and Tense* [Oxford: Clarendon, 1968], pp. 26–44, and in *Readings in the Philosophy of Religion*, ed. Baruch Brody [Englewood Cliffs, N.J.: Prentice-Hall, 1974], pp. 413–27); Norman Kretzmann, "Omniscience and Immutability," *Journal of Philosophy* 63 (1966): 409–21 (repr. in *Readings in the Philosophy of Religion*, ed. Baruch Brody [Englewood Cliffs, N.J.: Prentice-Hall, 1974], pp. 366–76).

4. John Perry, "The Problem of the Essential Indexical," *Noûs* 13 (1979): 3–21 (repr. in *The Philosopher's Annual*, vol. 3, ed. David L. Boyer, Patrick Grim, and John T. Sanders [Atascadero, Calif.: Ridgeview, 1980], pp. 155–74); David Lewis, "Attitudes *De Dicto* and *De Se*," *Philosophical Review* 88 (1979): 513–43 (repr. in *The Philosopher's Annual*, vol. 3, pp. 89–119); Roderick Chisholm, *The First Person* (Minneapolis: University of Minnesota Press, 1981).

5. Prior, "The Formalities of Omniscience." See also A. N. Prior: "Thank Goodness That's Over," *Philosophy* 34 (1959): 12–17 (repr. in *Papers in Logic and Ethics*, ed. P. T. Geach and A. J. P. Kenny [London: Duckworth, 1976]); "On Spurious Egocentricity," *Philosophy* 42 (1967): 326–35 (repr. in *Papers on Time and Tense* [Oxford: Clarendon, 1968], pp. 15–25); *Past, Present, and Future* (Oxford: Clarendon, 1967); "Now," *Noûs* 2 (1968): 101–109. There is, however, a medieval form of the problem in terms of tensed statements which appears in Aquinas (*Summa Theologiae* Ia, 14, 15) and is discussed by Anthony Kenny, *The God of the Philosophers* (Oxford: Clarendon, 1979), pp. 42 ff.

6. Hector-Neri Castañeda: "'He': A Study of the Logic of Self-Consciousness," *Ratio* 8 (1966): 130–57; "Indicator and Quasi-Indicators," *American Philosophical Quarterly* 4 (1967): 85–100; "On the Logic of Self-Reference," *Noûs* 1 (1967): 9–21; "On the Logic of Attributions of Self-Knowledge to Others," *Journal of Philosophy* 65 (1968): 439–56.

7. P. T. Geach, "On Beliefs About Oneself," *Analysis* 18 (1957): 23–24 (repr. in *Logic Matters* [Berkeley: University of California Press, 1972], pp. 128–29).

8. Castañeda, "Omniscience and Indexical Reference."

9. See for example Richard Swinburne's discussion of the debate in *The Coherence of Theism* (Oxford: Clarendon, 1977), pp. 162–67. Kenny is an exception in this regard in that he sides with Kretzmann, at least with regard to temporal indexicals (see Kenny, *The God of the Philosophers*, pp. 39–48).

10. Castañeda, "'He': A Study" and "Indicator and Quasi-Indicators."

11. Perry, "The Problem of the Essential Indexical"; Lewis, "Attitudes"; Chisholm, *The First Person*. Perry's, Lewis's, and some aspects of Chisholm's recent work might in fact be thought of as developments of Castañeda's basic work on indexicals. The central argument of Perry's "Frege On Demonstratives," for example, which I in turn rely on in the present paper, is anticipated in Castañeda's "'He': A Study," pp. 141–42, complete with the use of mirrors.

12. Perry, "The Problem of the Essential Indexical."

13. Ibid.; Lewis, "Attitudes"; Chisholm, *The First Person*; Castañeda, "'He': A Study" and "Indicator and Quasi-Indicators."

14. This argument is stated most clearly, I think, in Perry's "Frege On Demonstratives," although earlier forms of the argument appear there and are discussed in Lewis, "Attitudes." The argument does not appear in Chisholm's *The First Person*, oddly enough, although Chisholm's case would be stronger if it did, as Sydney Shoemaker has noted in

his review "Me and My Attributes," *London Times Literary Supplement* 4,096 (October 2, 1981): 1137.

15. Prior's argument, from which this is adapted, concerns tense, and is quoted in part in the following section. See Prior, "The Formalities of Omniscience," p. 116.

16. This argument, like many philosophical arguments, takes the form of a challenge. If there *is* something that others may know that *is* what I know in knowing (1)—that I am making a mess—what could that something possibly be? I have argued explicitly here against what seem to be the only plausible candidates: (3), that Patrick Grim is making a mess, and (4), that *he* is making a mess, known *de re* of me.

We might also consider a Russellian suggestion, however: what of that proposition in which a logically proper name for Patrick Grim replaces his indexical 'I' in "I am making a mess"?

This takes us into the thick of Russell. What is a logically proper name? It is a name that designates directly by "simply standing for an object of acquaintance" (Bertrand Russell, *The Problems of Philosophy* [New York: Oxford University Press, 1959], p. 54), and "names it by a convention ad hoc, not by a description" (Bertrand Russell, *An Inquiry into Meaning and Truth* [Baltimore: Penguin Books, 1967], p. 30). The standard example of a logically proper name is 'this' used to designate a present sense-datum, but Russell also proposes universals (*The Problems*, pp. 51–52), the past (*An Inquiry*, p. 37), and perhaps the 'I' (*The Problems*, pp. 50–51) as objects of direct acquaintance capable of logically proper names.

Now might not others know what I know in knowing (1)—that I am making a mess—by knowing, say that L. P. N. is making a mess, where 'L. P. N.' is a logically proper name for me?

On Russell's account, of course, others can have no logically proper name for me because I am not for them (and perhaps am not even for myself) an object of direct acquaintance. But this would seem to be merely an epistemological barrier, and a contingent epistemological barrier at that. Let us suppose that some other being *could* know me by direct acquaintance and so could use a logically proper name for me. Wouldn't such a being then be capable of knowing what I know in knowing (1)—that I am making a mess —in virtue of knowing that L. P. N. is making a mess?

No. For what are now at issue are logically proper names which an individual need not *bear* in order to *use*, and which any number of beings might use. In order to know that L. P. N. is making a mess, then, a being need not himself be making a mess and need not know himself to be making a mess. But if that is the case, *I* might know what other beings might know—that L. P. N. is making a mess—without knowing that I am making a mess. Whatever another being knows in knowing that L. P. N. is making a mess, then—using any particular candidate for L. P. N.—it cannot be what I know in knowing (1). For given any candidate L. P. N. as a logically proper name available to others, I might know that L. P. N. is making a mess without yet knowing that *I* am.

Logically proper names, despite their interesting peculiarities, appear to fall victim to the same pattern of argument as that presented above. The same would be true, I think, for the arguments of the next section and any attempt to introduce logically proper names for times.

17. On a view such as Frege's, *de re* belief itself causes difficulties for a proposi-

tional account. My belief *de re* that my wife is kind will surely have no adequate place in a propositional account if propositions are taken to be so like sentences—so obsessively *de dicto*—that I must be said to believe two distinct propositions in believing that the woman who loves me is kind and in believing that the woman who lives with me is kind. In order to include even *de re* belief, then, the propositions of a propositional account must be stretched to include *de re* conglomerates composed of objects together with parts of propositions in the more traditional sense. On this see Perry, "Frege On Demonstratives."

18. In several places Castañeda has argued against taking the *de re/de dicto* distinction as exhaustive, precisely because of quasi-indicators. This is perhaps clearest in Hector-Neri Castañeda, "Reference, Reality, and Perceptual Fields," *Proceedings and Addresses of the American Philosophical Association* 53 (1980): 763–823.

19. Prior, "The Formalities of Omniscience," p. 116.

20. We will be safe in our deception unless Q presses the fast forward again in order to watch what will not occur until later this afternoon. In that case we will have to fake a mechanical failure of some type.

21. In *The Coherence of Theism* Swinburne offers a definition of omniscience which does include a mention of times and which may be intended to be time-bound in this sense: "to say of a person P that he is at time *t* omniscient is to say that at *t* P knows of every true proposition that it is true" (p. 162). It is not clear, however, whether Swinburne intends this to be read such that a person omniscient at *t* is required only to know of every proposition true at *t* that it is true. Since in the context Swinburne follows Castañeda in arguing against Kretzmann's treatment of a time and tense, this is perhaps not what is intended.

22. Anselm, *Proslogium*, chap. 19 in *St. Anselm: Basic Writings*, trans. S. N. Deane (La Salle, Ill.: Open Court, 1968), p. 25.

23. Pike, *God and Timelessness*, p. 7.

24. Anthony Kenny, *Aquinas: A Collection of Critical Essays* (Garden City, N.Y.: Anchor Books, 1969), p. 264, and Kenny, *The God of the Philosophers*, pp. 38 ff.

25. Prior, "The Formalities of Omniscience," p. 116.

26. My discussion of this issue here is of necessity fairly limited. See also Kenny, chap. 4 in *The God of the Philosophers*.

27. See P. T. Geach, *God and the Souls* (London: Routledge and Kegan Paul, 1969), p. 71. A classic example of a Cambridge change is Socrates' coming to be shorter than Theatetus as Theatetus grows.

28. On this see Joseph Almog, "Dthis and Dthat: Indexicality Goes Beyond That," *Philosophical Studies* 39 (1981): 347–81, and Castañeda, "Indicator and Quasi-Indicators." Castañeda argues that various indexicals call for a similar treatment and suggests five irreducible indexical roles: first-person, second-person, third-person, (specious) present-time, and (speciously) presented place.

29. Pike, *God and Timelessness*, p. 95.

30. Ibid., p. 92.

31. Ibid., pp. 92–93.

32. Castañeda, "Omniscience and Indexical Reference," p. 204. This and the following quotation are phrased to apply to cases involving the use of the indexical 'I' by other people. In context it is clear that the general point is also to apply to cases involving the use of 'now' at other times.

33. Ibid.

34. Swinburne, quoted with approval by Kenny, offers the following as a gloss of Castañeda's argument in "Omniscience and Indexical Reference":

A knows on 2 October the proposition 'it is now 2 October'. Surely *B* on 3 October can know that *A* knew what he did on 2 October. How can *B* report his knowledge? By words such as 'I know that *A* knew yesterday that it was then 2 October'. How can we report *B*'s knowledge? As follows: *B* knew on 3 October that on the previous day *A* knew that it was then 2 October. Hence, . . . *B* knows on 3 October what *A* knew on 2 October, although *B* will use different words to express the latter knowledge. In reporting *B*'s knowledge of this item, we need a different referring expression to pick out the day of which being 2 October is predicted; but what is known is the same. . . . What *A* knows on 2 October and *B* knows on 3 October is that a certain day which can be picked out in many and various ways, according to our location in time as 'today' or 'yesterday' or 'the day on which *A* thought it was 2 October' (or even as '2 October') is 2 October. (Richard Swinburne, "Omnipotence," *American Philosophical Quarterly* 10 [1973]: 165–66, cited in Kenny, *The God of the Philosophers*, p. 46.)

This view, as noted, is adequately disposed of by arguments offered in preceding sections against a treatment of knowledge *de presenti* in terms of merely knowledge *de re* concerning a time. But as also noted this is *not* in fact Castañeda's view.

Castañeda is still more radically misinterpreted by Chisholm:

Castañeda also assumes that there are first-person propositions. He tells us that, when a person uses an 'I'-sentence, then he is expressing a first-person proposition which 'is different from every third-person proposition about him and, of course, different from any third-person proposition about anything else'. Castañeda thus seems to suggest the view that he could never express *my* 'I'-propositions, and I believe he would say that, strictly speaking, he could not even grasp them (Chisholm, *The First Person*, p. 33).

The view attributed to him in the last sentence here is explicitly denied by Castañeda in almost everything he has written on the topic. Castañeda repeatedly states that what is expressed by first-person 'I'-sentences *can* be expressed by others in *oratio obliqua* by means of quasi-indicators. See for example Castañeda's "Indicator and Quasi-Indicators," "On the Logic of Self-Reference," "Omniscience and Indexical Reference," and "On the Logic of Attributions of Self-Knowledge to Others." This position is again stated explicitly, moreover, on the page immediately preceding that from which Chisholm draws the quotation used (see Hector-Neri Castañeda, *Thinking and Doing: The Philosophical Foundations of Institutions* [Boston: Reidel, 1975], pp. 158–59).

35. This paragraph represents a quite basic Castañeda claim, repeatedly presented in "'He': A Study," "Indicator and Quasi-Indicators," "On the Logic of Self-Reference," "Omniscience and Indexical Reference," "On the Logic of Attributions," and *Thinking and Doing*.

36. Castañeda, "Omniscience and Indexical Reference," p. 207.

37. In context it is clear, I think, that (P) is to be read flexibly both with respect to tenses of 'know'—so as to apply, for example, to "Joe will know that Jane had known that . . ."—and with respect to pronouns, names, or referring expressions in substitution for '*S*' and '*Y*'. I am at any rate so using it here. Without that flexibility it is not clear that (P) would serve even Castañeda's immediate purposes.

38. See for example Castañeda, "Omniscience and Indexical Reference," pp. 207–208, and "Indicator and Quasi-Indicators," p. 93.

39. Quasi-indicators, in fact—the mechanisms Castañeda proposes for catching others' indexical references intact—cannot even *appear* in *oratio recta*. See esp. (H*1), p. 154 of "'He': A Study."

The argument offered in the preceding paragraph is not, I think, entirely without force. It does rely on an assumption, however, that everything known is in some way known in *oratio recta*. I do not consider that an implausible assumption, but I do not know either how one would attempt to demonstrate it.

40. This is put particularly straightforwardly on p. 158 of Castañeda's *Thinking and Doing*.

41. Castañeda proposes a very similar tenseless rendering in "Omniscience and Indexical Reference."

42. Robert Merrihew Adams and Hector-Neri Castañeda, "Knowledge and Self: A Correspondence between Robert M. Adams and Hector-Neri Castañeda," *Agent, Language, and the Structure of the World: Essays Presented to Hector-Neri Castañeda, with his Replies*, ed. James Tomberlin (Cambridge, Mass.: Hackett, 1983), p. 294. Adams's and Albritton's examples are discussed in Adams and Castañeda, "Knowledge and Self," *Agent, Language, and the Structure of the World*, pp. 293–309, and Hector-Neri Castañeda, "Reply to John Perry," *Agent, Language, and the Structure of the World*, pp. 313–27. Castañeda now recognizes the weakness of his argument against Kretzmann and in particular has abandoned his earlier view that the proposition expressed by Tiresias's "I am the blind Tiresias," for example, is also expressed as part of "Tiresias believes that he himself is the blind Tiresias."

43. With regard to these examples, some discussion of a further principle which appears in Castañeda's work is perhaps also in order.

Castañeda has repeatedly noted that indicators even in *oratio obliqua* express indexical references by the *speaker* and leave it open whether the person spoken about refers to the same objects indexically or not (see "'He': A Study," "Indicator and Quasi-Indicators," "On the Logic of Self-Reference," "Omniscience and Indexical Reference," and "On the Logic of Attributions"). In "On the Logic of Attributions," p. 440, this point appears in the form of principles (I.1) and (I.2).

(I.1) An indexical reference in *oratio obliqua* is made by the speaker and is presented by the oratio obliqua as being made by him and not as being made by the person to whom knowledge (belief, conjecture, assertion, etc.) is attributed; and indicator always has the largest scope in a sentence containing it.

(I.2) An indexical reference *R* in *oratio obliqua*, that is not part of an attribution of self-knowledge (self-belief, self-conjecture, etc.) leaves it by itself wholly unspecified how the person to whom knowledge (belief, etc.) is attributed refers to the person or object to whom R is made.

In "Indicator and Quasi-Indicators," pp. 89–90, the point is made in terms of an example:

> Suppose now that Privatus asserts of a dead friend of his:
> (2)   Once it occurred to Jones that I buried a letter here. . . . One thing is clear. In spite of their misleading position in the *oratio obliqua* of (2), the indicators of (2) serve to mark the positions occupied by some unspecified referring expressions in the sentence formulating the unspecified proposition that, according to (2), Jones once took to be true. Those referring expressions that Jones used were, of course, either
>   (a)   single indicators; or
>   (b)   names; or
>   (c)   indexical descriptions, like 'this man', 'my friend', or 'five years ago today (now)'; or
>   (d)   Leibnizian descriptions, i.e. descriptions that contain no indicators.
> The actual proposition that, by (2), Jones once took to be true can be one of eight different types, depending on which sort of reference Jones made to Privatus and the place in question. And now we must raise another question: Is Privatus's statement (2) definite enough on this point? And the answer seems to be that it is not: Privatus's statement (2) is simply the statement to the effect that *one* of the eight types of propositions allowed by the two positions occupied by indicators was taken by Jones to be true. That is, Privatus's statement (2) is to be conceived of as a disjunction of certain statements which we proceed to identify.

Castañeda's main point here is both clearly correct and crucially important: neither the 'I' nor the 'here' of Privatus's (2) need indicate that Jones referred *indexically* to Privatus or to the spot in question. It is on this basis that Castañeda in "Omniscience and Indexical Reference" criticizes Kretzmann's formulation of his argument against omniscience in "Omniscience and Immutability." But it is also on this basis, interestingly enough, that Castañeda suggests a limitation to God's omniscience and omnipotence: God can neither know nor formulate all propositions indexically in *oratio recta* (Castañeda, "Omniscience and Indexical Reference," p. 210).

Castañeda's presentation in both passages above, however, may be liable to misinterpretation. The 'I' and 'here' of Privatus's (2), we have said, need not indicate indexical reference on Jones's part, and (2) may be true although Jones referred *non*indexically to Privatus and the place in question. But this should not be taken the other way around, as it were. It does *not* follow and it is *not* the case that just any form of reference by Jones to Privatus and the place in question will suffice to make (2) true. Consider for example a case in which it one day occurs to Jones, quite out of the blue, that:

(15) The shortest person to bury a letter in the second-largest state buried a letter in the second-largest state.

Let us also suppose—although Jones is unaware of this—that (1) Privatus buried a letter in Texas, that (2) as it happens he is the shortest person to do so, and that (3) Texas is the second-largest state. If Privatus is speaking in Texas, does that make his statement *true*?:

(2)   Once it occurred to Jones that I buried a letter here.

No. Nor, were Jones to *know* that (15):

(15) The shortest person to bury a letter in the second-largest state buried a letter in the second-largest state.

would Privatus's statement (16) necessarily hold:

(16) Jones knows that I buried a letter here.

Why *don't* (2) and (16) hold in these circumstances, and why *doesn't* Castañeda's principle apply 'in reverse', as it were? The basic reason, I think, is a quite general one which Castañeda mentions in discussing *knowing who*:

A sentence like 'Peter knows who his neighbor is' really formulates different statements, not only because of the multiplicity of persons named 'Peter', but also because of the different criteria involved in identifying a certain person, i.e. knowing who a certain person is. The criteria vary from case to case depending on purposes and circumstances (Castañeda, "On the Logic of Attributions," p. 446).

This is also, I think, what underlies both the examples above and those offered by Adams and Albritton (see Adams and Castañeda, "Knowledge and Self," and Castañeda, "Reply to John Perry").

44. See especially Perry's "The Problem of the Essential Indexical," but also "Frege on Demonstratives." David Lewis characterizes Perry as holding that belief has *two* objects (see Lewis, "Attitudes," p. 536). But this seems to me to obscure both the strengths and the weaknesses of Perry's account.

45. Perry, "The Problem of the Essential Indexical," p. 19.

46. Ibid.

47. Lewis, "Attitudes," p. 523.

48. Chisholm, *The First Person*, p. 27.

49. Belief *de re* is a more complicated matter on both Lewis's and Chisholm's accounts and is not of immediate relevance here.

50. The relation of this account to Perry's is fairly obvious: I know what X knows, on Lewis's account, if and only if X and I are in the same belief state, on Perry's account.

51. Lewis, "Attitudes," pp. 525–26. Lewis does concede almost parenthetically that "Doubtless it is true in *some* sense that Heimson does not believe what Hume did" (p. 525). But this seems to play no role at all in his final position.

52. Lewis, "Attitudes," pp. 514, 522; Chisholm, *The First Person*, p. 27.

53. Lewis, "Attitudes," pp. 538–43, 552; Chisholm, *The First Person*, pp. 29–30, 38.

54. Lewis, "Attitudes," p. 526; Chisholm, *The First Person*, p. 44.

55. Lewis, "Attitudes," p. 525; Chisholm, *The First Person*, p. 58, pp. 7–8.

56. Shoemaker, "Me and My Attributes."

57. Chisholm, *The First Person*, p. 35.

58. A number of classic pieces on omnipotence and its difficulties appear in *Readings in the Philosophy of Religion*, ed. Baruch Brody (Englewood Cliffs, N.J.: Prentice-Hall, 1974). More recent pieces of note in the controversy include: Swinburne, "Omnipotence"; Richard R. La Croix, "Swinburne on Omnipotence," *International Journal for Philosophy of Religion* 6 (1975): 251–55, and "The Impossibility of Defining 'Omnipotence,'" *Philosophical Studies* 32 (1977): 181–90; George I. Mavrodes, "Defining Omnipotence," *Philosophical Studies* 32 (1977): 191–202; Joshua Hoffman, "Mavrodes on Defining Omnipotence," *Philosophical Studies* 35 (1979): 311–13; and Bruce R. Reichenbach, "Mavrodes on Omnipotence," *Philosophical Studies* 37 (1980): 211–14. The most recent exchange is represented by Edward Wierenga, "Omnipotence Defined," presented at the 78th Annual Meeting of the American Philosophical Association, Eastern Division, Philadelphia, December 29, 1981 (abstacted in *Journal of Philosophy* 78 [1981]: 617), and Joshua Hoffman, Commentary on Edward Wierenga's "Omnipotence Defined," presented at the 78th Annual Meeting of the American Philosophical Association, Eastern Division, Philadelphia, December 29, 1981.

59. I am grateful to Michael Slote, Kriste Taylor, David Pomerant, and an anonymous referee for *Noûs* for very helpful comments on earlier versions of this paper. Thanks also to Lee Miller for the use of his Latin.

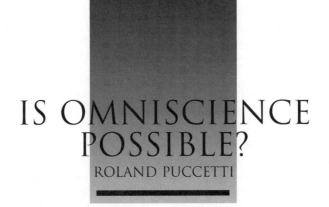

IS OMNISCIENCE POSSIBLE?

ROLAND PUCCETTI

In another place[1] I have argued that omnipotence, omniscience, and perfect goodness are requirements of the God-concept, and that such a concept is not only inconsistent with the actual world but in a sense self-contradictory. It follows that God does not exist. The present paper is designed to afford a kind of short-cut to the same conclusion: what I want to show here is that our notion of an omniscient being *itself* contains a contradiction.

The idea for this argument is really inspired by a remark of Wittgenstein's in the *Tractatus*. There he notes that one "cannot set a limit to thought," for in order to do so "we should have to be able to think both sides of this limit, that is, we should have to be able to think what is unthinkable."[2] What I shall argue is that the notion of omniscience implies being able to do just this.

Let 'X' stand for a hypothetical omniscient being, and 'Y' for the totality of facts (Wittgenstein's phrase) constituting the world. In order for X to be omniscient, he would have to know Y fully. Another way of saying this is that in order for an X to exist, Y would have to be fully known. But included in the totality of facts known by such an X, if he existed, would surely be his own existence as an omniscient being. This is where the difficulty begins. For in order to know he is omniscient, X would have to be certain there are no facts beyond those he knows. Thus he needs to know *something besides* Y. He needs to know the truth of the negative existential statement: "There are no facts unknown to me." Let us call

From *Australasian Journal of Philosophy* 41 (1963): 92–93. Copyright © 1963 Oxford University Press. Reprinted by permission of *Australasian Journal of Philosophy*.

knowing the truth of this statement knowing 'Z'. The question then arises, is it possible to know Z?

Now we all know the truth of some negative existential statements. I know, for example, there is no elephant in this room at the present moment. But the negative existential statements we know to be true have reference to limited factual situations. Z is quite another kind of statement. It makes an existential claim which is completely uncircumscribed, spatially and temporally. Knowing Z, then, would be like knowing it is true no centaurs exist *anywhere, at any time.*

This is where we come back to the point of Wittgenstein's remark. In order for X to know he is omniscient, if an X exists, he has to set a limit to the knowable. He has to ascertain that the limit of the known, so to speak, is also the limit of the factual. Yet he can only arrive at the limit of the known. It makes no sense to imagine X arriving at this limit, peering beyond it (at what?), and satisfying himself no further facts exist. So long as he, like us, can conceive there being facts still unknown it will never be contradictory to deny he knows Z. For the same reason our hypothetical X can never ascertain his own omniscience. And since as I said before he would have to know he is an X in order to know Y, it is obvious he could not know Y. But in that case he is not omniscient.

A theist, of course, might deny this conclusion on special grounds. He might say that if our hypothetical X were also God he *will* know Z because He is the sole creator of the totality of facts (other than Himself) constituting the world. The trouble with this reply is that it begs the question. God could not know He is the sole creator (or that nothing exists beyond Himself and His creation) unless He also knew Z. Since Z cannot be known, God cannot be omniscient.

But if I was right in the first part of my earlier argument,[3] God *must* be conceived as omniscient. From this it follows that the totality of facts constituting the world does not include God.

NOTES

1. Roland Puccetti, "The Concept of God," *Philosophical Quarterly* 14 (1964): 237–45.

2. L. Wittgenstein, Author's Preface in *Tractatus Logico-Philosophicus*, p. 2. The German text reads: "Denn um dem Denken eine Grenze zu ziehen, müssten wir beide Seiten dieser Grenze denken können (wir müssten also denken können, was sich nicht denken lässt)."

3. See note 1.

32

LOGIC AND LIMITS
OF KNOWLEDGE
AND TRUTH
PATRICK GRIM

Though my ultimate concern is with issues in epistemology and metaphysics, let me phrase the central question I will pursue in terms evocative of philosophy of religion: What are the implications of our logic—in particular, of Cantor and Gödel—for the possibility of omniscience?[1]

The attempt to draw philosophical lessons from metalogical texts is a notoriously perilous business.[2] With that in mind let me frame what follows as a *suggestion*, or offer it as an argument worthy of consideration, rather than trumpet it as a proof. What I want to suggest is that within any logic we have—in particular, in terms of systems and sets—omniscience appears to be simply impossible. In that sense Cantor and Gödel offer at least a suggestive case against the possibility of omniscience.

The path to this conclusion will be somewhat more circuitous than this introductory statement might suggest, however. In the first section that follows, I consider the standard Gödel result, and in the second, some intriguing nonconstructive extensions, neither of which suggests so definitive a negative conclusion regarding omniscience. In section III, however, I offer a more general argument for 'expressive' incompleteness of relevant systems, supplemented in section IV by a general argument for 'internal' incompleteness closer in spirit to Gödel. Each form of incompleteness appears again in section V as the basis of a first argument against omniscience.

The work of the paper to this point concerns formal *systems* as analogues of

From *Noûs* 22 (1988): 341–67. Copyright © 1988 by Blackwell Publishing. Reprinted by permission of Blackwell Publishing.

omniscience.[3] In section VI, I offer a more direct Cantorian argument against a *set* of all truths and hence against omniscience, digressing slightly to consider implications for possible worlds. Here alternative set theories may seem promising as a way out, however, and these are briefly considered—with negative results—in section VII.

Perhaps in the end there really *cannot* be any totality of truths and really *cannot* be any omniscience. Plantinga and Wittgenstein are used in a final section to summarize major epistemological and metaphysical suggestions.

I. OMNISCIENCE AND THE STANDARD GÖDEL RESULT

Many a body of knowledge may be thought of—at least ideally—on the model of an interpreted formal system. To the admissible formulae of the system, on this analogy, correspond all statements in the general domain of the body of knowledge, true or false, known or unknown. Formulae interpreted as *basic* truths or *basic* items of knowledge are chosen as axioms, and formulae interpreted as *derivative* truths—given appropriate transformation rules—will appear as theorems.[4] Axiomatic geometries are prime examples here, of course. But given a liberal-enough attitude toward sets of axioms, types of transformation rules, and the like, it appears that *any* body of knowledge might ideally be conceived on the model of a formal system.[5]

If bodies of knowledge might be so conceived, might not *knowers*? Here we need not suggest that processes of knowing or patterns of epistemic justification must somehow correspond to demonstrations within a formal system. But might not at least *what* a knower knows—the mere content of his knowledge—be conceived on the model of a formal system?

There is a major obstacle here, at least for familiar types of knowers and familiar types of systems. A formal system contains as a theorem every formula obtainable from its axioms by its specified transformation rules. If the transformation rules of such a system correspond to standard patterns of logical inference, then, a corresponding knower would have to know—as derivative truths—every truth derivable from his basic items of knowledge. None of us is such a knower.[6]

This is precisely the difficulty which seems to arise concerning Hintikka's work in *Knowledge and Belief.* Once rules which appear indispensable from a formal point of view are adopted, we seem to be saddled with the following result. Given any '$p \supset q$' valid in ordinary propositional logic, we appear to be committed to:

Kap $\supset$ *Kaq*,

where '*Kap*' is initially glossed as '*a* knows that *p*'.[7]

But this does *not* appear to hold for ordinary knowers, who may well *not* know all that what they know entails. Hintikka originally responded to the problem as follows:

> Our results are not directly applicable to what is true or false in the actual world of ours. They tell us something definite about the truth and falsity of statements only in a world in which everybody follows the consequences of what he knows as far as they lead him.[8]

On this approach, then, Hintikka's knowers are *ideal* knowers. So too are those knowers envisaged above, modelable on formal systems transformation rules of which correspond to standard patterns of logical inference. This limitation to ideal knowers is not the worrisome constraint for our purposes that it is commonly held to be for Hintikka's, however. For here it *is* ideal knowers—in fact divine knowers—that are at issue.[9]

Let us thus construct in imagination an ideal knower whose knowledge *can* be conceived on the model of a formal system G. The transformation rules of G, we suppose, do include on interpretation all standard rules of logical inference, so our ideal knower *will* know all that follows from what he knows. We will also suppose that his rules of inference operate only on workably finite sets of premises, that formulae of G are kept finite as well, and that the alphabet of G is kept manageably denumerable.

What of the *basic* knowledge of our ideal knower, corresponding to the axioms of G? Here we might insist that the axioms of G be finite as well, but we will instead impose only the weaker stipulation that they be recursively enumerable.

If an ideal knower so constructed is to have even a pretense of *divine* knowledge, of course, he must have at least a working knowledge of number theory. We will then suppose all statements of number theory to be expressible in his corresponding system, and we will expect to find among the axioms of G the mere handful required for predicate calculus with identity and the five Peano postulates. But of course we can also build in much more: a googolplex of basic propositions of biochemistry, perhaps, an infinite (though recursively enumerable) set of basic propositions of physics, and all seven true propositions of macroeconomics.

What Gödel's standard incompleteness result shows, however, is that no matter what other basic knowledge we imagine building into such an ideal knower—no matter what else is included among the recursively enumerable axioms of G—such an ideal knower *cannot* be omniscient. If, as specified, he knows enough to handle basic number theory, in fact—no matter what *else* he knows—he already knows too *much* to know everything.[10]

Gödel numbering for G is assured by the fact that formulae of G are finite and the axioms of G are adequate for number theory. Given Gödel numbering and these axioms a substitution predicate can be introduced, and—since the axioms of G are recursively enumerable and its rules of inference operate only on finite sets of premises—a proof predicate as well. These are in essence all we need to construct an undecidable sentence for G: a formula which, if G is omega-consistent,[11] demonstrably cannot appear as a theorem of G—and so cannot represent anything our ideal knower knows—and yet *does* represent a number-theoretical truth.

A similar incompleteness result will hold, moreover, for any improved model of an ideal knower we attempt to construct within the confines of the basic conditions above. It is tempting, for example, to try adding as an axiom to G the formula for G's missing truth. When this in turn gives us an incomplete system it is tempting to try adding an infinite series of missing truths, or an infinite series of infinite series of missing truths. As long as what we add remains recursively enumerable, however, any improved system we build will still be incomplete, and for basically the same reasons.[12] All systems within the basic conditions above are *essentially* incomplete and the ideal knowers to which they correspond are *essentially* nonomniscient.[13]

II. BEYOND STANDARD SYSTEMS

The ideal knowers considered above are analogous to formal systems adequate at least for the general purposes of number theory and which have (1) recursively enumerable axioms, (2) formulae of finite length and a denumerable alphabet, and (3) rules of inference from only finitely many premises.

On the grounds of Gödel's standard incompleteness result, no such ideal knower can be omniscient. But God *is* standardly conceived as omniscient. So God—if there be such a being—must not be an ideal knower of this kind.

Should this be considered a negative theological conclusion? Not necessarily. The work of the preceding section might instead be considered a positive theological contribution in the spirit of the *via negativa*—an approach to God by way of an understanding of what he is not. God's knowledge is quite standardly said, for example, to be infinite. But this would clearly be inadequate as a characterization of omniscience, since knowledge of many a mere ideal knower of the lowly sort considered above is literally infinite. *God's* knowledge would have to be much *more* than merely infinite, essentially incapable of being captured at all within the systematic confines laid down above. Some have argued in effect that those confines are our confines as well.[14] If so, our work to this point might be welcomed with open arms in theological circles as a particularly precise vindication of the doctrine that a divine mind must be humanly incomprehensible.

But what lies *beyond* the type of system considered above? What happens if we weaken one or more of the constraints imposed above on systems and on corresponding knowers?

That is a question for which no general and exhaustive answer can be said to exist. The systematic constraints outlined above are essentially the limits of constructive methods, and to go beyond them is to leave constructive methods behind. Beyond such constraints 'formal systems' cease to be genuinely 'formal' at all, and conceptions of 'proof' and 'demonstration' must change at the border. Beyond lies not logic in the familiar sense but what Geoffrey Hellman has not inappropriately termed 'theologic'.[15]

Important attempts to cross over have been made, however. Among the most promising for our purposes are the following.[16]

Barkley Rosser was the first to propose relaxing that condition which limits rules of inference to finite premises, introducing a form of transfinite induction instead. Rosser considered only systems allowing up to ω^2 uses of a non-constructive rule of inference from $f(0)$, $f(1)$, $f(2)$, ... to $(x)f(x)$, however, and within that limitation systems still prove incomplete in the standard ways: each system still contains an undecidable sentence and a consistency formula unprovable in the system.[17]

Transfinite induction is taken further in a system S_∞ developed in various forms by G. Gentzen, W. Ackerman, P. Lorenzen, K. Schutte, and I. Hlodovskii.[18] 'Proof' within S_∞ is redefined in terms of proof trees. To each formula of a proof tree an ordinal is assigned—the result of applying a weak rule in the system is given the same ordinal as its premise, but the result of applying a strong rule or cut is given an ordinal greater than that of its premises.

Restriction on the ordinals assignable to the formulae of proof trees restricts the notion of proof accordingly. But if *no* restriction is placed on the class of ordinals which can be attached to proofs, we get a system S_∞ that is both ω-consistent and complete.[19]

This may make it appear as if omniscience can escape the curse of Gödel on the wings of transfinite induction. But here some important limitations of S_∞ should be noted. The proof of S_∞'s consistency, first of all, is not formalizable internally; as Gentzen himself showed, transfinite induction up to ϵ_0 cannot be formalized in S_∞.[20] A second difficulty is perhaps more crucial. S_∞, obtained from a more standard system S for number theory by the addition of a rule of inference permitting transfinite induction, is still capable of dealing only with finite sets. For systems dealing with infinite sets as well, an obvious desideratum in any system intended to mirror omniscience, even transfinite induction will not be enough—those systems will *still* be incomplete.[21]

A somewhat different nonconstructive approach appears in the work of Solomon Feferman.[22] In 1939 A. M. Turing dealt with collections of axiom systems under the name *ordinal logics*. Feferman's work, although related, is extended to transfinite *sequences* of recursively enumerable axiom systems. Building on an initial axiom system A_0, we construct a progression of systems; for each successor ordinal we add a formula asserting the consistency of the preceding system, taking unions at each limit ordinal. Consider then the theorems of an entire transfinite progression of axiom systems of this sort. Might not *these* offer a promise of completeness?

So it might seem. Feferman notes that a general incompleteness result for such progressions would have been dramatic proof of the far-reaching extent of incompleteness phenomena. "However, the situation has not turned out this way."[23] For progressions based on a particular reflection principle, all true statements of elementary number theory *are* provable in the progression. It *is* possible, moreover, to select a path through the ordinals along which all theorems of the progression are provable.

But here again it would be rash to think that crucial limitations had finally been overcome.

As Feferman emphasizes, the construction of progressions at issue is intensional in character. This gives us a peculiar nonuniqueness result: two systems A_d and $A_{d'}$ may yield radically different theorems even though they are associated with the same progression function and even though $|d| = |d'|$.[24] It is the intensional character of Feferman's progressions that allows for proofs of consistency and the appearance of completeness. These rely, however, on what Michael Resnik has termed 'pathological' consistency predicates.[25] As R. G. Jeroslow notes,

> The issue is that a non-standard designator s(w) may so mysteriously describe
> S that S can prove consistent whatever s(w) may designate, not "knowing" that
> s(w) designates S itself.[26]

Those features of such progressions which seem initially to transcend Gödelian limits, then, rest ultimately on the progressions' basic ignorance—a strongly presumptive disqualification for any system intended to model omniscience.

Even the initially attractive features of such progressions, moreover, are lost for sequences based on higher than first-order calculi. Here Feferman does demonstrate a quite general incompleteness result: For any consistent progression based on at least the second-order calculus, either there is a true Π_1^1 sentence or there is a true Σ_1^1 sentence which is not provable from $U_{d \in 0} A_d$.[27]

Feferman's work has been incorporated and extended in R. G. Jeroslow's 'experimental logics'.[28] These logics transcend the limits of standard systems in being in effect dynamic rather than static, progressively building by trial and error. As such a system develops, axioms and even rules of inference can be withdrawn or supplemented. Thus experimental logics model not merely ideal knowers but ideal learners.

As might be expected from the link with Feferman's work, there *are* experimental logics capable of proving their own consistency. But this is not enough to offer much hope for modeling omniscience.

A logic of this sort is termed *convergent* if its recurring formulae do not vacillate indefinitely—if eventually "the conceptual superstructure settles down."[29] To model an (eventually) *omniscient* being, then, we would need a system which converged on all truth—on at least, say, all truths of the form $(\forall x)R(x)$ for recursive predicates R. But this does not appear to be possible. For systems at issue Jeroslow has shown that joint requirements of consistency, convergence, and closure under reasoning are in fact inconsistent with the goal of obtaining all truths $(\forall x)R(x)$.[30]

None of the nonconstructive attempts we've considered, then, seems to offer an acceptable model for omniscience. Is that enough, with the results of section I, to show that there simply *is* no such model?

Certainly not. The standard Gödel result stops at the limit of standard systems, and there are options for nonconstructive systems that have not yet been developed.[31] In the next section we will consider a more general negative result, the first of a series which does seem to suggest the genuine impossibility of omniscience.

III. EXPRESSIVE INCOMPLETENESS

The knowledge of an omniscient being can correspond to no system yet considered. But we have not yet shown that it can correspond to no system at all.

A quite simple but powerful Cantorian argument seems to show just that. For at least a particular type of incompleteness—what we will term 'expressive incompleteness'—*any* system meeting certain minimal conditions will prove incomplete. Those minimal conditions would seem clearly necessary in any system intended to model omniscience. But no system which meets those conditions can be complete, and no *in*complete system can model omniscience. To the knowledge of an omniscient being, it appears, will correspond no system at all.

It should perhaps be noted that what follows is not a form of Gödel's argument, and that expressive incompleteness is not the familiar form that incompleteness takes in his work. A broad but more strictly Gödelian treatment will be left to the following section.

We have offered above a very general statement of the conclusion of the argument. But let us begin with a proof of expressive incompleteness for a particular and particularly familiar type of system.

Consider the standard systems of number theory to which Gödel's theorems apply. In such systems, basic strings of formulae correspond on interpretation to the natural numbers, and it is these that such systems are taken to be *about.* Fairly intuitively, then, the natural numbers are what we will term the *objects* of such systems.

Within such systems appear formulae of various kinds, among which are formulae of one variable. These, in accord with common parlance, we will call *predicates.*[32]

Suppose now such a system with the following characteristics:

(1) It can, first of all, take each predicate expressible in its language as an object. A system with this capacity we will call *self-reflective,* for fairly obvious reasons. The systems immediately at issue are of course self-reflective by virtue of Gödel numbering: to each predicate corresponds a Gödel number which can be taken as an object of the system.

(2) Second, the system is designed to be capable of at least expressing all properties of its individual objects, the natural numbers.

Here's the rub: conditions (1) and (2) cannot both be satisfied for any system of the sort at issue. For consider the following questions: How many objects would be at issue for such a system? How many properties of individual objects? How many expressible predicates?

There must first of all be at least as many objects of such a system as there are predicates within it, since each predicate can be taken as an object. The device of Gödel numbering assigns a distinct number to each open formula of one variable, so there must be at least as many numbers—the objects of such a system—as there are predicates within it.

But there must also be more *properties* of individual objects of the system than there are objects. For consider the set of objects of the system—numbers—which we might envisage as the set O:

$$O = \{\ o_1, o_2, o_3, \ldots\ \}.$$

If we treat properties purely extensionally, possession of distinct properties will amount to membership in distinct sets. The properties of objects at issue, then, will correspond to subsets of the set of objects—to elements of the power set ρO of the set of objects at issue. A complete listing of such properties we might envisage as follows:

P^1,	corresponding to	$\varnothing$
P^2,	corresponding to	$\{\ o_1\ \}$
P^3,	corresponding to	$\{\ o_2\ \}$
P^4,	corresponding to	$\{\ o_3\ \}$

.

.

.

P'^1, corresponding to $\{\ o_1, o_2\ \}$
P'^2, corresponding to $\{\ o_1, o_3\ \}$

.

.

.

P''^1, corresponding to $\{\ o_1, o_2, o_3\ \}$

.

.

.

Intensionally construed, of course, a number of coextensional properties may correspond to each set.

There will then be as many properties applicable to individual objects as there are elements in the power set of objects. But by Cantor's power set theorem we know that the power set of any set is larger than the set itself.[33] Thus, there must be more properties applicable to individual objects than there are objects.

Let us sum up. By the first part of the argument, for any system of the sort specified, there are as many objects of the system—numbers—as expressible predicates—open formulae of one variable. But by the second part of the argument there must be more *properties* of individual objects than there are objects.

For any such system, then, there will be more properties of individual objects of the system than there will be appropriate predicates with which to express them. Properties will outnumber corresponding predicates. Some genuine property of the objects of a self-reflective system must thus go unexpressed, and so condition (2) above—that each property of its objects be at least expressible in the system—cannot be satisfied.

Correspondingly, of course, some *truth* regarding an object of the system—that it does (or does not) have a particular property—will be incapable even of *expression* in the system. All such systems will be expressively incomplete.[34]

As presented above, the argument for expressive incompleteness is tied to particular features of familiar systems; numbers are taken as *objects* in the argument, open formulae of one variable as *predicates*, and it is by the device of Gödel numbering that such systems can take their own predicates as objects.

The argument will hold, however, for any system interpreted as applying to a domain of objects—those things the system is taken to be about—and including a range of predicates applicable within the system. If any such system is self-reflective—if each of its predicates can also be taken as an object to which the system applies—it will have at least as many objects as predicates. But taking properties purely extensionally, by Cantor's power set theorem there will be more properties of individual objects of the system than corresponding predicates with which to express them. Some genuine property of some object of the system—and thus some truth—will be inexpressible, and any such system will prove expressively incomplete.

Expressive incompleteness, then, is by no means limited to the standard systems of section I: it will apply for any system which meets the basic condition of self-reflection.

At least no *system*, it appears, can achieve omniscience. For any system intended to model omniscience would surely have to include its own predicates among the objects it knows things about—it would have to be self-reflective in the sense outlined above. But any self-reflective system, we've seen, will be expressively incomplete: some property of its objects, and thus some truth, will be incapable even of expression within the system.

Note also how very thin a notion of 'system' is in fact required in the basic argument above. Nothing has been said to indicate that any system at issue must be formal or axiomatic, that it must generate theorems by means of demonstrations or even that it must contain a category of assertions or asserted theses.

All the argument requires, in fact, is a system of *expression*—in a word, a *language*. This first result might then be put as follows. Given even minimal requirements of expressible self-reflection, it appears, any system of expression must prove expressively incomplete. In that sense there could not even be a language adequate for the expression of all truths.

IV. GÖDEL GENERALIZED

Expressive incompleteness, because it does appear to hold for every self-reflective system, may pose real difficulties for omniscience.

As noted above, however, this is not Gödel's argument and expressive incompleteness is not the form that incompleteness takes in his work. *Expressive* incompleteness is a pervasive limitation on what can even be expressed within certain systems. What Gödel shows is that for a wide range of systems, on the assumption of consistency,[35] some formula which *is* expressible in the system and represents a truth on interpretation nonetheless cannot be captured as a theorem of the system. This more familiar form we might term *internal* incompleteness.

These two forms of incompleteness are not coextensive; internal incompleteness holds only for a somewhat more restricted class of systems than does expressive incompleteness. In the basic spirit of the preceding section, however, we can also offer a fairly general argument for internal incompleteness—an argument general enough to indicate that even internal incompleteness applies far beyond its usual association with the standard systems of section I.[36]

Let us start, as before, with a self-reflective system, capable of taking each of its expressible predicates as a particular object of the system.

For any self-reflective system, consider the set P of expressible predicates:

$$P = \{P_1, P_2, P_3, \ldots\}$$

and the corresponding set P^o of *predicate objects*—those objects of the system which are expressible predicates taken as objects:

$$P^o = \{P^o_1, P^o_2, P^o_3, \ldots\}^{37}$$

Clearly these two sets will be the same size. A one-to-one function f will be possible between them, then, which assigns each predicate object P^o to an expressible predicate $f(P^o)$ and such that to each expressible predicate of the system some predicate object is assigned. An obvious candidate for such a function, of course, would be that which assigns each predicate object to the predicate of which it *is* the object. Within the specified conditions there will be many other possibilities for f as well, however.

For any such f, now, consider any individual predicate object P^o and its associated predicate by f, namely, $f(P^o)$. That predicate may or may not in fact apply to the object at issue. The predicate $f(P^o)$ applied to the object P^o, in other words—giving us the formula $f(P^o)P^o$—may or may not represent a *truth* on the intended interpretation. $f(P^o)P^o$ may also, or may not, appear as a *theorem* within the system at issue.

For any choice of f, then, consider the following set:

$$P^{o\prime} = \{ \ P^o : f(P^o)P^o \text{ is not a theorem} \ \}.$$

Here P^o is any predicate object, and $f(P^o)$ its associated predicate by our chosen function f. $P^{o\prime}$, then, is the set of those predicate objects to which the corresponding predicates $f(P^o)$ do not apply as theorems.

Note however that P^o is explicitly just a set of objects of the system, and in that regard might seem a plausible candidate for the extension of a predicate. Such a predicate would apply to precisely those objects which are members of $P^{o\prime}$: to all and only predicate objects P^o to which the associated predicate $f(P^o)$ does not apply as a theorem.

The crucial question here is this: Is such a predicate—a predicate of which this is the extension—*expressible* in the system?

If not, of course, the system is expressively impoverished in certain respects. But if such a predicate *is* expressible, for *any* f of the sort indicated, and if the system at issue is also consistent, then it must be internally incomplete. Some truth expressible within the system will not be captured as a theorem.

For suppose that such a predicate, for some appropriate f, *is* expressible in the system. f, it will be remembered, has been chosen as a function mapping some predicate object P^o onto each predicate expressible in the system. If *this* predicate is expressible, f must then also map some P^o onto *it*.

Consider then the predicate at issue and any P^o which our chosen f assigns to it. Does the predicate at issue in fact apply to *that* P^o or not? We have two options:

Let us suppose first that the predicate at issue will *not* apply to its correlated object. Here we will bring in our final assumption—of consistency—in the following form: that it is only truths on the intended interpretation that are taken as theorems of the system.[38]

We are supposing that the predicate at issue will *not* apply to its associated P^o. Since only truths are captured as theorems, then, $f(P^o)$ applied to P^o in this case— the formula $f(P^o)P^o$—will not be a theorem. The predicate at issue, however, is specified as having $P^{o\prime}$ as its extension—as applying to *every* P^o for which $f(P^o)P^o$ is not a theorem. Contrary to our initial negative supposition, then, we are forced to conclude that the predicate at issue *will* apply to its associated object.

The only option left here is the second: that the predicate at issue *does* apply to that P^o with which it is correlated.

It is then true in this case that P^o's correlate—$f(P^o)$—in fact applies to P^o; $f(P^o)P^o$ represents a truth. The predicate at issue, however, has been specified as applying only to those objects P^o for which $f(P^o)P^o$ is not a theorem. Since the predicate at issue does apply to its corresponding P^o in this case—since $f(P^o)P^o$ is true—it is also true that $f(P^o)P^o$ is not a theorem of the system.

At least one truth expressible within the system, then, is not captured as a theorem; any such system must be internally incomplete.

The argument can be repeated, of course, for any choice of a one-to-one function f which assigns to each expressible predicate a corresponding object. For any such f there will be a predicate which if expressible in the system will give us the same result.

Note also that although the argument concerns systems conceived as containing expressible predicates, objects, and theorems, little else has been said to constrain that class of systems for which the argument will apply. Nothing has been said, in particular, to limit relevant systems to those meeting the formal constraints imposed in section I.

Where then does this leave us? Despite the surface complexities of the argument above, the assumptions we have made regarding any system at issue have been genuinely minimal: that it is self-reflective, consistent, and capable of expressing at least one of a range of predicates that we have specified in terms of their extensions. For any system which satisfies these basic conditions the argument above can be repeated, and thus any such system will prove internally incomplete.

How general then is the phenomenon of incompleteness? Expressive incompleteness, we've seen, will hold for any self-reflective system. Internal incompleteness will hold for any self-reflective and consistent system capable of expressing any of a range of particular predicates.

Here we can also say a bit more, however, about precisely how little expressive capacity is actually required for internal incompleteness. Just two elements will basically suffice: (1) that a system be capable of expressing theoremhood within the system—that a formula is or is not a theorem—as a predicate, and (2) that it be capable of expressing at least one function f which assigns an object P^o of the system to each expressible predicate $f(P^o)$. Given essentially these two elements a predicate can be constructed with extension $P^{o'}$:

$$P^{o'} = \{ \ P^o : f(P^o)P^o \text{ is not a theorem } \},$$

and with such a predicate expressible any self-reflective and consistent system will also prove internally incomplete.

V. FIRST ARGUMENTS AGAINST OMNISCIENCE

Let us return to the analogy between systems and knowers and in particular to systems and the notion of an omniscient knower.

Do the incompleteness results of the preceding sections offer an argument that omniscience is impossible?

Consider first an argument which follows the pattern of expressive incompleteness. Here we'll speak of conceptions of properties instead of predicates, and will use 'objects of knowledge' somewhat irregularly to indicate those things a knower knows something *about.*

Any omniscient mind would surely be self-reflective in at least the following sense: among its objects of knowledge—among those things it knows something about—would be its own conceptions of properties. But here the argument of section III can be rephrased to show that the knowledge of no such mind can be complete. It will have at least as many objects of knowledge as conceptions of properties, since each of the latter is also an object of knowledge. But by Cantor's argument there will be more actual properties of its objects than objects themselves. Actual properties will outnumber its conceptions of properties, and thus some genuine property of its objects of knowledge—and so some truth—will remain *inconceivable* for such a being.

Any omniscient being, so the argument goes, would have to be self-reflective in the sense specified. But no self-reflective being can be omniscient. There can be no omniscient being.

Whatever our final verdict, I think, the argument from expressive incompleteness is an elegantly simple one. Although significantly more awkward, we can also offer an argument from internal incompleteness:

An omniscient mind, we've suggested above, must be self-reflective in at least the sense of being able to take its conceptions of properties as objects of knowledge. But we might also argue that a genuinely omniscient mind would have to be self-aware in deeper senses as well. Among the things that such a being will know, of course, is *that* it knows certain things, and thus '. . . is known by me' or the like will be among its conceivable properties. Such a mind, we might insist, will surely also be cognizant of obvious aspects of its own conceptual structure—it will for example be aware of one-to-one mappings between its conceptions of properties and these taken self-reflectively as objects of knowledge.

Omniscience, then—so the argument goes—has formal features analogous to those outlined for systems in the preceding section: self-reflectivity, expressible theoremhood, and the expressibility of some one-to-one mapping f from predicate objects to predicates of the system. The knowledge of any omniscient being would of course also be consistent. But any *system* with these formal features will be internally incomplete: some truth expressible in the system will not be captured as a theorem. For the same reasons, it appears, the knowledge of any being proposed as omniscient must be correspondingly incomplete: there will be some truth which *is* expressible or conceivable by such a being and yet will *not* appear among those things it knows.

Or so the argument goes.

How good are these arguments as, say, genuine disproofs of omniscience?

The argument from expressive incompleteness seems by far the more persuasive of the two, if only because it is significantly simpler and more direct. The argument from internal incompleteness demands more points of comparison between systems and knowers, and here conviction may fade as the analogy begins to show the strain.

Both arguments presented rely on *some* points of analogy between knowers and systems, however. An objector might then take the following tack: "*If* analogous to a system in the sense required, the knowledge of any being proposed as omniscient *would* be demonstrably incomplete. But perhaps that merely indicates that omniscience is *not* analogous to any system. Perhaps the knowledge of an omniscient being not only cannot be conceived of on the model of a standard system such as those of section I but also cannot be conceived of in terms of any *system* at all."

Full vindication of the arguments above against such a reply would call for further work. One option here would be to carefully strengthen, strand by strand, the relevant analogy between systems and knowers—to emphasize how little is really required by the notion of 'system' at issue, how a set of propositions known *will* have the crucial formal properties of a set of theorems, and so forth. Another option would be to rephrase the incompleteness arguments of the preceding sections entirely in terms of knowers and what they know, thereby avoiding talk of 'systems' entirely.

With patience, I think, even the more complex second argument above could be defended in one of these ways. But perhaps none of this is necessary. A short and direct Cantorian argument, offered below, seems to give us the same conclusion while avoiding the complications of systems altogether.

Consider also a related objection. Even where not tied to formal systems, an objector might claim, the arguments above are at least tied to formal *languages* in some way. "Perhaps the arguments above indicate only that there can be no language adequate for the representation of all truths, or indicate only that there can be no divine *language* in the relevant sense."[39]

This, I think, would be a mistake. What the arguments above require is not formal languages but merely certain features analogous to those of formal languages—features which may themselves be quite natural and *non*linguistic features of knowers, minds, or sets of things known. The first argument against omniscience above, for example, is phrased entirely in terms of just objects of knowledge—things about which something is known—and conceptions of properties.[40]

We can, at any rate, sidestep this second objection in the same way as the first. The Cantorian argument of the following section seems to cut quite neatly through complications of either systems or languages.

VI. THERE IS NO SET OF ALL TRUTHS

There is no set of all truths.

For suppose there *were* a set **T** of all truths, and consider all subsets of **T**, elements of the power set $\mathcal{P}\mathbf{T}$.

To each element of this power set will correspond a truth. To each set of the power set, for example, a particular truth T_1 either will or will not belong as a member. In either case we will have a truth: that T_1 is a member of that set, or that it is not.[41]

There will then be at least as many truths as there are elements of the power set $\mathcal{P}\mathbf{T}$. But by Cantor's power set theorem the power set of any set will be larger than the original. There will then be *more* truths than there are members of **T**, and for *any* set of truths **T** there will be some truth left out.

There can be no set of all truths.

One thing this gives us is a short and sweet Cantorian argument against omniscience, uncomplicated by systems or formal languages:

Were there an omniscient being, what that being would know would constitute a set of all truths. But there can be no set of all truths and so can be no omniscient being.[42]

Let me digress slightly in order to mention some further implications of the argument as well, however. One victim of such an argument, it appears, is a common approach to the notion of *possible worlds* and in particular to the notion of an *actual* world.

Possible worlds are often introduced as maximal consistent sets of propositions—proposition-saturated sets to which no further proposition can be added without precipitating inconsistency—or as some sort of fleshed-out correlates to such sets. The *actual* world, on such an account, is that maximal consistent set of propositions all members of which actually obtain—a maximal and consistent set of all and only *truths*—or is an appropriately fleshed-out correlate to such a set.[43]

By the argument above, however, there is not and cannot be any set of all truths. *Any* set of true propositions will leave some true proposition out, and thus there can be no maximal set of truths. In this sense of 'actual world', then, there is and can be no actual world.[44]

It should perhaps not be too surprising that the notion of an actual world outlined above faces difficulties similar to those that can be raised against omniscience. These are, after all, largely correlative notions. That which would be known in omniscience is that which would obtain in such an actual world—omniscience is the epistemic correlate to this metaphysical conception of the actual world.

It should also be noted that the argument above can be applied against the existence of some 'smaller' sets as well. Consider for example the set not of all truths but merely of all *metamathematical* truths. *Is* there such a set?

Here we first have to answer a clarificatory question. Does each truth regarding the membership of a set of metamathematical truths itself qualify as a metamathematical truth? If so, by an argument perfectly analogous to that offered above, there will be no set of all metamathematical truths; each set of metamathematical truths will leave out some metamathematical truth.[45]

The same will hold for any set of truths of a type θ, where truths regarding membership in sets of truths of type θ themselves qualify as truths of that type. For no such type of truths will there be a set of *all* truths of such a type.

VII. ALTERNATIVE SET THEORIES: A POSSIBLE WAY OUT?

The simple Cantorian argument runs as follows:

Were there an omniscient being, what that being would know would constitute a set of all truths. But there can be no set of all truths, and so can be no omniscient being.

Might we not give up the idea of a *set* of all truths, however, or of what an omniscient being knows as a *set* of things known, and substitute something else here instead? Perhaps there is no set of all truths, but there *is* a *class* of all truths (or *proper class* or *ultimate class*) in the sense of alternative set theories. Will this offer a way out?

The short answer, I think, is no.[46]

All axiomatic set theory, standard or alternative, is essentially a response to two paradoxes: Cantor's paradox regarding a set of all sets and Russell's paradox regarding a set of all non-self-membered sets. By the Aussonderung axiom of standard ZF set theory, of course, there simply *are* no such sets. What we've suggested in preceding sections, in effect, is that a "set of all truths" leads to similar difficulties and should be similarly abandoned.

In some alternative set theories something like Cantor's and Russell's sets do appear, however—though in the guise of 'classes' or 'ultimate classes' or 'proper classes', carefully distinguished from sets and for which different principles hold. But in one way or another all such alternatives seem to come to grief.

Quine's "New Foundations" and the von Neumann-Bernays system, for example, both avoid paradox by effectively crippling the mechanism of Cantor's theorem, and in that sense may seem to offer hope for something like a class of all truths. NF and VNB also share one crucial and quite exorbitant cost, however: both entail a sacrifice of general mathematical induction.[47] As Quine concludes with respect to NF,

> the fact remains that mathematical induction of unstratified conditions is not generally provided for. . . . This omission seems needless and arbitrary. It hints that the standards of class existence . . . approximate insufficiently, after all, to the considerations that are really central to the paradoxes and their avoidance.[48]

Quine's system in *Mathematical Logic* and a modified VNB he suggests, on the other hand, both manage to remedy this glaring inadequacy with respect to mathematical induction. In order to do so, however, both restore the basic mechanism of the Cantorian argument just enough to dash any hopes for either a class of all classes or a class of all truths.

If these are any sample, then, alternative set theories do not seem a very promising route of escape. For our purposes, moreover, these technical problems are only one of the marks against them.

Ultimate classes in general, in whatever alternative system, are introduced as classes which are not members of further classes. But a "class of all truths" would surely not qualify as ultimate in that sense. Wouldn't it be a member of the class of classes of propositions? Wouldn't it form an ordered pair with the class of all false propositions?

Consider also the class of classes of things known by existent beings—wouldn't what God knows be a member of *that* class?

In the end, I think, the ultimate classes of alternative set theory turn out to be an unacceptable option even on simple intuitive grounds. This last difficulty is closely related to Quine's general objection:

> [VNB modified] shares a serious drawback with ML, and with von Neumann's unextended system, and with any other system that invokes ultimate classes . . . We want to be able to form finite classes, in all ways, of all things there are assumed to be . . . and the trouble is that ultimate classes will not belong.[49]

VIII. VERSUS PLANTINGA AND WITTGENSTEIN: CONCLUSION

I have attempted above to use Cantor and Gödel in suggesting an argument, or group of arguments, against omniscience—that there can in principle be no being that knows everything. There can in fact be no set of all truths, and alternative set theory offers little hope for even an ultimate *class* of all truths as an alternative.

Does the work above actually show that omniscience is impossible?

As noted in the introduction, philosophical speculation regarding metalogical results is a notoriously risky business. With that in mind I have confined myself throughout to *suggesting* Cantorian and Gödelian arguments against omniscience, offering these as arguments worthy of consideration, but without trumpeting them as proofs.

Nonetheless, philosophical speculation—however risky—also has its place. In that spirit let me stick my neck out at least this far:

Is omniscience impossible?

Within any logic we have, I think, the answer is yes.

What I mean is this. In terms of either systems or sets, on the basis of work presented above, omniscience appears to be simply incoherent. All the logic we have, however, is essentially a matter of systems and sets. Within any logic we have there appears to be no coherent notion of omniscience.

The theist, of course, can be expected to pounce on the crucial qualifying phrase above—"within any logic we have." "Perhaps our logic is merely inadequate to do justice to the notion of omniscience. Perhaps some other logic, *not* a matter of mere systems and sets, eventually within our grasp or forever beyond our grasp, *would* allow us a coherent notion of omniscience."

What gives this response plausibility is the fact that new logics *have* been developed to serve special needs. And perhaps it could be done again. Perhaps despite appearances it would be possible to specify a 'bunch' or 'gob' that *would* coherently collect all truths in a way that neither sets nor their alternative classes can. Perhaps. As things stand, however, the theist's invocation of that "perhaps" is merely a promissory note on a debt of coherence—a second or third or fourth mortgage on omniscience.

Note also that the same response could be made in behalf of *any* position, however ludicrous, and in the face of *any* argument, however rigorous. Perhaps our logic is merely inadequate to do justice to the notion of circular squares or married bachelors.[50] As it stands, then, the theist's response does nothing to distinguish omniscience from any of various incoherent notions that fall victim to logical argument.

Epistemological and metaphysical aspects of the work above have of course been mentioned throughout. Let me summarize these suggestions, however, by way of points regarding Plantinga and Wittgenstein respectively.

Gaunilo, a contemporary of Anselm's, parodied Anselm's ontological argument for the existence of God by constructing a parallel argument for a greatest possible island. In defending a form of Anselm's argument for Anselm's God, Plantinga attempts to avoid Gaunilo's argument for Gaunilo's island. He does so by insisting that the great-making characteristics of islands, unlike those of God, are without *intrinsic maxima*:

> The idea of an island than which it's not possible that there be a greater is like the idea of a natural number than which it's not possible that there be a greater. . . . There neither is nor could be a greatest possible natural number; indeed, there isn't a greatest *actual* number, let alone a greatest possible. And the same goes for islands. No matter how great an island is, no matter how many Nubian maidens and dancing girls adorn it, there could always be a greater—one with twice as many, for example. The qualities that make for greatness in islands— numbers of palm trees, amount and quality of coconuts, for example—most of these qualities have no *intrinsic maximum*. That is, there is no degree of productivity or number of palm trees (or of dancing girls) such that it is impossible that an island display more of that quality. So the idea of a greatest possible island is an inconsistent or incoherent idea; it's not possible that there be such a thing. . . .
>
> But doesn't Anselm's argument founder on the same rock? If the idea of a greatest possible island is inconsistent, won't the same hold for the idea of a greatest possible being? Perhaps not. . . . Anselm clearly has in mind such properties as wisdom, knowledge, power, and moral excellence or moral perfection. And certainly knowledge, for example, does have an intrinsic maximum. . . .[51]

What the argument of the preceding sections suggests, however, is that knowledge does *not* have an intrinsic maximum. The case of a "greatest possible number" would in fact be perfectly analogous here. For any natural number, there is a greater. What the Cantorian argument suggests is that for any body of knowledge—that possessed by any particular being, for example—there is some truth it leaves out, and so some body of knowledge beyond it.

If knowledge has no intrinsic maximum, of course, the notion of an omniscient being itself becomes "an inconsistent or incoherent idea; it's not possible that there be such a thing."

Metaphysical aspects of the work above can be summarized using Wittgenstein. The opening lines of the *Tractatus* run as follows:

1* The world is all that is the case.

1.1 The world is the totality of facts, not of things.

1.11 The world is determined by the facts, and by their being *all* the facts.[52]

What the arguments of the preceding sections suggest is that these famous lines must be dead wrong.[53] Given Cantor and Gödel, it appears, there simply *is* no totality of facts or of all that is the case. The universe itself, on such a view— like any knowledge or description of it—is essentially open and incomplete.[54]

NOTES

1. Defining omniscience is harder than it looks. In the first section of "Some Neglected Problems of Omniscience," *American Philosophical Quarterly* 20 (1983): 265–76, I argue that definitions offered by Peter Geach, A. N. Prior, Richard Swinburne, James F. Ross, and William E. Mann are inadequate. As a replacement I there suggest the following:

x is *omniscient* $=_{df.}$ for all p, p is true IFF x believes that p,
AND x believes that p IFF x knows that p.

For the purposes of this paper, however, all that is crucial is that any omniscient being will believe all and only truths.

2. Witness for example the checkered history of J. R. Lucas, "Minds, Machines, and Gödel," *Philosophy* 36 (1961): 112–27 (repr. in Alan Ross Anderson, *Minds and Machines* [Englewood Cliffs, N.J.: Prentice-Hall, 1964], pp. 43–59). Among its many replies, see esp. Judson Webb, "Metamathematics and the Philosophy of Mind," *Philosophy of Science* 35 (1968): 156–78, and Paul Benacerraf, "God, the Devil, and Gödel," *Monist* 51 (1967): 9–32.

3. The notion of a 'formal system' is stretched well beyond familiar limits in the course of the discussion, however.

4. Which are the *basic* truths of a body of knowledge, of course, may be relative to the choice of transformation rules. Even given a particular set of transformation rules, moreover, there may be alternative sets of truths any of which might be taken as basic.

5. Judson Webb notes in "Metamathematics," p. 167, that

whether or not a discipline regarding a given subject matter can be deductively systematized is simply the question whether or not the set T of true sentences about the subject matter is recursively enumerable . . .

If requirements on 'systems' are relaxed beyond recursive enumerability, even this will not restrict those bodies of knowledge which might be captured as 'systems'.

6. It might be thought that the following is an additional obstacle to any comparison between knowers and formal systems: a (standard) formal system, if it is to exclude any formula as a nontheorem, must be consistent. Knowers, on the other hand, are rarely if ever perfectly consistent.

There are unusual systems in which inconsistency does not result in the inclusion of everything as a theorem—see for example: Nicholas Rescher and Robert Brandom, *The Logic of Inconsistency* (Totowa, N.J.: Rowman and Littlefield, 1979); *Paraconsistent Logic: Essays on the Inconsistent*, ed. Graham Priest, Richard Routley, and Jean Norman (New York: Philosophia-Verlag, 1990); Richard Routley, *Relevant Logics and Their Rivals* (Atascadero: Ridgeview, 1984); and N. C. A. Da Costa, "On the Theory of Inconsistent Formal Systems," *Notre Dame Journal of Formal Logic* 15 (1974): 497–510. But at any rate inconsistency cannot pose a problem if we limit ourselves to formal systems analogous to merely *what a knower knows*. For no matter how inconsistent I—a knower—may be in my beliefs, *what I know* must be perfectly consistent. It must be consistent simply because what I know must all be true.

7. Jaakko Hintikka, *Knowledge and Belief* (Ithaca, N.Y.: Cornell University Press, 1962), p. 29. The rules at issue here are the following:

(A.~K) If λ is consistent and if "~*Kap*" ∈ λ, then λ + {"*Pa~p*"} is also consistent.
(A.~P) If λ is consistent and if "~*Pap*" ∈ λ, then λ + {"*Ka~p*"} is also consistent.

8. Ibid., p. 36. Alternatively, Hintikka proposes a reinterpretation of his operators; that "*Kap*" should perhaps be read not as "*a* knows that *p*" but "it follows from what *a* knows that *p*" (p. 38).

But Hintikka has since changed his tune. He now emphasizes that the difficulty above arises only if we insist that every epistemically possible world is logically possible. See Kriste Taylor, "Worlds in Collision," *Philosophia* 13 (1983): 289–97, and Jaakko Hintikka, "Impossible Possible Worlds Vindicated," *Journal of Philosophical Logic* 4 (1975): 475–84.

9. This point actually applies to bodies of knowledge as well—it is only *ideal* bodies of knowledge that are to be captured by standard systems.

We might be able to simulate *non*ideal knowers, and *non*ideal bodies of knowledge, by means of crippled transformation rules. This is in fact one way of characterizing Nicholas Rescher and Robert Brandom's intriguing work on belief in esp. chapter 19 of *The Logic of Inconsistency*. Here, however, it *is* ideal knowers and bodies of knowledge that are at issue.

10. A more standard statement of the standard Gödel incompleteness result is the following. Consider any formal system with recursively recognizable formulae and axioms, rules of inference only from finite sets of premises, and which is adequate at least for the purposes of number theory. If any such system is omega-consistent, it is unavoid-

ably incomplete; something will be left out. Syntactically put: for some formula expressible in the system, neither that formula nor its negation will appear as a theorem. Semantically put: some truth of number theory will not be captured as a theorem in the system.

I do not consider my purpose here to be that of a general introduction to Gödel—that has been done wonderfully elsewhere by others. I have in mind particularly Ernest Nagel and James R. Newman, "Gödel's Proof," *Scientific American* 194, no. 6 (June 1956): 71–86 (repr. in *Contemporary Philosophical Logic*, ed. Irving M. Copi and James A. Gould [New York: St. Martin's Press, 1978], pp. 14–34; expanded as *Gödel's Proof* [New York: New York University Press, 1958]), and of course Douglas Hofstadter, *Gödel, Escher, Bach: An Eternal Golden Braid* (New York: Vintage Books, 1979).

11. In Rosser's extension of Gödel's theorems, Gödel's stronger hypothesis of omega-consistency is replaced with the weaker hypothesis of mere consistency. See Barkley Rosser, "Extensions of Some Theorems of Gödel and Church," *Journal of Symbolic Logic* 1 (1936): 87–91.

12. The attempt to 'fill in' incompleteness holes in such a manner eventually leads one to a progression which corresponds to that of the constructive ordinals. But by a result due to Alonzo Church and Stephen C. Kleene, "Formal Definitions in the Theory of Ordinal Numbers," *Fundamenta Mathematicae* 28 (1936): 11–21, there is no recursively related notation system adequate even for *naming* each of the constructive ordinals.

13. On essential undecidability in this sense see Alfred Tarski, Andrzej Mostowski, and Raphael M. Robinson, *Undecidable Theories* (Amsterdam: North-Holland, 1968), and R. L. Goodstein, "The Significance of Incompleteness Theorems," *British Journal for the Philosophy of Science* 14 (1963): 208–20.

14. See for example Benacerraf, "God, the Devil, and Gödel."

15. Geoffrey Hellman, "How to Gödel a Frege-Russell: Gödel's Incompleteness Theorems and Logicism," *Noûs* 15 (1981): 451–68. Similar comments on the peculiarity of nonconstructive methods appear in Hofstadter, *Gödel, Escher, Bach*, p. 470, and Hao Wang, *A Survey of Mathematical Logic* (Peking and Amsterdam: Science Press and North Holland, 1964), pp. 318–19.

16. I have not here included work involving nondenumerable alphabets or formulae of infinite length, each of which seems to fizzle out at the level of first-order predicate calculus.

Nondenumerably many symbols appeared in a system Leon Henkin used to show completeness for first-order functional calculus ("The Completeness of First-Order Functional Calculus," *Journal of Symbolic Logic* 14 [1949]: 159–66). The limitations of the system even in that context are comparable to those of S_∞ in Gentzen's consistency proof for first-order number theory, considered below.

Henkin originally considered three ways in which infinite formulae might be introduced: (1) by means of infinitary predicate symbols and hence infinitely long primitive formulae, (2) by means of infinitely long conjunctions and disjunctions together with quantification over infinitely many variables, and (3) infinitely alternating quantifiers of a peculiar type (Leon Henkin, "Some Remarks on Infinitely Long Formulas," *Infinitistic Methods*, ed. International Mathematical Union and Mathematical Institute of the Polish Academy of Sciences (New York: Pergamon Press, 1961). It is the second of these that has been most developed, in particular in the work of Carol R. Karp, especially *Languages with Expressions of Infinite Length* (Amsterdam: North Holland, 1964).

For some such predicate systems $L_{\alpha\beta}$, in which conjunctions of fewer than α formulae and quantifications of fewer than β variables are permitted, completeness can be proven. A fairly uninteresting case here is $L_{\omega\omega}$, which is simply the standard predicate calculus without extension to infinite formulae. Where genuinely infinite formulae are at issue, completeness holds only for those predicate systems in which an ability to handle conjunctions outstrips an ability to handle quantifications. Jon Barwise, G. Kreisel, and Dana Scott have expressed doubts about any such system admitting infinite quantifiers (Jon Barwise, "Infinitary Logic and Admissible Sets," *Journal of Symbolic Logic* 34 [1969]: 227). But at any rate no definable system in which $\alpha = \beta = \gamma^{+}$, where γ is infinite—even if the underlying system has only one two-place predicate in addition to equality—will be complete (see Karp, *Languages*, pp. 166–74).

17. Barkley Rosser, "Gödel Theorems for Non-Constructive Logics," *Journal of Symbolic Logic* 2 (1937): 129–37.

18. The standard use of S_∞—to prove consistency for first-order numbers theory—is not here of much importance. In my sketch of S_∞ I follow Elliot Mendelson, *Introduction to Mathematical Logic* (Princeton, N.J.: D. Van Nostrand, 1964), pp. 258–70. But see also Wang, *A Survey*, pp. 362–75.

19. Mendelson, *Introduction to Mathematical Logic*, p. 270.

20. See Mendelson, *Introduction to Mathematical Logic*, p. 270; Wang, *A Survey*, pp. 369–70; and Webb, "Metamathematics," p. 177.

21. A result attributed to Rosser in Wang, *A Survey*, p. 45.

22. Solomon Feferman, "Transfinite Recursive Progressions of Axiomatic Theories," *Journal of Symbolic Logic* 27 (1962): 259–316; see also Solomon Feferman, "Arithmetization of Metamathematics in a General Setting," *Fundamenta Mathematicae* 49 (1960): 3–92, and Solomon Feferman and C. Spector, "Incompleteness Along Paths in Progressions of Theories," *Journal of Symbolic Logic* 27 (1962): 383–90.

23. Feferman, "Transfinite Recursive Progressions," p. 261.

24. Ibid., pp. 261–62, 286.

25. Michael D. Resnik, "On the Philosophical Significance of Consistency Proofs," *Journal of Philosophical Logic* 3 (1974): 133–47.

26. R. G. Jeroslow, "Consistency Statements in Formal Theories," *Fundamenta Mathematicae* 72 (1971): 25. Jeroslow also shows that consistency statements which differ from Feferman's can be proven in extraordinarily weak systems.

27. Feferman, "Transfinite Recursive Progressions," p. 314.

28. R. G. Jeroslow, "Experimental Logics and Δ_2^0-Theories," *Journal of Philosophical Logic* 4 (1975): 253–67; see also Peter Hajek, "Experimental Logics and Π_3^0 Theories," *Journal of Symbolic Logic* 42 (1977): 515–22.

29. Jeroslow, "Experimental Logics," p. 256. The systems at issue, however, are still in some sense mechanical. See esp. p. 255.

30. Ibid., pp. 257, 264–65.

31. The most promising candidates here would seem to be systems with nonrecursively enumerable sets of axioms.

32. As specified here these include only one-place predicates, for the sake of simplicity. The basic structure of the argument would be the same, however, if all n-ary predicates were included.

33. There are of course many standard presentations. See for example Irving M. Copi, *Symbolic Logic*, Fifth Edition (New York: Macmillan, 1979), pp. 185–90. My treatment below follows Copi's closely.

34. This argument is related to an incompleteness argument for finitary formal systems presented in Geoffrey Hunter, *Metalogic* (Berkeley: University of California Press, 1971), pp. 28–30, and to some wonderful work by Hans Herzberger, "Paradoxes of Grounding in Semantics," *Journal of Philosophy* 67 (1970): 145–69, and "New Paradoxes for Old," *Proceedings of the Aristotelian Society* 81 (1981): 109–23, and Hans Herzberger and Radhika Herzberger, "Bhartrhari's Paradox," *Journal of Indian Philosophy* 9 (1981): 1–17. The form of the argument offered here, however, is perhaps most similar to Johannes Baagoe, "God, Ghosts, and Gödel," *Second Order* 4 (1975): 32–35. Baagoe's is a marvelous piece of work to which I owe a very great debt.

35. See note 11.

36. That form of Gödel's proof that the argument of this section most closely resembles, perhaps, is Gödel's own less formal presentation in the opening pages of Kurt Gödel, "On Formally Undecidable Propositions of *Principia Mathematica* and Related Systems I," *From Frege to Gödel: A Source Book in Mathematical Logic: 1879–1931*, ed. Jean van Heijenoort (Cambridge, Mass.: Harvard University Press, 1967), pp. 596–616. Gödel himself notes a resemblance to Richard's paradox, itself but a step away from some of the Cantorian techniques employed here.

37. Here and throughout the argument, for noble motives of simplicity, I will unabashedly exploit a particular ambiguity: P^o will sometimes be referred to as an object of the system—that to which a predicate on interpretation *applies*—and yet will also appear as a term *for* such an object in formulae such as $f(P^o)P^o$. A similar ambiguity appears in many informal presentations of Gödel, and with good reason: the attempt to avoid it adds merely one more subtlety for the reader to try to keep track of. As a corrective for this type of subterfuge, however, see F. J. Fitzpatrick, "To Gödel via Babel," *Mind* 75 (1966): 232–50.

38. Strictly speaking, this is a somewhat stronger assumption than mere consistency, but such a simplification is fairly standard in informal presentations of Gödel and seems harmless in the present context.

39. The expressive incompleteness argument of section III was of course characterized as showing that no language can be adequate for the expression of all truths. The objector's suggestion here is that perhaps that is all that any of the arguments really show.

40. There is no need here to treat 'truths' as linguistic entities in any sense. The argument would be the same against any supposed set of all true propositions or of all facts—at least in the ordinary sense of 'fact' in which it's a fact that $7 + 5 = 12$.

With regard to truths and linguistic entities, another Cantorian argument should also be noted. In *Thinking and Doing: The Philosophical Foundations of Institutions* (Boston: Reidel, 1975), pp. 34 ff., Hector-Neri Castañeda uses a Cantorian argument to show that propositions are not reducible to classes of sentences.

41. There is of course nothing special about T_1 here—we could have used any particular truth in its place. There are also myriad other ways of constructing a truth for each element $\mathcal{P}T$.

For a slightly expanded form of the argument, see Patrick Grim, "There Is No Set of All Truths," *Analysis* 44 (1984): 206–208.

42. In personal correspondence, J. H. Sobel has outlined a very similar Cantorian argument against omniscience, developed independently. Sobel has also pointed out that such an argument can be constructed against even a *non*omniscient being of a certain type. Consider any being which, although perhaps *not* omniscient, does know *itself* very well: it knows (*de re*, let us say), for each set that contains only propositions that it knows, *that* that set contains only propositions that it knows. Consider now the set of all propositions that that being knows and the power set of that set. To each set of the power set will correspond a proposition that our being, as specified, knows—that that set consists only of propositions it knows. But by Cantor's theorem there are more elements of the power set, and thus more propositions our being knows, than in the original set—the set of *all* propositions that the being knows. There can be no such being, then, and even 'Know thyself' has Cantorian limits.

David L. Boyer has pointed out that the argument against omniscience can also be presented without explicit mention of sets of truths:

Let us assume there is an omniscient God. Consider all that such a being would know, and consider further what would be known by each of a chorus of archangels meeting the following conditions:

Each archangel knows something, no two archangels know precisely the same thing, and for each archangel there is something that God knows and it does not.

Let us also add two more 'archangels', in a somewhat extended sense: an archangel who knows absolutely nothing and God himself. (This is not entirely without theological precedent, by the way: Aquinas claims that to each degree of being there corresponds a being.)

Now for each of the archangels envisaged there would be something that an omniscient being would know: that it is possible that such a being exists, perhaps, or that it is not possible; that the knowledge of that archangel would include the fact that seven is prime, perhaps, or that it would not. There will then be at least as many things God knows as envisaged archangels.

By the basic mechanisms of Cantor's power set theorem, however, there will be *more* archangels than things God knows. Our initial assumption leads to contradiction, then, and so must be rejected: there is no omniscient God.

43. See Robert M. Adams, "Theories of Actuality," *Noûs* 17 (1974): 211–31; Alvin Plantinga, *The Nature of Necessity* (Oxford: Clarendon, 1974) and *God, Freedom, and Evil* (Grand Rapids, Michigan: Wm. B. Eerdmans, 1980). This is not, however, the only way that possible worlds have been introduced. In David Lewis, *Counterfactuals* (Cambridge, Mass.: Harvard University Press, 1973), for example, possible worlds are ways things might have been. In Michael Slote, *Metaphysics and Essence* (Oxford: Basil Blackwell, 1975), they are possible histories of *the* world. Whether possible worlds in these senses must be analogously incomplete is a question I leave to others or to another paper.

44. For a similar argument against possible worlds using a variation on the paradox of the Liar, see Grim, "Some Neglected Problems of Omniscience."

45. Does every conjunction of mathematical truths, even if transfinite, correspond to a mathematical truth? If so, there is not even a set of all *mathematical* truths. Here the argument would be the same as the above except that to each element of the power set of a supposed set of all mathematical truths would correspond that mathematical truth represented by the conjunction of all members of that set.

46. For a longer answer, see especially: W. V. O. Quine, *Set Theory and Its Logic* (Cambridge, Mass.: Harvard University Press, 1963); Abraham A. Fraenkel, Yehoshua Bar-Hillel, and Azriel Levy, *Foundations of Set Theory*, Second Revised Edition (Amsterdam: North-Holland, 1973); and K. Kuratowski and A. Mostowski, *Set Theory* (Amsterdam: North-Holland; Warsaw: PWN, 1966).

I have not included here a section on many-valued set theories. But these don't seem to offer a plausible way out either; many-valued logics exhibit many-valued forms of the Liar and of Russell's paradox, and for essentially the same reasons can be expected to exhibit many-valued forms of the Cantorian argument above as well. In this regard see Nicholas Rescher, *Many-valued Logic* (New York: McGraw-Hill, 1969), esp. pp. 87–90 and 206–12.

47. NF has other difficulties as well. Barkley Rosser and Hao Wang, "Non-Standard Models for Formal Logic," *Journal of Symbolic Logic* 15 (1950): 113–29, initially showed that no model of NF—no interpretation of '$\in$' compatible with the axioms— could make well-orderings of both the lesser-to-greater relation among ordinals and that among finite cardinals, except by interpreting ' $=$ ' as something other than identity. Ernest Specker, "The Axiom of Choice in Quine's New Foundations for Mathematical Logic," *Proceedings of the National Academy of Sciences* 39 (1953): 972–75, went on to show that those sets of NF which are non-Cantorian cause the relations of lesser to greater among cardinals to fail of being a well-ordering, and thereby produced a disproof of the axiom of choice within NF.

48. Quine, *Set Theory and Its Logic*, p. 199. In a similar spirit Fraenkel, Bar-Hillel, and Levy note in *Foundations of Set Theory*, p. 139, drawing on work by Mostowski:

A particularly embarrassing fact about VNB is that in VNB . . . one cannot prove all instances of the induction schema, "If 0 fulfils the condition $D(x)$ and for every natural number n, if n fulfils $?(x)$ then $n + 1$ fulfils $D(x)$ too, then every number fulfils $D(x)$."

49. Quine, *Set Theory and Its Logic*, p. 312.

50. With regard to circular squares, serious work in a Meinongian tradition should perhaps be mentioned, including: Terence Parsons, *Nonexistent Objects* (New Haven: Yale University Press, 1980); William J. Rapaport, "Meinongian Theories and a Russellian Paradox," *Noûs* 12 (1978): 153–80 (errata, *Noûs* 13 [1979]: 125) and "An Adverbial Meinongian Theory," *Analysis* 39 (1979): 75–81; Richard Routley, *Exploring Meinong's Jungle and Beyond* (Canberra: Philosophy Dept., Research School of Social Studies, Australian National University, 1980); Edward N. Zalta, *Abstract Objects* (Boston: Reidel, 1983); and Castañeda's guise theory (see esp. Alvin Plantinga's "Guise Theory," and Castañeda's reply, in *Agent, Language, and the Structure of the World: Essays Presented to Hector-Neri Castañeda, with his Replies*, ed. James Tomberlin [Indianapolis: Hackett, 1983]). Regarding paraconsistent logics, designed to incorporate carefully quarantined contradictions, see esp.: Da Costa, "On the Theory of Inconsistent Formal Systems," and references; *Paraconsistent Logic*, ed. Graham Priest, Richard Routley, and Jean Norman; Routley, *Relevant Logics*; and related work in Rescher and Brandom, *The Logic of Inconsistency*.

51. Plantinga, *God, Freedom, and Evil*, pp. 90–91. For further crucial work on Plantinga's treatment of Gaunilo, see Patrick Grim, "Plantinga's God and Other Monstrosities," *Religious Studies* 15 (1979): 91–97, and "In Behalf of 'In Behalf of the Fool,'" *International Journal for Philosophy of Religion* 42 (1982): 33–42.

52. Ludwig Wittgenstein, *Tractatus Logico-Philosophicus* (London: Routledge and Kegan Paul, 1961), p. 7.

53. To quote Wittgenstein is to risk contradiction by Wittgensteinian scholars, however. Evan W. Conyers has argued in personal correspondence that 'facts' appear in the *Tractatus* in a technical sense that does not include '7 + 5 = 12' or truths regarding set membership such as those relied on in the arguments above.

54. I have many people to thank for tolerating me at various points in the long development of this set of ideas. I am grateful to Hector-Neri Castañeda, Geoffrey Hunter, and A. J. Stenner for encouragement at crucial points, and to David Auerbach, David L. Boyer, Robert F. Barnes, Evan W. Conyers, and Christopher Martin for more recent help.

I would like to dedicate this paper to the memory of my father.

33

THE BEING THAT KNEW TOO MUCH

PATRICK GRIM

INTRODUCTION

John Abbruzzese has recently attempted a defense of omniscience against a series of my attacks.[1] This affords me a welcome occasion to clarify some of the arguments, to pursue some neglected subtleties, and to rethink some important complications. In the end, however, I must insist that at least three of four crucial arguments really do show an omniscient being to be impossible. Abbruzzese sometimes misunderstands the forms of the arguments themselves and quite generally misunderstands their force.

The fourth argument—the Cantorian argument against omniscience—has a more complicated status. The possibility that such an argument is somehow self-defeating is an intriguing one, with deep philosophical implications for propositional quantification in general.[2] This is the one aspect of my earlier work about which I've come to have the gravest second thoughts. But the second thoughts I have to offer here are second thoughts about the nature of a particular class of arguments and perhaps about the character of argument in general. I don't believe those second thoughts ultimately offer any hope for omniscience.

From *International Journal for Philosophy of Religion* 47 (2000): 141–54. Copyright © 2000 by Kluwer Academic Publishers. Reprinted with kind permission of Kluwer Academic Publishers.

THE ESSENTIAL INDEXICAL ARGUMENT

No one else—no one other than me—knows what I know in knowing that:

(1) I am making a mess.

The closest others may get is knowing that

(2) Patrick Grim is making a mess,

or perhaps

(3) He (indicating me *de re*) is making a mess.

But what they know when they know (2) or (3) is not what I know in knowing (1).

It is easy to construct cases which make it clear that I might know what others know in knowing (2) without knowing what I know in knowing (1). I might know that Patrick Grim is making a mess without knowing that *I* am making a mess, for example, simply because I fail to realize that I am Patrick Grim.

It is also easy to construct cases with fish-eye mirrors which make it clear that I might know what others know in knowing (3) without knowing what I know in knowing (1). I might know that *he* is making a mess without knowing that *I* am making a mess simply because I fail to realize that *he*—that clumsy oaf in the mirror—is *me*.

The argument can be constructed for indexicals other than 'I' as well. What I come to realize when I realize the meeting is starting *now* is not simply what others know when they know that the meeting starts (timelessly) at noon. The fact that I know the meeting is starting *now* fully explains my hurry to gather up materials required for the meeting. My knowing that the meeting starts at noon would *not* explain that hurry, unless we added that I also knew that it is *now* noon, thereby reintroducing the indexical. What I know now explains something that my knowing what others might know timelessly or at other times could not explain. The two things must therefore be different: what I know now is not merely what they know then. A similar argument using indexicals of place can be rehearsed regarding my knowledge that the bomb is scheduled to fall *here*.

It thus appears that there are things that can be known *now* that simply cannot be known timelessly. No timeless being can therefore be omniscient. It appears there are things that I know—when I know I am making a mess, for example—that others simply cannot know. If so, since I am not omniscient, there are things that I know that no omniscient being could know. But an omniscient being would have to know at least all that I know. There can therefore be no omniscient being.

Abbruzzese's defense of omniscience in such cases amounts to the observation that

> . . . feelings of any kind, I would think, are not included in what we would call knowledge.

> . . . what this knowledge does *not* contain is the feelings of guilt or embarrassment I experienced. . . .

> In light of this, there appears to be an easier way to resolve the problem of essential indexicals and the omniscience of the MPB ['Most Perfect Being']. By definition, the nature of the MPB's knowledge is perfect and would contain, as Grim should admit, all facts. But as we have seen, the knowledge that I have . . . comprises only factual, not emotional parts.[3]

This seems to be a simple misunderstanding of the character of the argument from essential indexicals, not only in my treatment but in Castañeda's, David Lewis's, John Perry's, or Steven Boër and William Lycan's.[4] None of the arguments above suggest that my feelings about anything—my mess-making, the meeting starting, or the bomb dropping—are part of what I know. The structure of the argument would be the same for cases in which I had no particular feeling at all about what was at issue—cases in which I realized that I am the man wearing a purple tie (ho hum), or that it is now 1:00, or that it is here that I bought a paper a week ago.

The argument can be presented by calling attention to certain feelings *explained* by what I know. Beyond that, feelings simply have nothing to do with it. What the argument shows is that two pieces of knowledge cannot be the same because (1) I can know one thing without knowing the other, or (2) my having one explains things that my having the other could not. We don't need feelings to go on to argue that these two pieces of knowledge cannot be the same. The nonidentity of discernibles will suffice.

Although entirely different than Abbruzzese's defense, it should be noted that there *are* some proposals in the later work on essential indexicals that might appear to offer a loophole for omniscience.[5] John Perry, as well as Steven Boër and William Lycan, suggests that what I know when I know that I am making a mess, and what others know when they know that *he* is making a mess, *is* after all the same thing known. What differs, Perry proposes, is not what is known but simply the 'belief state' in which it is known. What differs, Boër and Lycan propose, is not the semantic content of what is believed but merely the pragmatics of terms used to express it. What I know in knowing *de se* that I am making a mess and what you know in knowing *de re* of me that I am making a mess are precisely the same thing, though known in a different 'belief state' or expressed in language with different pragmatics.

On either approach, omniscience might again seem possible. God might, after all, know precisely what I know in knowing that I am making a mess. What he couldn't do is express it in language with the same pragmatics (Boër and Lycan), or know it in the same 'belief state' (Perry).

Neither approach, however, ultimately seems very promising.

When I suddenly realize that the man in the mirror is *me*, there is clearly something that I've learned. There is something that I didn't know before that I do know now. There is indeed a piece of crucial information that I've just acquired that I didn't have before—the fact that it is *me* who is making a mess. But the simple fact that there is something learned, or recognized, or realized in such a case is a simple fact to which neither Perry's nor Boër and Lycan's accounts can do justice, since on both accounts it is emphatically *not* the case that there would be anything new to learn. Perry's analysis of such a case would call for a change in 'belief state'. But Perry is careful to distinguish 'belief states' from what is believed, and thus can't do justice to the fact that some new piece of information is acquired. Boër and Lycan's analysis attempts to explain away differences between *de se* and *de re* in terms of pragmatics alone. But they carefully distinguish the pragmatics of expression from the semantic content of what is believed and thus can't do justice to the fact that there is something that comes to be believed in such a case that wasn't believed before.

Similar comments apply to other indexicals. When I suddenly realize not only that the meeting starts at noon, but that it starts *now*, there is something that I realize for the first time. When I merely knew that the bomb was going to fall at a spot marked on the map, there was a crucial piece of information I lacked— I didn't yet realize that it was going to fall *here*.

We can also appeal to the fact that what I know carries over to other propositional attitudes. What I come to realize in the mess-making case is precisely the thing that I am then ashamed of—the fact that it is *me* that is making a mess. For a case without 'feelings', we can note that what I come to realize in realizing it is me who is wearing the blue tie is precisely one of those facts about my own apparel to which I am so indifferent. What I know in knowing that the meeting is starting now is precisely the thing that surprises me—that the meeting is starting *now*. And what I come to know about the bomb's fall is precisely what I was afraid of—that it would fall *here*.

The straightforward lesson seems to be that it is *not* merely a 'belief state' that changes when I come to recognize, for example, that it is *me* that is making a mess. Nor is the difference to be written off as pragmatics of expression. At least part of what has changed is what I know. In the straightforward ontology of what is known, then—in the straightforward sense of what I know—the argument from indexicals does show quite explicitly that no being can know what I know. In defining 'omniscience' we would expect 'knowledge' to be used in the familiar sense. But in that familiar sense there can be no being that knows everything. There can be no omniscient being.

THE STRENGTHENED DIVINE LIAR

Consider the following:

(4) God doesn't believe that (4) is true.

Is that true or false? If it's true, God doesn't believe it—and thus cannot be said to know all truths. If it's false, on the other hand, it's false that God doesn't believe it. It must then be true that he believes it. God therefore believes a falsehood. If omniscience is not defined to exclude belief in falsehoods, it clearly should be.[6]

(4) is a strengthened version of the Divine Liar. Using 'MPB' for 'Most Perfect Being', Abbruzzese considers merely an unstrengthened version:

(5) The MPB believes that (5) is false.

With that version in mind, Abbruzzese seems to think the Divine Liar is particularly easy to dispose of:

> Grim's use of the Liar paradox to impugn the coherence of omniscience is an illegitimate challenge to the coherence of omniscience simply because it is logically impossible to answer the question whether [5] is true or false, since [5] does not express anything at all; it merely contradicts itself. Indeed, statement [5] is, as Swinburne would say, no more than a garble of words. . . .[7]

There is some fairly basic confusion here; Abbruzzese seems to think that contradictions fail to express anything at all, which leaves one wondering what it is that makes them contradictions. That problem aside, however, it is clear that this reasoning does *not* escape the Strengthened Divine Liar as it appears in (4) above. If (4) fails to express anything at all, or is merely a garble of words, then it clearly is not true. Since Abbruzzese holds that God believes only truths, he must conclude that:

God doesn't believe that (4) is true.

Simple observation, however, makes it clear that this *is* (4).

It thus appears that the Strengthened Divine Liar follows quite directly from

Abbruzzese's own reasoning. He must therefore be committed to its truth. But if (4) is true, God doesn't believe it—and thus cannot be said to know all truths.

We can construct a sentence like this for any being whatsoever. There can therefore be no omniscient being.[8]

OMNISCIENCE AND THE KNOWER

One argument which Abbruzzese does not address is that which builds on the Paradox of the Knower.

Consider any formal system with axioms adequate for arithmetic. Those axioms formalize statements as simple as the principle that zero is the successor of no natural number. We take them to be true on their face, and moreover true because we take arithmetic to be true.

For any such system, we can encode formulae as numbers; here we will use $\bar{A}$ to refer to the numbered encoding for a formula A. It's well known that for any such system we will be able to define a derivability relation I such that $\vdash$ I($\bar{A}$, $\bar{B}$) just in case A is derivable from B.

Let us also introduce a symbol 'Δ' within such a system, applicable in the same way to numerical encodings $\bar{A}$ for formulae A. We might introduce 'Δ' as a way of representing universal knowledge, for example—the knowledge of an omniscient being within at least this limited formal system. Given any such symbol with any such use we would clearly want to maintain each of the following:

If something is known by such a being, it is so. $\Delta\,(\bar{A}) \to A$

This itself is known by such a being. $\overline{\Delta(\Delta\,(\bar{A}) \to A)}$

If A is derivable from B in our system,
and A is known by such a being,
B is known by such a being as well. $I\,(\bar{A}, \bar{B}) \to .\; \Delta\,(\bar{A}) \to \Delta\,(\bar{B})$

The simple truth, however, is that no symbol *can* consistently mean what we have proposed 'Δ' to mean, even in a context as limited as the formal system at issue. The addition of these axioms simply renders the system as a whole inconsistent.[9] One way to put the point is this: that omniscience proves inconsistent in any world adequate for arithmetic.

Both the Knower and the Strengthened Divine Liar, it should be noted, *can* be finessed by familiar hierarchical techniques. The proposal in Russell, Tarski, Kripke, and others is that truth and related predicates form a hierarchy of different levels, each of which applies only to statements (including statements involving truth) on lower levels. On such an approach we know precisely what goes wrong with the Strengthened Divine Liar and the 'Δ' predicate: each attempts to apply a truth-related predicate beyond its hierarchically regulated reach.

The formal charms of a hierarchical approach are many. One thing such an approach doesn't offer, however, is any hope for omniscience. If truth forms such a hierarchy, there can be no notion that applies to truths on *all* levels. That is precisely what the notion of an omniscient being would require.

SECOND THOUGHTS ON THE CANTORIAN ARGUMENT

One thing seems to be established: There can be no set of all truths.

For suppose any set of truths **T**, and consider its power set $\mathcal{P}\mathbf{T}$. For each element of the power set there will be a unique truth—at least the truth that that element contains a particular truth T_1 as a member, for example, or that it does not contain T_1 as a member. By Cantor's Theorem we know that the power set of any set is larger—contains more members—than the set itself. There will then be more truths than are contained in **T**. But **T** was any set of truths. There can therefore be no set of *all* truths.[10]

The argument against omniscience requires one further step. Were there an omniscient being, what such a being knew would constitute a set of all truths. There can be no set of all truths, and therefore can be no omniscient being.

Abbruzzese offers several critiques of the Cantorian argument.

Completed totalities

> Grim . . . [assumes] that the multiplicity of truths, **T**, is a completed totality. This, however, need not be so, for the multiplicity of all truths may be, and in fact seems to be, infinite. . . . Indeed, the totality of all truths, I think, *must* be infinite because, as Grim argues, all truths cannot compose one set, for one can always add another truth to the multiplicity even if only by self-referential propositions, e.g. 'T_1 is true', and 'It is true that "T_1 is true",' and 'It is true that "it is true that" T_1 is true",' *ad infinitum*.[11]

Here again there are some elementary confusions. The argument against a set of all truths holds, precisely as Cantor's Theorem holds, regarding an infinite set of any suggested cardinality. It is indeed clear that there are infinite sets of distinct truths, and it is easy to conjure up sets of truths of higher cardinality than the countable set Abbruzzese exhibits. But no matter what infinite cardinality one proposes for a set of *all* truths, there will be a truth of each element of its power set and thus will be more truths than it contains. Appeal to infinity does nothing to guard against the argument against a set of all truths.

In the passage quoted, Abbruzzese also restricts 'completed totalities' to finite sets, which is simply a mistake—there are plenty of 'completed totalities' in Cantor's sense which are fully infinite. But what of the suggestion that the real target of the argument is not all truths in their plurality but merely the notion that they can somehow be thought of as a 'completed totality'—as a single set? Much the same suggestion, without some of the confusions, appears also in pieces by Richard Cartwright, D. A. Martin, and Keith Simmons.[12]

Although tempting, this kind of appeal to truth as a 'many' rather than a 'one' turns out to be ineffective against Cantorian argument. The argument does not in the end depend in any essential way on reference to a single set, class, or collection of all truths. It can be phrased directly in terms of the 'many', entirely in the plural, and using only a notion of relations between things.

For properties P_1 and P_2, the formal properties of relations we require can be outlined as follows. Those things which are P_1 can be mapped one-to-one *into* those things which are P_2 just in case there is a relation R such that:

$$\forall x \forall y [P_1 x \wedge P_1 y \wedge \exists z (P_2 z \wedge Rxz \wedge Ryz) \rightarrow x = y] \wedge$$
$$\forall x [P_1 x \rightarrow \exists y \forall z (P_2 z \wedge Rxz \leftrightarrow z = y)]$$

Those things which are P_1 can be mapped one-to-one *onto* those things which are P_2 just in case (here we simply add a conjunct):

$$\forall x \forall y [P_1 x \wedge P_1 y \wedge \exists z (P_2 z \wedge Rxz \wedge Ryz) \rightarrow x = y] \wedge$$
$$\forall x [P_1 x \rightarrow \exists y \forall z (P_2 z \wedge Rxz \leftrightarrow z = y)] \wedge$$
$$\forall y [P_2 y \rightarrow \exists x (P_1 x \wedge Rxy)]$$

It will be true for some P_1 and P_2 that a mapping *into* is possible but a mapping *onto* is not; relative to the things that are P_1 there will be too many things that are P_2 to allow a full mapping of those things that are P_1 *onto* those things that are P_2.

Consider, now, any 'many' truths you like—the truths that any particular being knows, for example. Consider also truths about one or more of those truths. Using the notions above, phrased entirely in the plural, it is possible to show that the first truths can be mapped *into* but not *onto* the second truths.[13] There are more of the latter. No matter what truths are at issue, therefore, they cannot be *all* the truths. Appeal to a plural 'many' rather than a single set, like 'one', thus offers no escape. It is still true that there can be no omniscient being.

Alternative set theories

There have also been attempts to rescue omniscience from the grips of the Cantorian argument by appeal to alternative set theories. I consider all such attempts to date unsuccessful, simply because the set theories appealed to bring with them other commitments that are radically counterintuitive with regard to notions of truth. Gary Mar questions the appeal to Cantor, for example, because Cantor's Theorem does not hold in some set theories—it does not hold, in particular, in the system NF.[14] Contrary to Mar's representation, however, the argument need not pause midstride and defer to a set-theoretical theorem. It can be phrased throughout quite simply as a philosophical argument regarding truths. The proposal that we shift to a system such as NF, therefore, is really the proposal that we abandon some of the claims about truth that are instrumental in the argument and adopt others, NF-like, instead.

The technical disappointments of NF are well known—in particular, mathematical induction fails in NF for unstratified conditions.[15] But here it is more relevant that the reason why Cantor's Theorem fails in NF is because the notion of 'sets' is restricted in such a way that only stratified conditions guarantee the existence of corresponding sets. That doesn't mean that other conditions are in any way illicit or ungrammatical in NF, or in any way fail to apply to the things they appear to apply to. All it means is that we are prohibited from referring to those things to which such conditions apply in terms of 'sets'. If we are to carry this over into the context of a fully philosophical argument concerning *truths*, however—an argument that as we have seen need not be phrased in terms of sets at all—the corresponding principle we would have to embrace is that there will be certain pluralities about which there are no *truths*. In the philosophical context, an NF-like 'solution' would have us cheerfully admit that there are certain things—precisely those things that satisfy the diagonal condition of the argument, for example—but would force us to conclude that there can nonetheless be no *truth* about precisely those things. The things themselves fully exist, on such an approach, and they are indeed precisely those things that satisfy the relevant condition. It's just that there is no truth about them—no truth whatsoever.

As a purely formal system, NF can be regarded as an interesting experiment in set-theoretical axiomatics. The claim that there really are things about which there are no truths, on the other hand, is much more serious. The latter is a fully philosophical claim, one that violates our basic concept of truth. In a philosophical context, it is that claim that any NF-like 'defense' of omniscience against the philosophical argument would demand. For that reason, I think, any NF-like defense must prove philosophically unacceptable. It is of course true that we can block some of the problems at issue by radically reconstituting our notion of truth. In terms of the notion of truth that we in fact use, however, and in terms of any notion of omniscience defined in terms of that notion of truth, the problems remain.[16]

Is the Cantorian argument self-defeating?

I come at last to a difficulty with the Cantorian argument that seems significantly more serious. Although already anticipated in *The Incomplete Universe*, the objection appears forcefully in Plantinga and Grim, "Truth, Omniscience and Cantorian Arguments: An Exchange,"[17] and is repeated in Abbruzzese:

> Aside from these points, however, there is a more important logical flaw in Grim's Cantorian argument: it is self-reflexivity inconsistent. The conclusion that there can be no set of all truths implicitly denies the existence of a set of all propositions, and by denying the existence of such universal propositions, Grim is denying existence to the very conclusion of his argument, a conclusion that, to be meaningful, requires quantification over the totality of all things.

As noted, Abbruzzese uses 'MPB' for 'Most Perfect Being':

> Consider now Grim's original argument. His conclusion that 'There is no set of all truths' is equivalent to the universal proposition 'for all X, if X is a set, then X is not a set of all truths'. Moreover, his ultimate conclusion that the MPB does not exist is equivalent to the universal proposition 'for all x, if x exists, then x is not the MPB'. But these propositions involve universal quantification: the former over sets and truths, the latter over the totality of all things. If Grim's conclusion is true, and hence denies existence to these types of propositions, then by that very conclusion, it cannot be meaningfully expressed. Thus, it seems to me that Grim's final objection to omniscience is unsound.[18]

The problem can be tightened. Parallel to the Cantorian argument against a set of all truths is a Cantorian argument to the effect that there can be no proposition about all propositions.[19] But the immediate way of attempting to symbolize that claim, using 'Px' for 'x is a proposition' and 'Axy' for 'x is about y', would appear to be:

$$\neg\exists x(Px \wedge \forall y(Py \rightarrow Axy))$$

or equivalently:

$$\forall x(Px \rightarrow \neg\forall y(Py \rightarrow Axy))$$

or

$$\forall x(Px \rightarrow \exists y(Py \wedge \neg Axy))$$

But such a conclusion has all the marks of a quantification over all propositions—a proposition about all propositions. If there can be no propositions about all propositions, there can be no proposition which expresses such a conclusion. If the Cantorian argument at issue were sound, in other words, it could have no true proposition about all propositions as its conclusion. As an argument for any of the conclusions above, therefore, the Cantorian argument cannot be sound. We have reason to be equally suspicious of parallel arguments, one might suggest, including the original Cantorian argument against a set of all truths.

This is indeed an intriguing logical case. It seems to me that there are two obvious responses, each of which breaks some new logical ground but neither of which ultimately affords any consolation for omniscience.

The first response is simply to reject the attempt to phrase the argument's conclusion in terms of universal quantification over propositions. The argument is, after all, a reductio, demonstrating that the assumption of a proposition genuinely about all propositions leads to contradiction. We might be forgiven for having thought that a reductio from a premise R allows us in all cases to conclude straightforwardly that ¬R. This will not be the case, however, where the reductio turns on the inconsistency of a concept which appears in both R and its negation. In the present case, interestingly enough, the target of the argument—propositional quantification in general—is of such wide scope that the principle usually applicable to reductios cannot be applied.[20]

If someone proposes that a particular proposition P is genuinely about all propositions, however, we will still be able to force him to contradiction by the moves of the argument outlined. We can even see that the argument has a schematic form which will allow us to repeat the argument against the next candidate P′ offered as a proposition about all propositions. What we can't do, interestingly enough, short of falling victim to our own argument, is to draw as conclusion some universal proposition about all propositions.

There may be other ways in which we can express what it is that the argument shows, however. What it shows is that a particular notion of propositional 'aboutness', if blown to extremes—the notion of a proposition about *all* propositions—leads directly to contradiction. Any such notion proves inconsistent, as does the notion of omniscience along with it. Here we do have to be careful to express conclusions about such a notion without ourselves *using* it, but in cases of existential rather than universal quantification such a need for careful expression has long been clear. Ponce de Leon sought the fountain of youth. But we quite rightly resist the temptation to represent that as the claim that

$$\exists x(Fx \wedge Spx)$$

Mythical beasts abound in the pages of Revelation. But we must be wary of representing that as an existential quantification over beasts.

The force of the Cantorian argument, it seems to me, stands unimpugned. The interesting logical point is merely that its conclusion cannot be represented in the manner we might first attempt.

Suppose, however, that the case were worse than this. Suppose, purely for the sake of argument, that it could be shown that there was *no* way to draw a general conclusion from such an argument. I don't believe that is so. But even if it were, it would provide no consolation for the defender of omniscience. It would still be true, given the next claim P' proposed as about all propositions, about all truths, or asserting omniscience, that we could show P' to lead quite directly to contradiction.[21] The Cantorian argument could be used not to generate some general conclusion, in other words, but merely as a 'logic bomb', applied case by case to demolish the next omniscience claim that comes down the line. Even if it in fact afforded us no general positive conclusion, in other words, the Cantorian argument would remain a decisive and devastating tool against claims for omniscience.

CONCLUSION

None of Abbruzzese's defenses of omniscience seems adequate to save it.

Rightly understood, the core of the Essential Indexicals argument has nothing to do with feelings. The argument stands that others cannot know what I know in knowing that I am making a mess, for example, and thus stands as an argument that omniscience is impossible.

In a strengthened form, the Divine Liar still seems to show omniscience to be impossible. Abbruzzese's claim that it "expresses nothing at all" forces him to draw the Strengthened Divine Liar itself as a conclusion.

The negative conclusion regarding omniscience is further underscored by the reasoning of the Knower.

Of all of Abbruzzese's attacks, the critiques of the Cantorian argument are the most interesting, and the question of whether the argument is self-defeating is the most interesting of those. It does indeed appear that one cannot represent the conclusion of that argument as a proposition regarding the nonexistence of any proposition about all propositions. But that doesn't mean that the conclusion might not be represented in plenty of other ways. Even if it couldn't, moreover—even if the Cantorian argument allowed us *no* positive conclusion—the argument structure would remain within reach to use as a 'logic bomb' against the next omniscience claim that comes down the line.

There is no hope yet for the being that knew too much.[22]

NOTES

1. John Abbruzzese, "The Coherence of Omniscience: A Defense," *International Journal for Philosophy of Religion* 41 (1997): 25–34.

2. See particularly chapter 4 of Patrick Grim, *The Incomplete Universe* (Cambridge, Mass.: MIT Press, 1991), and Alvin Plantinga and Patrick Grim, "Truth, Omniscience and Cantorian Arguments: An Exchange," *Philosophical Studies* 71 (1993): 267–306.

3. Abbruzzese, "The Coherence of Omniscience," p. 28.

4. Hector-Neri Castañeda, "'He': A Study of the Logic of Self-Consciousness," *Ratio* 8 (1966): 130–57, John Perry, "The Problem of the Essential Indexical," *Noûs* 13 (1979): 3–21, David Lewis, "Attitudes *De Dicto* and *De Se*," *Philosophical Review Philosophical Review* 88 (1979): 513–43, Steven Boër and William Lycan, "Who, Me?" *Philosophical Review* 88 (1980): 427–66.

5. Here I don't address Hector-Neri Castañeda's proposal in "Omniscience and Indexical Reference," *Journal of Philosophy* 64 (1967): 203–10, which relies on the roundly rejected principle P: that if X knows that Y knows that . . . , X knows what is expressed *in situ* by the phrase. . . . Castañeda had at any rate given up such an approach, and any associated defense of omniscience, by the time of Perry's "The Problem of the Essential Indexical." For further discussion of Castañeda with regard to omniscience, see Patrick Grim, "Against Omniscience: The Case from Essential Indexicals," *Noûs* 29 (1985): 151–80.

6. See particularly Patrick Grim, "Some Neglected Problems of Omniscience," *American Philosophical Quarterly* 20 (1983): 265–77.

7. Abbruzzese, "The Coherence of Omniscience," p. 29.

8. The Swinburne approach that Abbruzzese quotes with approval is a propositionalist response to the Liar. But difficulties for propositionalist approaches also continue well beyond this point. See particularly Grim, *The Incomplete Universe,* chapter 1, section 6.

9. For details see David Kaplan and Richard Montague, "A Paradox Regained," *Notre Dame Journal of Formal Logic* 1 (1960): 79–90; C. Anthony Anderson, "The Paradox of the Knower," *Journal of Philosophy* 80 (1983): 338–55, and Patrick Grim, "Truth, Omniscience, and the Knower," *Philosophical Studies* 54 (1988): 9–41. In the present context I have passed over several arguments against omniscience related to Gödel's results that appear in chapter 3 of *The Incomplete Universe.*

10. See Grim, "There Is No Set of All Truths," *Analysis* 44 (1984): 206–208.

11. Abbruzzese, "The Coherence of Omniscience," p. 32, his punctuation.

12. Richard Cartwright, "Speaking of Everything," *Noûs* 28 (1994): 1–20; D. A. Martin, "Sets versus Classes," quoted in Keith Simmons, "On an Argument Against Omniscience," *Noûs* 27 (1993): 22–33.

13. The full diagonal argument isn't given here. For details see chapter 4 of Grim, *The Incomplete Universe,* and Plantinga and Grim, "Truth, Omniscience and Cantorian Arguments."

14. Gary Mar, "Why 'Cantorian' Arguments against the Existence of God Do Not Work," *International Philosophical Quarterly* 33 (1993): 429–42. A less formal presenta-

tion, though with precisely the same central difficulty, appeared as Keith Simmons, "On an Argument Against Omniscience," APA Central Division, April 1990. The importance of that particular objection is significantly reduced in the published form (see note 12). System NF, for 'New Foundations', first appears in W. V. O. Quine, "New Foundations for Mathematical Logic," *American Mathematical Monthly* 44 (1937): 70–80.

15. W. V. O. Quine, *Set Theory and its Logic* (Cambridge, Mass.: Harvard University Press, 1969). J. B. Rosser and Hao Wang, "Non-Standard Models for Formal Logic," *Journal of Symbolic Logic* 15 (1950): 113–29, showed that no interpretation of '∈' compatible with the axioms of NF could make well-orderings of both the lesser-to-greater relation among ordinals and that among finite cardinals except by interpreting '=' as something other than identity. Ernest Specker, "The Axiom of Choice in Quine's New Foundations for Mathematical Logic," *Proceedings of the National Academy of Sciences* 39 (1953): 972–75, went on to show that the non-Cantorian sets of NF cause the relations of lesser-to-greater among cardinals to fail of a well-ordering, entailing the falsehood of the axiom of choice.

16. A consideration of other alternative set theories appears in chapter 4 of *The Incomplete Universe*.

17. See note 2.

18. Abbruzzese, "The Coherence of Omniscience," p. 32.

19. See esp. Grim, *The Incomplete Universe*, pp. 119 ff.

20. Here I assume classical logic throughout. An intriguing alternative is to borrow elements of the formal structure of intuitionistic logics, which limit the consequences to be drawn from the negation of a universal quantification.

21. In Plantinga and Grim, "Truth, Omniscience and Cantorian Arguments," Alvin Plantinga charges that the premises of the Cantorian argument might also fall victim to the same objection: that if the argument were sound, they couldn't be true. This seems irrelevant from the perspective of the 'logic bomb'. It is the defender of omniscience who buys into the notion of a proposition about all propositions, and he can hardly object to the premises on the grounds that they invoke such a notion. The person who builds the bomb, on the other hand, need himself have no such commitments regarding the coherence of the premises. It is thus only the defender of omniscience who ends up making the universal claim, buying the premises, and facing contradiction and consternation as a result. Plantinga's other alternative—to deny the diagonal—seems to me a much better option in this case, but it is not one that Abbruzzese pursues.

22. I am grateful to the participants of *The Disproof Atheism Society* for helpful comments on an earlier draft. I am also grateful for helpful comments to an anonymous referee for the *International Journal for Philosophy of Religion*.

APPENDIX

OF THE CONFUSED AND CONTRADICTORY IDEAS OF THEOLOGY

PAUL THIRY D'HOLBACH

lthough man has originally borrowed from himself the traits, the colors, the primitive lineaments of which he composed his God, although he has made him a jealous, powerful, vindictive monarch, his theology, by force of dreaming, entirely lost sight of human nature. In order to render his Divinities still more different from their creatures, it assigned them, over and above the usual qualities of man, properties so marvelous, so uncommon, so far removed from everything of which his mind could form a conception, that he lost sight of them himself. From thence he persuaded himself these qualities were divine because he could no longer comprehend them; he believed them worthy of God because no man could figure to himself any one distinct idea of him. Thus, theology obtained the point of persuading man he must believe that which he could not conceive; that he must receive with submission improbable systems; that he must adopt with pious deference conjectures contrary to his reason; that this reason itself was the most agreeable sacrifice he could make on the altars of his fantastical master who was unwilling he should use the gift he had bestowed upon him. In short, it had made mortals implicitly believe that they were not formed to comprehend the thing of all others the most important to themselves.[1] On the other hand, man persuaded himself that the gigantic, the truly incomprehensible, attributes which were assigned to his celestial monarch placed between him and his slaves a distance so immense that this proud master could not be by

From Baron d'Holbach, in chap. 1, vol. 2 of *The System of Nature* (1770), 2 vols. in 1, trans. H. D. Robinson (New York: Burt Franklin, 1970), pp. 191–202.

any means offended with the comparison; that these distinctions rendered him still greater, made him more powerful, more marvelous, more inaccessible to observation. Man always entertains the idea that what he is not in a condition to conceive is much more noble, much more respectable, than that which he has the capacity to comprehend: he imagines that his God, like tyrants, does not wish to be examined too closely.

These prejudices in man for the marvelous appear to have been the source that gave birth to those wonderful, unintelligible qualities with which theology clothed the sovereign of the world. The invincible ignorance of the human mind, whose fears reduced him to despair, engendered those obscure, vague notions with which he decorated his God. He believed he could never displease him provided he rendered him incommensurable, impossible to be compared with anything of which he had a knowledge, either with that which was most sublime or that which possessed the greatest magnitude. From hence the multitude of negative attributes with which ingenious dreamers have successively embellished their phantom God, to the end that they might more surely form a being distinguished from all others or which possessed nothing in common with that which the human mind had the faculty of being acquainted with.

The theological metaphysical attributes were in fact nothing but pure negations of the qualities found in man or in those beings of which he has a knowledge; by these attributes their God was supposed exempted from everything which they considered weakness or imperfection in him or in the beings by whom he is surrounded. To say that God is infinite [. . .] is only to affirm that, unlike man or the beings with whom he is acquainted, he is not circumscribed by the limits of space; this, however, is what he can never in any manner comprehend, because he is himself finite.[2] When it is said that God is eternal, it signifies he has not had, like man or like everything that exists, a beginning and he will never have an end; to say he is immutable is to say that, unlike man or everything which he sees, God is not subject to change; to say he is immaterial is to advance that his substance or essence is of a nature not conceivable by man, but which must from that very circumstance be totally different from everything of which he has cognizance.

It is from the confused collection of these negative qualities that has resulted the theological God; the metaphysical whole of which it is impossible for man to form to himself any correct idea. In this abstract being, everything is infinity, immensity, spirituality, omniscience, order, wisdom, intelligence, omnipotence. In combining these vague terms, or these modifications, the priests believed they formed something; they extended these qualities by thought and they imagined they made a God, while they only composed a chimera. They imagined that these perfections or these qualities must be suitable to this God because they were not suitable to anything of which they had a knowledge; they believed that an incomprehensible being must have inconceivable qualities. These were the materials of which theology availed itself to compose the inexplicable phantom before which they commanded the human race to bend the knee.

Nevertheless, a being so vague, so impossible to be conceived, so incapable of definition, so far removed from everything of which man could have any knowledge, was but little calculated to fix his restless views; his mind requires to be arrested by qualities which he is capacitated to ascertain—of which he is in a condition to form a judgment. Thus after it had subtleized this metaphysical God, after it had rendered him so different in idea from everything that acts upon the senses, theology found itself under the necessity of again assimilating him to man, from whom it had so far removed him: it therefore again made him human by the moral qualities which it assigned him; it felt that without this it would not be able to persuade men there could possibly exist any relation between them and the vague, ethereal, fugitive, incommensurable being they are called upon to adore. They perceived that this marvelous God was only calculated to exercise the imagination of some few thinkers, whose minds were accustomed to labor upon chimerical subjects or to take words for realities; in short, it found that for the greater number of the material children of the earth it was necessary to have a God more analogous to themselves, more sensible, more known to them. In consequence the Divinity was reclothed with human qualities; theology never felt the incompatibility of these qualities with a being it had made essentially different from man, who consequently could neither have his properties nor be modified like himself. It did not see that a God who was immaterial, destitute of corporeal organs, was neither able to think nor to act as material beings, whose peculiar organizations render them susceptible of the qualities, the feelings, the will, the virtues, that are found in them. The necessity it felt to assimilate God to their worshipers, to make an affinity between them, made it pass over without consideration these palpable contradictions, and thus theology obstinately continued to unite those incompatible qualities, that discrepancy of character, which the human mind attempted in vain either to conceive or to reconcile. According to it, a pure spirit was the mover of the material world; an immense being was enabled to occupy space, without however excluding nature; an immutable deity was the cause of those continual changes operated in the world: an omnipotent being did not prevent those evils which were displeasing to him; the source of order submitted to confusion: in short, the wonderful properties of this theological being every moment contradicted themselves.

There is not less discrepancy, less incompatibility, less discordance in the human perfections, less contradiction in the moral qualities attributed to them, to the end that man might be enabled to form to himself some idea of this being. These were all said to be *eminently* possessed by God, although they every moment contradicted each other: by this means they formed a kind of patchwork character, a heterogeneous being, entirely inconceivable to man, because nature had never constructed anything like him whereby he was enabled to form a judgment. Man was assured that God was eminently good—that it was visible in all his actions. Now goodness is a known quality, recognizable in some beings of the human species; this is, above every other, a property he is desirous to find in all those upon whom he is in a state of dependence; but he is unable to bestow the title of good on any among his fellows, except their actions produce on him those effects which he approves—that he finds in unison with his existence—in conformity with his own peculiar modes of thinking. It was evident, according to this reasoning, that God did not impress him with this idea; he was said to be equally the author of his pleasures as of his pains, which were to be either secured or averted by sacrifices or prayers. But when man suffered by contagion, when he was the victim of shipwreck, when his country was desolated by war, when he saw whole nations devoured by rapacious earthquakes, when he was a prey to the keenest sorrows, how could he conceive the bounty of that being? How could he perceive the order he had introduced into the world, while he groaned under such a multitude of calamities? How was he able to discern the beneficence of a God whom he beheld sporting as it were with his species? How could he conceive the consistency of that being who destroyed that which he was assured he had taken such pains to establish, solely for his own peculiar happiness? What becomes of those final causes which, without any ground, they give as the most incontestable proof of the existence of an omnipotent and wise God who, nevertheless, can preserve his work only by destroying it, and who has not been able to give it all at once that degree of perfection and consistency of which it was susceptible. God is said to have created the universe only for man, and was willing that, under him, he should be king of nature. Feeble monarch! Of whom a grain of sand, some atoms of bile, some misplaced humors, destroy at once the existence and the reign: yet thou pretendest that a good God has made everything for thee! Thou desirest that the entire of nature should be thy domain, and thou canst not even defend thyself from the slightest of her shocks! Thou makest to thyself a God for thyself alone; thou supposest that he watcheth for thy preservation; thou supposest that he unceasingly occupieth himself only for thy peculiar happiness; thou imaginest everything was made solely for thy pleasure; and, following up thy presumptuous ideas, thou hast the audacity to call him good! Seest thou not that the kindness exhibited toward thee, in common with other beings, is contradicted? Dost thou not see that those beasts which thou supposest submitted to thine empire, frequently devour thy fellow creatures; that fire consumeth them; that the ocean swalloweth them up; that those elements of which thou admirest the order, frequently sweep them off the face of the earth? Dost thou not see that this power, which thou callest God, which thou pretendest laboureth only for thee, which thou supposest entirely occupied with thy species, flattered by thy homage, touched with thy prayers, cannot be called good, since he acts necessarily? Indeed, according to thy own ideas, dost thou not admit that thy God is the universal cause of all, who must think of maintaining the great whole, from which thou hast so foolishly distinguished him. Is he not then, according to thyself, the God of nature—of the ocean—of rivers—of mountains—of the earth, in which thou occupiest so very small a space—of all those other globes that thou seest roll in the regions of space—of those orbs that revolve round the sun that enlighteneth thee?—Cease, then, obstinately to persist in beholding nothing but thyself in nature; do not flatter thyself that the human race, which reneweth itself, which disappeareth like the leaves on the trees, can absorb all the care, can engross all the tenderness of the universal being, who, according to thyself, ruleth the destiny of all things.

What is the human race compared to the earth? What is this earth compared to the sun? What is our sun compared to those myriad suns which at immense distances occupy the regions of space? Not for the purpose of diverting thy weak eyes; not with a view to excite thy stupid admiration, as thou vainly imaginest, since multitudes of them are placed out of the range of thy visual organs, but to occupy the place which necessity hath assigned them. Mortal, feeble and vain! Restore thyself to thy proper sphere; acknowledge everywhere the effect of necessity; recognize in thy benefits, behold in thy sorrows, the different modes of action of those various beings endowed with such a variety of properties of which nature is the assemblage, and do not any longer suppose that its pretended mover can possess such incompatible qualities as would be the result of human views, or of visionary ideas, which have no existence but in thyself.

Notwithstanding experience, which contradicts at each moment the beneficent views which man supposes in his God, theologians do not cease to call him good: when he complains of the disorders and calamities of which he is so frequently the victim, they assure him that these evils are only apparent: they tell him, that if his limited mind were capable of fathoming the depths of divine wisdom and the treasures of his goodness, he would always find the greatest benefits to result from that which he calls evil. But in spite of these frivolous answers, man will never be able to find good but in those objects which impel him in a manner favorable to his actual mode of existence; he shall always be obliged to find confusion and evil in everything that painfully affects him, even cursorily: if God is the author of those two modes of feeling, so very opposite to each other, he must naturally conclude that this being is sometimes good and sometimes wicked; at least, if he will not allow either the one or the other, it must be admitted that he acts necessarily. A world where man experiences so much evil cannot be submitted to a God who is perfectly good; on the other hand, a world where he experiences so many benefits cannot be governed by a wicked God. Thus, he is obliged to admit of two principles equally powerful that are in hostility with each other; or rather, he must agree that the same God is alternately kind and unkind; this after all is nothing more than avowing he cannot be otherwise than he is; in this case is it not useless to sacrifice to him, to pray, seeing it would be nothing but *destiny*—the necessity of things submitted to invariable rules.

In order to justify this God from the evils the human species experiences, the deist is reduced to the necessity of calling them punishments inflicted by a *just* God for the transgressions of man. If so, man has the power to make his God suffer. To offend presupposes relations between the one who offends and another who is offended; but what relations can exist between the infinite being who has created the world and feeble mortals? To offend anyone is to diminish the sum of his happiness; it is to afflict him, to deprive him of something, to make him experience a painful sensation. How is it possible man can operate on the well-being of the omnipotent sovereign of nature, whose happiness is unalterable? How can the physical actions of a material substance have any influence over an immaterial substance, devoid of parts, having no point of contact? How can a corporeal being make an incorporeal being experience incommodious sensations? On the other hand, *justice*, according to the only ideas man can ever form of it, supposes a permanent disposition to render to each what is due to him; the theologian will not admit that God owes anything to man; he insists that the benefits he bestows are all the gratuitous effects of his own goodness; that he has the right to dispose of the work of his hands according to his own pleasure, to plunge it if he please into the abyss of misery. But it is easy to see that, according to man's idea of justice, this does not even contain the shadow of it; that it is, in fact, the mode of action adopted by what he calls the most frightful tyrants. How then can he be induced to call God just who acts after this manner? Indeed, while he sees innocence suffering, virtue in tears, crime triumphant, vice recompensed, and at the same time is told the being whom theology has invented is the author, he will never be able to acknowledge them to have *justice*.[3] But, says the deist, these evils are transient; they will only last for a time: very well, but then your God is unjust, at least for a time. It is for their good that he chastises his friends. But if he is good, how can he consent to let them suffer even for a time? If he knows everything, why reprove his favorites from whom he has nothing to fear? If he is really omnipotent, why not spare them these transitory pains and procure them at once a durable and permanent felicity? If his power cannot be shaken, why make himself uneasy at the vain conspiracies they would form against him?

Where is the man filled with kindness, endowed with humanity, who does not desire with all his heart to render his fellow creatures happy? If God really had man's qualities augmented, would he not by the same reasoning exercise his infinite power to render them all happy? Nevertheless we scarcely find anyone who is perfectly satisfied with his condition on earth: for one mortal who enjoys, we behold a thousand who suffer; for one rich man who lives in the midst of abundance, there are thousands of poor who want common necessaries: whole nations groan in indigence to satisfy the passions of some avaricious princes, of some few nobles, who are not thereby rendered more contented—who do not acknowledge themselves more fortunate on that account. In short, under the dominion of an omnipotent God, whose goodness is infinite, the earth is drenched with the tears of the miserable. What must be the inference from all this? That God is either negligent of, or incompetent to, his happiness. But the deist will tell you coolly that the judgments of his God are impenetrable! How do we understand this term? Not to be taught—not to be informed—impervious—not to be pierced: in this case it would be an unreasonable question to inquire by what authority do you reason upon them? How do you become acquainted with these impenetrable mysteries? Upon what foundation do you attribute virtues which you cannot penetrate? What idea do you form to yourself of a justice that never resembles that of man?

To withdraw themselves from this, deists will affirm that the justice of their God is tempered with mercy, with compassion, with goodness. These again are human qualities; what, therefore, shall we understand by them? What idea do we attach to mercy? Is it not a derogation from the severe rules of an exact, a rigorous justice, which causes a remission of some part of a merited punishment? In a prince clemency is either a violation of justice or the exemption from a too-severe law; but the laws of a God infinitely good, equitable, and wise, can they ever be too severe and, if immutable, can he alter them? Nevertheless, man approves of clemency in a sovereign when its too-great facility does not become prejudicial to society; he esteems it because it announces humanity, mildness, a compassionate, noble soul; qualities he prefers in his governors to rigor, cruelty, inflexibility. Besides, human laws are defective; they are frequently too severe; they are not competent to foresee all the circumstances of every case: the punishments they decree are not always commensurate with the offense: he therefore does not always think them just; but he feels very well, he understands distinctly, that when the sovereign extends his mercy, he relaxes from his justice—that if mercy be merited, the punishment ought not to take place—that then its exercise is no longer clemency, but justice: thus he feels that in his fellow creatures these two qualities cannot exist at the same moment. How then is he to form his judgment of a being who is represented to possess both in the extremest degree?

They then say, well, but in the next world this God will reward you for all the evils you suffer in this: this, indeed, is something to look to, if it had not been invented to shelter divine justice and to exculpate him from those evils which he so frequently causes his greatest favorites to experience in this world. It is there, deists tell us, that the celestial monarch will procure for his elect that unalterable happiness which he has refused them on earth; it is there he will indemnify those whom he loves for that transitory injustice, those afflicting trials, which he makes them suffer here below. In the meantime, is this invention calculated to give us those clear ideas suitable to justify providence? If God owes nothing to his creatures, upon what ground can they expect in a future life a happiness more real, more constant, than that which they at present enjoy? It will be founded, say theologians, upon his promises contained in his revealed oracles. But are they quite certain that these oracles have emanated from him? On the other hand, the system of another life does not justify this God for the most fleeting and transitory injustice; for does not injustice, even when it is transient, destroy that immutability which they attribute to the Divinity? In short, is not that omnipotent being, whom they have made the author of all things, himself the first cause or accomplice of the offenses which they commit against him? Is he not the true author of evil or of the sin which he permits, while he is able to prevent it; and in this case can he, consistently with justice, punish those whom he himself renders culpable?

We have already seen the multitude of contradictions, the extravagant hypotheses, which the attributes theology gives to its God must necessarily produce. A being clothed at one time with so many discordant qualities will always be indefinable; they only present a train of ideas which will destroy each other, and he will in consequence remain a being of the imagination. This God has, say they, created the heavens, the earth, and the creatures who inhabit it to manifest his own peculiar glory: but a monarch who is superior to all beings, who has neither rivals nor equals in nature, who cannot be compared to any of his creatures, is he susceptible of the desire of glory? Can he fear to be debased and degraded in the eyes of his fellow creatures? Has he occasion for the esteem, the homage, or the admiration of men? The love of glory is in us only the desire of giving our fellow creatures a high opinion of ourselves; this passion is laudable, when it stimulates us to perform great and useful actions; but more frequently it is only a weakness attached to our nature, it is only a desire in us to be distinguished from those beings with whom we compare ourselves. The God of whom they speak to us ought to be exempt from this passion; according to theology he has no fellow creatures, he has no competitors, he cannot be offended with those ideas which we form of him. His power cannot suffer any diminution, nothing is able to disturb his eternal felicity; must we not conclude from this that he cannot be either susceptible of desiring glory or sensible to the praises and esteem of men? If this God is jealous of his prerogatives, of his titles, of his rank, and of his glory, wherefore does he suffer that so many men should offend him? Why does he permit so many others to have such unfavorable opinions of him? Why allows he others to have the temerity to refuse him that incense which is so flattering to his pride? How comes he to permit that a mortal like me should dare attack his rights, his titles, and even his existence? It is in order to punish thee, you will say, for having made a bad use of his favors. But why does he permit

me to abuse his kindness? Or why are not the favors which he confers on me sufficient to make me act agreeably to his views? It is because he has made thee free.
Why has he given me liberty, of which he must have foreseen that I should be
inclined to make an improper use? Is it then a present worthy of his goodness to
give me a faculty that enables me to brave his omnipotence, to detach from him
his adorers, and thus render myself eternally miserable? Would it not have been
much more advantageous for me never to have been born, or at least to have been
placed in the rank of brutes or stones, than to have been in spite of myself placed
among intelligent beings, there to exercise the fatal power of losing myself
without redemption by offending or mistaking the arbiter of my fate? Had not
God much better have shown his omnipotent goodness, and would he not have
labored much more efficaciously to his true glory, if he had obliged me to render
him homage and thereby to have merited an ineffable happiness?

The system of the liberty of man, which we have already destroyed, was visibly imagined to wipe from the author of nature the reproach which they must
offer him in being the author, the source, the first cause of the crimes of his creatures. In consequence of this fatal present given by a beneficent God, men,
according to the sinister ideas of theology, will for the most part be eternally punished for their faults in this world. Farfetched and endless torments are by the
justice of a merciful and compassionate God reserved for fragile beings, for transitory offenses, for false reasonings, for involuntary errors, for necessary passions, which depend on the temperament this God has given them, circumstances
in which he has placed them, or, if they will, the abuse of this pretended liberty,
which a provident God ought never to have accorded to beings capable of
abusing it. Should we call that father good, rational, just, clement, or compassionate, who should arm with a dangerous and sharp knife the hands of a petulant child, with whose imprudence he was acquainted, and who should punish
him all his life, for having wounded himself with it? Should we call that prince
just, merciful, and compassionate, who did not proportion the punishment to the
offense, who should put no end to the torments of that subject who in a state of
inebriety should have transiently wounded his vanity, without however causing
him any real injustice—above all, after having himself taken pains to intoxicate
him? Should we look upon that monarch as all-powerful, whose dominions
should be in such a state of anarchy, that, with the exception of a small number
of faithful subjects, all the others should have the power every instant to despise
his laws, insult him, and frustrate his will? O, theologians! Confess that your God
is nothing but a heap of qualities, which form a whole as perfectly incomprehensible to your mind as to mine; by dint of overburdening him with incompatible
qualities, ye have made him truly a chimera, which all your hypotheses cannot
maintain in the existence you are anxious to give him.

They will, however, reply to these difficulties that goodness, wisdom, and justice are in God qualities so eminent, or have such little similarity to ours, that they have no relation with these qualities when found in men. But I shall answer, how shall I form to myself ideas of these divine perfections if they bear no resemblance to those of the virtues which I find in my fellow creatures or to the dispositions which I feel in myself? If the justice of God is not that of men; if it operates in that mode which men call injustice; if his goodness, his clemency, and his wisdom do not manifest themselves by such signs that we are able to recognize them; if all his divine qualities are contrary to received ideas; if in theology all the human actions are obscured or overthrown, how can mortals like myself pretend to announce them, to have a knowledge of them, or to explain them to others? Can theology give to the mind the ineffable boon of conceiving that which no man is in a capacity to comprehend? Can it procure to its agents the marvelous faculty of having precise ideas of a God composed of so many contradictory qualities? In short, is the theologian himself a God?

They silence us by saying that God himself has spoken, that he has made himself known to men. But when, where, and to whom has he spoken? Where are these divine oracles? A hundred voices raise themselves in the same moment, a hundred hands show them to me in absurd and discordant collections. I run them over, and through the whole I find that the *God of wisdom* has spoken an obscure, insidious, and irrational language. I see that the *God of goodness* has been cruel and sanguinary; that the *God of justice* has been unjust and partial, has ordered iniquity; that the *God of mercies* destines the most hideous punishments to the unhappy victims of his anger. Besides, obstacles present themselves when men attempt to verify the pretended relations of a Divinity who, in two countries, has never literally held the same language; who has spoken in so many places, at so many times, and always so variously that he appears everywhere to have shown himself only with the determined design of throwing the human mind into the strangest perplexity.

Thus, the relations which they suppose between men and their God can only be founded on the moral qualities of this being; if these are not known to men, they cannot serve them for models. It is needful that these qualities were natural in a known being in order to be imitated; how can I imitate a God of whom the goodness and the justice do not resemble mine in anything, or rather are directly contrary to that which I call either just or good? If God partakes in nothing of that which forms us, how can we even distantly propose to ourselves the imitating him, the resembling him, the following a conduct necessary to please him by conforming ourselves to him? What can in effect be the motives of that worship, of that homage, and of that obedience which we are told to render to the Supreme Being, if we do not establish them upon his goodness, upon his veracity, upon his justice—in short, upon qualities which we are able to understand? How can we have clear ideas of these qualities in God if they are no longer of the same nature as our own?

They will no doubt tell us that there cannot be any proportion between the creator and his work, that the clay has no right to demand of the potter who has formed it, *why have you fashioned me thus*? But if there be no proportion between the workman and his work, if there be no analogy between them, what can be the relations which will subsist between them? If God is incorporeal, how does he act upon bodies, or how can corporeal beings be able to act upon him, offend him, disturb his repose, excite in him emotions of anger? If man is relatively to God only an *earthen vase*, this *vase* owes neither prayers nor thanks to the potter for the form which he has been pleased to give it. If this potter irritates himself against his *vase* for having formed it badly, or for having rendered it incapable of the uses to which he had destined it, the potter, if he is not an irrational being, ought to take to himself the defects which he finds in it. He certainly has the power to break it, and the *vase* cannot prevent him; it will neither have motives nor means to soften his anger, but will be obliged to submit to its destiny; and the potter would be completely deprived of reason if he were to punish his vase, rather than, by forming it anew, give it a figure more suitable to his designs.

We see that, according to these notions, men have no more relation with God than stones. But if God owes nothing to men, if he is not bound to show them either justice or goodness, men cannot possibly owe anything to him. We have no knowledge of any relations between beings which are not reciprocal; the duties of men among themselves are founded upon their mutual wants; if God has not occasion for them, they cannot owe him anything, and men cannot possibly offend him. In the meantime, the authority of God can only be founded on the good which he does to men, and the duties of these toward God can have no other motives than the hope of that happiness which they expect from him; if he does not owe them this happiness, all their relations are annihilated, and their duties no longer exist. Thus, in whatever manner we view the theological system, it destroys itself. Will theology never feel that the more it endeavors to exalt its God, to exaggerate his grandeur, the more incomprehensible it renders him to us? That the further it removes him from man, or the more it debases this man, the more it weakens the relations which they have supposed between this God and him? If the sovereign of nature is an infinite being and totally different from our species, and if man is only in his eyes a worm or a speck of dirt, it is clear there cannot be any *moral relations* between two beings so little analogous to each other; and again, it is still more evident that the *vase* which he has formed is not capable of reasoning upon him.

It is, however, upon the relation subsisting between man and his God that all worship is founded, and all the religions of the world have a despotic God for their basis; but is not despotism an unjust and unreasonable power? Is it not equally to undermine his goodness, his justice, and his infinite wisdom, to attribute to the Divinity the exercise of such a power? Men in seeing the evils with which they are frequently assailed in this world, without being able to guess by what means they have deserved the divine anger, will always be tempted to believe that the master of nature is a *sultan*, who owes nothing to his subjects, who is not obliged to render them any account of his actions, who is not bound to conform himself to any law, and who is not himself subjected to those rules which he prescribes for others; who in consequence can be unjust, who has the right to carry his vengeance beyond all bounds. In short, the theologians pretend that God would have the right of destroying the universe and replunging it into the chaos from whence his wisdom has withdrawn it; while the same theologians quote to us the order and marvelous arrangement of this world as the most convincing proof of his existence.[4]

In short, theology invests its God with the incommunicable privilege of acting contrary to all the laws of nature and of reason, while it is upon his reason, his justice, his wisdom, and his fidelity in the fulfilling his pretended engagements that they are willing to establish the worship which we owe him and the duties of morality. What an ocean of contradictions! A being who can do everything, and who owes nothing to anyone, who, in his eternal decrees, can elect or reject, predestine to happiness or to misery, who has the right of making men the playthings of his caprice, and to afflict them without reason, who could go so far as even to destroy and annihilate the universe, is he not a tyrant or a demon? Is there anything more frightful than the immediate consequences to be drawn from these revolting ideas given to us of their God by those who tell us to love him, to serve him, to imitate him, and to obey his orders? Would it not be a thousand times better to depend upon blind matter, upon a nature destitute of intelligence, upon chance, or upon nothing, upon a God of stone or of wood, than upon a God who is laying snares for men, inviting them to sin, and permitting them to commit those crimes which he could prevent, to the end that he may have the barbarous pleasure of punishing them without measure, without utility to himself, without correction to them, and without their example serving to reclaim others? A gloomy terror must necessarily result from the idea of such a being; his power will wrest from us much servile homage; we shall call him good to flatter him or to disarm his malice; but, without overturning the essence of things, such a God will never be able to make himself beloved by us, when we shall reflect that he owes us nothing, that he has the right of being unjust, that he has the power to punish his creatures for making a bad use of the liberty which he grants them, or for not having had that grace which he has been pleased to refuse them.

Thus, in supposing that God is not bound toward us by any rules, theologians visibly sap the foundation of all religion. A theology which assures us that God has been able to create men for the purpose of rendering them eternally miserable shows us nothing but an evil and malicious genius, whose malice is inconceivable and infinitely surpasses the cruelty of the most depraved beings of our species. Such is nevertheless the God which they have the confidence to propose for a model to the human species! Such is the Divinity which is adored even by those nations who boast of being the most enlightened in this world!

It is, however, upon the moral character of the Divinity, that is to say upon his goodness, his wisdom, his equity, and his love of order, that they pretend to establish our morals or the science of those duties which connect us to the beings of our species. But as his perfections and his goodness are contradicted very frequently and give place to weakness, to injustice, and to cruelties, we are obliged to pronounce him changeable, fickle, capricious, unequal in his conduct, and in contradiction with himself, according to the various modes of action which they attribute to him. Indeed, we sometimes see him favorable to and sometimes disposed to injure the human species; sometimes a friend to reason and the happiness of society; sometimes he interdicts the use of reason, he acts as the enemy of all virtue, and he is flattered with seeing society disturbed. However, as we have seen mortals crushed by fear, hardly ever daring to avow that their God was unjust or wicked, to persuade themselves that he authorized them to be so, it was concluded simply that everything which they did according to his pretended order or with the view of pleasing him was always good, however prejudicial it might otherwise appear in the eyes of reason. They supposed him the master of creating the just and the unjust, of changing good into evil, and evil into good, truth into falsehood, and falsehood into truth: in short, they gave him the right of changing the eternal essence of things; they made this God superior to the laws of nature, of reason, and virtue; they believed they could never do wrong in following his precepts, although the most absurd, the most contrary to morals, the most opposite to good sense, and the most prejudicial to the repose of society. With such principles do not let us be surprised at those horrors which religion causes to be committed on the earth. The most atrocious religion was the most consistent.[5]

In founding morals upon the immoral character of a God who changes his conduct, man will never be able to ascertain what conduct he ought to pursue with regard to that which he owes to God, or to others. Nothing then was more dangerous than to persuade him there existed a being superior to nature, before whom reason must remain silent; to whom, to be happy hereafter, he must sacrifice everything here. His pretended orders and his example must necessarily be much stronger than the precepts of human morals; the adorers of this God cannot then listen to nature and good sense, but when by chance they accord with the caprice of their God, in whom they suppose the power of annihilating the invariable relation of beings, of changing reason into folly, justice into injustice, and even crime into virtue. By a consequence of these ideas, the religious man never examines the will and the conduct of this celestial despot according to ordinary rules; every inspired man that comes from him, and those who shall pretend they are charged with interpreting his oracles, will always assume the right of rendering him irrational and criminal; his first duty will always be to obey his God without murmuring.

Such are the fatal and necessary consequences of the moral character which they give to the Divinity, and of the opinion which persuades mortals they ought to pay a blind obedience to the absolute sovereign whose arbitrary and fluctuating will regulates all duties. Those who first had the confidence to tell men that in matters of religion it was not permitted them to consult their reason, nor the interests of society, evidently proposed to themselves to make them the sport of the instruments of their own peculiar wickedness. It is from this radical error, then, that have sprung all those extravagances which the different religions have introduced upon the earth; that sacred fury which has deluged it in blood; those inhuman persecutions which have so frequently desolated nations; in short, all those horrid tragedies, of which the name of the Most High have the cause and the pretext. Whenever they have been desirous to render men unsociable, they have cried out that it was the will of God they should be so. Thus, the theologians themselves have taken pains to calumniate and to defame the phantom which they have erected upon the ruins of human reason, of a nature well known, and a thousand times preferable to a tyrannical God, whom they render odious to every honest man. These theologians are the true destroyers of their own peculiar idol by the contradictory qualities which they accumulate on him: it is these theologians, as we shall yet prove in the sequel, who render morals uncertain and fluctuating by founding them upon a changeable and capricious God, much more frequently unjust and cruel, than good: it is they who overturn and annihilate him by commanding crime, carnage, and barbarity in the name of the sovereign of the universe and who interdict us the use of reason, which alone ought to regulate all our actions and ideas.

However, admitting for a moment that God possesses all the human virtues in an infinite degree of perfection, we shall presently be obliged to acknowledge that he cannot connect them with those metaphysical, theological, and negative attributes of which we have already spoken. If God is a *spirit*, how can he act like man, who is a corporeal being? A pure spirit sees nothing; it neither hears our prayers nor our cries; it cannot be conceived to have compassion for our miseries, being destitute of those organs by which the sentiments of pity can be excited in us. He is not *immutable* if his disposition can change; he is not *infinite* if the totality of nature, without being him, can exist conjointly with him; he is not *omnipotent* if he permits or if he does not prevent disorder in the world; he is not *omnipresent* if he is not in the man who sins, or if he leaves at the moment in which he commits the sin. Thus, in whatever manner we consider this God, the human qualities which they assign him necessarily destroy each other; and these same qualities cannot, in any possible manner, combine themselves with the supernatural attributes given him by theology.

With respect to the pretended *revelation* of the will of God, far from being a proof of his goodness, or of his commiseration for men, it would only be a proof of his malice. Indeed, all revelation supposes the Divinity guilty of leaving the human species, during a considerable time, unacquainted with truths the most important to their happiness. This revelation, made to a small number of chosen men, would moreover show a partiality in this being, an unjust predilection but little compatible with the goodness of the common Father of the human race. This revelation destroys also the divine immutability, since, by it, God would have permitted at one time that men should be ignorant of his will and at another time that they should be instructed in it. This granted, all revelation is contrary to the notions which they give us of the justice or of the goodness of a God who they tell us is immutable and who, without having occasion to reveal himself or to make himself known to them by miracles, could easily instruct and convince men and inspire them with those ideas which he desires—in short, dispose of their minds and of their hearts. What if we should examine in detail all those pretended revelations which they assure us have been made to mortals? We shall see that this God only retails fables unworthy of a wise being; acts in them in a manner contrary to the natural notions of equity; announces enigmas and oracles impossible to be comprehended; paints himself under traits incompatible with his infinite perfections; exacts puerilities which degrade him in the eyes of reason; deranges the order which he has established in nature to convince creatures whom he will never cause to adopt those ideas, those sentiments, and that conduct with which he would inspire them. In short, we shall find that God has never manifested himself but to announce inexplicable mysteries, unintelligible doctrines, ridiculous practices; to throw the human mind into fear, distrust, perplexity, and, above all, to furnish a never-failing source of dispute to mortals.[6]

We see then that the ideas which theology gives us of the Divinity will always be confused and incompatible and will necessarily disturb the repose of human nature.

NOTES

1. It is quite evident that every religion is founded upon the absurd principle that man is obliged to accredit finally that which he is in the most complete impossibility of comprehending. According even to theological notions man, by his nature, must be in an *invincible ignorance* relatively to God.

2. Hobbes in his *Leviathan* says: "Whatsoever we imagine is finite. Therefore there is no idea or conception of anything we call infinite. No man can have in his mind an image of infinite magnitude, nor conceive infinite swiftness, infinite time, infinite force, or infinite power. When we say anything is infinite, we signify only that we are not able to conceive the ends and bound of the thing named, having no conception of the thing, but

of our own inability." Sherlock says: "The word infinite is only a negation, which signifies that which has neither end, nor limits, nor extent, and, consequently, that which has no positive and determinate nature, and is therefore nothing"; he adds, "that nothing but custom has caused this word to he adopted, which without that would appear devoid of sense, and a contradiction."

3. *Dies deficiet si velim numerare quibus bonis male evenerit; nec minus si commemorem quibus malis optime.*

— Cicer. de Nat. Deor. lib. iii.

If a virtuous king possessed the ring of *Gyges*, that is to say, had the faculty of rendering himself invisible, would he not make use of it to remedy abuses to reward the good, to prevent the conspiracies of the wicked, to make order and happiness reign throughout his states? God is an invisible and all-powerful monarch, nevertheless his states are the theater of crime, of confusion: he remedies nothing.

4. "We conceive, at least," says Doctor Castrill, "that God is able to overturn the universe, and replunge it into chaos." See his *Defense of Religion, Natural and Revealed.*

5. The modern religion of Europe has visibly caused more ravages and troubles than any other known superstition; it was in that respect very consistent with its principles. They may well preach tolerance and mildness in the name of a despotic God, who alone has a right to the homage of the earth, who is extremely jealous, who wills that they should admit some doctrines, who punishes cruelly for erroneous opinions, who demands zeal from his adorers; such a God must make fanatical persecutors of all consistent men. The theology of the present day is a subtle venom, calculated to infect all by the importance which is attached to it. By dint of *metaphysics* modern theologians have become systematically absurd and wicked: by once admitting the odious ideas which they gave of the Divinity, it was impossible to make them understand that they ought to be humane, equitable, pacific, indulgent, or tolerant. They pretended and proved that these humane and social virtues were not seasonable in the cause of religion and would be treason and crimes in the eyes of the celestial Monarch, to whom everything ought to be sacrificed.

6. It is evident that all revelation which is not clear or which teaches *mysteries* cannot be the work of a wise and intelligent being: as soon as he speaks, we ought to presume, it is for the purpose of being understood by those to whom he manifests himself. To speak so as not to be understood only shows folly or want of good faith. It is, then, very clear that all things which the priesthood have called *mysteries* are inventions, made to throw a thick veil over their own peculiar contradictions and their own peculiar ignorance of the Divinity. But they think to solve all difficulties by saying *it is a mystery*; taking care, however, that men should know nothing of that pretended science of which they have made themselves the depositaries.